Peter Aitken

 CORIOLIS GROUP BOOKS

Publisher	*Keith Weiskamp*
Editor	*Maggy Miskell*
Proofreader	*Diane Green Cook*
Cover Design	*Anthony Stock*
Interior Design	*Bradley Grannis*
Layout Production	*Sue Tynan*
Publicist	*Shannon Bounds*
Indexer	*Kirsten Dewey*

Distributed to the book trade by IDG Books Worldwide, Inc.

Library of Congress Cataloging-in-Publication Data

Aitken, Peter
    Visual Basic 4 Programming Explorer / Peter Aitken
        p. cm.
    Includes Index
    ISBN 1-883577-21-7 : $39.99

Printed in the United States of America

10 9 8 7 6 5 4 3 2 1

CONTENTS

Chapter 6   Text Processing 117

Chapter 7   Graphics   145

Chapter 8   File Access and Management   189

Chapter 9   Serial Communication   229

Chapter 12   Preliminary Considerations   307

Chapter 13   Beyond the Basics: Tools for Developing Database Applications   321

Chapter 14   Back to the Beginning: Designing the Database   331

Chapter 16　Wrapping It Up: Validation Code and the Invoices Form　389

Chapter 17　Dynamic Data Exchange　417

Chapter 18   Object Linking and Embedding   449

Chapter 19   Error Handling   487

More Faster, More Better

CHAPTER 1

For fast application development, you can't beat Visual Basic.

Welcome! Join me as we explore the world of Visual Basic. We're going to jump right in and start our adventure by creating a small Visual Basic program. Learn by doing; I believe that's the best approach—and the most fun. There will be some theoretical stuff later—there's no avoiding that, if you want to become a skilled Visual Basic programmer. But first, it will help you to have a look at what Visual Basic is and how it works. In other words, start with the *what,* and later deal with the *how come.* You'll also get a feel for how *fast* Visual Basic is in getting a working program up and running.

Did I say *fast?* Indeed I did. Quick, rapid, speedy—after all, this seems to be the "I need it yesterday" era. Rarely can you take a leisurely approach to program development. Whether you're programming for yourself, your boss, or a paying client, no one ever complained because the project was completed too soon. Visual Basic is unexcelled for *rapid application development,* or RAD. As you'll soon see, however, making the best use of

Visual Basic's capabilities requires an understanding of the how and why of its workings. But every exploration must start somewhere, and that's the purpose of this chapter.

I assume that you already have Visual Basic installed on your system. If not, follow the installation instructions in your Visual Basic package. We'll start by learning how to use some of Visual Basic's tools, then we'll get to the sample program that I promised you.

VISUAL BASIC BASICS

When you start Windows after installing Visual Basic on your system, a Visual Basic program group should appear on your screen, which will look something like Figure 1.1. To start Visual Basic, point at the "Visual Basic 4.0 - 32-bit" icon and double click.

eXPLORER TIP — Can't Find the Visual Basic Program Group?

Look on the Windows Task Bar, which is normally displayed along the bottom of the screen. If there's a button labeled Visual Basic 4.0, click it to display the program group. Still no luck? Right-button click the Start button on the Task Bar, then select Open to display the Start Menu group. Double click the Programs icon to display the Programs group, then double click the Visual Basic 4.0 icon to display the Visual Basic program group. If there's no Visual Basic icon in the Program group, it probably means that Visual Basic has not yet been installed.

When Visual Basic starts, it displays several windows on the screen—five windows, to be exact. This can be somewhat disconcerting to someone used to working with the more common type of Windows program that organizes all of its components neatly in one master window. For one thing, you may

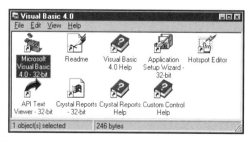

Figure 1.1   *The Visual Basic program group.*

need to move and resize the Visual Basic windows to make everything visible. In addition, the background—whatever was on the screen before you started Visual Basic—will show through between the Visual Basic windows. Usually this is the Windows Desktop, and it can be quite distracting to have Desktop elements, such as program groups, peeking out at you as you're working on a Visual Basic project. You can't get rid of the Desktop, but you can minimize all the program group windows by right-button clicking a blank area on the Task Bar and selecting Minimize All Windows. Once you get everything arranged the way you like it, your screen will look more or less like Figure 1.2.

There are five different elements, or windows, on the initial Visual Basic screen.

Menu Window

Along the top of the screen is what I'll call, for lack of an official name, the *menu window*. It contains the main Visual Basic menu, from which you select commands, and the Toolbar that contains buttons you can click to carry out commonly needed menu commands. Note that if you position the mouse pointer over a Toolbar button for a moment (don't click!) Visual Basic will display a brief description, called a *tool tip*, of the button's function. At the right end of the Toolbar are two dimension boxes that give the screen position and size of the current screen object (you'll see how to use these soon).

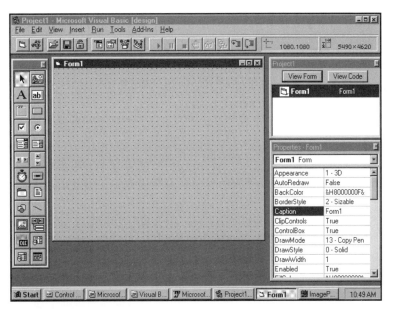

Figure 1.2   The Visual Basic screen.

Form Window

Near the center of the screen is the *form window*, where you will draw your program's visual interface. You start each new project with one blank form and can add as many others as you need. Each form corresponds to a window or dialog box in the final program. During program design a grid of dots aids you in aligning the elements placed on the form. These dots do not display in the final program.

Toolbox Window

On the left side of the screen is the *Toolbox*. This window contains icons representing the various visual objects, called *controls*, that you can place on a Visual Basic form. To place a control, you click the corresponding toolbox button, then point and drag on the form to specify the position and location of the control. The toolbox buttons display tool tips just like the toolbar buttons. The top left button in the toolbox, the arrow, is not a control but represents the pointer. Select this toolbox button when you want to edit controls that you have already placed on the form.

Project Window

The small window with the title *Project 1* in its title bar is the *project window*. This window lists all the modules in the current project. The term *project* simply means a Visual Basic program under development, with all its component objects. A *module* is simply a component of a Visual Basic project. For example, each form is a module. When you start a new project, it contains only a single module, a form with the default name *Form1*. Likewise, the project itself has the default name *Project1*. You'll assign more meaningful names to modules and the project as you work.

Properties Window

The final window is the *properties window*. This window lists the properties of the currently selected object, the name of which is displayed in the box at the top of the properties window. A form is an object, and the controls you place on it are objects too. An object's properties control its appearance and behavior—for example, the color of a form's background is one of its properties. Since you'll be learning a lot about object properties throughout this book, I won't go into detail now.

Other Windows

Visual Basic has a number of other windows to use during program development. For the most part, we'll deal with these other windows as the need arises. There's one type of window, however, that is so central to Visual Basic programming that I'll introduce it here. In a *code window*, you enter and edit Basic code. It works pretty much like any other Windows text editor—you can type text, delete it, move and copy it from place to place, and so on. If you want to see what a code window looks like, click the View Code button in the Project window, and an empty code window will open.

 **Using Visual Basic Windows**

Remember that Visual Basic's windows are just like any other window. You have the same freedom to move them, change their size, close and minimize them as in any program running under the Windows operating environment. After you have worked with Visual Basic for a while, you will develop the screen layout—window sizes and positions—that best suits the way *you* work.

AN OVERVIEW

Now that you've had a look at the most important parts of Visual Basic, you may be wondering how it all fits together. With Visual Basic more than with other programming tools, understanding how all the parts fit together is essential to realizing its full potential. We'll be delving into this topic in considerable detail in the next chapter, but I think it is worthwhile to go over the main points before we get to your first Visual Basic project.

- A Visual Basic program consists of one or more windows, or *forms*. Each form contains a number of *controls*. A wide variety of different controls is available, providing just about any functionality your program could need—entering and editing text, selecting options, displaying graphics, and so on. Together, the forms and controls comprise a program's *visual interface*.

- Each *object* (form or control) in a Visual Basic program has a number of *properties* associated with it. An object's properties control the way it behaves and looks.

- Visual Basic objects have the ability to detect *events* such as mouse clicks and key presses. This ability is built-in, and requires no effort on your part. What *happens* when an event is detected, however, is up to the programmer.

- Basic *code* written by the programmer defines the functionality of the program—in other words, what the program does. Whether it's text processing, graphical display, or numerical calculations, it's the programmer's job to write the code to perform the desired actions. Basic code also serves to link the program's visual interface to the program's functionality—to control what happens in response to those events that Visual Basic objects can automatically detect.

YOUR FIRST VISUAL BASIC PROGRAM

All right, enough talk! It's time to dive in and get your fingers dirty. We're going to create a real, live Visual Basic program. And it won't be some silly demonstration program, either—it will be a real program that does something useful. We'll write a mortgage calculator, which will display the monthly payment on a mortgage or other loan. The process of creating the program is divided into four steps.

Step 1: Planning Ahead

Programming projects always benefit from a bit of planning, and Visual Basic is no different. What will a mortgage calculator require? Put on your thinking cap and get out your paper and pencil. (Yes, even in this computerized age, paper and pencil are still best for some tasks!) A few moments of thought yields the conclusion that the program will need to do three things: Gather input information from the user, perform the calculations, and display the answer.

Let's start with the input. Three pieces of information are needed to perform the calculations: the amount of the loan, the interest rate that is being charged, and the duration, or *term*, of the loan. Right away we know the program will need places for the user to enter these three items. One of Visual Basic's controls, the Text Box, is intended for entering and displaying information of this sort. This completes the first planning step—we know the project will need three Text Box controls for input.

As for program output, the program will generate only one piece of information, the monthly loan payment. Again, a Text Box control is ideal for this purpose, so we'll add one output Text Box to the three input Text Boxes, for a total of four.

We also need some way to identify the Text Box controls to determine which one is for the interest rate, which for the loan term, and so on. The Label control is just what we need, and we'll need one for each input Text Box.

Finally, we need some way for the users to quit the program. Yes, we could let them quit by using the default window controls, clicking the X button in the upper right corner, but we want to be more elegant and provide a "Quit" button. Visual Basic's Command Button control is suited for such a task, and we'll need only one.

Our planning is now complete. Well, almost. We also need to know how to calculate the mortgage payment, given the amount, term, and rate. Fortunately, I happen to have a Handbook of Financial Formulas on my shelf. Here's the needed formula; if we define the following:

rate = interest rate per period

amount = loan amount

nper = term of loan in periods

then

monthly payment = (amount * rate) / (1 - (1 + rate) ^ -nper)

The formula is written in Basic, so it may not be clear to you. You'll learn all about "Basic-speak" in later chapters. For now all you need to know is that * means multiply, / means divide, and ^ means raised to the power of.

Okay, the planning is really complete. Of course, planning ahead does not mean that your plan is engraved in stone—you always have the freedom to change things later (this is one of the beauties of Visual Basic). But now it's time to get to work.

Step 2: Designing the Interface

The next step in creating a Visual Basic program is usually the design of the visual interface. This means we are going to start with a blank form and put the needed controls on it. Since we were wise enough to plan ahead, we already know what controls will be on the form. All we need to do now is decide on the visual layout—where the controls are located, how big they are, and so on.

Adding the Label Controls

Fire up Visual Basic, and, if necessary, arrange its windows in a convenient manner. We'll be working with the blank form and the Toolbox, and the first thing we'll do is place the four Label controls on the form. Here are the steps to follow for the first one:

1. Point the mouse cursor at the Label button in the Toolbox and click. The Label button is in the second row, and has a large "A" on it.

2. Move the mouse pointer to the form, where it will display as a cross. Point at the location where you want the top left corner of the first label to be located.

3. Click and hold the left mouse button, and move the pointer to the opposite corner of the Label. As you do this, you'll see a rectangular outline follow the pointer, indicating the label size. This technique is called *dragging*.

4. When the outline size is as you want it, release the mouse button. Visual Basic will place a Label with the caption *Label1* on the form, as shown in Figure 1.3. Don't worry if your form size or label location is not exactly like the figure.

Now that the Label control is on the form, let me call your attention to two things. First, the new control has eight small black boxes displayed around its perimeter. These are called *handles*, and are used to change the size and shape of the control. Go ahead and try it—point at one of the handles, and you'll see the mouse pointer change to a double-headed arrow. Click and hold the mouse button, drag the control outline to the desired size and shape, then release the mouse button. You can also move the control without changing its size by pointing inside the control (not at a handle) and dragging to the new location.

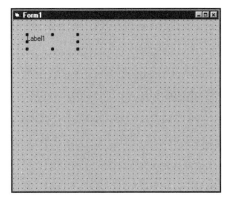

Figure 1.3 *A Label control placed on a form.*

Figure 1.4 *The Properties window displays the properties of the selected object.*

Second, the Properties window is displaying the new control's properties, as shown in Figure 1.4. Make the Properties window active by clicking its title bar (the bar at the top of the window that says "Properties - Form1"). You can now scroll through the list of properties using the scroll bar at the right of the window. The left column lists the property names, and the right column lists the current value, or setting, of each property. There sure are a lot of properties, no? Don't be intimidated—you'll learn about these properties while working through the book.

Changing the Control Properties

For now we are interested in the **Caption** property. This controls the text that the label displays on the form. We'll need to change the current value of this property, *Label1*, so the label will identify one of the Text Box controls that we will be placing on the form. Use the following steps:

1. Be sure that the Label control you just placed on the form has handles displayed around it. If not, click on the control to activate it.

2. Double click on the **Caption** property name in the left column of the Properties window. The current caption *Label1* in the right column of the Properties window will become highlighted. (That is, it will display as white letters on a dark background.)

3. Type the new caption *Annual interest rate:*. The old caption will be replaced by what you type. If you make an error, press the Backspace key to erase it.

4. When you finish, press Enter.

You may find that the new caption is too long for the Label control, and that the end of the text is cut off. No problem, simply point at the handle on the right border of the control, and click, hold, and drag to stretch it until it's big enough.

Okay, the first Label is done. We need three more for this project, which you can create by using the techniques I just described. Change their **Caption** properties to read the following:

```
Loan period (months):
Loan amount:
Monthly payment:
```

After you've added the Label controls, your form will look similar to Figure 1.5. Note that you can change the size of the form itself at any time by pointing at the form border (the mouse pointer will change to a double-headed arrow) and dragging it to the desired size.

Adding the Text Box Controls

With the Label controls in place, the next step is to add the four Text Box controls outlined in our planning stage. The procedure is similar what you just learned, but I'll walk you through it anyway.

1. Click on the Text Box icon in the Toolbox. This icon has a white box with "ab" in it, and is usually located just to the right of the Label icon.

2. Point at the form where you want the Text Box located and press and hold the mouse button.

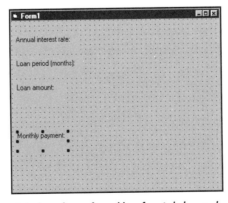

Figure 1.5 *The Mortgage Calculator form after adding four Label controls.*

3. Drag to place the Text Box.

4. Release the mouse button.

Repeat these steps to place all four Text Boxes. Each Text Box should be placed to the right of a Label. You'll see that each Text Box is assigned a default caption *Text1*, *Text2*, and so on. We'll change those next.

Changing Text Box Properties

As with the Label controls, we'll need to modify some properties of the Text Box controls that we just placed on the Mortgage Calculator form. This time, however, there are two properties that need changing for each of the four Text Boxes. One is the **Text** property, which controls the text that is displayed in the Text Box—we want to specify a blank **Text** property so the Text Box control is empty when the program starts. The other is the **Name** property, which specifies the identifying name associated with the control. For this property we want to assign a meaningful name to the control. Here are the steps to follow for the first Text Box:

1. Click the Text Box that is next to the *Annual interest rate:* label so that its handles are displayed.

2. Double click the **Text** property in the Properties window (you may have to scroll the Properties window to bring the desired property into view). The current setting *Text1* will be highlighted.

3. Press the Del key to erase the text.

4. Press Enter.

5. Double click the **Name** property in the Properties window.

6. Type "InterestRate."

7. Press Enter.

The procedure for changing the properties of the other Text Box controls is the same: Click the Text Box to select it, then change the properties in the Properties window. All of the Text Box controls should be given a blank **Text** property; the proper values for the **Name** properties are given in Table 1.1.

Table 1.1 *Proper Values For the Name Properties*

For the Text Box next to This Label	Assign This Name property
Loan period (months):	LoanPeriod
Loan amount:	LoanAmount
Monthly payment:	MonthlyPayment

There's one more property to change. While the first three Text Boxes are designed to accept input from the user, the last one, MonthlyPayment, does not need to accept user input. To prevent errors, therefore, we will *lock* it, which means it cannot be changed by the user while the program is running. (The program will still be able to display the answer there, of course.) Click the Text Box next to the *Monthly payment* label, then click the **Locked** property in the Properties window. The property setting in the right column will display False with a small button displaying a downward pointing arrow, as shown in Figure 1.6. Click the button to display a list of possible settings for the property; in this case there are only two, True and False. Click True to lock the Text Box.

Once all of the Text Box controls have been finished, there's one more step required to complete the visual interface.

> **Note:** *Why didn't we change the Name property of the Label controls? Since there is no need to refer to the Label controls in the program's code, their names are unimportant and the default names assigned by Visual Basic (Label1, Label2, and so on) are perfectly adequate.*

Adding a Command Button

During the planning stage we decided that the Mortgage Calculator should have a "Quit" button that the user could use to exit the program. Visual Basic's

Figure 1.6 *Setting the MonthlyPayment Text Box's Locked property.*

Command Button control is what we need. A Command Button is placed on the form in the same manner as the other controls. Click its icon in the Toolbox (the icon is a small gray rectangle, normally located just below the Text Box icon) then drag on the form to place the control. You'll need to change the Command Button's **Name** and **Caption** properties, too. Use the Properties window to do this as you learned above; both properties should be set to "Exit".

Adjusting the Form Size

You may find that the form's size is too big or too small for the controls you have placed on it. This is easily fixed. All you need do is point at one of the form's borders, making sure that the mouse pointer has changed into a two-headed arrow. Then, simply drag the form to the desired size. This might be a good time to fine-tune the position and sizes of the controls as well. Click each control that you want to adjust, dragging it to its new position, or dragging its handles to change its size.

Changing the Form's Caption

While not strictly necessary for the program to function, there's one more thing we can do to improve its appearance. It would be nice to have the main program window—the form—display the name of the program while it's running. As you might guess by now, the text displayed in the window's title bar is controlled by a property. In this case it's a property of the form, and here's how to change it:

1. Click anywhere on the form between the controls. When selected, the Properties window will display "Form1 form" on the first line below its title bar.

2. Double click the **Caption** property.

3. Type "Mortgage Calculator".

4. Press Enter.

The visual design stage of this project is complete, and your Visual Basic design screen will look more or less like Figure 1.7. We can now move to the third stage of development, writing the code. But first, saving the project to disk will safeguard our work against your 3-year-old tripping over the computer's power cord, or some other unexpected disaster.

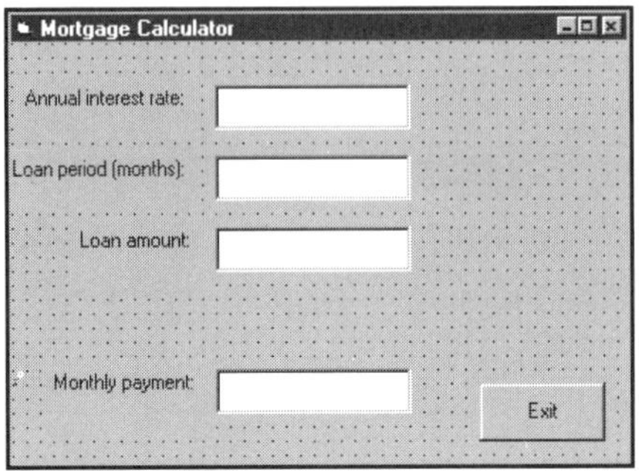

Figure 1.7 *The completed Mortgage Calculator form.*

Saving the Project

As you work on a Visual Basic project, all associated information is stored in your computer's random access memory (RAM). The problem with RAM is that it loses its information when the power is turned off. If you want your project to be there tomorrow, you must save it to disk. If you have any experience with other Windows programs, you probably already know how to do this, but I'll run through the procedure just in case. There are two parts to this step: saving the form and saving the project.

Pull down the File menu by clicking on File in the Menu window or by pressing Alt+F. Next, select the Save Project command from the menu by clicking it or by pressing "v". Visual Basic will display the Save File As dialog box, in which you specify a name for the disk file that the form is stored in. In the dialog box's File Name box, Visual Basic suggests a default file name that is the same as the form's Name property. Since we have not changed the form's Name property from its default value of Form1, that's what Visual Basic will suggest as a file name. We can do much better, however. Type "Mortgage Form" and press Enter.

Next, Visual Basic displays the Save Project As dialog box. Again, there's a File Name box with a default project name, typically Project1. Type "Mortgage Calculator" and press Enter.

That's all there is to it. Your project is now saved to disk, and you'll be able to load and continue working on it the next time you use your computer. Now that you have assigned file names to your project and form, pressing Ctrl+S automatically saves them under the existing names. It's a good idea to do this once in a while as you work on a project, and of course when you are finished and ready to quit Visual Basic.

Step 3: Writing the Code

The Mortgage Calculator's visual interface is complete. The next step is to write the code that does the actual work of the project. In this case the "work" consists of retrieving the input data that the user has entered in the three input Text Boxes, calculating the corresponding mortgage payment, and displaying the result in the fourth Text Box.

The code required to do this is relatively simple, requiring only a dozen lines or so. You can see it in Listing 1.1. Some readers are familiar with Basic code, while others are not, and I will not bore you by explaining how the code works. You may be able to decipher some of it on your own. I will, of course, be explaining all the details of Basic code later in the book. For now, however, I think it's more important for you to get a quick look at a working Visual Basic program, so I'll ask you to trust me on the code and just type it as shown in the listing.

The first step in adding the code is to switch Visual Basic from form design mode to code editing mode. You can do this two ways: by double clicking anywhere on the mortgage calculator form, or by clicking the View Code button in the Project window. Visual Basic will open a code editing window, as shown in Figure 1.8. Don't worry about any code that may be displayed in this window; we don't need it.

Next, display the Insert menu and select Procedure. Visual Basic displays the Insert Procedure dialog box, which is shown in Figure 1.9.

In the dialog box, type "Calculate" into the Name box, then press Enter. Don't worry about the options in the dialog box. We'll use the default settings.

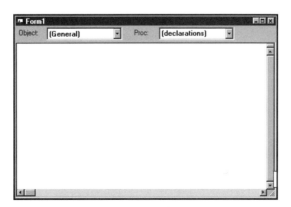

Figure 1.8 *A Visual Basic code editing window.*

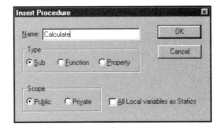

Figure 1.9 *You use the Insert Procedure dialog box to add a Basic procedure to your project.*

Visual Basic will open a new code editing window with the following two code statements already entered:

```
Public Sub Calculate()

End Sub
```

These two code statements define the beginning and end of a Basic *procedure*, a discrete section of code that has been assigned a name (in this case, the name is Calculate). In later chapters you'll see how Basic procedures are central to Visual Basic programming. For now, however, we are concentrating on finishing the project—explanations will come later. You need to type the remaining code from Listing 1.1 into the code editing window. Be careful with spelling, and remember not to duplicate the first and last lines of code. The code editing window is used like a word processor. Here are the basics:

- Text you type appears at the cursor (the blinking vertical line).

- Use the arrow keys to move the cursor.

- Press Enter to start a new line.

- Use Backspace to delete characters to the left of the cursor.

Listing 1.1   The Sub Calculate Procedure

```
Public Sub Calculate()

Dim answer As Currency, rate As Single
Dim months As Integer, amount As Single

If Val(InterestRate.Text) > 0 Then
    If Val(LoanPeriod.Text) > 0 Then
```

```
    If Val(LoanAmount.Text) > 0 Then
        rate = Val(InterestRate.Text) / 12
        months = Val(LoanPeriod)
        amount = Val(LoanAmount)
        answer = (amount * rate) / (1 - (1 + rate) ^ -months)
        MonthlyPayment.Text = Format(answer, "Currency")
      End If
    End If
End If

End Sub
```

Once the code has been entered, you should hit Ctrl+S to save the additions to the project. The Mortgage Calculator is now ready to take for a spin. You may be thinking "Hold on—it isn't finished yet!" That's absolutely correct, but running the program now will illustrate an important point about Visual Basic programming.

To run the program, press F5 or select Start from the Run menu. The program will start and display its dialog box. You can move the blinking cursor between Text Boxes by pressing Tab or Shift+Tab or by clicking the desired box with the mouse, and you can enter numbers in the three input Text Boxes, just like a real Windows program. (Well, of course, it *is* a real Windows program!) Funny thing, though—no answer appears in the Monthly Payment box! Also, nothing happens if you click on the Exit button (you'll have to press Alt+F4 or click the "X" button in the title bar to exit the program). What's wrong?

Nothing's wrong, but something is missing. We're written the code to perform the program's calculations, and we've created the visual interface. What's missing is the *connection* between the interface and the code. That's our next task.

Step 4: Connecting the Code to the Interface

When I say "connecting the code to the interface" it may sound rather technical. It's not, though—all it means is enabling the program to respond to the user. Think about what happened when you ran the incomplete Mortgage Calculator. The program ran, but didn't respond to your input. Whether you entered numbers in the input boxes, or clicked the Exit button, the program just sat there like a bump on a log. We need the program to respond to *events*—things the user does. What events, exactly, are we interested in? We'll deal with them one at a time.

Exiting the Program

Let's take the Exit button first. The event of interest, of course, is when the user clicks the button. We want:

- To write code that causes the program to terminate.

- To cause that code to be executed when the user clicks the button.

We accomplish this by creating an *event handler*, a procedure that executes when the event (the click) occurs. Dealing with user events such as button clicks is one of Visual Basic's strong points. You'll learn a lot more about it in later chapters, but for now I just want to show you how easy it is.

We need to work with the form. If it is hidden behind the code editing window, close the code window by clicking the Close button (the one with the "X") in the upper right corner. Now, double click the Exit Command Button control. Visual Basic displays a code editing window with the following two lines of code in it:

```
Private Sub Exit_Click()

End Sub
```

Now, add the following single line of code between those two lines:

```
End
```

The **End** statement is the Basic command to terminate a program. The job of this event handling procedure can be ascertained from its name. The first part of the name, **Exit**, is the name of the Command Button control—remember, we assigned this name earlier when we placed the Command Button on the form. The second part, **Click**, is the name of the event that we are interested in. Thus, we know that the code in this procedure will be executed when the control named Exit receives a click event. Note that the detection of the click is done automatically by Visual Basic. All we needed to do is write the code to be executed when the event occurs.

Try running the program (remember, press F5). Now when you click the Exit button, the program ends, just like it should. The mortgage calculations are still not working, however. We'll fix this problem next.

Performing the Calculations

You may have caught on already that getting the program to perform the mortgage calculation and display the answer will be triggered by some event. But what event? There is no "Calculate" button to click, so we can't use the Click event. But think for a moment about what the user will be doing; he or she will be entering or changing information in the three input Text Boxes. Can we use this as the "event" to trigger the program's calculations? Indeed we can. Text Box controls have a Change event that is automatically triggered whenever the data in the box changes.

Our strategy is clear. We will write an event handling procedure for each of the three input Text Box controls. Since we have already written the **Calculate** procedure that does the work of performing the mortgage calculations and displaying the answer, all that the code in the Change event procedures will need to do is execute the **Calculate** procedure.

As before, we begin by double clicking the control of interest, in this case, the Annual interest rate Text Box control. Visual Basic displays a code editing window with these lines of code in it:

```
Private Sub InterestRate_Change()

End Sub
```

You can see from the event procedure name that it will be executed when the control named **InterestRate** receives a **Change** event. Add the following line of code between the two existing lines:

```
Call Calculate
```

This line says, in effect, "Execute the code in the procedure named **Calculate**." After adding the code, you can close the code editing window by clicking the "X" button in the top right corner.

We want the program to respond to changes in all three input Text Boxes, so repeat the above steps—double clicking the control and adding the same line of code—on the other two input Text Box controls. When you're done, press Ctrl+S to save the project.

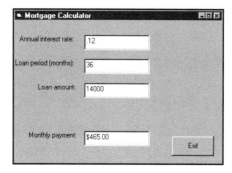

Figure 1.10 *The mortgage calculator in action.*

Trying it Out

Congratulations! You have just completed your first Visual Basic program. Press F5 to run the program. Enter values in the three input Text Boxes. As soon as there is something in each box, the program will display an answer in the Monthly Payment box. As you change your input values, the answer automatically changes to provide the correct answer. Click the Exit button to quit the program.

Remember that the interest rate values must be entered as decimals—.08 for 8%, for example. You can have fun seeing just how much the payments on that $500,000 house would be! Note that the Mortgage Calculator is not limited to mortgages. It can be used for any type of loan with a fixed interest rate and regular payments, such as a car loan.

WHAT'S NEXT?

Now that you have joined the ranks of Windows programmers, where do you go from here? There's a lot more to learn about Visual Basic, of course, since this first program has only scratched the surface. I hope that this quick introduction to the power of Visual Basic has whetted your appetite for more. If you think that the Mortgage Calculator is cool, wait until you see what else Visual Basic can do!

A Whole New Way of Programming

CHAPTER 2

Visual Basic introduced an entirely new programming paradigm. You need to understand the underlying concepts if you are going to master it.

After taking a look at Visual Basic, you might be ready to move on and learn more, or you might may be a bit puzzled. If the latter is true, you probably have some programming experience under your belt (non-Visual Basic experience, that is). This seems strange—shouldn't previous programming experience make it *easier* to pick up Visual Basic? Not necessarily. Sit back a minute and I'll explain.

OUT WITH THE OLD, IN WITH THE NEW

Prior to Visual Basic, all programming languages were conceptually pretty much the same. Sure, there were differences in language keywords, syntax, and other details, but beneath these surface distinctions, programming in C was pretty much the same as programming in Pascal, FORTRAN, or COBOL. Programmers could, and often did, move from language to language with little difficulty.

Then along came Visual Basic with its radically different approach to programming. Experienced programmers not only had to learn something new, they had to wrap their brains around a variety of programming principles that were in distinct contrast to what they already knew. Not everyone found this to be a problem, but some of us—and I speak from experience—required some time and effort to get the hang of Visual Basic.

For other people, however, Visual Basic was their first foray into computer programming. They had no old concepts to "unlearn" and no old programming habits to break. Visual Basic was not puzzling or different to them, it was simply the way to program. The result was that, in many cases, newcomers were able to catch on to the Visual Basic way of doing things more easily than the old pros.

There's more to this story. Believe it or not, part of the problem is that Visual Basic makes it so easy to create Windows programs. I am using the term "easy" in the comparative sense, of course—writing a large, complex Windows program in Visual Basic is no walk in the park, but it is an order of magnitude easier than doing it the old way. This is great, and was in fact one of the goals behind the development of Visual Basic—programming should be accessible to any reasonably intelligent computer user, and no longer be limited to the trained professionals. But this resulted in many users obtaining only a surface knowledge of Visual Basic, enough to create working programs but not sufficient to take full advantage of its features and power. The result? Wasted time and effort, and programs that don't perform as well as they could. Sort of like the guy who fancies himself to be "Mr. Fix It" and then goes around using his screwdriver for a chisel.

We'll have none of that here! My goal is to teach you not only the nuts and bolts of Visual Basic programming, but also show you the underlying structure of Visual Basic so you can use those nuts and bolts to your best advantage. When we're done, you'll not only have a full set of chisels *and* screwdrivers in your toolkit, but you'll know exactly when and how to use each one.

GET TO KNOW WINDOWS

Before we get started on our Visual Basic adventure, it's important that you have some familiarity with Windows applications and Windows itself. I'm not talking about programming, and I'm not talking about being any sort of expert. All I mean is that you should have some experience, if only a couple of hours worth, using Windows programs. And it doesn't really matter which programs you use, because the objective here is to give you a feel for the commonalities between Windows programs. The sample programs that are supplied with Windows are excellent choices—the games and the Paint program, for example. Since you'll be using Visual Basic to create Windows programs, it's helpful to have some idea of what the end product will be like!

UNDER THE HOOD

From your brief look at Visual Basic in Chapter 1, you have probably guessed that there's a lot going on behind the scenes in Visual Basic. You're absolutely correct—but what exactly is going on, and what is it for? The answer to the second question is easy—it's for *you*, the programmer, and the purpose is to make your life easier! But what is this stuff that goes on?

Think for a moment about the various Windows programs that you use. Sure, they are different in many ways, but there are plenty of similarities too. They all have screen windows, for one thing, and the windows can be resized, moved, minimized, and so on. They also all have a subset of the same fundamental components: pull-down menus, option buttons that can be turned on or off, command buttons that carry out an action when clicked, text boxes for display and entry of text…. The list could go on and on. But the conclusion is clear: *Windows programs consist largely of the same basic components put together in different ways.*

Now let's go a step further and ask: What is it that these components do? Of course their specific tasks vary from one program to the next, so consider this question at a more fundamental level. A menu drops down when its title is clicked, a text box permits text entry and editing, an option button switches between "on" and "off" when selected…. Again, I could go on and on, but I hope the point is made: *Windows components respond to the user.*

Putting these two insights together, we see that a significant part of any Windows program consists of these "responsive components"—that is, the fundamental Windows objects through which the user interacts with the program. And *that's* the main job of Visual Basic, *that's* what's going on behind the scenes—a whole lot of stuff just to make it easy for you to include these responsive components in your program.

The Skeleton in Your Program

To use some "official" terminology, we can say that Visual Basic is an *applications framework*. It provides the bones—the skeleton, if you will—for your applications. All the fundamental building blocks of a Windows program are there in Visual Basic, waiting for you to use them. No longer do you have to write dozens of lines of code to display a dialog box or an option button. (Yes, this is the way Windows programs used to be written!) The process is so simple that you are free to spend almost all of your time and mental energy working on the important parts of your program—the things that make it unique in the world of Windows programs.

The idea here—and I know I'm repeating myself, but this is important—is that a lot of what goes on in any Windows program goes on in all other Windows programs too. Every time you put a text box or a menu in a program, a thousand other programmers are doing the same thing—from London to Sydney, from Bombay to Cherepovets. (Look it up! Hint: it's not in Silicon Valley.) The folks at Microsoft reasoned, "Why should every programmer have to spend time writing the same code for the same program elements? Let's do all that basic stuff for them." Thus was born one of the fundamental ideas behind Visual Basic, that of the applications framework: Let the development tool—that is, Visual Basic—do all the boring, repetitive work, freeing the programmer to work on the creative aspects of the program. Which brings us to:

AITKEN'S RULE #1: *Don't Reinvent the Wheel*

Visual Basic's job, then, is to provide a whole bunch of the "wheels" that your Windows programs need. The time you might have spent reinventing these wheels will be better spent in creating the meaningful program features that make your program unique. I hope you'll forgive my terrible mixing of metaphors—one minute Visual Basic is a framework, next it's a skeleton, and now it's wheels—but this is an important point that you need to understand. When you're creating a Visual Basic application, and you need to add some feature or capability to the program, the first thing to do is to see whether Visual Basic provides what you need. Visual Basic doesn't have everything, but you will be surprised to see just how much it does have!

A Framework Is Not Enough

The framework provided by Visual Basic is pretty darned amazing. Visual Basic's framework is so complete, in fact, that you can create a very impressive looking program without writing a single line of code (or, at most, a very few lines). The program could have multiple windows, each containing an impressive array of Option Buttons, lists, Text Boxes, and so on. Menus would display when needed, dialog boxes would come and go, and everything would look terrific. Only one thing would be lacking, but it's a very important thing—the program wouldn't *do* anything (other than look nice). The meaningful parts of the program—the parts that make it into a word processor, a stock market analyzer, or a multimedia presentation—are missing. This is what you, the programmer, must add. To teach you how to do this is the main goal of this book. As you'll see in this and subsequent chapters, there are two main parts to this task:

- Selecting those components from the Visual Basic framework that are best suited to your program

- Writing Basic code to tie the framework components together and provide the needed functionality

In the remainder of this chapter, we'll take a closer look at the different parts of Visual Basic. I know you're probably itching to sit down at your computer and get to work with Visual Basic, and I promise that we will in the next chapter. But please try to stay with me for the next few pages; I think you'll find this theoretical material to be a real help down the road.

OBJECTS IS OBJECTS

The framework that Visual Basic provides comes in the shape of *objects*. You had an introduction to Visual Basic objects in Chapter 1. Because you've seen objects in action, you'll be better able to understand the following material on what goes on behind the scene with objects.

eXPLORER TIP

Is Visual Basic Object-Oriented Programming (OOP)?

In a word, no. With all the talk of objects in Visual Basic, you might well think that Visual Basic lets you do OOP. Not true. While Visual Basic lets you do some things that are similar to OOP, it does not have the characteristics of a true object-oriented language such as C++ or SmallTalk. The term "object" is used differently in Visual Basic. This does not mean that Visual Basic is lacking in some way—it's just a different approach to programming (and for many purposes, a better one).

Two Kinds of Objects

There are two basic kinds of objects: *forms*, which are simply screen windows, and *controls*, which are placed on forms to provide functionality. There are many different kinds of controls, including text boxes, option buttons, and command buttons. A Visual Basic program consists of one or more forms; each form usually contains one or more controls. I say "usually" because it is possible to do things with a blank form, although this is not common. A form can also contain a menu, just like the menus you find in other Windows programs. Visual Basic has a menu editor that makes menu design easy.

You can see that a large part of creating a Visual Basic program consists of working with objects. You must decide how many forms your program needs, and which controls to place on each form. The mechanics of creating the forms and placing controls is quite easy, as you saw if you worked through the project in Chapter 1. This technique of visual interface design—painting your program's screens—is one of the two landmark innovations that Visual Basic brought to programming. We'll meet the other technique later in the chapter.

Properties

All Visual Basic objects have properties. An object's properties determine the way it looks and behaves. For example, almost all objects have **Top** and **Left** properties, which specify the screen position of the upper-left corner of the object. Likewise, the **Height** and **Width** properties specify the size of the object. Each type of object has its own set of properties, often running to a couple of dozen or more. While some properties, such as those just mentioned, are common to many or all objects, there are other more specialized properties that are relevant to only one or, at most, a few types of objects.

Object properties are also an important part of a Visual Basic program's interactions with the user. For example, if the user has entered text in a Text Box control, the program can access that text via the control's **Text** property. In a similar manner, by reading a Check Box control's **Value** property the program can determine whether the user has turned the corresponding program option on or off. Note that when I say "the program," I am referring to the Basic code in the program, code that you write.

You can change object properties during program design (referred to as *design-time*). Properties can also be read and modified at runtime, while the program is executing. The ability to read and modify properties at runtime may sound trivial, but in fact it is a central part of Visual Basic's power. It permits a program to be *self-modifying*, to change its appearance and behavior in response to current conditions and user input. You'll see plenty of examples of this throughout the book.

You'll find that a significant proportion of your Visual Basic programming time will be spent dealing with these properties. This fact is an indication of the importance of object properties. We can think of properties as the edges, or skin, of objects. Our knowledge and control of an object is limited to the properties the object makes available to us. There may be all sorts of complicated stuff going on inside an object, but we have no way of knowing about it. More important, we don't *want* to know about it. All we need is access to the object's properties in order to make full use of its capabilities.

Methods

Most Visual Basic objects have one or more *methods* associated with them. A method can be thought of as a chunk of code that does something to, or with, the object. Instead of you having to write the code, however, it is an integral part of the object.

The methods that are available differ from object to object. For example, the **Move** method, which moves an object to a different location on screen, is available for most objects. In contrast, the **Print** method, which displays text on an object, is available only for forms and a few other objects where the display of text makes sense.

EVENTS MAKE IT HAPPEN

The second major innovation that Visual Basic introduced is *event-driven programming*. (The first, in case you were dozing for the first part of the chapter, is the use of visual objects.) So what are events, and how do they work? The first part is easy. With a few exceptions, events are things the user does with the mouse or the keyboard while the program is running. In other words, "event" means user input. So far so good, and hardly surprising. "Of course a program must respond to user input, so what's the big deal?" I can hear you saying. The big deal is *how* a Visual Basic program responds to user input, and how *easy* is it for the programmer. I'll explain by comparing how a DOS program deals with events with the Windows approach.

DOS Event Handling

When you write a program to run under DOS, it is necessary to explicitly write code for detection of all user events (mouse or keyboard input). And that's a lot of work. In a sense, the title of this section is inaccurate because the DOS operating system does no event detection—it is totally up to the program code. For example, if you wanted the user to be able to select from a menu with the mouse, you would need to write code to perform the following steps:

1. Display the menu text.

2. Query the mouse driver to see if a click has occurred.

3. If yes, go to step 4. If no, return to step 2.

4. Query the mouse driver to obtain the screen coordinates where the click occurred.

5. Do the click coordinates match up with the screen locations of one of the menu items?

6. If no, return to step 2. If yes, branch to the code associated with the menu item.

The procedure for responding to keyboard input is similar—look for each keystroke and then compare it with the list of keys the program is interested in. This event-detection process is illustrated in Figure 2.1.

This method of event handling has two consequences:

- The program can respond only to those events that are explicitly programmed. If a keystroke or a mouse location is not included in the code, the program is oblivious to them.

- The program can respond to events only while the event-detection code is executing. At other times—while the program is performing calculations or printing, for example, it is unresponsive.

It's true that over the years clever programmers have developed methods to partially overcome these limitations. This was typically accomplished by using the PC's interrupts or memory-resident programs, advanced programming techniques that have driven many a programmer to drink (if only a tenth can of

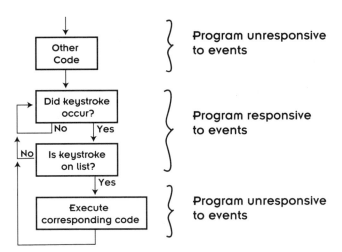

Figure 2.1   *DOS's linear method of responding to events.*

Jolt cola!). The fact remains that DOS input handling is still a linear, do-one-thing-at-a-time process. Some programmers have done things this way for so long that they think it's the only way to do it, and, as a result, have difficulty adapting to Visual Basic.

Windows Does it Differently

If you've used Windows at all, and given some thought to how it works, you are probably already aware that the way Windows handles user input, or events, is totally different. (If you haven't used Windows much, I'll repeat my suggestion that you do so before continuing.) With rare exceptions, Windows is *always* responsive to events. Even if the currently active program is not responding, Windows itself is—whether you press Alt+Tab to switch to the next task, click a button on the task bar, or whatever, the event is detected. Of course every user event is not responded to—that would lead to chaos—but some are. To be completely accurate, every event is detected, but only certain ones are responded to. How does Windows do this?

Hello, Western Union?

At the heart of Windows' event-detection capabilities is its messaging architecture. In fact, messages play a vital role in just about everything Windows does, but we will limit ourselves to a very basic look at messages and events.

Whenever Windows is running, Windows is running. Now this may seem like a nonsensical statement, but it serves to emphasize the fact that there is a much more intimate relationship between the Windows operating system and programs than there is between DOS and programs. Many, if not most of the things a program does are actually done by Windows, at the program's request. Among these tasks is complete management of user input via the keyboard and mouse. When any mouse or keyboard event happens, Windows knows about it. A message identifying the event is dispatched to Windows' message queue. The message might say, in effect, "The mouse was clicked at screen coordinates such-and-such." All of the running programs, or processes, can receive the message. This includes application programs as well as Windows' own processes. The message is available to all processes, but only the process that is interested in the event will bother to "read" the message and respond. Sort of like a mother going to the front porch and yelling "Herman, if you don't get yourself home for dinner this instant I'll tan your behind." All the kids in the neighborhood have access to the message, but only Herman will respond (at least he will if he knows what's good for him!).

Figure 2.2 shows a simplified diagram of the Windows messaging system. My account is simplified as well, and the actual system is really quite complex. But you don't need to understand all the details; it's enough if you grasp the basics of messaging.

Just remember that Windows does all the work of event detection, and dispatches messages identifying each event that occurs. All your program needs to do is keep an eye on the message stream and latch on to the messages of interest. How is this done? As you'll see next, it's ridiculously easy.

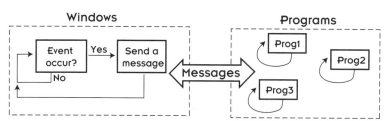

Figure 2.2 *Windows is continually looking for events. When one is detected, a message is dispatched that running programs can respond to.*

Event Procedures

Earlier in this chapter, I said that there were two ground-breaking innovations that Visual Basic brought to Windows programming, with the first one being visual interface design. Now we'll meet the second one, event detection. Well, not event detection itself, since that's nothing new. Rather it's the ease with which a programmer can make his or her program respond to events that is the innovation. It is all done with *event procedures*.

An event procedure is a procedure, or block of Basic code, that is associated with an event. When the event is detected, the code in the procedure is automatically executed. Creating an event procedure in Visual Basic is a simple two step process:

1. Select the object (Text Box, Command Cutton, etc.) that will respond to the event.

2. Choose the desired event from a list of events that the selected object can detect.

It's really that simple! Carrying out these steps creates the skeleton of an event procedure that looks something like this:

```
Sub ExitButton_Click()

End Sub
```

The name of the event procedure identifies both the visual object and the event. In this case, the object is a Command Button to which we have assigned a **Name** property of *ExitButton,* and the event is a mouse click. When the program executes and the user clicks the button, this procedure will be executed. There is nothing more involved in getting the program to respond to events.

Of course, you must still write the code that will be executed within the event procedure. The skeleton procedure above is empty, so it does not do anything when it executes. We'll be spending a lot of time learning Basic code, so you'll soon be able to write event procedures that perform useful tasks. Actually, event procedure code usually does not perform the task itself, but rather calls code that is located elsewhere, outside the event procedure, to do the work. The reasons for this will be explained in a later chapter. In any event (pardon the pun!), the result is the same—the program responds to user input. Visual Basic puts the whole range of user events at your fingertips. When creating a program, you need only decide which events the program should respond to, and what the response will be.

COMPONENTS, ANYONE?

Another avenue of programming that has been receiving increased attention, thanks in part to Visual Basic, is the use of software components. This is nothing new, of course—software components have been around for a long time, sometimes under another name. However, the complexity of Windows programming and the continued development of sophisticated programming tools, such as Visual Basic, have made an increased reliance on software components not only possible, but necessary.

A software component is nothing more than a self-contained chunk of software that performs a specific task. The task can be just about anything, from the very simple, such as calculating a cube root, to the very complex, such as providing a spreadsheet-like grid in a window. The "self-contained" part is important. To get the maximum benefits from a software component, you should be able to take it off the shelf, so to speak, and drop it directly into your program without any fuss. The more software components you have at your disposal, the easier your programming will be. Instead of writing, testing, debugging, and rewriting the code yourself, all you do is pop the component into your program. Remember the "wheels" I was talking about earlier in the chapter, and Aitken's rule #1, don't reinvent the wheel? Software components are those ready-made wheels.

Some of you may be thinking that Visual Basic's objects are software components, and you are 100 percent correct. This is one of the three levels of software component use in Visual Basic. By themselves they are very powerful, but there's more.

On a second level, Visual Basic permits you to create your own software components. As you gain more programming experience, you'll probably find that there are things you are doing over and over in different programs. This is particularly true if all your programming tends to fall in a specialized category, such as graphics or database. For example, many of your programs may need a dialog box that lets the user select from a palette of background patterns.Whatever the specifics, Visual Basic provides the tools that permit you to wrap the functionality in a self-contained component that you can then easily drop into future programs.

The third level at which Visual Basic uses software components is that of custom controls, sometimes called OCX controls. These controls are not supplied with the Visual Basic package, but you use them just like the controls that come with Visual Basic; you place them on your forms and interact with them by means of their properties. You can purchase some custom controls commercially, others are available as freeware or shareware, and some are provided on the disk that accompanies this book. (See *Appendix* for a description of the controls supplied on the companion disk.)

The Software Component Mindset

Sure, software components sound like a good idea, and anyone can see the advantages of using them. But to really get the maximum benefit from components, you will have to develop a specific way of thinking when creating Visual Basic programs, something I call the *software component mindset*. It's more than just thinking, "Oh yeah, maybe I can use a software component here." Rather, it's the habit of starting at the very beginning, when the structure of your Visual Basic program first starts to take shape in your mind, with the goal of using as many software components as possible—in other words, you want to invent as few wheels as possible.

Not only do you want to maximize the use of existing components in your program, you also want to remain aware of creating your own components. In almost all of the programs you write, there will be certain functions for which you will not be able to use an existing component, so you'll have to write them yourself. With a bit of planning, you can create components for these functions, components that will be available to you in the future. After a while you'll find yourself with a small library of software components that perform the functions you need most often in your programs.

As for using custom controls, you can't use them if you don't know what's available. Dozens of publishers and private programmers are continually devising new custom controls, so there is a wide variety available. To keep aware of what's out there, you may want to subscribe to a Visual Basic programming magazine, get on some manufacturer's mailing lists, attend Visual Basic trade shows, and frequent the Visual Basic programming forums on CompuServe and other online services. As for the cost of commercial custom controls, some of the prices may seem high at first, but they all turn out to be relatively inexpensive when you figure in the time and aggravation you'll save. This is particularly true if you are writing Visual Basic programs for paying clients, who can be mighty impressed when you deliver a robust, powerful program ahead of schedule!

THE ROLE OF CODE

What's the role of Basic code in Visual Basic? Isn't programming supposed to require writing lots of code? So far I've been talking about just about anything *besides* code in this chapter—objects, properties, components, and what-not. Where's the code?

Don't worry, you'll be writing plenty of code for your Visual Basic programs. While some programs require less code than others, there is always some code needed behind the scenes to tie everything together and perform the real work of the program. If you want to perform mathematical calculations, read data from disk, display graphics or text on-screen, or send data over a modem, you'll have to write the code for it. If you want to display a form, change an object's properties, or respond to an event, you'll have to write code. If you want your program to recover gracefully from errors, you'll have to write code. Code ties all a program's objects together, linking them to each other, to the user, and to the outside world. Don't worry! Code has a plenty big role in Visual Basic!

ENOUGH TALK — LET'S PROGRAM!

If you've managed to slog though this entire chapter, you are probably raring to go. If you'll bear with me, I'd like to finish with a few suggestions and reminders about Visual Basic programming:

- *Plan ahead.* Like all types of programming, creating a Visual Basic program will always go more smoothly if you spend some time planning ahead. Think about what you need to do in the context of Visual Basic's available tools. This sort of planning is more difficult when you're just starting out with Visual Basic, because you are unfamiliar with its capabilities. But as you gain expertise, planning should become a top priority.

- *Think like a user.* Design your program from the user's perspective. Don't base program design on what's easy for you to program. What data will the user want to see? How will he or she want it displayed? What tasks, and in what order, will the user need to perform? Many technically talented programmers have seen their work collect dust on user's shelves because they neglected to follow this advice.

- *Think components!* Once you have some idea of what your program will do, start looking for existing software components that can do parts of the job. When you're doing it yourself, make an effort to encapsulate your interface and code elements in self-contained components that you'll be able to reuse.

- *Learn by doing.* Programming is like surgery (except for the pay, of course!): you can read all the books you want, but you'll never learn how to do it, except by doing it. That's the approach I take in this book, and you should too. Yes, you should definitely read the rest of this book, but you should also spend as much time as you can working with Visual Basic. You'll be pleasantly surprised by how quickly your programming skills improve.

- *Learn from other Visual Basic programs.* Take time to examine other people's Visual Basic programs. You never know when you'll come across an idea or technique that you can use in your own work. Sources for Visual Basic programs include the sample programs provided with the Visual Basic package, Visual Basic programming forums provided by online services, such as CompuServe, and books and magazines.

And now, friend, into the fray.

VISUAL DESIGN— DRAWING YOUR PROGRAM

Part of Visual Basic programming involves drawing rather than writing code. In this chapter, I'll show you the techniques of visual interface design, and how an object's properties define it.

In Chapter 1, you had an introduction to Visual Basic by creating and running a simple project. Then, in Chapter 2, you learned some of the concepts and theory behind Visual Basic, and how it differs from earlier methods of programming. I hope that you're excited and ready to learn more, because we've just begun to scratch the surface. Now it's time to learn more about controls and properties.

I cannot overemphasize the close relationship between objects and properties. There's really no separating them—an object *is* its properties, to a very large degree. To get the most out of Visual Basic's objects, you need to develop an intimate knowledge of their properties. And since objects are central to the whole idea of Visual Basic programming...well, you get the idea!

Let's start with the fairly simple subject of drawing your interface—in other words, placing controls on forms. Then, we'll explore properties, and work through a demonstration project to illustrate these concepts.

DRAWING YOUR WAY TO SUCCESS

When Visual Basic burst onto the scene, the thing that most amazed programmers was the way it let you draw the program's visual interface. No more writing long and complex code statements to display something on-screen—point, click, drag, and that's all there was to it! Now that Visual Basic has been around a while, and has spawned a whole fleet of copycats, the idea of drawing a program's interface has become accepted as the norm. Even so, I still think it's fun. In this section, I'll describe the tools and techniques Visual Basic provides for interface design.

The controls available to you are represented by buttons in the Visual Basic toolbox. The picture on each button makes an attempt to represent the corresponding control, but if you're still not sure, just rest the mouse pointer over the button for a second or two, and a *tooltip* will display next to the mouse pointer, describing the button's control.

Placing Controls on a Form

When you start Visual Basic, a new project and a blank form will display in the Project window. Generally you will just start working with this form, but if you need another blank form, simply select Form from the Insert menu. A Visual Basic program can contain multiple forms, although we will be limiting ourselves to single form projects for now.

There are two methods for placing controls on a form. If you double click on a button in the toolbox, Visual Basic will place a default-size control in the center of the form. Your alternative method is to click on the desired button and then drag to place the control on the form. The click-and-drag method has the advantage of letting you place the control and set its position and size in one step, but you can use whichever technique you prefer.

If you've placed a control on the form and want to place more controls of the same size and type, you can copy the original. Be sure that the control you want to copy is selected (small black *handles* will appear around the edges of a selected control). If not, click on the control to select it, and follow these steps.

1. Press Ctrl+C (or select Copy from the Edit menu) to place a copy of the control on the Windows Clipboard.

2. Press Ctrl+V (or select Paste from the Edit menu). Visual Basic displays a dialog box asking if you want to create a control array.

3. Select No (we'll learn about control arrays later).

4. A duplicate control is placed on the form.

5. Repeat steps 2 through 4 to place additional copies of the control on the form.

Manipulating the Form

The size and position of a form during program design is the size and position it will have when the final program runs (unless you modify the size or position in code). You can change the form's position by dragging its title bar to the new location. To change size, point at one of the form's borders (the mouse pointer will change to a double-headed arrow) and drag to the new size. If you drag one of the corners of the form, you can change its height and width at the same time.

As you may have guessed, a form's size and position are properties, and can therefore be changed by the program's code when the program executes. Most Visual Basic programmers don't worry about form position during design. If it is necessary to display the window at a specific position when the program runs, it is better done in code. Size is a different matter. Forms that contain a lot of controls, like most dialog boxes, will have their "proper" size dictated by their contents. Too small will hide some of the controls; too large and you're wasting valuable screen space. The usual approach here is to adjust the size of the form visually during design, then set the form's **BorderStyle** property to *Fixed Dialog* so the user will not be able to change its size while the program is running.

Moving, Sizing, and Aligning Controls

Once you have placed controls on a form, you will probably need to tweak them a bit to get their sizes and position just right. A sloppily constructed form, with controls that are poorly aligned and inconsistent sizes, will *not* impress your customers!

To work with controls on a form, you must select the control or controls that you are interested in. To select multiple controls, click on the first one, then press and hold the Shift key while you click on the others. As I mentioned previously, selected controls have handles displayed on their edges. If only one control is selected, its handles are black. If two or more controls are selected, the handles on each control are gray. To delete the selected controls, press Del.

Selecting the Form

To select the form itself, click on the form between controls. The form won't display handles, but you can tell it's selected because the Properties window will display the form name in its title bar.

When you have one control selected, you can change its size by pointing at one of its handles and dragging the outline to the desired size. You can change its position by pointing to the control (not a handle) and dragging. With more than one control selected, you can move them as a group, with the individual controls retaining their positions relative to each other. You cannot, however, change the size of multiple selected controls.

Alignment of controls is another pesky design issue. However, the Visual Basic design grid makes things easier. Note that the design form has a grid of dots displayed on it. Visual Basic's normal behavior is to "snap" controls to this grid. In other words, when you are moving or sizing a control, its edges always align with the grid—they cannot take intermediate positions. By aligning controls to the grid, it is relatively simple to ensure that a group of controls are all the same size and are also equally spaced.

The design grid is controlled by the Options dialog box, which you display by selecting Options from the Tools menu. In the dialog box click on the Environment tab, and look for the Form Design Grid section. You have several options to set here:

- **Show Grid** determines whether the grid dots are displayed. Controls will align to the grid whether or not the grid is displayed.

- **Width and Height** sets the spacing of grid dots in a Visual Basic unit called *twips* (more on twips soon).

- **Align Controls to Grid** specifies whether controls snap to the grid or are free to be positioned at any location.

Changing the width or height of the grid does not affect controls already on the form—only controls added after the grid has been modified. The same is true of turning alignment on or off.

There are a few other visual design tricks you should know. You can overlap controls; normally, the one that was placed on the form first will be totally or partially hidden by the one placed later. You can modify the relationship of overlapped controls with the Bring to Front and Send to Back commands, both located on the Edit menu. Bring to Front makes the selected control the top one in the "pile" of overlapping controls, so it will be visible and hide the other controls. Send to Back has the opposite effect.

Finally, you can lock the controls on a form to prevent them from being modified. Select the Lock Controls command on the Edit menu, and all controls on the form—both existing ones and ones you add subsequently—are locked and cannot be moved or resized (but they can be deleted). Select the command again to unlock the controls. When locked, selected controls display white handles.

A CONTROL GALLERY

Now that you know how to place and arrange controls on a form, it's time to give you a brief overview of some of the controls that Visual Basic provides. This is not intended to be an detailed summary of the entire Visual Basic control set; rather, my intention is simply to make you aware of the most fundamental of the controls, those that are used most often. You'll meet the other controls later in the book. Figure 3.1 illustrates the more common Visual Basic controls.

- The *Command Button* provides a way for the user to tell the program "go" or "start." Its most typical use is to cause the program to take some action when the user clicks on the button or selects it using the keyboard.

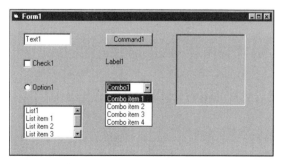

Figure 3.1 *Some of Visual Basic's most useful controls.*

- The *Text Box* is used for the display, input, and editing of text. A Text Box can display anything from a single word to a document containing a hundred lines of text. You'll find that the Text Box is one of Visual Basic's most useful and powerful controls.

- The *Check Box* lets the user turn an option on or off. A Check Box consists of a small box with an adjacent label. Check boxes toggle on and off using the same keystroke; clicking on the box or selecting it with the keyboard puts (or removes) an "X" in the box. The program can query the Check Box's **Value** property to see if it is in the "on" or "off" state.

- The *Option Button* is similar to the Check Box in that it provides an option that can be turned on or off by the user. The difference is that Option Buttons are always arranged in groups of two or more, and only one option in the group can be on at any time.

- The *Picture Box* does just what its name suggests—displays a picture. You can also create graphics in a Picture Box using Basic statements. The Picture Box control has a lot of hidden power that greatly simplifies the otherwise complex task of handling and displaying graphics and images. In Figure 3.1, the Picture Box displays as a blank rectangle because it has not yet been loaded with a picture.

- The *Label* is perhaps the simplest control, with the main purpose of displaying fixed text on a form. By "fixed," I mean that the user cannot edit or modify the text, so Labels are generally used to identify other items on a form.

- A *List Box* displays a scrollable list of text items from which the user can select. With automatic sorting of its contents, it is a common method of presenting a list of options, such as font names, to the user.

- A *Combo Box* can be thought of as a combination of a Text Box and a List Box. It normally displays like a single-line Text Box, but clicking its arrow opens a list of items from which the user can choose.

This list includes only eight of Visual Basic's twenty primary controls. The primary controls are an integral part of the Visual Basic development environment, and are always displayed in the toolbox. Visual Basic also supports *custom controls*, drop-in components that represent one of the legs of the software component philosophy (as covered in Chapter 2).

The custom controls you have available to you may vary. Some are provided with Visual Basic. In the past, Visual Basic was sold in two versions, the Standard Edition and the more expensive Professional Edition, which provided various additional capabilities, including additional custom controls. At the time of this writing it was not clear whether Visual Basic 4.0 would be sold in two versions also, but if it is, I strongly recommend that you purchase the Professional Edition—the extra features are well worth the cost.

You can control which of the available custom controls are displayed in the toolbox by selecting Custom Controls from the Tools menu (or pressing Ctrl+T). The Custom Controls dialog box, shown in Figure 3.2, lists all of the custom controls and insertable objects that you have available. (I'll explain what an insertable object is in a minute). Only those controls and objects with an "X" in the box next to their name will be displayed as buttons in the toolbox. Click in the boxes to turn the option on or off. My system offers 39 custom controls and objects, and displaying all of them all the time, along with the 20 primary controls, would result in a confusing and unwieldy toolbox. So you can see why Visual Basic lets you determine which controls are displayed in the toolbox.

Now for the difference between a custom control and an insertable object. In one sense they are equivalent, because they both represent a software component that you can drop into your Visual Basic programs. A custom control is a self-contained component that depends only on its OCX file, and has no use except for being dropped in a Visual Basic program (or a program created with another development tool that supports custom controls).

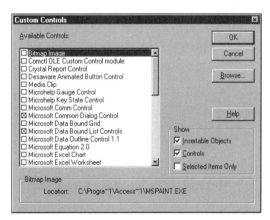

Figure 3.2 *The Custom Controls dialog box.*

In contrast, an insertable object represents a data object that is supported by an existing application on your system. An insertable object is available to your Visual Basic programs only if the corresponding application is installed on your system. For example, you can create a chart in Microsoft Excel and then insert the chart data into your Visual Basic program. However, people using your programs will be able to use the inserted object only if they also have the application on their system.

PROPERTIES MAKE THE OBJECT

Every Visual Basic object has a set of properties that control how it looks and behaves. This is true even of insertable objects, although their property sets are relatively small because so much of their behavior is determined by the parent application and not by Visual Basic. But rather than talking about properties, let's create a simple Visual Basic project that shows you how properties work. This program will display text in a Text Box, and permit the user to change the size of the Text Box and the color of the text.

Starting to Design the Interface

Our project will consist of a single dialog box with eight controls. Start by firing up Visual Basic. The first control we'll place is a Text Box. Using the techniques you learned earlier in this chapter, place a text box in the upper-left corner of the form. The exact size doesn't matter—perhaps one grid unit high by six units wide. Of course, you can always adjust it later. Before placing the other controls, let's set the properties for the Text Box that we just added.

Changing the Text Property

Make sure that the Text Box is selected, then take a look at the Properties window (if it's not displayed, press F4). The Properties window displays the properties of the selected object, with the object's name displayed in the title bar and also in the box just below the title bar. This box is like a Visual Basic Combo Box control—you can click on the arrow at the right end of the box to see a list of all the controls on the current form. You can select a control by choosing it from the list, just as if you had clicked on it on the form.

The lower section of the Properties window lists all of the control's properties, in alphabetical order. The property names are in the left column, and the property values in the right column. You use the scroll bar to display different properties. Scroll until the **Text** property is visible. The default value for this is

Text1, as shown in Figure 3.3. The **Text** property of a Text Box specifies the text that is displayed in the control.

We need to change the **Text** property of this control. Follow these steps:

1. Scroll the Properties list to bring the **Text** property into view.

2. Double click on the **Text** property name to highlight the property value in the right column.

3. Type in the new text. I used "Visual Basic" but you are welcome to use any short phrase you like. The text you type will replace the highlighted text.

4. Press Esc or Enter to end editing.

Notice that the new property is reflected not only in the Properties window but also in the Text Box control on the form.

Now let's suppose that you made a typing error while entering the **Text** property. Do you have to go back and retype the whole thing? Not at all. If you double click on the property value in the right column of the Properties window, Visual Basic will display an editing cursor at the end of the text, allowing you to edit the text using the regular editing keys. Here is a brief description of the keys:

• The left arrow and right arrow move the cursor one character at a time.

• Ctrl+Left arrow and Ctrl+Right arrow move the cursor one word at a time.

• The Home and End keys move the cursor to the start or end of the text.

Figure 3.3 *The Properties window showing the Text Box's properties.*

- New text is inserted at the cursor.

- To select text, drag over it with the cursor.

- The Del key erases selected text or the character to the right of the cursor.

- The Backspace key erases the character to the left of the cursor.

Changing the Font Property

Next, we'll change the Text Box's **Font** property. As you can guess, this property determines the font used for the text in the control. Scroll the Properties list to bring the **Font** property into view, and click once on the property name. A small button with three dots on it displays next to the current font value. Click on the button to display the Font dialog box, which is shown in Figure 3.4. You can also double click on the **Font** property name to go directly to the dialog box. Select from the Font, Font Style, and Size lists to specify the font you want, then click on OK. I suggest something 12 points in size. The new font is reflected immediately in the Text Box on the form.

Adding the Other Controls

Now that the first control is complete, we'll add all of the remaining controls and then change their properties as needed. We need three Command Buttons, three Option Buttons, and one Frame.

What is the Frame control for? Remember our discussion of Option Button controls? I mentioned then that only one Option Button in a group can be set

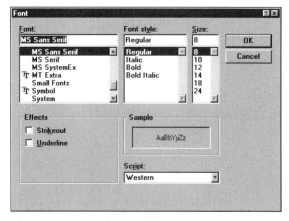

Figure 3.4 *Setting the Font property in the Font dialog box.*

to "on" at any time. The obvious question is, "How does one define a group of option buttons?" By placing them in a Frame, that's how. If you want more than one group of Option Buttons on a form, you need one Frame for each group.

Placing Option Buttons on a Frame requires a specific technique. If you add some Option Buttons to a form, then add a frame, and finally drag the Option Buttons onto the Frame, they will certainly look like they are in the Frame but Visual Basic will not treat them as a group. Here's what you have to do:

1. In the lower-left corner of the form, place a Frame large enough to hold three Option Buttons.

2. Click on the Option Button icon in the toolbox.

3. Point at the interior of the Frame and drag to place the Option Button.

4. Repeat steps 2 and 3 to place the additional Option Buttons.

Next, add the three Command Buttons, placing them in the lower-right area of the form, as shown in Figure 3.5.

Before changing the properties of these newly added controls, it will be wise to save the project. Select Save Project from the File menu. Since the project and form files have not been given names yet, Visual Basic will prompt you for names for both the form and the project. I used "Properties Demo" for the project and "Properties" for the form, but you can assign other names if you like. Near the end of this chapter, I provide detailed information on file management in Visual Basic.

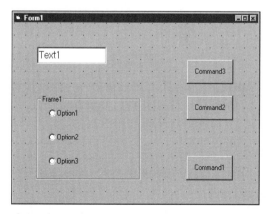

Figure 3.5   *The form during design.*

Setting the Remaining Properties

The last part of creating the project's visual interface is setting the properties of the controls. Start by selecting the Frame, then scroll the Properties list to bring its **Caption** property into view. Double click on the **Caption** property name, type *Text Colors,* and press Enter. Note that this is the same method you used to set the **Text** property for the Text Box. Visual Basic maintains as much consistency as possible in the techniques for dealing with properties, which makes the learning process go as quickly as possible.

Next, select the top Option button. Set its **Name** property to *OptionBlack* and its **Caption** property to *Blac&k*. That's not a typo—there is an ampersand before the *k*. What's that for? And what is the **Name** property?

If you place an ampersand in a control's **Caption** property, it does not display on the form but causes the following letter—in this case the k—to be underlined. This defines an *access key* for the control. When the program is running the user can select the control by pressing Alt+*letter*, and the effect will be the same as clicking on the control. Because some people prefer to use the keyboard rather than the mouse, it's wise to provide keyboard alternatives for as many program tasks as possible, and access keys are one way to do this.

A control's **Name** property is what you use to refer to the control in Basic code. While all controls are given a default name when you create them, it's a good idea to assign names that reflect both the type of control and its specific function. Thus, the name **OptionBlack** identifies an Option Button that sets the Black option. Note that we did not change the default names of the Text Box or the Frame controls. We will not need to refer to the Frame in code, so its **Name** property is irrelevant. And, since there's only one Text Box in the project, there is no chance of confusion, so its default name of "Text1" will be okay.

We need to change one more property for this control. Scroll the Properties list to display the **Value** property, click on it, and then click on the down arrow in the right column. You'll see two possible values for this property, True and False, corresponding to "on" and "off" states for the Option Button. The default value is False, but we want to set this one to True.

Change the properties for the remaining two Option Buttons as follows:

Second Option Button
>   *Caption*: &Red
>   *Name:* OptionRed

Third Option Button
> *Caption*: &Blue
> *Name*: OptionBlue

We'll leave the **Value** property at *False* for these two buttons. We really have no choice here, since we've already set the **Value** property of the first Option Button in this group (OptionBlack) to *True*, and only one button in a group can be "on" at a time. If you did set the **Value** property of one of the other buttons to *True*, the **Value** property of the OptionBlack button would automatically switch to False.

We also need to change the **ForeColor** property of the second and the third Option Buttons. The **ForeColor** property controls the color of the control's caption text (the first Option Button will be left at its default **ForeColor** property of Black). Scroll down to the **ForeColor** property. You'll see that the property value is a weird-looking combination of letters and numbers, something like this:

&H800000012&

What kind of color is this? Actually, it's a number that represents a color—in this case black. The leading &H identifies it as a hexadecimal number, and the trailing & indicates that it's a type Long number. If you don't know what I'm talking about here, don't fret—you'll learn about these things in Chapter 4. But why does Visual Basic use a number to represent a color? Couldn't they have used something easier to work with, like a color name or a sample of the color?

Well, I agree, the numbers are useless, but fortunately you don't need to work with them directly. If you select the **ForeColor** property, then click on the down arrow in the property value column, Visual Basic displays a palette of the available colors, which is shown in Figure 3.6.

Select a shade of Blue for the OptionBlue button and a shade of red for the OptionRed button.

The final properties you need to set are those for the three Command Buttons. I'm sure by now you're well acquainted with the process, so I won't repeat the steps. Here are the properties to set:

Upper Command Button
> *Caption*: &Bigger
> *Name*: CmdBigger

Figure 3.6 *You select colors from a palette.*

Middle Command Button
> *Caption*: &Smaller
> *Name*: CmdSmaller

Lower Command Button
> *Caption*: &Quit
> *Name*: CmdQuit

Our Command Buttons will allow the user to resize the Text Box control or quit the program entirely.

The final step in our form design is to set a couple of properties for the form itself. Select the form by clicking on it between the controls, or by selecting Form1 from the objects list in the Properties window (Form1 is the default name that Visual Basic assigned to the form). Set its **Caption** property to *Playing With Properties* and its **BorderStyle** property to *3-Fixed Dialog*. The **Caption** property specifies the text that is displayed in the form's title bar, and the **BorderStyle** property controls the form's border and whether or not it can be resized by the user.

You're done with the visual design part of the project. Your form should look more or less like Figure 3.7. Select Save File from the File menu (or press Ctrl+S) to save the changes you've made to the form. You can run your program now if you like. Select Start from the Run menu (or press F5). You'll see the dialog box you just designed pop up on the screen, minus the design grid. But when you click on the various buttons, nothing happens. You have a beautiful interface, but it is brain dead—it doesn't respond to anything. Our next task it to add the code that will respond to user input.

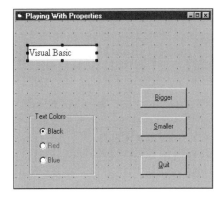

Figure 3.7 *The completed form.*

Adding the Code

What exactly do we want the program to do? Let's make a list:

- When the user selects one of the Option Buttons, change the color of the text in the Text Box accordingly.

- Each time the user selects the Bigger Command Button, enlarge the size of the Text Box by 20 percent.

- Each time the user selects the Smaller Command Button, reduce the size of the Text Box by 20 percent.

- When the user selects the Quit Command Button, end the program.

We'll start with the last item in the list. The Basic statement to end a program is

```
End
```

and we want it executed when the user selects (clicks on) the Quit button. In other words, we want the **End** statement in the **Click** event procedure. For a refresher on event procedures in general, take another look at Chapter 2. To create this procedure, double click on the Quit Command Button to open the code editing window with the skeleton of the event procedure already entered, as shown in Figure 3.8. (Double clicking on a object automatically brings up its **Click** event procedure.)

What do I mean by "skeleton?" It refers to the first and last statements of the event procedure, the statements that actually define the start and the end of the procedure. The last statement **End Sub** is common to all event procedures, and does nothing more than mark the end of the procedure. Of more interest is the first statement:

```
Private Sub CmdQuit_Click()
```

Don't worry about the **Private** and the **Sub** keywords—all event procedures have them and you'll learn about them later in the book. Look at the actual name of the procedure, **CmdQuit_Click**. The first part is the name of the control, and the second part is the event. Visual Basic names event procedures to identify both the control and the event. If you later change the control's **Name** property, the names of its event procedures are automatically changed too. You can't much more user-friendly than that!

If you want to work with another event or another object, you can select from the Object list or the Proc list at the top of the code editing window. But for now, it's the **Click** event procedure we want. All you need to do to make this procedure functional is to add the statement **End**, so it reads as follows:

```
Private Sub CmdQuit_Click()

End

End Sub
```

If you run the program now (press F5 or select Start from the Run menu), you'll see the dialog box you designed. Click on the Quit button (or press Alt+Q) to end the program. Cool! Your event procedure really works. But we have a few more event procedures to add before the project is complete.

We'll do the Option Buttons next. We'll start with the OptionBlack button. Create the **Click** event procedure skeleton for this button by selecting the ob-

Figure 3.8 *Visual Basic creates the skeleton of the Click event procedure.*

ject from the Object list at the top of the code editing window (or by returning to the form and double clicking on the control). When this control is selected, we want the color of the text in the Text Box—its **ForeColor** property—set to *Black*. But Visual Basic uses those weird numbers to represent colors. Do we have to figure out the number for Black? No—there's a better way.

Remember that we have already set the color of all the Option Buttons to the correct color. The number we need is already present in the Option Button's **ForeColor** property. All we need to do is copy that number from the Option Button's **ForeColor** property to the Text Box's **ForeColor** property, and we accomplish our task without having to worry about the exact color number. Here's the event procedure with the single necessary line of code added:

```
Private Sub OptionBlack_Click()

Text1.ForeColor = OptionBlack.ForeColor

End Sub
```

> *Note: As you create these event procedures, be careful with the spelling and punctuation in the code; the computer is very literal-minded and will catch even the smallest mistake!*

You can see here how Visual Basic represents object properties in code: the name of the object (that is, its **Name** property) followed by a period and the property name. The equal sign is Basic's *assignment* operator. In effect it says, "Make the thing on the left (in this case the **ForeColor** property of the Text1 object) equal to the thing on the right (the OptionBlack object's **ForeColor** property)."

We use the same technique for the other two Option Buttons. The code for the OptionBlue button **Click** event procedure is shown here:

```
Private Sub OptionBlue_Click()

Text1.ForeColor = OptionBlue.ForeColor

End Sub
```

And here is the code for the **Click** event procedure of the OptionRed button:

```
Private Sub OptionRed_Click()

Text1.ForeColor = OptionRed.ForeColor

End Sub
```

The last steps in creating this project are writing the event procedures for the other two Command Buttons. Each time the user clicks the Bigger button, we want to increase the size of the Text Box by 20 percent. The size of a control is determined by its **Width** and **Height** properties. So, to increase the width by 20 percent, we would perform the following steps:

1. Obtain the current width from the control's **Width** property.

2. Multiply the value by 1.2.

3. Set the **Width** property equal to the new value.

In code, we can accomplish all three steps with a single Basic statement:

```
Text1.Width = Text1.Width * 1.2
```

The asterisk is Basic's multiplication operator, and the equal sign is the assignment operator we discussed earlier. We also want to increase the height, which we can do by using the same formula, so the complete event procedure for the CmdBigger button looks like this:

```
Private Sub CmdBigger_Click()

Text1.Width = Text1.Width * 1.2
Text1.Height = Text1.Height * 1.2

End Sub
```

The final step for our project is to create the event procedure for the Smaller button. We'll use the same approach as we did for the Bigger button, except this time we need a multiplication factor of 0.8 to decrease the control size by 20 percent. Here's the completed event procedure:

```
Private Sub CmdSmaller_Click()

Text1.Width = Text1.Width * 0.8
Text1.Height = Text1.Height * 0.8

End Sub
```

That's it! The project is complete. Let's take it for a spin. Press F5 to execute the project, and you'll see the dialog box shown in Figure 3.9. Click on the Option Buttons to change the color of the text in the Text Box. Click on the Bigger and Smaller Command Buttons to resize the Text Box. This may not be the most exciting program in the world, but I think it's a pretty effective demonstration of the use of properties in Visual Basic.

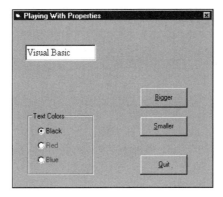

Figure 3.9 *The project in action.*

Note that you can click in the Text Box control and edit the text there. How can this be? We didn't program any editing capabilities. Actually, you are just seeing the built-in capabilities of the Text Box control.

And here's another example of the built-in power of Visual Basic controls. If you click the Smaller button several times, you will see that the Text Box height reaches a certain size and then does not change. A Text Box always maintains at least the minimum height necessary to display text. This height will depend on the size of the font in use, which you set in the Font property.

Summing Up

The project in this chapter is fairly simple, but it illustrates some important Visual Basic concepts. You've seen how an object's properties control its appearance and behavior, and how these properties can be manipulated both during program design and by code during program execution. We've touched on only a few object properties, and it's obvious from browsing through the Properties list that there are lots more! We'll be visiting many of them in the following chapters, but it's hardly possible to cover them all.

If you highlight a property name in the list and press F1, the Visual Basic Help system will display a page of information about the property. A typical Help screen is shown in Figure 3.10. Click on the underlined keywords to view related information. Among the useful things that the Help system provides are examples of how various properties are used (click on the Example keyword). You can also do experiments on your own. It's so easy to whip up a small project, that experimenting with various property settings should be a regular part of your Visual Basic explorations. Remember, to learn by doing is our approach!

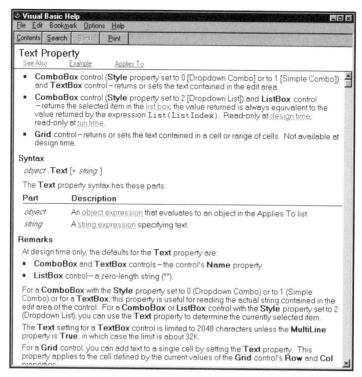

Figure 3.10 *A property Help screen.*

We're almost ready to close this chapter and move on to Basic code. But first, you need to know a bit more about file management in Visual Basic.

FILE MANAGEMENT

The various parts that go into creating a Visual Basic application are collectively called a *project*. A small simple project may contain only a single form, while complex projects can contain dozens of forms. Each form is stored in its own file on disk, and the filenames are automatically given the .FRM extension by Visual Basic. Some projects also use Basic modules. These are files that contain only Basic code, and they have the .BAS extension. Each project is stored in a project file with the .VBP (Visual Basic Project) extension.

> ***Note:*** *Previous versions of Visual Basic used the .MAK extension for their project files. The current Visual Basic can read these files, of course, and keeps the .MAK extension when subsequently saving them.*

When you select Save File from the File menu, Visual Basic saves the form or module that you are currently working on. If it is a new file, and has not yet been named, you will be asked to enter a name for the file before it is saved. Selecting Save Project from the File menu saves the *project definition,* as well as all of the project's form and module files. The project definition consists of the names of all the form and Basic module files in the project, plus some additional information about Visual Basic option settings, window positions, and so on. Again, you'll be prompted to name the project file the first time it is saved.

It's important to remember that a Visual Basic project file does not contain the actual parts of the project, but just a list of these parts. The parts themselves— the form and module files—exist in their own independent disk files. This arrangement makes it possible to use a given form or module in more than one project, an ability that is an important part of the Visual Basic programming concept (see Chapter 2 for more information). One of the things that I'll be emphasizing throughout the book is the advantage of designing your programs so that the individual modules are reusable in other programs.

THE BASICS OF BASIC

Underneath Visual Basic's fancy objects and events there's a foundation of Basic code doing the grunt work. Let's take a comprehensive look at just what Basic is and what you can do with it.

While someday you may be able to create a complete applications program by doing nothing more than sticking a few software components together, that day is not here yet. By now, I hope you are convinced of the power and flexibility of Visual Basic's objects. Despite all this power, it still requires a bit of glue to stick them together into a functioning program. As you saw in the example in the previous chapter, that glue is Basic code.

What exactly is Basic? The name is an acronym for Beginner's All-purpose Symbolic Instruction Code, a language that was originally developed at Dartmouth College for instructional purposes, many moons ago. While Basic may have had its uses as a teaching aid, for many years it had the reputation among programmers for being slow and inflexible. The reason for this unpleasant reputation was that Basic *was* slow and inflexible, at least in its early days. "Greasy kid stuff," snorted real programmers as they went off to struggle with C or FORTRAN.

Over the years, however, Basic gradually improved. With Microsoft QuickBasic leading the way, Basic evolved from a language suited only for students and hobbyists to a powerful tool that was up to the task of creating full-fledged business and scientific applications. This is the Basic that's inside Visual Basic. The fundamentals of the language are fairly easy to learn, and that's the goal of this chapter.

I am not going to cover the complete Basic language here. That could be—and, in fact, has been—the subject of complete books. If I tried to squeeze any sort of complete coverage of Basic into one chapter, I'd end up with a very long and boring chapter with lots of turned off readers. Instead, I'll cover what I feel are the real basics (again, no pun intended!) of the language, the tools you need to get started writing Basic code. Then, as more advanced language topics arise during the remainder of this book, I'll provide you with more information.

NOW WHERE DID I PUT THAT DATA?

Almost every program works with data, or information, of one kind or another. Whether it's a chunk of text to be edited, a graphic image, or a table of numbers, the program needs a place to keep the data while the program is executing. Although an important topic, I'm not talking about disk files—I'm talking about something different here.

During execution, a program stores its data in *variables* and, to a lesser degree, in *constants*. A variable gets its name from the fact that the information stored there can change, or vary, during program execution. In contrast, the information stored in a constant does not change. Visual Basic offers a rich variety of variables and constants to suit all your programming needs.

Visual Basic's variables can be divided into two general categories. *Numeric variables* store numbers, while *string variables* store text. Within each of these categories, things are broken down even further. Let's start with the numbers.

Numeric Variables

Computers work with numbers a lot, so we certainly need a type of variable to store them. Visual Basic actually has several types of numeric variables: Byte, Integer, Long, Single, Double, and Currency (more on these variable types in a moment). Why not just have a single numeric variable that can hold any number? Efficiency. The number 5 can be stored in less memory space, and can be manipulated more quickly, than 123,513,465,760.74666. By providing several subtypes of numeric variables, each suited for a certain numerical range and accuracy, program efficiency can be improved.

Numbers can be divided into two types. *Integers* have no fractional part (any digits to the right of the decimal point). Floating point numbers can contain a fractional part. There are three integer variable types, called **Byte**, **Integer**, and **Long**, and there are also two floating point types, called **Single** and **Double**. The types differ in the ranges of values, the largest and the smallest, they can hold. The two floating point types also differ in their precision, or accuracy, which refers to the number of digits to the right of the decimal point. There's also a sixth type of numeric variable called **Currency**, which is designed specifically to work with financial figures. As Table 4.1 shows, Visual Basic numeric variable types provide for just about any imaginable situation.

So, how do you decide which type of numeric variable to use in a particular situation? The general rule is to use the smallest type that will suffice. For an integer variable, use a type **Integer** in preference to a **Long**, but only if you're sure that the data stored there will never exceed the limits of a type **Integer**. Because of its extremely limited range, type Byte can be used only in special situations (but can be very useful indeed). Similarly, use a **Single** in preference to a **Double** whenever possible. Type **Currency** is almost always the best choice if you're working with money amounts.

The next logical questions are "How do you create variable names?" and "How do you inform Visual Basic of the type of variable you want?" We'll answer these questions in our next topic.

Table 4.1 *Numeric Variables*

Variable Type	Minimum Value	Maximum Value	Precision	Storage Space
Byte	0	255	N/A	1 byte
Integer	-32,768	32,767	N/A	2 bytes
Long	-2,147,483,648	2,147,483,647	N/A	4 bytes
Single	-3.4×10^{38} *	3.4×10^{38} *	6 digits	4 bytes
Double	-1.79×10^{308} *	1.79×10^{308} *	14 digits	8 bytes
Currency	-9.22×10^{11} *	9.22×10^{11} *	4 digits	8 bytes

* An approximate value. See Visual Basic Help for exact figures.

Naming and Declaring Variables

Each variable that you use in your program must have a unique name. You must follow several rules when creating variable names:

- The maximum length is 255 characters

- The first character must be a letter

- The name cannot contain a period, space, or any of the following characters: ! @ # & % $

There's another rule concerning variable names that, while not an absolute requirement, is nonetheless important enough to merit to be dubbed:

AITKEN'S RULE #2: *Use Descriptive Variable Names*

What does this mean? Simply, that the name of a variable should describe the data it holds. For example, if your program deals with the population genetics of bats, and you need a variable to hold the number of bats, you should use a name such as Bat_Count or NumberOfBats. You could legally name the variable XY, J89, or BillClinton, and Visual Basic wouldn't care. But when working on the program later, you'll find that descriptive variable names make a big difference in the readability of your code. It's a good habit to get into right from the get-go.

eXPLORER TIP

Standardizing Variable Naming Conventions

Visual Basic does not care one whit about the case of variable names. As far as Basic is concerned, Count, count, and COUNT all references to the same variable. For the sake of code readability, I suggest that you adopt a standard variable naming scheme and stick to it. My method is to use a combination of upper- and lowercase letters for variable names. This approach makes the names easier to read, particularly when a variable name has been constructed by combining two or more words. For example, I think that MaxDataCount is a lot easier to read than maxdatacount. And, as I'll soon explain, I reserve names that are all uppercase for constants.

Visual Basic's code editor makes it easy to be consistent with your use of capitalization. Once you've entered the first instance of a variable name, which is usually in a **Dim** statement, Visual Basic automatically corrects future instances of the name to match the original capitalization.

How is the type of a variable determined? You have two choices. You can explicitly declare the variable in a **Dim** statement, or you can use a type declaration character at the end of the variable name. An explicit declaration takes the following form:

```
Dim X As Integer, Y As Single, Z As Currency
```

Each variable name is listed, followed by the **As** keyword and the type name. You can have one or more variables in a single **Dim** statement, and you can have as many **Dim** statements as you need.

The use of type declaration characters makes **Dim** statements unnecessary. I'll explain in a minute why I think that the use of type declaration characters is a bad idea, but you do need to know about them. To use the type declaration characters, simply place the character corresponding to the desired variable type at the end of the variable name. The characters are shown in Table 4.2.

Then, since no **Dim** statement is necessary, you simply use the variable in code as needed. For example, if you need a type **Integer** variable to hold the value 100, you would write as follows:

```
Count% = 100
```

In other words, all you do is use the variables when and where they are needed—there's no need to declare them first. This sounds quite convenient, but now I'll explain why it's a bad idea.

Table 4.2 *Type Declaration Characters*

Type	Declaration Character
Integer	%
Long	&
Single	!
Double	#
Currency	@

To Declare or Not To Declare

This question—to declare or not—is an easy one. Always declare your variables. In fact, you can tell Visual Basic to require variable declaration. To do so, select Options from the Tools menu, click the Environment tab, and turn on the Require Variable Declaration option. When this option is active, Visual Basic will report a Variable Not Defined error if you try to use a variable that has not been declared in a **Dim** statement.

> **Note:** *When this option is on, Visual Basic inserts the **Option Explicit** statement in your code.*

Why am I so adamant that you must always declare your variables? Isn't the use of type declaration characters easier? It may seem easier at first, but it always seems to lead to problems. Here's why. Let's say you've created a variable, but at some point in the code where you refer to it you misspell its name. Without **Option Explicit** active, Visual Basic will simply create a new variable using the misspelled name (as far as Visual Basic's concerned, you are creating a new variable). New variables are automatically given the value of 0. Since the program is using this new variable instead of the one it should be using, you are almost sure to get program errors that are extremely hard to track down. If **Option Explicit** were active, however, Visual Basic would immediately flag the misspelled variable name as an undeclared variable, and the problem would never arise.

But this isn't the *only* reason to declare your variables. Some of Visual Basic's variable types, such as types **Byte**, **Boolean**, and **Date** (I'll get to the last two soon) do not have a type declaration character associated with them. If you want to create a variable with one of those types, you must use a **Dim** statement. If you are not requiring variable declarations, you'll find yourself in a situation where some of your program's variables are declared in **Dim** statements, while others are not. This is a recipe for confusion, and any seasoned programmer knows potential confusion should be nipped in the bud.

Heed my advice: Turn on the Require Variable Declaration option, and leave it on. In fact, I feel this so strongly that I'll elevate it to the exalted status of:

AITKEN'S RULE #3: *Always Require Variable Declarations*

There is one minor shortcoming involved in requiring variable declarations. Without type declaration characters, variable names do not provide any information about their type. If you see a variable named Index in your code, for example, you have no way of knowing if it's a type **Integer**, **Double**, or what have you. Some programmers don't find this a problem, but if you do, it can be surmounted by using a type prefix similar to the Hungarian notation so beloved of C programmers. Simply decide on a single letter to represent each variable type—i for Integer, d for Double, for example—then prefix each variable name with the corresponding letter. This way you'll know that iCount is an **Integer**, sRatio is a **Single**, and so on.

String Variables

The second major category of variables is *strings*. This is simply computer-talk for text, but I am guessing this use of "string" comes from the fact that text is nothing more than a string of characters. A string variable can hold a single character or thousands of characters, and it can also be empty. Depending on the needs of your program, you can choose from Visual Basic's two types of string variables. A *fixed length string* has a maximum capacity that you set when you declare it. A fixed length string can hold any number of characters up to this maximum length, but not over it. In contrast, a *variable length string* is sort of like a rubber bag that automatically adjusts its size to hold however many characters you put in it. For both types of string variables the maximum capacity is some 2 billion characters—that's right, billion!

Fixed length string variables *must* be declared (another argument for using **Option Explicit**). The declaration takes the following form:

```
Dim LastName As String * 5
```

The number in the declaration, in this example, 5, specifies the string length. Remember, this is the maximum number of characters that you can store in the string. If you try to put more characters in the variable, they will be lost. For example, if you execute the following statement

```
LastName = "Aitken"
```

then only the first five characters will be stored—the "n" will be lost.

You can create a variable length string by using its type declaration character $, but, of course, the preferred method of declaring it is to use the **Dim** statement:

```
Dim FirstName As String
```

Now you have a string variable named FirstName into which you can stuff as big a string as you like—up to that 2 billion character limit, of course, which I really don't consider too limiting!

Which type of string variable should you use? For the most part it's up to you, and should be decided based on your program's data. It's true that fixed length strings can be manipulated a bit more quickly, but with today's lightning-fast processors it won't make any noticeable difference unless your program performs an enormous amount of text processing. If you are sure your string data won't ever exceed a certain length, then a fixed length string is probably best. Otherwise, use a variable length string.

Other Variable Types

Three more Visual Basic data types are used in special situations: **Boolean**, **Date**, and **Variant**. The *Boolean* type is used to hold information that takes the form of yes/no or on/off. In other words, a Boolean variable can hold only two possible values, referred to by the Basic keywords **True** and **False**. You'll see that **Boolean** variables are closely related to logical expressions, which I'll cover later in the chapter. A **Boolean** variable requires 2 bytes of storage, the same as type **Integer**.

The *Date* type is used to hold date and time information. It is a floating point type, with the whole-number portion representing the date and the fractional portion representing the time. The date is encoded as the number of days since December 30, 1899, with negative numbers representing earlier dates. The time is encoded as fraction of the 24 hour day, with 0.0 representing midnight, 0.25 representing 6:00 AM, 0.5 representing noon, and so on.

The *Variant* data type is Visual Basic's catchall data type. A type **Variant** can be assigned any of Visual Basic's data types except fixed length strings. The main use of **Variant** variables is to simplify dealing with numerical data that sometimes needs to be treated as a string. There are some other specialized uses of type **Variant** that I'll explain as necessary later in the book.

None of these three data types has a type declaration character associated with it. The **Date** and **Boolean** types *must* be declared in a **Dim** statement:

```
Dim Answer As Boolean, OrderDate As Date
```

The Variant type can also be declared in a **Dim** statement. If, however, you are not requiring variable declarations, and you use a variable name without a type declaration character, then Visual Basic makes it a type **Variant**.

User-Defined Types

One of Basic's handiest features is the ability to create user-defined data types. A user-defined type, also called a *structure*, is a compound data type containing two or more other data types. You can define exactly what does into a structure, designing it to exactly meet the needs of your program. You use the **Type...End Type** statement to define a structure. Here's how it looks:

```
Type StructureName
   element1 As Type
   element2 As Type
   ...
End Type
```

For example, if you were writing a program to maintain an inventory list, you could define a structure as follows:

```
Type StockItem
   Name As String * 25
   PartNumber As String * 12
   Cost As Currency
   NumberOnHand As Integer
End Type
```

The individual elements of a structure can be any of Basic's fundamental data types *except* variable length strings. You can even use one structure type as an element in another structure type. And while I haven't introduced you to arrays yet (that comes in the next chapter), I will mention that an array can be an element of a structure, and you can also create arrays of structures.

When you define a structure with the **Type...End Type** statement that's all you are doing—defining it. The **Type...End Type** statement does not create any actual variables of the defined type. You must use the **Dim** statement to create *instances* of the structure—actual variables with names and with memory space allocated to them. Using our previous example, once we have defined the **StockItem** type, we can then create an instance of the type as follows:

```
Dim NewPart As StockItem
```

Now that you have a structure of type **StockItem** named **NewPart** to work with, how do you get at its various elements? By using the variable name followed by a period and the element name, as shown here:

```
NewPart.Name = "cam tensioning spring"
NewPart.PartNumber = "L-101-6J"
NewPart.Cost = 99.76
NewPart.NumberOnHand = 8
```

To define a structure that contains another structure as an element, follow the same syntax. The definition of the embedded structure—in this case **StockItem**—must come first in the code.

```
Type OrderData
   Part As StockItem
   Supplier As String * 30
End Type
```

Then to access elements of the embedded structure use the period syntax as follows:

```
Dim LastOrder As OrderData
LastOrder.Part.Name = "cam tensioning spring"
LastOrder.Part.Cost = 99.76
```

User-defined structures must be defined at the module level. In other words, you cannot include a **Type...End Type** statement inside a procedure. There are no special rules for using the elements of structures in your program—you can use them anywhere a simple variable of the same type could be used. You'll learn about using arrays *of* user-defined types and arrays *in* user-defined types in Chapter 5.

Constants

There are two types of constants that can be used in a Visual Basic program: literal and symbolic. A *literal constant* is nothing more than the number or string typed directly into your source code. Look at the following lines of code:

```
Dim MyString As String * 10, MyNumber As Integer
MyString = "New York"
MyNumber = 123
```

Here, the "New York" and the 123 are literal constants. You type them in while you are editing your source code, and they (of course) do not change during program execution—they are "constant."

Much more useful is the so-called *symbolic constant.* A symbolic constant has a name and a data type just like a variable, and generally follows the same rules. The differences are that a symbolic constant is assigned a value when it is declared, and this value cannot change during program execution. To create a symbolic constant, use the **Const** keyword in the declaration statement:

```
Const MAXIMUM As Integer = 100
```

This statement creates a constant named MAXIMUM with the value 100. You can then use the name MAXIMUM anywhere in the program where you could use a literal constant 100, and the result is the same. Note that the **As** part of the **Const** declaration is optional. If you do not specify a data type, Visual Basic will automatically use the type most appropriate for the specified value. For example, the declaration

```
Const RATIO = 15.12
```

will result in RATIO being assigned type **Single**.

What's the value of symbolic constants? Why not just type in literal constants wherever they are needed? The major advantage is that you can change the value of a symbolic constant throughout the program simply by editing its declaration statement. Another advantage is that the constant's name can help in making the program easier to read.

You may have noticed that in the above two examples I used all uppercase for the constant names. This is *not* required by Visual Basic, and in fact the rules for naming constants are the same as the rules for naming variables. However, I find it very useful to use all uppercase for constant names, with variable names in a combination of upper- and lowercase. This makes it easy to distinguish constants from variables when reading your own code, a distinction that would not otherwise be apparent.

This wraps up our introduction to Visual Basic variables and constants. You now have the fundamentals under your belt, although there's quite a bit more to Visual Basic data storage. In particular, arrays and the **Type** statement are indispensable tools, but as mentioned earlier, I will cover these and other topics later in the book, as the need arises.

Commenting Your Code

It's a good idea to use comments liberally in your Basic code. A comment is ignored by Visual Basic; its only purpose is to provide anyone reading the code with a reminder or explanation of what's going on. Some programmers don't use comments, or they use them sparingly. They are usually sorry later! Aspects of your code design and program structure that seem perfectly clear as you are writing it may not seem clear to you a month or a year later when you need to modify the code.

To insert a comment, type an apostrophe anywhere in your code except within a literal string (that is, inside double quotation marks). Anything from the apostrophe to the end of the line is treated as a comment and is ignored by the Visual Basic compiler.

I'm the Manipulative Type

Now that you know how to store data in your program, you'd probably like to know what you can do with the the data. Lots of things, and some of the most important ones involve Visual Basic's *operators*. An operator is a symbol or word that instructs Visual Basic to manipulate data in a certain way. You've already been introduced to the assignment operator (=), which tells Visual Basic to make the variable or object property on the left of the operator equal to the expression on the right side of the operator.

What's an Expression?

You'll see the term *expression* used frequently, and you're probably wondering just what exactly it refers to. It is quite simple, actually. An expression is anything that evaluates to a number, a string, or a logical value. Thus, the literal constant 5 is an expression, as is 5+2.

Arithmetic Operators

The arithmetic operators perform mathematical manipulations. There are seven of them. The first four, listed in Table 4.3, are the common operations that I'm sure you are familiar with.

The other arithmetic operators may be unfamiliar to you. Integer division, represented by the \ symbol, divides two numbers and returns an integer result, discarding any fractional part of the answer. Thus, 7 \ 2 evaluates to 3, as does 6 \ 2. There is no rounding—the fraction part of the answer is simply discarded. Thus, both 21 \ 10 and 29 \ 10 evaluate to 2.

The exponentiation operator raises a number to a power. The symbol for this operation is ^. In Basic, therefore, X ^ Y means the same thing as the more common notation X^Y. If X is negative, then Y must be an integer; otherwise, both X and Y can be floating point values.

The modulus operator, represented by the keyword **Mod**, divides two numbers and returns only the remainder. The expression 7 Mod 2 evaluates to 1, 23 Mod 4 evaluates to 3, and 25 Mod 5 evaluates to 0. Any fractional part of the answer is truncated, so 23.5 Mod 4 evaluates to 3 and not to 3.5.

String Manipulation

There is only one operator that works with string data, called the *concatenation* operator, the symbol &. Concatenation simply means to tack one string on the end of another. For example, if MyString is a string variable, then executing the statement

```
MyString = "Visual " & "Basic"
```

results in the string "Visual Basic" being stored in the variable. You can also use the + symbol for string concatenation, but this is provided for compatibility with old Basic programs, and there's no reason to use it in new programs—stick with &.

Operator Precedence

What happens if an expression contains more than one operator? And what difference does it make? An example will illustrate. Look at this expression:

```
5 + 3 * 2
```

What does it evaluate to? If we perform the addition first, it evaluates to 16,

Table 4.3 *Arithmetic Operators*

Operation	Symbol	Example	Result
Addition	+	2 + 5	7
Subtraction	-	18 - 10	8
Multiplication	*	2 * 5	10
Division	/	10 / 2	5

but if we perform the multiplication first, the result is 11. Which is correct? Because of potentially ambiguous expressions such as this, Visual Basic includes strict rules of operator precedence. This is just a fancy way of determining which operations are performed first. The precedence of Visual Basic's operators is given in Table 4.4. Operators with low precedence numbers are performed first.

If we return to the original example, we can see that multiplication has a higher precedence than addition, so it will be performed first and the expression will evaluate to 11. For operators that have the same precedence level, such as multiplication and division, the order of execution is always left to right.

What if the order of execution specified by the operator precedence rules isn't what you want? Let's say you want to add variables A and B, then multiply the sum by variable C. Can this be done? Yes! Parentheses come to the rescue. By including parentheses in an expression, you force operators inside parentheses to be evaluated first. If you write

```
A + B * C
```

the precedence rules will cause the multiplication to be performed first and the result will not be what you want. If, however, you write the expression like this

```
(A + B) * C
```

the parentheses force the addition to be performed first, and the expression evaluates properly. You can use as many parentheses in an expression as you need, as long as they always come in pairs; each left parenthesis *must* have a matching right parenthesis. If you create an expression with an unmatched

Table 4.4 *Operator Precedence*

Operator	Precedence
Exponentiation ^	1
Multiplication (*), division (/)	2
Integer division (\)	3
Modulus (MOD)	4
Addition (+), subtraction (-)	5
String concatenation (&)	6

parenthesis, Visual Basic displays an error message when you try to move the editing cursor off the line. When there are nested parentheses (one set inside another set) execution starts with the innermost set and proceeds outward.

You can use parentheses in an expression even when they are not needed to modify the order of operator precedence. Particularly with long, complex expressions, the use of parentheses can help to make the expression easier to read and understand.

A NEED TO CONTROL

You've seen that Basic code consists of a series of statements, one to a line. When a chunk of Basic code executes, the normal execution order is to start with the first statement and then execute all the statements in order, top-to-bottom. Sometimes, however, this just won't do. One of the most powerful Basic programming tools available to you is the ability to control program execution—to determine which Basic statements execute, when they execute, and how many times they execute. Before I show you how to do this, however, you need to know about logical expressions and Visual Basic's comparison and logical operators.

Logical Expressions

Computer programs often need to deal with yes/no questions. When a question or an expression has only these two possible outcomes, it is called a *logical expression*. In computer programming, the two possible outcomes are referred to as TRUE and FALSE. As an example, consider the question "Is the value stored in the variable X larger than the value stored in the variable Y?" Clearly, either it is (answer = TRUE) or it is not (answer = FALSE). Since computers use numbers for everything, it has become standard practice to use 0 for FALSE and -1 for TRUE. Now let's take a look at how to construct and manipulate logical expressions.

Comparison Operators

Visual Basic provides a number of operators that you can use to construct logical expressions by asking questions about the data in your programs. Specifically, these operators perform comparisons between expressions, and then return a value of TRUE or FALSE, depending on the result of the comparison. Table 4.5 lists the *comparison operators*.

Table 4.5   *Comparison Operators*

Operator	Comparison	Example	Meaning
=	Equal to	X = Y	Is X equal to Y?
>	Greater than	X > Y	Is X greater than Y?
<	Less than	X < Y	Is X less than Y?
>=	Greater than or equal to	X >= Y	Is X greater than or equal to Y?
<=	Less than or equal to	X <= Y	Is X less than or equal to Y?
<>	Not equal to	X <> Y	Is X not equal to Y?

We can see that if X is equal to 10 and Y is equal to 5, then expression X < Y will evaluate as FALSE and X <> Y will evaluate as TRUE. We can utilize the numerical value of a logical expression, like this

```
Q = X < Y
Z = X <> Y
```

which would result in the variable Q having the value 0 and Z having the value -1. More often, however, logical expressions are used in program control, as you'll see soon. But first we need to take a look at how you can combine two or more logical expressions to get a single TRUE/FALSE answer.

Logical Operators

The logical operators work to combine logical expressions. Why would one want to do this? Here's an example from everyday life. You receive a call inviting you to join a group of friends for dinner. If Mary is coming along, you'd like to go because you're a bit sweet on her, but otherwise, you'll pass. This is a single logical condition, and easy to understand. But assume for a moment that you also like Helen, and if she's coming with the group you'd also like to go. But, if both Mary and Helen are coming, things will get a bit too complicated, so you again will pass. In this situation there are two TRUE/FALSE questions (Mary coming? Helen coming?) that you need to combine somehow to answer the TRUE/FALSE question, are you going?

Similar situations arise in computer programming. For example, you need an answer to the question "Are X and Y both greater than 0?" Here's where the logical operators come in, letting you combine and manipulate logical expressions to get the answer you need. The six logical operators, shown in Table 4.6, are designated by a keyword. As you review the table, assume that X and Y are both logical expressions.

Table 4.6   *Logical Operators*

Operator	Example	Evaluation
And	X And Y	TRUE if both X and Y are TRUE; FALSE otherwise
Or	X Or Y	TRUE if X or Y, or both of them, are TRUE; FALSE only if both X *and* Y are FALSE
Xor (exclusive Or)	X Xor Y	TRUE if X and Y are different (one TRUE and the other FALSE); FALSE if both are TRUE or both are FALSE
Eqv (Equivalence)	X Eqv Y	True if X and Y are the same (both TRUE or both FALSE); False otherwise
Imp (Implication)	X Imp Y	FALSE only if X is TRUE and Y is FALSE; TRUE otherwise
Not	Not X	TRUE if X is FALSE, FALSE if X is TRUE

Now we can cast the earlier question using the comparison operators and the logical operators. The expression

```
(X > 0) And (Y > 0)
```

will evaluate as TRUE if and only if both X and Y are greater than 0. Likewise, if you need to know whether at least one of these two variables is greater than 0, you would write

```
(X > 0) Or (Y > 0)
```

Of course, the comparison and logical operators can be used to ask questions about object properties too. Let's say you have two Check Box controls on a form, and want to determine if one or both of them are checked. Here's the expression to do so:

```
(Check1.Value = TRUE) Or (Check2.Value = TRUE)
```

I have been talking about comparison and logical operators for a while now, but I haven't really showed you how to do anything useful with them. Don't worry; that's our next topic: How to use logical expressions in conjunction with Basic's decision and loop structures to control program execution.

Basic Code Line Wrapping

Some lines of Basic code can get rather long. While the Visual Basic editor can handle long lines, it can be a nuisance to have your lines of code running off the right edge of the editor window where you can't see them without scrolling. You can avoid this problem by using the line continuation character to break a long line of code into two or more lines. All you need to do is type a space followed by an underscore, then press Enter. All code on the new line will be treated by Visual Basic as part of the first line. The only restriction is that the line continuation character cannot be placed in a literal string within double quotation marks.

Decision Structures

Visual Basic's *decision structures* control program execution based on whether certain logical conditions are met. In other words, program statements are either executed or not executed based on the evaluation of logical expressions.

If...Then...Else

The **If** structure executes a block of one of more statements only if a specified logical expression evaluates as TRUE. Optionally, you can include a second block of statements that is executed only if the logical expression is FALSE. An **If** structure has the following form:

```
If X Then
   ...
   Statements to be executed if X is TRUE go here.
   ...
Else
   ...
   Statements to be executed if X is FALSE go here.
   ...
End If
```

The **Else** keyword and the block of statements between it and the **End If** keyword are optional. If there are no statements to be executed when X is FALSE, you can write as follows:

```
If X Then
   ...
   Statements to be executed if X is TRUE go here.
   ...
End If
```

If your blocks of statements are only single statements, you can use the concise single-line form of the **If** structure:

```
If X then Statement1 Else Statement2
```

For more involved situations, you can include the **ElseIf** keyword to create what are effectively nested **If** structures:

```
If X Then
   ...
   Statements to be executed if X is TRUE go here.
   ...
ElseIf Y Then
   ...
   Statements to be executed if Y is TRUE go here.
   ...
Else
   ...
   Statements to be executed if both X and Y are FALSE go here.
   ...
End If
```

You can have as many **ElseIf** statements as you like. You must realize, however, that at most one of the blocks of statements in an **If** structure will be executed. In the preceding example, if both X and Y are TRUE, only the statements associated with the X condition are executed. The rule is that only the statements associated with the first TRUE condition are executed. Note, however, that for situations that would require more than one or two **ElseIf** clauses, you are usually better off using the **Select Case** structure, which I'll cover next.

You might have noticed the indentation style I used in the previous code samples; within each block, all statements are indented with respect to the statements that mark the beginning and the end of the block. This is not required by Visual Basic, but I think that it makes the code more readable.

Select Case

You will find that the **Select Case** structure is more appropriate than the **If** structure when you have more than a couple of conditions to be tested:

```
Select Case TestExpression
   Case Comparison1
      ...
      Block1
      ...
   Case Comparison2
      ...
      Block2
      ...
   Case Else
      ...
```

```
      ElseBlock
      ...
End Select
```

The TestExpression is any numeric or string expression. The way **Select Case** works is to go through the list of **Case** statements, comparing TextExpression with each Comparison until a match is found. Then the statements in the associated block are executed. If no match is found, the statements associated with the optional Case Else statement are executed. If there is no **Case Else** and no match is found, none of the statements will be executed. There is no limit to the number of **Case** statements allowed in a **Select Case** structure.

In the simplest situation, each Comparison is a numeric or string expression against which TestExpression is compared for equality. You can also use the **To** keyword to check TestExpression against a range of values, and the **Is** keyword in conjunction with one of the comparison operators to make a relational comparison. Thus, if you want a match when TestExpression is between 1 and 5 you would write

```
Case 1 To 5
```

and if you want a match if TestExpression is greater than 10, you would write this:

```
Case Is > 10
```

You can use multiple Comparison expressions that are associated with one **Case** statement by separating them with commas. For example, here's a **Case** statement that would match TestExpression if it is equal to -1 or to -2, between 8 and 12, or greater than 100:

```
Case -1, -2, 8 To 12, Is > 100
```

Loop Structures

You've seen that Basic's decision structures determine whether a block of statements is executed. In contrast, Basic's loop structures control how many times a block of statements is executed. You can accomplish "looping" in one of two ways: by executing a block of statements a fixed number of times, or executing the block repeatedly until a specified condition is met.

For...Next

In its most common use, the **For...Next** loop executes a block of statements a fixed number of times:

```
For Counter = Start To Stop
   ...
   statement block
   ...
Next Counter
```

Counter is a numeric variable that can be any type, although type **Integer** is generally used unless there is a specific reason to use another type. **Start** and **Stop** are the values that specify the start and stop of the loop—they can be any numeric expression. A **For...Next** loop begins by setting Counter equal to **Start**. Then, as the statements in the block are executed, Counter is incremented by 1 and compared with **Stop**. If Counter is greater than **Stop**, the loop terminates and execution passes to the first statement following the **Next** statement. Otherwise, the loop repeats.

 ***Never Change the Counter Variable***
Basic will not prevent you from changing the value of Counter inside the loop. However, this practice should be avoided. It can lead to pesky program bugs and code that is difficult to understand.

Here's an example of **For...Next** that will execute the number of times specified by the variable X.

```
For Count = 1 to X
   ...
Next X
```

You are not limited to starting the loop at 1, of course. You can also use the **Step** keyword to specify that the Counter variable be incremented by a value other than 1 with each cycle of the loop. Here's a loop that will execute 4 times, with the Counter variable taking the values 4, 7, 10, and 13:

```
For I = 4 To 13 Step 3
   ...
Next I
```

You can use negative **Step** values to count backwards, which of course requires that the **Stop** value be smaller than **Start**. You can also use fractional values as long as Counter is a floating point type. The following loop will count backwards from 4 to 1 by increments of 0.25 (4, 3.75, 3.5, ... , 1.25, 1):

```
For I = 4 To 1 Step -0.25
   ...
Next I
```

If you want to terminate a loop early—that is, before Counter exceeds Stop—you can use the **Exit For** statement. This is an extremely useful statement because it lets you specify a variety of conditions that will terminate the loop in addition to the loop's own count programming. Here's a loop that will execute 10 times or until the variable X is less than 0:

```
For I = 1 to 10
   ...
   If X < 0 Then Exit For
   ...
Next I
```

Strictly speaking, you do not have to include the name of the Counter variable in the **Next** statement. Basic will automatically associate each **Next** statement with the immediately preceding **For** statement. However, I suggest that you develop the habit of always including the Counter variable name with **Next**, to improve readability of the code.

Do...Loop

The **Do...Loop** structure is the most flexible of Basic's loops. It allows the loop to execute until a specified condition is either TRUE or FALSE, and it also allows the condition to be evaluated either at the start or the end of the loop. In its simplest form, a **Do...Loop** executes as long as a condition is TRUE:

```
Do While Condition
   ...
   statement block
   ...
Loop
```

Condition is any logical expression. When execution first reaches the **Do** statement, Condition is evaluated. If it is FALSE, execution passes to the statement following the **Loop** statement. If it is TRUE, the block of statements is executed, execution returns to the **Do** statement, and Condition is evaluated again. You can also use the **While** or the **Until** keyword to continue execution for as long as Condition is FALSE:

```
Do Until Condition
   ...
   statement block
   ...
Loop
```

Both of the previous examples perform the comparison at the start of the loop, which means it is possible for the statement block *not* to be executed, even once. If you want to be sure that the loop executes at least once, you can place the Condition at the end of the loop. As before, you can use either the **While** or the **Until** keyword:

```
Do
   ...
   statement block
   ...
Loop While Condition

Do
   ...
   statement block
   ...
Loop Until Condition
```

To terminate the loop early, use **Exit Do**. Here's a loop that will execute until Y is greater than 0 or X is less than 0:

```
Do
   ...
   If X < 0 Then Exit Do
   ...
Loop Until Y > 0
```

You may be thinking that the same result could have been obtained by writing the loop like this:

```
Do
   ...
Loop Until Y > 0 Or X < 0
```

You are correct, but there is a subtle difference between these two loops. In the first example, the statements between the If X < 0 statement and the **Loop** statement are not executed during the last loop iteration, when X becomes less than 0. In the second example, all of the statements in the loop are executed during the last execution.

While... Wend

The **While...Wend** loop executes a block of statements as long as a specified condition is TRUE. It is not nearly as flexible as **Do...Loop**, and, in fact, anything that **While...Wend** can do can also be accomplished with **Do...Loop**. You may find **While...Wend** in older Basic programs because earlier versions of Basic did not support **Do...Loop**.

Here's how you write a **While...Wend** loop:

```
While Condition
   ...
   statement block
   ...
Wend
```

You can write all of your Basic programs without ever needing a **While...Wend** loop. Take a look at the following variant of **Do...Loop**, which does exactly the same this as a **While...Wend** loop:

```
Do While Condition
   ...
   statement block
   ...
Loop
```

Because of the added flexibility, I recommend that you use **Do...Loop** rather than the **While...Wend** structure found in older programs.

Nested and Infinite Loops

A *nested loop* is a loop that is contained within another loop. There is no limit to nesting of loops in Visual Basic, although I think that nesting beyond four or five levels is rarely advisable. If your program seems to need such deep nesting then you probably should re-examine its structure to see if the same task can be accomplished more simply. The only restriction on nesting of loops is that each inner loop must be enclosed entirely within the outer loop. The following example is illegal because the **For...Next** loop is not contained entirely within the **Do...Loop** loop:

```
Do While X > 0
   For I = 1 to 10
      ...
Loop
   Next I
```

The following example, however, is okay:

```
Do While X > 0
   For I = 1 to 10
      ...
   Next I
Loop
```

An *infinite loop* is one that executes forever (or until you halt the program!). Clearly, if a loop's terminating condition is never met, it will loop indefinitely. This situation can arise from faulty program logic or from unexpected user input. Keep a sharp eye out for this sort of problem, and if your program seems to "hang" during execution, you might want to examine your loops.

BUT WAIT, THERE'S MORE

If you've managed to read this entire chapter—and I suggest that you do read it closely—you should come away with a good introduction to the foundations of the Basic programming language. There's more to Basic—quite a bit more, in fact. Does that mean this chapter is going to stretch on for another 40 pages? Not to worry! I suspect that your patience is wearing thin and you are itching to try some of the things you have learned. The remaining details of Basic will be covered as individual topics arise. Now it's time to move on to the next chapter, where we will put together a Visual Basic application that demonstrates how Basic code, objects, and properties are put together to create an application.

Visual Design + Basic Code = Visual Basic

By adding a few more fundamentals to what you've already learned, you'll be well on your way to becoming Captain of the good ship Visual Basic.

We've covered a lot of ground in the first four chapters, and I hope you're beginning to get your Visual Basic sea legs. If I've been doing my job well, you're starting to develop at least a hazy picture in your head of how the various parts of Visual Basic—objects, properties, and code—work together to form a fully functioning application program. To bring this picture into sharper focus, we're going to tackle a somewhat more ambitious project in this chapter—an on-screen calculator. As you work through this project, you will see how all of the stuff I've crammed into your head in the past four chapters comes together. Along the way, I'll present a few more useful Visual Basic tools and techniques.

PLANNING THE CALCULATOR

The first step in planning a calculator is deciding what type of logic it will use. Calculator logic comes in two types: algebraic and reverse Polish notation (RPN). Algebraic calculators are more common. With this type of calculator, you perform calculations electronically in the same way you would on paper. For example, to add 4 to 7 on paper, you would write:

4 + 7 = 11

Using an algebraic calculator to perform this calculation, you would press 4, press +, press 7, and press =, and the answer would be displayed. In contrast, to perform this calculation using an RPN calculator, you would press 4, press Enter, press 7, then press +. If you are not accustomed to RPN calculators, I am sure that this seems weird to you. It makes a lot of sense, however, and is actually quite similar to internal computer logic. Let's take a look at how it works.

RPN Notation and Stacks

RPN notation is based on the concept of a *stack*. A stack is a data storage method that uses the "last in, first out" method. In other words, when you retrieve a data item from the stack, you'll get the item that was most recently placed on the stack. If you then retrieve another item, you'll get the one before that, and so on. The most common analogy to a data stack is the way cafeteria plates are often stacked, in a spring-loaded tube. As you retrieve plates, they come out in the reverse of the order in which they were inserted. Here's what happens, then, when you add 4 and 7 on an RPN calculator:

Press 4:   Put 4 in the display

Press Enter: Put the display number (4) on the stack

Press 7:   Put 7 in the display

Press +:   Add the number in the display (7) to the number at the top of the stack (4), display the result, and place the result on the stack.

For short calculations, the RPN method really has no advantage over the algebraic method. With longer calculations, however, it really comes into its own. Let's say you want to add 4 to 7, multiply the result by 2.5, then square the result. Table 5.1 shows how you would enter this calculation, and how it would show in the display.

Table 5.1 *RPN Calculation*

Press	Display Reads
4	4
Enter	4
7	7
+	11
2.5	2.5
X	27.5
2	2
Y^x (Y to the X)	756.25

On an algebraic calculator, this equation requires a lot more keystrokes, and the order of execution is more difficult to follow. In any case, I'm not here to sell you on the advantages of an RPN calculator, but we will be using it for our project. Since we will have to implement a stack in the program, it's time to introduce you to Visual Basic arrays, the method we'll use to maintain the stack.

Arrays

An *array* stores a large number of variables under the same name. All the individual variables, or *elements*, of an array *must* have the same data type, and are distinguished from each other by a numerical *array index*. You create an array with the **Dim** statement, as shown here:

```
Dim Data[100] As Integer
```

This statement declares an array containing 101 type Integer elements. But then why does the statement indicate 100 elements? In Visual Basic, array indexes begin with 0, so this array starts at element Data[0] and ends at Data[100], for a total of 101 elements. An array can be any of Visual Basic's data types, including both variable length and fixed length strings. If the data type is not specified in the **Dim** statement, the type defaults to **Variant**.

The elements of an array can be used anywhere regular variables of the same type can be used. The real power of arrays becomes evident when you use variables as the array index, or subscript. In fact, any numerical expression that evaluates to a value within the array's index range can be used as the subscript. For example, here's a **For...Next** loop that fills all the elements of a 1000 element array with the values 1 through 1000:

```
For i = 0 To 999
   Array(i) = i + 1
Next I
```

You can create arrays of user-defined structures, and you can also include an array as an element of a structure. To create an array of structures you must first define the structure with the **Type...End Type** statement, as shown here:

```
Type Person
   FirstName As String * 15
   LastName As String * 20
End Type
```

Then, you use the **Dim** statement to create instances of the structure. For example, the line

```
Dim MyFriends(100) As Person
```

will create an array of 100 type **Person** structures. You access the elements of the structures within the array by using a combination of the structure's period notation (which we covered in Chapter 4) and the array subscript notation. Thus, the code

```
MyFriends(n).FirstName = "Bill"
MyFriends(n).LastName = "Gates"
```

would place data in both the **FirstName** and **LastName** elements of the *n*th structure in the array.

To use an array as an element of a structure, include it in the structure definition, as follows:

```
Type Person
   FirstName As String * 15
   LastName As String * 20
   Likes(10) As String * 20
End Type
```

If you create a single instance of the structure, you can access the elements of the array element by using array subscript notation on the right side of the period:

```
Dim MyBestFriend As Person
MyBestFriend.FirstName = "Pat"
```

```
MyBestFriend.LastName = "Smith"
MyBestFriend.Likes(1) = "chocolate"
MyBestFriend.Likes(2) = "old movies"
```

If you declare an array of a structure that includes an array as an element, things get a bit more complicated. For example, look at this code (assuming the definition of type **Person** shown previously):

```
Dim MyFriends(100) As Person
MyFriends(1).FirstName = "Pat"
MyFriends(1).LastName = "Smith"
MyFriends(1).Likes(1) = "chocolate"
MyFriends(1).Likes(2) = "old movies"
```

All you need to remember is that the subscript for an array *of* structures goes to the left of the period, and the subscript for an array that's *in* a structure goes to the right of the period.

There's a lot more to arrays, including multi-dimensional arrays, but you know enough now to implement the stack we need for our calculator project. I'll deal with the other array topics as we encounter them in the book. But first, we need to review a special data type that we'll find very useful in this project.

The Variant Data Type

The data types we have examined so far have been rather specific. That is, they could hold either string or numeric data, and the numeric types could hold either integer or floating point values. The **Variant** type is a different animal altogether. A type **Variant** variable can hold just about any kind of data, string, integer, or floating point. Even more amazing (at least to experienced programmers who are used to the standard fixed data types) is that the data in a type **Variant** is automatically treated in the appropriate way.

What does this mean? For the most part, it means that the data is treated either as a string or as a number, depending on how you are using the variable. Here's an example. Suppose that MyVariant is a type **Variant** and you assign data to it as follows:

```
MyVariant = 1234
```

If you then add this variable to a numeric variable, the data will be treated as a number. Thus, after the following statements execute (assuming X and Y are type **Integer**)

```
X = 111
Y = X + MyVariant
```

the variable Y will contain the numeric value 1345. Now, if S is a type **String** variable, then after executing the statement

```
S = "abc" & X & "def"
```

the variable S will contain the string "abc1234def." Throughout the book, you will see that the **Variant** type can be very useful when your program is working with numeric data that must also be treated as a string—formatting data for display in a calculator, for example.

To create a variable or an array of type **Variant** you can use the **Variant** keyword in your **Dim** statement, or you can simply omit the **As** part of the **Dim** statement because **Variant** is Visual Basic's default data type. The following two statements are equivalent:

```
Dim X As Variant
Dim X
```

Trying Out Code

You can use Visual Basic's **Debug.Print** method as a quick way to try out your Basic code. Create a new project, doubleclick in the form to bring up the **Form_Click()** event procedure, and place the code you want to test in the procedure. Press Ctrl+G to display Visual Basic's Debug window. (The Debug window is displayed every time you run a program inside the Visual Basic development environment, and is hidden when the program ends. To display the Debug window when a program is not running, as instructed here, simply press Ctrl+G.)

To check your code, enter the **Debug.Print** statement and then enter one or more variable names after the statement, separated by commas. Each **Debug.Print** statement displays on a new line. For example, the statements

```
Debug.Print X, Y
Debug.Print Z
```

will display the values of variables X and Y on one line and the value of variable Z on the next line.

Implementing the Stack

Now back to implementing the stack for the RPN calculator. Our stack will have two parts: a **Variant** array where the stack data is kept, and an **Integer** variable to serve as the *stack pointer*, indicating the current top of the stack. Let's see how this works.

Initially, the stack array is empty and the stack pointer points at element 0. Adding something to the stack requires that we increment the stack pointer to point at element 1, then store the data in that element. If we want to store a second item, we again increment the stack pointer by a value of 1 and store the data item in the array element that is now indicated, as shown in Figure 5.1.

You'll note that this method results in element 0 of the array never being used, but that's a small price to pay. If you want to be totally stingy about memory usage, you could use element 0 to store the stack pointer, although we won't use this approach in the project.

Retrieving data from the stack follows the opposite procedure. To read the item on the top of the stack without removing it from the stack, simply get the array element that the stack pointer points to. To remove the item from the stack, you must also decrement the stack pointer by 1. Figure 5.2 illustrates the removal of two data items from a stack.

You'll note that data items removed from the stack are not actually erased—they remain in the array, but are not part of the stack because the stack pointer is not pointing "below" them. If new items are added to the stack, the old ones will be overwritten.

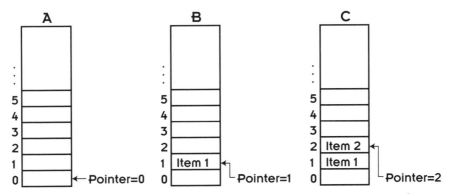

Figure 5.1 *Part A shows an empty stack, part B shows the stack after adding one item, and part C shows the stack after adding a second item.*

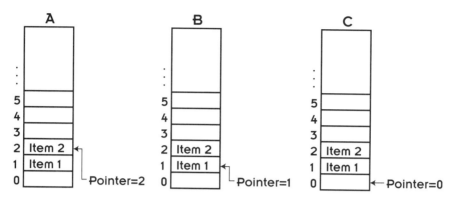

Figure 5.2 *Part A shows a stack containing two data items; parts B and C show the stack after removing one and then both items, respectively.*

CREATING THE CALCULATOR

We will start by creating a basic calculator that can add, subtract, multiply, and divide. Later in the chapter, we'll add several enhancements, but I think it's a good idea to start simple.

Declaring Global Variables and Constants

Create a new project. Double click in the blank form to open the code editing window. At the top of the editing window, open the Object list and select (General), then open the Proc list and select Declarations. We'll start by entering the required global variable and constant declarations into the form. The term *global* means that these data items will be available throughout all parts of the program. I will explain this in detail later in the chapter when I discuss variable scope. For now, enter the code show in Listing 5.1. **Option Explicit** should appear by default, but if you have changed any of the default settings and **Option Explicit** doesn't appear, make sure to enter this statement at the top of the code window.

Listing 5.1   Variable and Constant Declarations in the Declarations Section of the Calculator Form

```
Option Explicit

' The size of the stack.
Const STACKSIZE = 1000
```

```
' The format string for the display.
Const DISPLAY_FORMAT1 = "###,###,###,###.0000000000"
Const DISPLAY_FORMAT2 = "#.######E+000"

' The RPN stack; defaults to type Variant.
Dim Stack(STACKSIZE)

' Keeps track of current stack location.
Dim StackPointer As Integer

' Flag indicating whether we are starting a new entry.
Dim NewEntry As Boolean
```

You may be able to figure out what the various statements do just by reading the comments. But just in case you can't, I will explain them briefly. There are three constants included in the code. STACKSIZE specifies the number of elements in the stack. The two DISPLAY_FORMAT constants are used in formatting numbers for display by the calculator. I will discuss them in detail later in the chapter.

The first **Dim** statement declares the stack array. Note that the size of the array is specified by the STACKSIZE constant that we declared earlier. The other **Dim** statements declare a type **Integer** to serve as the stack pointer, and a type **Boolean** that serves as a flag indicating whether or not we are starting a new number entry on the calculator. The term *flag* is programmer-speak for a **Boolean** variable, one that is either True or False.

Designing the Form

Once the global variables and constants have been entered, we can start designing the form. Click on the View Form button in the Project window to display the still-blank form. Size the form so that it is about 50 percent wider than it is tall. Set the form properties as follows:

Caption: Calculator

Name: frmCalculator

BorderStyle: 1 - Fixed Single

MinButton: True

The **BorderStyle** property setting creates a calculator form that cannot be resized by the user, but the **MinButton** property setting allows users to minimize the calculator when it is not in use.

The first control we'll place is a Text Box that will serve as the calculator's display. Stretch it across the width of the form, near the top. Then set its properties as follows:

Name: txtDisplay

Alignment: 1 - Right Justify

Locked: True

A right justified **Alignment** setting causes the text in the Text Box to be aligned at the right edge of the box. Setting the **Locked** property to True prevents the user from editing the Text Box while the program is running. You also need to set the **Font** property of the Text Box, as well as its **ForeColor** and **BackColor** properties. These property settings are a matter of personal preference, so you can experiment to see what you like. I used the MS Sans Serif font in bold, 30 point size for the font, and I selected a black background with bright green text, to simulate the fluorescent display of some hand-held calculators. Once you're done setting font and colors, set the Text Box's **Text** property to blank. You'll find it helpful to leave the default text displayed while you are choosing your color schemes, so you can see the effect of your various attempts.

Creating the Control Array of Number Buttons

The next step in creating the calculator's interface is to place the ten command buttons for entering the digits 0 through 9. We will use a new technique called a *control array*. Once you've seen how this works, I think you'll agree that it is a very powerful tool.

When you place individual controls on a form, each one has its own name and each one has its own event procedures. In contrast, a control array contains two or more controls of the same type that have the same name and the same event procedures. Each control in an array still has its own set of properties, however. In the event procedure, Visual Basic provides an Index argument that specifies which of the controls in the array received the event. As a result, you can write a single event procedure that handles events to two or more controls.

This concept will be easier to understand if you try it out. Start by placing a Command Button on the form, in the position where you want the "0" button (in the lower-left corner, if you're following my design). Change the **Name** property of this button to *cmdNumbers*. With the new Command Button selected, press Ctrl+C to copy the control to the Clipboard, then press Ctrl+V to paste it on the form. Visual Basic displays a dialog box asking if you want to create a control array. Select Yes. The duplicate Command Button will be inserted in the top-left corner of the form. Drag it to the location where you want the "1" button to appear.

Before adding the remaining buttons, let's briefly look at the properties of the Command Button that was just added. Its name is cmdNumbers, the same as the original button that you copied. Its **Index** property, however, is 1. If you select the original Command Button you'll see that its **Index** property is 0. This is how Visual Basic distinguishes between controls in a control array.

Now you can finish inserting the eight remaining number buttons. For each one, simply press Ctrl+V to paste another copy of the button from the Clipboard, and drag it to the desired location. You should do this in order, beginning with the "2" button. You'll see the reason for this soon.

Once all ten number buttons have been added to the form, you should go through and select each one, changing its **Caption** property to the proper number—that is, the same as its **Index** property. When you're done, your form will look something like Figure 5.3.

Don't forget to save your project. I used the name Calculator for both the form and the project.

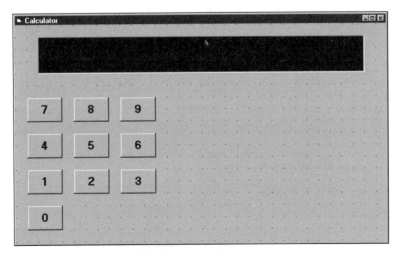

Figure 5.3 *The Calculator form, after adding the number buttons.*

Creating the Array of Operator Buttons

The calculator also needs four buttons for the basic arithmetic operations: addition, subtraction, multiplication, and division. We will use a control array for these buttons, as well. Place a new Command Button on the form, and change its **Name** property to *cmdOperators*. Then use the Copy and Paste technique from the previous section to create a control array of four buttons. Change the buttons' Caption properties as shown in Table 5.2.

Changing the Button Font

Visual Basic's default font is a bit too small for the Command Button captions, so you should change it. Rather than changing the **Font** property of each button individually—a tedious task to be sure—you can change a property for multiple controls at one time. First, select all the controls. (The controls do not have to be the same type, although, in this case, they will all be Command Buttons.) You can use the Shift+Click method, or you can select the Pointer tool and use the mouse to drag an outline (marquee) around the desired controls. When you release the mouse button, all controls that are completely within the rectangle will be selected. To deselect an individual control, press Shift and click on it.

When multiple controls are selected, the Properties window displays only those properties that all of the controls have in common. For example, if you selected a Text Box and a Command Button, you would not see the **Text** property displayed in the Properties window because only the Text Box control has this property. However, **BackColor** and **Font** (among others) are two properties that the control types have in common, so these properties would display in the Properties window. When you make a change to a common property, the change is reflected in all selected controls.

Use this technique now to change the **Font** property for all the Command Buttons you have placed on the form. Experiment to find a font that looks good to you.

Table 5.2 *Operator Button Caption Properties*

cmdOperators Index	Caption
0	+
1	–
2	X
3	/

Adding the Other Calculator Buttons

There are a few more buttons that any calculator needs: a Clear button to erase the display, a BackSpace button to delete the last number entered, a decimal point button, and a +/- button to change the sign of the number in the display. Don't forget the Enter button, to place values on the stack. Go ahead and add these five buttons, making the Enter button bigger than all the rest. Note that these are individual buttons and are *not* a control array. Set the properties as shown in Table 5.3.

You'll probably want to change the **Font** property for these new buttons also. When you are finished, your form will look like Figure 5.4.

Table 5.3   *Calculator Button Properties*

Button	Caption	Name
Plus/Minus	+/–	cmdPlusMinus
Decimal point	.	cmdDecimal
Clear	C	cmdClear
Backspace	<<	cmdBackspace
Enter	Enter	cmdEnter

Figure 5.4   *The partially completed Calculator form.*

The Number Button Event Procedures

We are done with the visual interface (at least for now). We can begin writing the code that will give the calculator its "smarts." Since the most basic thing a calculator must do is display numbers as the user clicks on the buttons, we'll start with that. Double click on one of the number buttons on the form to display the skeleton of the **Click()** event procedure. The first line looks like this:

```
Private Sub cmdNumbers_Click(Index As Integer)
```

The stuff in the parentheses shows that when this procedure is called in response to a button click, Visual Basic passes a variable named Index to the event procedure. Because the ten number buttons are all part of a control array, this one **Click()** event procedure is called when *any* one of them is clicked on. The value of Index (which is the same as the value stored in Index property) specifies which of the buttons was selected.

Let's begin by taking a look at what's going on when the user clicks one of the number buttons. The calculator could be in one of two states. In one state, the user has started entering a number and the just-clicked number should be tacked on to the end of what's already in the display. In the other state, the user has completed making the previous entry or calculation and the just-clicked number represents the start of a new entry, in which case the existing display should be erased. We will use the Boolean variable NewEntry that we declared earlier as a flag for the calculator's condition. This flag will be set to False if the user is continuing an existing entry, and set to True if the user is starting a new entry. Therefore, the procedure needs to perform two tasks:

- If NewEvent is True, erase the display and set NewEntry to False.

- Add the clicked number to the display.

The code for this procedure is shown in Listing 5.2. You can see that it's quite simple. You should also be able to see why I insisted that you match each button's Index property with its caption, which results in the Index argument to the event procedure holding the button's actual value. In this case, the program needs only to use the concatenation operator to tack Index onto the end of the calculator's display.

Listing 5.2   The Click Event Procedure for the Array of Number Buttons

```
Private Sub cmdNumbers_Click(Index As Integer)

' If we're starting a new entry, clear the text box.
If NewEntry Then
    txtDisplay.Text = ""
    NewEntry = False
End If

' Put the new digit at the end of the text.
txtDisplay.Text = txtDisplay.Text & Index

End Sub
```

You can test the project at this point by pressing F5. The calculator will display, and you can click on the number buttons to enter numbers in the display. Nothing else works yet, however, so clearly we have some more code to write!

The Display Procedure

Before getting to the other button event procedures, we are going to create a procedure that will display results in the calculator's display. This will be a *general* procedure, which is different from an event procedure.

General Basic Procedures

As you have learned, an event procedure is a separate, self-contained chunk of code that is automatically executed whenever the associated event occurs. A general procedure is similar, except that it is not linked to an event. Rather, a general procedure (or, from here on, simply *procedure*) is executed when code elsewhere in the program calls it. The use of procedures (a technique sometimes referred to as *structured programming*) is a central part of Visual Basic programming, and in all other programming languages. Procedures emphasize breaking a program into various partially independent tasks—each task being placed in its own procedure. Each time the program needs the task performed, it calls the procedure. This approach has a number of significant advantages:

- The program is easier to write because the entire project is broken down into a number of smaller, more easily managed tasks.

- The program is easier to debug, because you can localize the problem to a specific section of code.

- The program is easier to maintain, because modifications made in one part of the program are less likely to have unwanted side effects in other parts of the program.

Code that is inside a procedure (including event procedures) is called *procedure level code*. Code that is outside a procedure is called *module level code*. With a few exceptions, you can put any Basic statement in a procedure. There's no limit to the amount of code that you can put in a procedure, but it is good programming practice to keep procedures to a small or moderate size by splitting complex tasks into several smaller tasks. What's a moderate size? There's no strict definition, of course, but in my experience it's rare to find a procedure more than 25 or 30 lines of code that could not be profitably broken into two or more smaller procedures.

There are two types of procedures. A *function* returns a value to the calling program, whereas a *sub procedure* does not. Otherwise, the two types are identical. An important feature of procedures is the ability to define *procedure arguments*, which can be thought of as specialized variables that are used to pass information to the procedure when it is called. We will see how to create a sub procedure here. Functions aren't much different, and I'll cover them later on.

Creating a Procedure

Visual Basic automates much of the work of creating a procedure. Let's walk through the steps of creating the **DisplayResult()** procedure for the Calculator project.

1. Load the Calculator project, then open the code editing window (click on View Code from the Project window).

2. Select Procedure from the Insert menu. Visual Basic displays the Insert Procedure dialog box, shown in Figure 5.5.

3. Enter *DisplayResult* in the Name box. Procedure names follow the same rules as variable names, and, of course, the name should describe what the procedure does.

4. Be sure that the Sub option is selected in the Type section of the dialog box.

5. Click on OK.

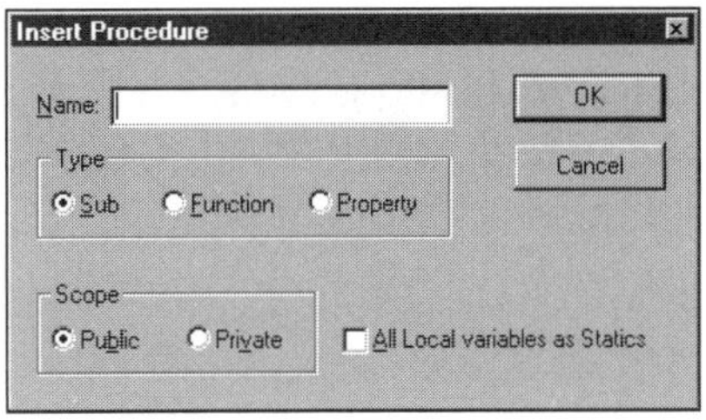

Figure 5.5 *You use the Insert Procedure dialog box to create a new procedure.*

Visual Basic opens a new editing window with the skeleton of the procedure entered in it, as shown here.

```
Public Sub DisplayResult( )

End Sub
```

Public versus Private

What's the meaning of the **Public** keyword in the procedure definition? There is one of two possibilities here. The **Public** and **Private** keywords shown in the previous code are relevant only for procedures that are located in a Basic module (a file that contains only Basic procedures, no forms or controls), but Visual Basic sticks the default **Public** keyword on *all* procedure definitions, even though it has no effect. A procedure declared **Public** in a Basic module can be called from any module in the project, whereas a **Private** procedure can be called only from within its own module. A procedure in a form module, such as the one we are creating here, can only be called from within its own module, regardless of whether the **Public** or the **Private** keyword (or no keyword at all) is used.

The next step is to specify the procedure arguments. A procedure can have no arguments, or as many arguments as are needed. Arguments can be any Basic data type. We will need only one for this procedure—a numeric argument that is used to pass the number to be displayed. Edit the first line of the procedure as follows:

```
Public Sub DisplayResult(X As Double)
```

We are specifying that the procedure **DisplayResult()** takes one type Double argument named X. If we needed to specify additional arguments, they would be separated by commas.

Now it's time to think about what the code in this procedure should do. First of all, the value being entered should be placed on the stack. If NewEntry is True the new number is placed at the top of the stack, replacing what's already there. Otherwise, the stack pointer is incremented before placing the new number on the stack.

How the number is displayed raises some more complicated questions. On most hand-held calculators, the number is displayed exactly as it is entered. We've seen how this is done in the event procedure for the number buttons. Once the Enter key is pressed, however, the number is displayed with full accuracy. For example, if you press 2.5 (but not Enter) the display reads "2.5." Once you press Enter, it reads "2.500000000." This enables the user to tell whether they are in the middle of an entry or whether the display is showing a calculated or entered number.

We also have to deal with very large and very small numbers. Our calculator display will show approximately 20 digits, with the exact capacity depending on the display Text Box size and the font used. For very large and very small numbers, however, it is better to use scientific notation, which greatly improves readability. This method expresses numbers as a value between 1 and 10, multiplied by 10 raised to a specified power. For example, a small number such as 120 would be expressed as 1.2 multiplied by 10^2 or, in computer notation, 1.2 E +002. A large number such as 1,234,756,000,000,000,000,000 would be expressed as 1.234756 E + 021.

What we'll do then, is test the number that is to be displayed and depending on its value, format it accordingly:

- If it's 0, simply display 0.00.

- If it's not too big (greater than 999,999,999) or too small (less than 0.000000001), we will display 10 decimal places with commas separating the thousands.

- If it's outside our other boundaries, we will display it in scientific notation, using 6 decimal places.

To implement this display scheme we will turn to two of Visual Basic's built-in functions. These functions are identical to user-defined functions, except they are part of Visual Basic instead of being written in your program. There are well over 100 functions that perform a wide variety of commonly needed tasks, such as trigonometric calculations, date and time manipulation, user input, and error handling. I can't cover all of these functions, but I will be explaining quite a few as we encounter them. For a complete function listing, select Contents from the Help menu, then select Functions (for an alphabetical listing) or Keywords by Task (for a listing by category).

The first function we will use is **Abs()**, which returns the absolute value of its argument. This means that negative numbers are converted to positive, and positive numbers are not changed. Thus, **Abs(8)** returns 8, and **Abs(-10)** returns 10.

The other function we'll be using is **Format()**. **Format()** takes two arguments, a number and a *format specifier*. The format specifier is a string that contains special characters that indicate how the number is to be formatted. The return value is a string containing the formatted number. For the full details on how to construct format specifiers, refer to Visual Basic's Help system. For our purposes, we simply need to know:

- A # character specifies a digit position that will be used if needed, and omitted if not needed.

- A 0 character specifies a digit position that will be displayed whether needed or not, being filled with a 0 as required.

- The E+ characters specify scientific notation.

Now you can see the purpose of the two constants that we declared in the declarations section of the form module. The first one

```
Const DISPLAY_FORMAT1 = "###,###,###,###.0000000000"
```

will format a number with up to 12 digits to the left of the decimal point, with thousands separators, and 10 digits to the right of the decimal point padded with 0s if needed. For example, the number 4098.998 would be formatted as 4,098.9980000000. We will use this format specifier for numbers that are not too big or too small. The second format specifier

```
Const DISPLAY_FORMAT2 = "#.######E+000"
```

will format a number in scientific notation, with up to 6 decimal places and a 3 digit exponent.

Now we have the tools needed to create the **DisplayResult()** procedure. Finish editing the procedure, as shown in Listing 5.3.

Listing 5.3   The DisplayResult() Procedure

```
Public Sub DisplayResult(X As Double)

' Put X on the top of the stack and display it.

If Not NewEntry Then StackPointer = StackPointer + 1

Stack(StackPointer) = X

If X = 0 Then
    txtDisplay.Text = "0.00"
ElseIf (Abs(X) < 999999999 And Abs(X) > 0.000000001) Then
    txtDisplay.Text = Format(X, DISPLAY_FORMAT1)
Else
    txtDisplay.Text = Format(X, DISPLAY_FORMAT2)
End If
NewEntry = True

End Sub
```

Visual Basic Helps You Out

I'm sure you have noticed that Visual Basic is keeping an eye on you as you enter code. Whenever you complete a line of code and move the cursor off it, Visual Basic reviews the line for certain syntax errors. For example, if the line contains an unmatched parenthesis, Visual Basic will catch it. When an error is detected Visual Basic pops up a dialog box with an description of the error and highlights the line of code and positions the cursor where it thinks the error might be. You can either close the dialog box and fix the error, or wait until you run the program. Certain kinds of syntax errors are caught only when the program runs (in the Visual Basic development environment, not as a stand-alone). Again, Visual Basic highlights the line with the error and displays a dialog box. After fixing the error, press F5 to restart the program.

Some programmers find the automatic syntax checking to be annoying. To turn it off, click on the Environment tab, and turn off the Auto Syntax Check option. This way, errors will be caught only when the program runs.

Programming the Enter Button

Now we will write the event procedure for the Enter button. You'll see that it is very simple because we already put most of the needed functionality in the **DisplayResult()** procedure. Double click on the Enter button to display its Click procedure, then add the code shown in Listing 5.4.

Listing 5.4 The Enter Button Event Procedure

```
Private Sub cmdEnter_Click()

' Call DisplayResults to put the number in the display on the stack.
' Set NewEntry to False to force the DisplayResult() procedure
' to increment the stack pointer. Code in DisplayResults will
' set NewEntry to True.

NewEntry = False
DisplayResult (txtDisplay.Text)

End Sub
```

Programming the +/−, Clear, Decimal, and BackSpace Buttons

The remaining buttons are also fairly easy to program. Remember, double-click on the button to display its **Click()** event procedure. You can also select the control and the event from the lists that display at the top of the code editing window.

The +/− button changes the sign of the displayed number, from negative to positive or positive to negative. First, we use the **Left()** function to check if the number already begins with a minus sign. To do this, you pass this function a string and a number, n, and it returns the leftmost n characters of the string. In this case, we obtain the first character of the text that is displayed. If it is not "−", then we know the number is positive and can make it negative by adding a leading "−". If the number is negative, we can use the **Len()** and **Right()** functions to remove the leading "−" and make the number positive. **Len()** is passed a string and returns its length (the number of characters). **Right()** works just like **Left()**, but returns the rightmost n characters of the string. Thus the expression

```
Right(txtDisplay.Text, Len(txtDisplay.Text) - 1)
```

has the effect of trimming the first character off the display. The full code for this function is presented in Listing 5.5.

Listing 5.5 The +/− Button Click Event Procedure

```
Private Sub cmdPlusMinus_Click()

If (Left(txtDisplay, 1) <> "-") Then
    txtDisplay.Text = "-" & txtDisplay
Else
    txtDisplay.Text = Right(txtDisplay.Text, Len(txtDisplay.Text) - 1)
End If
End Sub
```

The Clear button is an easy one. All we need to do is set the **Text** property of the txtDisplay Text Box to an empty string and set the **NewEntry** flag. The procedure is given in Listing 5.6.

Listing 5.6   The Clear Button Click Event Procedure

```
Private Sub cmdClear_Click()

txtDisplay.Text = "0"
NewEntry = True

End Sub
```

The BackSpace button has the task of removing the rightmost character from the display. If the **NewEntry** flag is set, we do nothing because we don't want to erase part of an entered or calculated number. Otherwise, we check to see that the display is not empty and, if not, we use the **Left()** and **Len()** functions to remove the last character from the display. The full event procedure is presented in Listing 5.7.

Listing 5.7   The BackSpace Button Click Event Procedure

```
Private Sub cmdBackSpace_Click()

' If we're in the process of making an
' entry, remove the rightmost character from the display.

If NewEntry Then Exit Sub

If txtDisplay.Text <> "" Then
    txtDisplay.Text = Left(txtDisplay.Text, Len(txtDisplay.Text) - 1)
End If

End Sub
```

The event procedure for the decimal button is a bit more complicated. As with the number keys, if a new entry is being started, the event procedure clears the text box and clears the **NewEntry** flag, then checks the entry for the following two conditions:

- If the display is empty (length = 0), the decimal is added as the first character.

- If the display is not empty, we then see if a decimal point already has been entered. If not, the decimal is added at the end of the displayed string.

To determine if one string is present in another string, use the **Instr()** function. It takes two arguments—the string to be searched and the string you are looking for. If the string is found, the function returns the position where it was found (with the first character in position 1). If the string is not found, the function returns 0. Complete code for this event procedure is shown in Listing 5.8.

Listing 5.8   The Decimal Button Click() Event Procedure

```
Private Sub cmdDecimal_Click()

' If we're starting a new entry, clear the text box.
If NewEntry Then
    txtDisplay.Text = ""
    NewEntry = False
End If

If Len(txtDisplay.Text) = 0 Then
    txtDisplay.Text = "."
Else
    If InStr(txtDisplay.Text, ".") = 0 Then
        txtDisplay.Text = txtDisplay.Text & "."
    End If
End If

End Sub
```

Go ahead and run the project. You'll be able to enter numbers, clear the display, backspace, and so on. Of course, the calculator won't calculate yet! Our next task is programming the operator buttons.

 **Watching the Stack**

By adding a few lines of code to the program, you'll be able to keep track of the calculator's stack, which will help you to get a better understanding for how the stack works. Use the techniques you learned in the section *Creating a Procedure* to create a new sub procedure called **ShowStack()**, and add the following code:

```
Public Sub ShowStack()

Dim i As Integer

Debug.Print "StackPointer = "; StackPointer

For i = 1 To 10
```

```
    Debug.Print i, Stack(i)
Next

End Sub
```

Then, to call the procedure at the end of **DisplayResults()**, insert the line

```
Call ShowStack
```

just before the End Sub statement in the **DisplayResults()** procedure. What **ShowStack()** does is display, in the Debug window, the value of the stack pointer and of the first 10 stack positions (to display more than ten, edit the **For** statement).

Programming the Operator Buttons

The last thing we need to do in order to have a functioning calculator is to write the event procedure for the operator buttons. Because we added these buttons to the form as a control array, we will need only a single procedure for all four buttons. As before with the number buttons, we will tell which button was clicked by looking at the Index argument that is passed to the procedure.

The code is actually rather simple. First, we declare a type **Double** variable named Result to hold the result of the calculation. It is also necessary to ensure that there is at least one value on the stack. Then, we perform the requested operation between the value on the top of the stack and the value in the display. For addition and multiplication, the order doesn't matter, but for division it is the stack value divided by the display value, and for subtraction it is the display value subtracted from the stack value.

One more thing is required. Since dividing by 0 is a definite no-no, we must be sure that the display value is not 0 before performing the division (or Visual Basic would report an error). If the display value is 0, we call the **MsgBox()** function to inform the user, then exit the procedure without performing the calculation. The **MsgBox()** function displays a small dialog box containing your message and an OK button. We'll be using this function regularly, and you can refer to Visual Basic Help for more information.

Once the calculation has been performed, all we need to do is pass the result to the **DisplayResult()** procedure, and *voilá!* the answer appears in the display. The full event procedure for the operator buttons is shown in Listing 5.9. Make sure that the Index property of each operator button matches the proper **Case** statement in the function.

Listing 5.9   The Operator Button Click Event Procedure

```
Private Sub cmdOperators_Click( Index As Integer)

Dim Result As Double

' See if there is at least 1 value on the stack.
If StackPointer < 1 Then Exit Sub

Select Case Index
    Case 0  ' plus
        Result = Stack(StackPointer) + Val(txtDisplay.Text)
    Case 1  ' minus
        Result = Stack(StackPointer) - Val(txtDisplay.Text)
    Case 2  ' multiply
        Result = Stack(StackPointer) * Val(txtDisplay.Text)
    Case 3  ' divide
        If (Val(txtDisplay.Text) <> 0) Then
            Result = Stack(StackPointer) / Val(txtDisplay.Text)
        Else
            MsgBox "Cannot divide by 0!"
            Exit Sub
        End If
End Select

DisplayResult (Result)

End Sub
```

The calculator is now complete. Well, at least it's working! We will be adding some enhancements to it later in the chapter. But first let's sit back and think about what we have done

ARE YOU IMPRESSED?

Well, I certainly am. And if you're not, you should be. Just look at what Visual Basic has let us accomplish. While it may have taken you, a Visual Basic programming newcomer, an hour or two to have finished the calculator project, even a moderately experienced Visual Basic programmer would have knocked it off in 15 to 30 minutes. So you can see that for a *very* modest expenditure of time we have a fully functional (albeit basic) calculator with a slick visual interface.

It makes me sweat just to think about how long this would have taken with the old ways of programming. If you are new to programming, you can't really know what I'm talking about. Just think of the differences between a horse and buggy and a 400 horsepower Jaguar with a wet bar and mink seats, and you may get some idea! Of course, you may not know any other way of programming, so to you the speed and power of Visual Basic is simply the way programming ought to be. And I agree completely—I just wish I had it ten years ago!

But enough complaining. Let's take a moment to review what we have done so far. The Calculator project helped to reinforce some of the Visual Basic tools and concepts you learned in previous chapters—drawing controls on a form, setting control properties, and writing event procedures. You've also been introduced to several powerful new techniques. Let's summarize:

- Data arrays are a very useful way of storing large quantities of data in an indexed fashion. Combining arrays with loops is a powerful technique that you'll see frequently in all kinds of Visual Basic programs.

- Control arrays group two or more controls under the same name. By sharing a name and event procedures, control arrays greatly reduce the coding required for certain tasks.

- General procedures are used to isolate individual program tasks, reducing coding and debugging effort and resulting in simpler and more robust programs.

- Visual Basic's built-in functions perform a wide variety of commonly needed tasks.

- The Debug window and the **Debug.Print** method provide a useful way for peeking at what's going on inside your program.

At this point, I think you have learned enough so you can start experimenting with Visual Basic on your own. Don't give up this book, of course! But, by combining further readings with experimentation, you'll learn more quickly than by doing just one or the other. I recommend that you spend some time browsing through Visual Basic's function library; it contains a great deal of useful stuff. If you're feeling ambitious, a good project for you to try would be a calculator that uses algebraic logic. Hint: It's more difficult than an RPN calculator.

While our new calculator is quite nice, I can think of a few additional features it might have. We will spend the remainder of this chapter polishing our project.

ENHANCING THE CALCULATOR

The enhancements I have in mind involve adding more functionality to the calculator. We would like to be able to calculate the trigonometric functions SIN, COS, and TAN, as well as the inverse (1 / X) and raising a number to a power. In addition, it can very useful to be able to copy the number in the calculator's display to the Windows Clipboard for use in other Windows applications. For example, you can perform calculations and paste the answer right into the letter you are writing with Word or WordPerfect. Finally, a Last X button that removes the top value from the stack can be useful for certain calculations.

For the Trig calculations we will use Visual Basic's built-in **Sin()**, **Cos()**, and **Tan()** functions. As you may already have guessed, we'll use a control array of Command Buttons. Use the techniques you learned earlier to create this array of three buttons. Name the array cmdTrig and set the **Caption** properties to Sin, Cos, and Tan. The code for the event procedure is shown in Listing 5.10. Again, you must be sure that the **Index** property of each button matches the corresponding **Case** statement in the procedure. After calculating the correct value, all that is required is calling the **DisplayResult()** function. (I told you we'd get a lot of mileage out of this function!)

Listing 5.10 The Trigonometric Command Button Click Event Procedure

```
Private Sub cmdTrig_Click(Index As Integer)

Dim Result As Double

Select Case Index
    Case 0  ' Sin
        Result = Sin(txtDisplay.Text)
    Case 1  ' Cos
        Result = Cos(txtDisplay.Text)
    Case 2  ' Tan
        Result = Tan(txtDisplay.Text)
End Select

DisplayResult (Result)

End Sub
```

The remaining buttons are all single buttons, not part of a control array. Add four more Command Buttons, assigning them the **Name** and **Caption** properties shown here.

Command Button 1

> *Caption:* 1 / X
> *Name:* cmdInverse

Command Button 2

> *Caption:* Y ∧ X
> *Name:* cmdPower

Command Button 3

> *Caption:* Last X
> *Name:* cmdLastX

Command Button 4

> *Caption:* Copy
> *Name:* cmdCopy

When you have finished adding the buttons, your form will look like Figure 5.6. You can change the **Font** property of the new buttons if you find the default font too small.

The event procedure for the Last X button is shown in Listing 5.11. After verifying that the stack has two or more values on it, the stack pointer is decremented by 1 and the new top value is displayed. You'll note that the display code looks very much like the code in the **DisplayResult()** function that we wrote earlier. Why not just call **DisplayResult()**? If you look at the code for **DisplayResult()**, you'll see that it does more than just display a

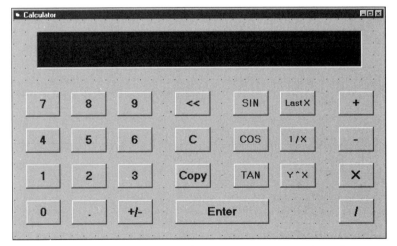

Figure 5.6 *The calculator with trig functions and Inverse, Power, Last X, and Copy buttons.*

number in the Text Box—it also increments the stack pointer, something we don't want to do here. Instead, we'll simply copy the display code from **DisplayResult()** to the **cmdLastX_Click()** procedure.

Listing 5.11   The Last X Button Click Event Procedure

```
Private Sub cmdLastX_Click()

' Discard the top stack value and display previous one.

If StackPointer > 1 Then
    StackPointer = StackPointer - 1
    If Stack(StackPointer) = 0 Then
        txtDisplay.Text = "0.00"
    ElseIf Stack(StackPointer) < 999999999 And _
      Stack(StackPointer) > 0.000000001 Then
        txtDisplay.Text = Format(Stack(StackPointer), DISPLAY_FORMAT1)
    Else
        txtDisplay.Text = Format(Stack(StackPointer), DISPLAY_FORMAT2)
    End If
End If

NewEntry = True

End Sub
```

The code to calculate the inverse of a number (1 / X) is very simple. The only possible catch is if the user tries to invert 0, so we'll test for that condition and display a message box if it occurs. Otherwise, all that's necessary is to divide 1 by the value in the display, and call **DisplayResult()** to display it and put it on the stack. The code for this event procedure is shown in Listing 5.12.

Listing 5.12   The 1/X Button Click Event Procedure

```
Private Sub cmdInverse_Click()

' Displays the inverse.

If txtDisplay.Text = 0 Then
    MsgBox "Cannot take inverse of 0!"
    Exit Sub
Else
    DisplayResult (1 / txtDisplay.Text)
    NewEntry = True
End If
End Sub
```

Raising a number to a power, the Y ^ X button, is an equally simple calculation requiring only Visual Basic's ^ operator. Note that the number on the stack is raised to the power of the number in the display, not the other way around. The code for this event procedure is shown in Listing 5.13.

Listing 5.13   The Y ^ X Button Click() Event Procedure

```
Private Sub cmdPower_Click()

' Raises the number on the stack to the power
' of the number in the display.

Dim Result As Double

If StackPointer < 1 Then Exit Sub

Result = Stack(StackPointer) txtDisplay.Text
DisplayResult (Result)
NewEntry = True

End Sub
```

Finally, we come to the Copy button's Click event procedure. Now, how the devil do you copy something to the Windows Clipboard? You may think it's complicated, but it's actually very simple. In a Visual Basic program, you have direct access to the Windows Clipboard object, which is named Clipboard. There are several methods by which you can work with the Clipboard object. One method is **SetText**, which places the specified text on the Clipboard where it can be retrieved by any Windows program with a Paste command. You can see from Listing 5.14 how simple the code is, requiring only a single line. There are several other Clipboard methods, and we'll be using some of them in other parts of the book. Take a look at the Visual Basic Help system for more information.

Listing 5.14   The Copy Button Click Event Procedure

```
Private Sub cmdCopy_Click()

' Put the display text on the Windows clipboard

Clipboard.SetText txtDisplay.Text

End Sub
```

The calculator is—believe it or not—done. Take it for a spin, I think it's pretty neat. Figure 5.7 shows the calculator in action.

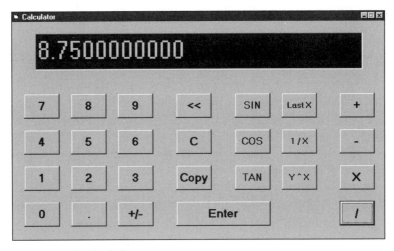

Figure 5.7 *The completed calculator in action.*

VARIABLE SCOPE

Before ending this chapter, we need to explore the concept of variable scope. The *scope* of a variable means what parts of the program it is visible in. When a variable is not visible, or is *out of scope*, it might as well not exist. You can't get at it until it comes back in scope.

What do I mean by "parts" of a program? In a Visual Basic module, some code is contained in procedures (both general and event procedures) and is called *procedure level code.* Most of the code in the Calculator project is procedure level code. Other code, such as Calculator's **Const** declarations, exists outside any procedure, and is called *module level code.* Although we haven't seen one yet, some Visual Basic programs contain more than one module, so which module code is within also matters.

The location of a variable's declaration (its **Dim** statement) determines the scope of a variable. If you declare a variable inside a procedure, its scope is limited to that one procedure. Module level code cannot access it, nor can code in other procedures. Such variables are called *local* variables because their scope is local to the procedure where they are declared. In fact, different procedures can have local variables of the same name and they exist as totally independent variables because their scopes do not overlap. For example, we used a variable named Result in more than one procedure in the Calculator project.

If you declare a variable in module level code, its scope is the entire module. The array Stack() is such a variable, and you can see that code in several of the program's procedures use it. Such variables are said to have *global* scope.

In a multiple module program, you can declare a global variable to be *public*. This means that the variable's scope includes not only the module it is declared in, but all other modules in the project. Use the **Public** keyword in a module-level declaration to create a public variable, as in this example:

```
Public Array(1000) As Integer
```

You may wonder why programmers don't simply make all their program's variables global or public, and then not have to worry about scope. Bad idea! Don't look at scope as a restriction, but a tool that helps you create bug-free programs. The ability to hide variables in procedures from the rest of the program is a major component of the power of structured programming. With local variables, a procedure can be completely independent from the rest of the program. It receives information via its arguments, and returns information (if it is a function) via its return value. No other part of the program can screw up what goes on in the procedure. Likewise, what goes on in the procedure cannot screw up the rest of the program. The rule to follow is to use local variables as much as possible. Global and public variables are reserved for situations where they are really needed.

WHAT NOW?

With the completion of this chapter, you have finished the first part of the book. You've come a long way, and learned a lot. With the material we have covered, you can do an awful lot with Visual Basic, but there's still a lot to come. We haven't touched on menus, common dialogs, class modules, and many other important topics. From here on, however, I will be a lot less "general" in my approach. Each chapter will delve into a specific area where you might want to apply Visual Basic—text processing and multimedia are two examples. We'll deal with the remaining Visual Basic tools as we go along.

TEXT PROCESSING

CHAPTER 6

Many programs that are created with Visual Basic deal with text in one form or another. In this chapter, we'll explore Visual Basic's text processing capabilities by creating a handy text editor.

Have you ever seen a program that doesn't deal with text in one form or another? They're pretty rare, that's for sure. Some programs, such as word processors, are designed specifically to work with text. Others, such as databases, utilize text as a means for displaying and organizing data. Whatever kinds of Visual Basic projects you find yourself taking on, it's a sure bet that you'll be dealing with text on a regular basis.

Fortunately for us, Visual Basic has a variety of powerful text-related tools. In this chapter's project, we'll use these tools to create a fully functional text editor. In addition, I'll show you some other important capabilities, including:

- Storing text data in disk files

- Adding a menu to a Visual Basic program

- Using the Common Dialog control

When we're finished, not only will you have learned a lot more about Visual Basic, but you'll have a pretty nice text editor. You can use the editor as a standalone program, or you can use it as a software component that you can add to your other Visual Basic projects that require text editing capabilities.

PLANNING THE EDITOR

As always, it pays to take a little time to plan the project before setting finger to keyboard. We are designing a text editor, which is quite different from a word processor. Word processors, such as Microsoft Word and WordPerfect, include an assortment of complex features for creating professionally formatted documents, including formatting, footnotes, graphics, and so on. Our project is much less ambitious. A text editor does nothing more than edit text files— that is, add, delete, and rearrange the text in the file. There's no formatting, no automatic word wrap (you must press Enter to start a new line), no fancy stuff.

Understanding Text Files

So what's a text file? A text file is one that contains nothing but the so-called standard characters—letters, numbers, punctuation marks, and so on. Text files are sometimes called ASCII files; the American Standard Code for Information Interchange (ASCII) specifies which numbers are used to represent the characters (remember, computers use numbers internally for data storage). For example, the letter *a* is represented by the number 97, and the percent symbol (%) is represented by the number 37. To view the ASCII codes, display the Visual Basic Help Contents screen. From there, first select Visual Basic Help, then select Reference Information, and then, under Other Information, select Character Set.

How do you tell a text file from a non-text file (such as a program file or a word processor document)? Sometimes the filename extension can help. The .TXT extension is (or at least should be) reserved for text files. DOS batch files (*.BAT), Windows INI files (*.INI), and all Visual Basic program files (*.VBP, *.FRM, and *.BAS) are text files too. The true test, however, is to view the file's contents, either using the Type command from the DOS prompt or by using a text editor. If the file displays nothing but recognizable characters, then it's a text file.

The editor we will create is what I call a *Baby Editor*—an editor that provides only the most basic editing functions, but is quick, simple to use, and is easy to customize should the need arise. What features should it have? Here are the bare essentials I would want in any editor:

- Basic editing: inserting and deleting text, moving the cursor, etc.

- Text selection capabilities

- Cut, copy, and paste capabilities

- Open any file that the user specifies

- Save a file under its original name or a new name

- Never lose unsaved changes without warning the user

These are the features that are included in our sample program. I have also added the ability to select the font that the text is displayed in. You may have a different list of "must have" features. But that's one of the beauties of the Baby Editor—you can easily customize it to your heart's desire!

PROGRAMMING THE EDITOR

Let's start with the editor's basic text-handling chores—entering and editing text. Sounds like we have some pretty serious programming ahead of us! Well, are you ever in for a pleasant surprise! All you have to do is drop a Text Box control on a form and most of the work is done. That's right, the Text Box control has many of the text-handling capabilities we need built in: cursor movement, selecting text, inserting and deleting characters. All we need to add is the ability to cut, copy, and paste text (using the Clipboard) to complete the editing part of the project.

Starting the Project

Start Visual Basic and select File | New. Resize the form to the size you want it to be when the program runs (the user can always change it), and set its properties as follows:

Name: frmBabyEditor

Caption: Text Editor - untitled

Next, place a Text Box control on the form. Don't worry about the size and position right now. When we execute the program, the Text Box will be adjusted to fill the entire form. Set the Text Box properties as shown here:

Multiline: True

ScrollBars: Both

These property settings give us a Text Box that can hold multiple lines of text (as opposed to the default single line) and has scroll bars that permit the user to scroll the text both vertically and horizontally using the mouse (the default is no scroll bars). Leave the other properties at their default setting. (Throughout the book, if I do not specifically say to change a property, you should assume that the default setting is preferred or that we will be changing the setting in code.)

Next, add a Common Dialog control to the form. This control provides several of Windows' standard dialog boxes; we'll see how it works later in the chapter. If the Common Dialog icon is not present in your toolbox, press Ctrl+T to display the Custom Controls dialog box. Scroll through the list and find the Microsoft Common Dialog Control entry, click on the corresponding Check Box to select the control, and then close the dialog box.

Your form should look something like the one shown in Figure 6.1. This figure also shows the File and Edit menus—creating them is our next task.

ADDING MENUS TO YOUR VISUAL BASIC APPS

One of the many things that most Windows applications have in common is a menu system. Visual Basic's menu editor makes it a snap to add menus to your programs—menus that are every bit as functional as the ones you see in any Windows program. You can add menus to any Visual Basic form, and in a multiple-form program each form can have its own menus. A menu is just another control, and like other controls it has properties and responds to events. Because of the special requirements of menus, however, you must design a menu and set its properties with the Menu Editor.

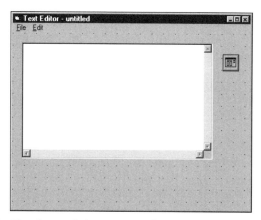

Figure 6.1　*The Baby Editor form with the Text Box and Common Dialog controls added.*

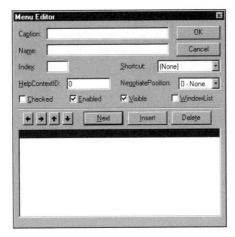

Figure 6.2 *The Menu Editor.*

To start the Menu Editor, which is shown in Figure 6.2, display a form then press Ctrl+E or select Menu Editor from the Tools menu. Rather than bore you with a long-winded description of how the editor works, I'll walk you through creation of the menus for our baby editor. Once we're done with that, you'll know most of what there is to know about the Menu Editor and menu design; the rest I can fill in quickly and easily.

Creating the Text Editor's Menu

What will our editor need in the way of menu commands? We are going to keep things simple, so we'll create only two menus: a File menu and an Edit menu. The File menu will contain the New, Open, Save, Save As, and Exit commands. The Edit menu will contain the Copy, Cut, Paste, and Font commands. Let's get to work.

Display the project's form, then press Ctrl+E or select Tools | Menu Editor to display the Menu Editor. Since this form does not yet have a menu, the editor is blank. We will start by adding the first menu command to display on the menu bar. Since we're following Windows conventions, this will be the File menu. In the Caption box enter *&File*; you'll see the menu caption appear in the large box at the bottom of the dialog box. Next, tab to the Name box and enter *mnuFile*, then click on the Next button. The highlight will move down a line in the menu outline, and the Text Boxes will be cleared, ready for you to enter the next menu item.

Before we do, however, I want to point out two things. First, menu captions can have access keys. In the menu display, an access key is designated by the underlined letter in the menu command. The user can quickly "access" the command by pressing that key when the menu is displayed. As with other control captions, you specify the access key by preceding it with *&*. Second, each menu item has a name. Just like with other types of controls, the name is used in the event procedures associated with the item. I have developed the habit of beginning all menu item names with *mnu*, then completing the name with the menu caption(s). Thus, the File menu is named *mnuFile*, and the Open command on the File menu will be named *mnuFileOpen*. This naming convention removes any possibility of confusion when dealing with menus.

Now, on to the next menu item. Enter *&New* in the Caption box and *mnuFileNew* in the Name box. Before clicking on the Next button, however, click on the right arrow button. You'll see the New caption—now displaying with an ellipsis in front of it—move over in the outline box. What we have done here is make the New command subsidiary to the File command. In other words, New will appear as an item on the File menu and not as a menu item on the menu bar.

Now click on Next. The new menu item (which is currently blank) is inserted at the same level as the item immediately preceding it (in this case, the New command). Enter *&Open* as the caption and *mnuFileOpen* as the name for this menu item. Open the Shortcut Key list and scroll down and select Ctrl+O to specify that the Ctrl+O key combination will be the shortcut for the File|Open command. Notice that Ctrl+O displays in the menu outline next to the Open caption.

Add the remaining two commands to the File menu:

- *&Save*, with the name *mnuFileSave* and the Ctrl+S shortcut key

- *Save File &As*, with the name *mnuFileSaveFileAs* and no shortcut key

At this point, your menu editor will look like Figure 6.3.

The next item we need to add to the File menu is not a menu command at all, but rather a *separator*, a horizontal line separating one section of the menu from another. To add a separator, create a menu item with a caption consisting of just a single dash, or hyphen. Because all menu items must be named, we'll assign the name *mnuFileSeparator* to this item. After clicking on Next, add the last item on the File menu, with the caption *E&xit* and the name *mnuFileExit*.

After entering the Exit command and clicking on Next, you are ready to start with the Edit menu. At this point, any entry you make will be subsidiary to the File menu. Since we want Edit to be a top-level menu, you need to click on the left arrow button to move up one level on the outline. Assign the caption

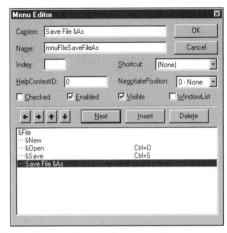

Figure 6.3 *The Menu Editor after partially completing the File menu.*

&Edit and the name *mnuEdit* to this menu item, then click on Next. Click on the right arrow to move down one level on the outline, and add the commands shown in Table 6.1 to the Edit menu.

Don't Stray from the Norm

If you have even a little experience using Windows programs, you have probably noticed that there are certain conventions that most programs follow when it comes to their menus. For example, if the program deals with files (and most programs do!), the file-related commands are on the File menu, which is the first item on the menu bar. Likewise, the first three entries on the File menu are usually New, Open, and Close.

Do yourself—and your users—a favor; follow these standards when it comes to menu organization in your Visual Basic programs. Sure, your unique menu design may be just as good from a functional point of view, but it will sure confuse the heck out of your users!

Table 6.1 *Edit Menu Commands*

Caption	Name	Shortcut Key
&Copy	mnuEditCopy	Ctrl+C
Cu&t	mnuEditCut	Ctrl+X
&Paste	mnuEditPaste	Ctrl+V
-	mnuEditSeparator	
&Font	mnuEditFont	Ctrl+F

Figure 6.4 *The completed menu in the Menu Editor.*

That's it—the menu is finished. Your Menu Editor will look like the one shown in Figure 6.4. Click on OK to close the Menu Editor and return to the form, as shown earlier in Figure 6.1. Your new menus now display on the form. You can open them to see what they look like. If you actually select a menu command Visual Basic will open the code editing window with that command's **Click()** event procedure displayed. We will be creating the event procedures later.

Before we continue creating the project, let's go over the other Menu Editor commands. Even though you didn't need them for this project, you will someday!

Other Menu Editor Options

The Menu Editor contains Check Boxes for setting several menu item properties. These properties control how the menu item is displayed when the program is running and the user pulls down the menu:

- *Checked*   Displays a check mark next to the menu item when the menu is displayed.

- *Enabled*   Indicates that a menu item is available. If a menu item is disabled, it is grayed out, indicating it is unavailable to the user.

- *Visible*   Toggles the display of a menu item.

You can also edit the structure of a menu as follows:

- Click on the up or down arrow to move the current menu item (the one highlighted in the hierarchical list) without changing its left-right position.

- Click on the left and right arrow to change a menu item's position in the hierarchy. You can have as many as four levels in a menu system.

- Click on the Insert button to add a new, blank menu item above the current item.

- Click on the Delete button to delete the current menu item.

There are some things in the Menu Editor that I have not explained. We'll get to them when and if they are needed later in the book.

PROGRAMMING THE EDITOR—PART 2

With the two controls placed and the menus designed, we are done with the visual design part of the Baby Editor project and it's time to turn our attention to the code. Let's start with the general declarations section, which is where the declarations of global variables and constants are placed—those variables and constants that must be available in all of the module's procedures. We require two type Boolean flags, plus two type String variables. The general declarations code is shown in Listing 6.1.

In case you don't remember how to display a specific part of a project's code, I'll refresh your memory. If the code editing window is not open, click on the View Code button in the Project window. Then, at the top of the window use the Object list to select the object whose code you want to view (in this case select General), and use the Proc list to select the specific procedure (in this case, Declarations).

Listing 6.1　General Declarations in BABYEDIT.FRM

```
Option Explicit

' True if the text being edited has changed.
Dim TextChanged As Boolean

' True if a file has just been loaded.
Dim JustLoaded As Boolean

Dim FileName As String, OldName As String
```

The next thing to write is the form's **Form_Load()** event procedure, which is triggered when the form is loaded. With a single-form program, such as this one, the form is loaded when the program begins execution. This procedure, then, is the ideal place to put program initialization code—code that does things like initializing variables and object properties. We have two tasks for **Form_Load()** to perform: setting the two flag variables to False, and setting the Common Dialog control's **Filter** property. I don't want to explain the details of this property setting now; I will devote a good deal of attention to the Common Dialog control later in the chapter. For now, restrain your curiosity! The code for the **Form_Load()** procedure is presented in Listing 6.2.

Listing 6.2   The Form_Load() Event Procedure

```
Private Sub Form_Load()

Dim Filter As String

' Clear flags.
TextChanged = False
JustLoaded = False

' Load filters into the common dialog box.
Filter = "Text files (*.txt) | *.txt"
Filter = Filter & "|Batch files (*.bat) | *.bat"
Filter = Filter & "|INI files (*.ini) | *.ini"
Filter = Filter & "|All files (*.*) | *.*"
CommonDialog1.Filter = Filter

End Sub
```

The next procedure, **Form_Resize()**, has the job of setting the size and position of the Text Box control to fill the form. The **Form_Resize()** event procedure is triggered every time the form's size is changed and also when it is first displayed. The code for this procedure is shown in Listing 6.3. By setting the Text Box's **Top** and **Left** properties to *0*, it positions the Text Box against the top and left edges of the form. By setting the Text Box's **Width** and **Height** properties to the values of the form's **ScaleWidth** and **ScaleHeight** properties, the Text Box's size is made equal to the form's internal display area.

Note that a form object also has **Width** and **Height** properties, but these differ from **ScaleWidth** and **ScaleHeight**. The former two properties give the outer dimensions of an object; in the case of a form object, these dimensions include its border, title bar, etc. The **ScaleHeight** and **ScaleWidth** properties refer specifically to the display area of the form—the area in which you place other objects.

Listing 6.3   The Form_Resize() Event Procedure

```
Private Sub Form_Resize()

' Size the Text Box to fill the form.

Text1.Top = 0
Text1.Left = 0
Text1.Width = ScaleWidth
Text1.Height = ScaleHeight

End Sub
```

You're probably wondering why we didn't specify an object for the **ScaleWidth** and **ScaleHeight** properties. Shouldn't I have written:

```
Text1.Width = frmBabyEditor.ScaleWidth
Text1.Height = frmBabyEditor.ScaleHeight
```

Well, I could have. This code would have worked fine, but was not necessary. In an object's own event procedures any reference to a property without an object name automatically refers to the object's own properties.

If you run the project now, you'll see that you can enter text into the Text Box and that you can select text using the standard methods (dragging with the mouse or holding Shift while using the cursor movement keys).

Implementing Cut, Copy, and Paste

The first requirement for the Cut, Copy, and Paste operations is taken care of for us by the Text Box's built-in capabilities. And, as we'll soon see, the other parts are also.

The Text Box control has a property named **SelLength** that gives us the length, in characters, of the selected text in the Text Box, and another property named **SelText** that returns the selected text itself. It's a trivial matter, therefore, to see if any text is selected (simply set **SelLength** to return lengths greater than 0) and if so, get the text itself.

As for the Copy operation, we will, of course, use the Windows Clipboard, which is represented in Visual Basic by the Clipboard object. This object is automatically available to all Visual Basic programs—you don't have to explicitly add it to the project. The Clipboard object has several methods, two of which we will use:

- **Clipboard.SetText** Places a specified block of text on the Clipboard, replacing any text that is already there.

- **Clipboard.GetText** Returns the text from the Clipboard.

With these tools, it is an easy matter to implement the Copy command. The code is placed in the Edit | Copy menu command's **Click** event procedure. You can display this procedure either by selecting it from the lists at the top of the code editing window or by selecting the command from the menus when the form is displayed. The code for this procedure is given in Listing 6.4. All it does is verify that there is text selected in the Text Box, which it then copies to the Clipboard.

Listing 6.4   The Edit|Copy Command Event Procedure

```
Private Sub mnuEditCopy_Click()

' If any text is selected copy it to the Clipboard.

If Text1.SelLength = 0 Then
    Beep
    Exit Sub
End If

Clipboard.SetText Text1.SelText

End Sub
```

Implementing the Cut command is very similar. In fact, the only difference is that the selected text is deleted from the Text Box after being copied to the Clipboard. This is accomplished by setting the Text Box's **SelText** property to an empty string. The code for the Edit | Cut command's **Click** event procedure is shown in Listing 6.5.

Listing 6.5   The Edit|Cut Command Event Procedure

```
Private Sub mnuEditCut_Click()

' If any text is selected copy it to the Clipboard,
' then delete it.

If Text1.SelLength = 0 Then
    Beep
    Exit Sub
End If

Clipboard.SetText Text1.SelText
Text1.SelText = ""

End Sub
```

Implementation of the Edit|Paste command is the simplest of all, requiring only a single line of code. Set the Text Box's **SelText** property equal to the text returned by the Clipboard's **GetText** method—that's it. Note that if there is text selected in the Text Box when the Paste command is executed, the selected text is replaced by the pasted text, which is the standard Windows way of doing things. If no text is selected, then the pasted text is inserted at the insertion point. The code for this event procedure is shown in Listing 6.6.

Listing 6.6 The Edit|Paste Command Event Procedure

```
Private Sub mnuEditPaste_Click()

' Paste Clipboard text.

Text1.SelText = Clipboard.GetText()

End Sub
```

You can run the baby editor now, and you'll be able to enter text and then cut and copy it to other locations (either within the editor's own text or into another Windows application). True, there are plenty of things we still have to add, such as file support and font selection, but I think you'll agree that we have a good deal of functionality with very little coding involved!

Enabling and Disabling Menu Items

There's one fairly minor problem with the editor as it stands. If you open the Edit menu, you will see that both the Cut and Copy commands are enabled even when no text is selected in the editor. Clearly, these commands are applicable only when there is text selected. While it's true that code in both the Edit|Cut and Edit|Copy command event procedures prevent anything from happening if either command is issued when there is no text selected, enabling the command only when appropriate adds a professional touch. Likewise, the Paste command should be enabled only when there is text in the Clipboard to be pasted. How is this done?

The enabling/disabling of the menu commands is easy, requiring only that we set the command's **Enabled** property to *True* or *False*. And determining whether to enable or disable these commands is equally easy. We can look at the value of the **SelLength** property to determine if there is text selected in the Text Box, and we can use the Clipboard object's **GetText** method to see if there is any text in the Clipboard. But where will we carry out these actions?

Obviously we don't care whether these menu items are enabled or disabled when the menu is not displayed. And what always happens before the menu is displayed? The top-level menu item (in this case Edit) is clicked on, that's what. Therefore the **Click** event procedure for the top-level menu item is the place to put this code. The code for the **mnuEdit_Click()** event procedure is given in Listing 6.7.

Listing 6.7 The mnuEdit_Click() Event Procedure

```
Private Sub mnuEdit_Click()

' Enable Paste command only if there is text on
' the Clipboard.

Dim x As String

x = Clipboard.GetText()

If x = "" Then
    mnuEditPaste.Enabled = False
Else
    mnuEditPaste.Enabled = True
End If

' Enable Cut and Copy commands only if
' there is text selected.

If Text1.SelLength <> 0 Then
    mnuEditCopy.Enabled = True
    mnuEditCut.Enabled = True
Else
    mnuEditCopy.Enabled = False
    mnuEditCut.Enabled = False
End If

End Sub
```

Run the project after adding this event procedure, and you'll see that the Copy, Cut, and Paste commands are enabled only when appropriate. Remember that the Paste command will be enabled if there's *anything* in the Clipboard, whether or not it was put there by this program.

The Common Dialog Control

Before continuing with the project we need to take a look at the Common Dialog control, one of the custom controls that is provided with Visual Basic. You added a Common Dialog control to the baby editor form earlier. What exactly is this control? I'll tell you right out, it's very cool.

The Common Dialog control provides your Visual Basic applications with several of the frequently needed Windows dialog boxes: Open, Save As, Font, Color, Help, and Printer. You specify which dialog box you want by the method you use to display it. If a particular dialog box offers options—a Color choice in the Font dialog box, for example—you can control their display by setting certain control properties before displaying the dialog box. Similarly, selections the user makes in the dialog box are returned to the calling program in properties.

The Common Dialog control is a terrific time saver. While you could certainly construct these dialog boxes yourself using Visual Basic controls, why bother? Remember Aitken's Rule #1: Don't reinvent the wheel! As you'll see, using the Common Dialog control is quite easy. And, you have the added advantage that your program's dialog boxes will be identical to those used by many other Windows programs that also use the Common Dialogs (which are actually a part of Windows, not Visual Basic).

Preventing Data Loss

One of the aspects of program design that we must set ourselves is to prevent data loss. This means that the user should not be able to inadvertently exit the editor program, load another file, or start a new file if the current file contains changes that have not been saved to disk. The program should warn the user, prompting to save the current file. Of course, the user can choose to exit without saving—the point is to prevent accidents.

We'll implement data loss insurance by maintaining a flag named **TextChanged** that is True if the contents of the editor's Text Box have changed since they were loaded or last saved. The obvious place to set this flag is in the Text Box control's **Change()** event procedure, which is executed whenever the contents of the Text Box change. The flag will then be cleared when the file is saved. Whenever the user tries to load a file, start a new file, or quit when this flag is True, a warning message will be displayed (we'll see how this is done later).

There's a fly in this ointment, however. When a file is read from disk and loaded into the Text Box, the **Change()** event procedure will be triggered and the **TextChanged** flag set even though the text has not actually been changed. This will trigger false warnings if the user loads a file then tries to exit without changing the file. The solution is to keep a second flag named **JustLoaded** that is True only when a file has just been loaded but not modified yet. Then the **Text1_Change()** event procedure is modified to set the **TextChanged** flag only if the **JustLoaded** flag is False. The code for this procedure, shown in Listing 6.8, executes whenever the contents of the Text Box changes.

Listing 6.8   The Text1_Change() Event Procedure

```
Private Sub Text1_Change()

' If the Text bBx's contents change, set global
' variable TextChanged to True unless we have
' just loaded a file.

If JustLoaded = True Then
    Just Loaded = False
Else
    TextChanged = True
End If

End Sub
```

Opening a File

Opening a file means to read the data from a text file on disk and display it in the program's Text Box. There are two main parts to this process:

- Using the Common Dialog control to let the user select the file

- Using Visual Basic's file access commands to open, read, and close the file

We'll deal with these issues in turn.

First, which files should we make available to the user? Rather than simply listing all of the files in the selected folder, it would be better to restrict the file listing to those files the user is likely to be interested in—in other words, text files. We already took care of this task in the **Form_Load()** event procedure (Listing 6.2) when we initialized the Common Dialog control's **Filter** property as follows:

```
Filter = "Text files (*.txt) | *.txt"
Filter = Filter & "|Batch files (*.bat) | *.bat"
Filter = Filter & "|INI files (*.ini) | *.ini"
Filter = Filter & "|All files (*.*) | *.*"
CommonDialog1.Filter = Filter
```

With this code, we have actually loaded four different filters into the dialog box; one that will display only text files (*.txt), and so on. When the dialog box is displayed, the user will be able to select the desired filter in the List Files of Type list. Note that one of the filters will list all files, a good idea since we cannot be sure what extensions will be associated with text files on the user's system.

Once the filter has been specified, displaying the Open dialog box requires only two lines of code:

```
CommonDialog1.FilterIndex = 1
CommonDialog1.ShowOpen
```

The first line specifies the filter that will be in effect initially, and the second displays the Common Dialog with the **ShowOpen** method, which specifies that the control is to act as an Open dialog box. Execution pauses until the user closes the dialog box, at which time the selected filename can be retrieved from the Common Dialog's **FileName** property. If the user canceled the dialog box without selecting a file, this property will contain a blank string.

Once we have the name of the file to open, we must open it, read the data, and close the file. To open a file, you must supply the filename and a number that will be associated with the file. Because a particular number can be associated with only one open file at one time, and because you have no way of knowing which numbers are in use (Windows can have multiple processes going on simultaneously, and processes other than your program can have numbers associated with open files), use the **FreeFile()** function to be sue you select an unused number for your file.The two lines of code required to open a file (whose name is stored in the variable **FileName**) are as follows:

```
FileNum = FreeFile
Open FileName For Input As FileNum
```

Note the syntax of the **Open** statement. It specifies the filename that it is being opened for input (since we are just reading the file, not writing any-thing to it), and the number of the file. Once the file is open, you use this number to refer to it in subsequent program statements.

Once the file is open we will read the text in one line at a time. The Basic statement designed for this task is **Line Input**, which reads a single line of text from the file. A "line" is defined as a sequence of characters that ends with either a carriage return (CR) character by itself or combined with a line feed (LF) character. If we repeatedly execute **Line Input** until we reach the end of the file, we will read in all lines of text in the file. Each line is put in a buffer, which is simply a string variable used for temporary storage of data. This buffer is then added to the end of another buffer, using the concatenation operator **&**. This second buffer then accumulates the entire contents of the file. Finally the second buffer is copied to the Text Box's **Text** property.

There's one minor complication. Windows text files are stored with a single CR character at the end of each line. While the CR character is sufficient for the **Line Input** statement to detect the end of the line, the Text Box requires the CRLF combination to break a line. If we simply copied the text file's contents directly to the Text Box, we would end up with one very long line of text. To get the text to break into separate lines we must add the CRLF combination to the end of each line before putting it in the buffer. We obtain these characters with Visual Basic's built-in **Chr$()** function, which returns the character corresponding to a specific numerical ASCII code. The ASCII codes for CR and LF are 13 and 10, respectively, so we can create a string variable holding the CRLF combination as follows:

```
CRLF = Chr$(13) + Chr$(10)
```

Then we can just concatenate this variable onto the end of the buffer after each line is read in from the file.

We also need some way to tell when we have reached the end of the file. The **EOF()** function serves this purpose. Passed a file number as its argument, this function returns True when the end of the file has been reached, False otherwise. We can set up a loop as follows (expressed in pseudocode):

```
Do While Not end of file
   Get next line
   Add to buffer
Loop
```

The final step is to use the **Close** statement to close the file. Then, copy the text to the Text Box, change the form's caption to display the name of the file, and we're done.

The code for the File|Open command's **Click()** event procedure is shown in Listing 6.9. Note that the first thing this procedure does is call the procedure **SaveChanges()**. This function has the job of ensuring that no editing changes are lost. We will look at its code later. For now, it's enough to know that the function returns True if there are no unsaved changes. If there are unsaved changes, the user is given the option to either save changes or discard them. **SaveChanges()** returns False if the user decides to cancel, in which case execution exits the **mnuFileOpen_Click()** procedure, leaving the original contents of the editor unchanged.

Listing 6.9   The FileIOpen Command Event Procedure

```
Private Sub mnuFileOpen_Click()

Dim Buffer1 As String, Buffer2 As String, CRLF As String
Dim Reply As Integer, Flags As Integer, FileNum As Integer

' Carriage return - line feed combination.
CRLF = Chr$(13) + Chr$(10)

' Verify that changes are saved, if user desires.

Reply = SaveChanges()
If Reply = False Then Exit Sub

' Get a filename from the user.

CommonDialog1.FilterIndex = 1
CommonDialog1.ShowOpen

' If user canceled
If CommonDialog1.FileName = "" Then Exit Sub
FileName = CommonDialog1.FileName

' Open the file and read in text.
FileNum = FreeFile
Open FileName For Input As FileNum

Do While Not EOF(FileNum)
    Line Input #FileNum, Buffer1
    Buffer2 = Buffer2 & Buffer1 & CRLF
Loop

Close FileNum

' Put the text in the Text Box.
Text1.TEXT = Buffer2

' Display the filename in the form's caption.
frmBabyEditor.Caption = "Text Editor - " & FileName

' Set flag.
JustLoaded = True

End Sub
```

Starting a New File

The File|New command erases the existing contents of the editor, if any, leaving the user with a blank, unnamed document. Again, we use the **SaveChanges()** function to guard against loosing unsaved data. The operation of this function is quite straightforward. Listing 6.10 shows the File|New command event procedure.

Listing 6.10 The File|New Command Event Procedure

```
Private Sub mnuFileNew_Click()

Dim Reply As Integer

' Verify that changes are saved, if user desires.
Reply = SaveChanges()
If Reply = False Then Exit Sub

' Erase the editor text and the filename.
Text1.TEXT = ""
FileName = ""

' Change the form caption and clear the TextChanged flag.
frmBabyEditor.Caption = "Text Editor - Untitled"
TextChanged = False

End Sub
```

Saving a File

Saving a file and ensuring against data loss gets a bit more complicated, although proper planning simplifies the task. There are two menu commands related to saving a file, File|Save and File|Save As. The first of these commands saves the file under its current name; if there is no name assigned yet, the user is prompted to enter one. The second command prompts the user for a filename regardless of whether it already has one. Remember, the global variable **FileName** holds the filename, which will be blank if either the user has started the editor and entered some text without saving it, or if the user has selected the File|New command.

We will design the code that does the actual job of saving the file (which we will call **SaveFile()**) to prompt the user for a filename only if the **FileName** variable is blank. Otherwise, the file will be saved under its existing name. We can then write the event procedures for the Save and Save As commands as shown in Listings 6.11 and 6.12. Both event procedures call **SaveFile()**. The difference is that the **mnuFileSaveFileAs_Click()** procedure first sets **FileName** to a blank (saving its original value in the variable **OldName**).

Listing 6.11   The File|Save Command Event Procedure

```
Private Sub mnuFileSave_Click()

Call SaveFile

End Sub
```

Listing 6.12   The File|Save As Command Event Procedure

```
Private Sub mnuFileSaveFileAs_Click()

OldName = FileName
FileName = ""
Call SaveFile

End Sub
```

As you know, the procedure that does the actual saving is **SaveFile()**, which is shown in Listing 6.13. Most of the code deals with the situation when **FileName** is blank, which, as we discussed a moment ago, occurs only when the user is saving a new file or has selected the Save As command. We again call on the Common Dialog control, using the **ShowSave** method to display the Save dialog box. In this dialog box, the user can enter the desired filename, changing to a different folder if desired. The name is returned in the Common Dialog's **FileName** property, which will be blank if the user canceled the dialog box. If the user entered a name, the file is saved under that name, and the form's caption is changed accordingly. If the user canceled, **FileName** is set back to its old value (which was saved in **OldName**), and execution exits the procedure.

The actual task of saving the file is in many respects identical to the procedure for reading a file. We use **FreeFile()** to obtain an unused file number, then use the **Open** command to open the file, this time using the **For Output** qualifier since we will be outputting data to the file. Unlike reading the file, however, we don't have to output it one line at a time. We can save the entire buffer in one step with the **Print** command. Closing the file and clearing the **TextChanged** flag complete the necessary steps.

Listing 6.13   The SaveFile() Procedure

```
Private Sub SaveFile()

' Saves current text under original filename.
' If no filename, prompts for one.

Dim FileNum As Integer, Buffer As String
```

```
Buffer = Text1.TEXT

' FileName will be blank only if we are saving a
' file for the first time or if user selected
' Save As.
If FileName = "" Then
    CommonDialog1.ShowSave
    FileName = CommonDialog1.FileName

    If FileName = "" Then
        FileName = OldName
        Exit Sub
    Else
        frmBabyEditor.Caption = "Text Editor - " + FileName
    End If
End If


FileNum = FreeFile

Open FileName For Output As FileNum
Print #FileNum, Buffer
Close FileNum

TextChanged = False

End Sub
```

Finally we get to the last file-related procedure, **SaveChanges()**. This procedure's job is to ensure that the user cannot lose unsaved changes to a file without being warned first. This procedure is called by both the File|Open and File|New event procedures. This is the first time you have seen a *function*, a type of procedure that returns a value to the calling program. You will also meet Visual Basic's handy **MsgBox()** function. Let's cover these two new topics before getting to the function itself.

Function Procedures

In most respects, a function procedure is identical to the sub procedures you learned about earlier. You create a function the same way you do a sub procedure, with the Insert Procedure command from the Visual Basic menu. Simply select the Function option in the Insert Procedure dialog box, and Visual Basic will create the function skeleton. You pass arguments to a function in the same way as for a sub procedure. If there are no arguments, leave the parentheses empty.

When creating a function, there are two things you need to be concerned with that are not relevant to sub procedures. One is the data type of the value returned to the calling program, called the *return type*. A function can return any of Visual Basic's data types except a fixed length string or an array. You declare the return type by putting an **As** clause after the function definition. For example, for a function named **MyFunc** that returns a type Long, the function skeleton would be:

```
Function MyFunc() As Long

End Function
```

If you omit the **As** clause the return type defaults to **Variant**.

The second concern is specifying the value to be returned. This is done by assigning a value to the function name in code inside the function. For example, this code segment

```
Function MyFunc() As Long

...
MyFunc = x / y

End Function
```

causes the function to return the result of dividing x by y. Note that assigning a return value does not terminate the function. Function execution continues until it reaches the terminating **End Function** statement or until it encounters an **Exit Function** statement in the body of the function. If you exit a function without assigning a return value, the function will return 0 or a blank string depending on its type.

The MsgBox() Function

The **MsgBox()** function is one of Visual Basic's most useful tools. You use it to display brief messages to the user and get a response. In its simplest form, **MsgBox()** displays your message in a small dialog box containing an OK button. The title of the dialog box is the same as the project name. For example, the statement

```
MsgBox("This is the message")
```

displays the box shown in Figure 6.5. Program execution pauses while the box is displayed, and continues once the user has selected OK.

Figure 6.5 *A basic message box.*

The **MsgBox()** function is a lot more flexible than this, however. You can specify your own title, and can also specify that different combinations of buttons be displayed (Yes and No buttons, for example). When more than one button is displayed, the return value of the **MsgBox()** function indicates which button the user selected. You can also have a graphical icon, such as a question mark, displayed in the message box as well. Here is the full syntax of the **MsgBox()** function:

```
return = MsgBox(message, flags, title)
```

Let's take a brief tour of the arguments:

message The string literal or variable specifying the message to be displayed.

title The string literal or variable specifying the message box title.

flags An integer value that controls the display of buttons and icons.

For the **flags** argument, you can use the predefined constants listed in Table 6.2. The last two constants determine which button is the default; that is, which one will be selected if the user simply presses Enter. The normal default is the first button. To combine constants—to specify buttons and an icon, for example—use the Or operator. The following call would display the Abort, Retry, and Ignore buttons, an exclamation icon, and make the Retry button the default:

```
x = MsgBox("Message Here", vbAbortRetryIgnore Or vbExclamation Or
        vbDefaultButton2, "Title Here")
```

The possible return values are also defined by constants, which are listed in Table 6.3.

Creating the Function

Go ahead now and create the **SaveChanges()** function, assigning it a return type of Boolean. The function code is shown in Listing 6.14. Note that the

Table 6.2 *Predefined Constants for the flags Argument*

Constant	Value	Description
vbOKCancel	1	Display OK and Cancel buttons
vbAbortRetryIgnore	2	Display Abort, Retry, and Ignore buttons
vbYesNoCancel	3	Display Yes, No, and Cancel buttons
vbYesNo	4	Display Yes and No buttons
vbRetryCancel	5	Display Retry and Cancel buttons
vbCritical	16	Display Critical Message icon
vbQuestion	32	Display Warning Query icon
vbExclamation	48	Display Warning Message icon
vbInformation	64	Display Information Message icon
vbDefaultButton2	256	Second button is default
vbDefaultButton3	512	Third button is default

Table 6.3 *Predefined Constants for Return Values of the flags Argument*

Constant	Value	Button chosen
vbOK	1	OK
vbCancel	2	Cancel
vbAbort	3	Abort
vbRetry	4	Retry
vbIgnore	5	Ignore
vbYes	6	Yes
vbNo	7	No

code does not explicitly test for a return from the message box of vbNo. If the user selects No (the only possibility besides Yes and Cancel), execution falls through the **If** block and the function terminates with a return value of True.

Listing 6.14   The SaveChanges() Function

```
Private Function SaveChanges() As Boolean

' Determines if the text being edited has changed since the
' last File|Save command. If so, the function offers the user the option of
  saving the file.
' Function returns True if there have been no changes or if
' the user saves the changes; returns False if the user
' selects Cancel.
```

```
Dim Title As String, Msg As String
Dim Reply As Integer, Flags As Integer

If TextChanged = True Then
    Title = "Text has changed"
    Msg = "Save changes to text?"
    Flags = MB_YESNOCANCEL + MB_ICONQUESTION
    Reply = MsgBox(Msg, Flags, Title)

    If Reply = vbYES Then
        Call SaveFile
    ElseIf Reply = vbCANCEL Then
        SaveChanges = False
        Exit Function
    End If
End If

SaveChanges = True

End Function
```

Selecting Fonts

Selecting fonts is the third place where our baby editor program will make use of the Common Dialog control. When used as a Font dialog box, the Common Dialog control has a **Flags** property that you set to determine what is displayed in the dialog box. You must specify one of the following flags:

cdlCFPrinterFonts   Displays only printer fonts

cdlCFScreenFonts   Displays only screen fonts

cdlCFBOTH   Displays both screen and printer fonts

You can combine one of these flags with **cdlCFEffects**, which specifies that the Font dialog box display underline, strikethrough, and color choices as well.

Before displaying the Font dialog box, it is good practice to load it with the current font settings; that is, the settings currently in effect in the Text Box control. You can accomplish this task easily by copying the relevant properties from one control to the other. Then, use the **ShowFont** method to display the font version of the Common Dialog control. When the user closes the dialog box, we check the **FontName** property of the Common Dialog. If this is a blank string, it means that the user canceled the dialog box, so we exit the procedure without making any changes to the Text Box's font. Otherwise, we reverse the property copying operation, making the Text Box's font-related properties equal to the corresponding settings in the Font dialog box.

The code for the Edit | Font command's **Click()** event procedure is shown in Listing 6.15. The font selected applies immediately to all of the text in the editor. The font setting affects the display only, since font information is not saved in the file along with the text.

Listing 6.15   The Edit|Font Command Event Procedure

```
Private Sub mnuEditFont_Click()

' Set flags.
CommonDialog1.Flags = cdlCFBoth Or cdlCFEffects

' Set initial values for the dialog box.
CommonDialog1.FontName = Text1.FontName
CommonDialog1.FontSize = Text1.FontSize
CommonDialog1.FontBold = Text1.FontBold
CommonDialog1.FontItalic = Text1.FontItalic
CommonDialog1.FontUnderline = Text1.FontUnderline
CommonDialog1.FontStrikethru = Text1.FontStrikethru
CommonDialog1.Color = Text1.ForeColor

' Display Choose Font dialog box.
CommonDialog1.ShowFont

' If canceled, exit.
If CommonDialog1.FontName = "" Then Exit Sub

' Change the text font according to options selected.
Text1.FontName = CommonDialog1.FontName
Text1.FontSize = CommonDialog1.FontSize
Text1.FontBold = CommonDialog1.FontBold
Text1.FontItalic = CommonDialog1.FontItalic
Text1.FontUnderline = CommonDialog1.FontUnderline
Text1.FontStrikethru = CommonDialog1.FontStrikethru
Text1.ForeColor = CommonDialog1.Color

End Sub
```

Exiting the Program

To exit the program all that is required is the **End** statement, and, of course, we should place it in the event procedure for the File | Exit command. As before, however, we need to be sure that unsaved data is not lost, so we need to call the **SaveChanges()** function. After that, we either exit the sub procedure or end the program, depending on the return value of the function. The code for **mnuFileExit_Click()** is shown in Listing 6.16.

Listing 6.16 The File|Exit Command Event Procedure

```
Private Sub mnuFileExit_Click()

' Verify that changes are saved, if user desires.

Dim Reply As Integer

Reply = SaveChanges()
If Reply = False Then Exit Sub

End

End Sub
```

CREATING AN EXE FILE

Until now you have been running your Visual Basic programs from inside the Visual Basic development environment. This is great while you're working on the program because the environment's debugging capabilities make it easy to track down problems with the program. Once the program is in final form, however, you will want to make an *executable* file. This is a standalone program that runs on its own, without any help from the Visual Basic environment. You need an executable file to distribute your program, of course.

Creating an executable file is easy. Select Make EXE File from the File menu to display the dialog box shown in Figure 6.6. Change to a different folder, if desired, then enter the name for the EXE file in the File name box and click on OK. Visual Basic will crank away for a while, its speed dependent on the size of the project and the speed of your computer. When it's done there will be an EXE file on your disk that can be used like any other Windows program. You can create a shortcut for it, put it on the Start menu, and so on. It's a real Windows program!

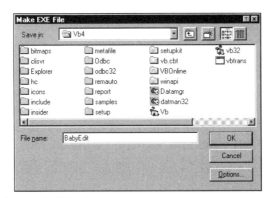

Figure 6.6 *The Make EXE File dialog box.*

GRAPHICS

Visual Basic
is a graphics
programmer's
paradise. Many
difficult graphics
tasks are made
easy with Visual
Basic's controls
and methods.

When it comes to graphics, only a few objects are involved: the Picture Box, Image, Shape, and Line controls, and the Printer and Form objects. This may seem like a small cast of characters, but you'll soon see that they provide a rich and powerful set of graphics capabilities.

TWIDDLING YOUR TWIPS—THE VISUAL BASIC COORDINATE SYSTEM

Before we get to the meat and potatoes of the chapter, you need to understand Visual Basic's coordinate system. *Coordinates* are used to define the position of any object displayed on the screen. For some objects, the coordinate system is also used to define the object's size (its height and width). An object's position is always expressed as the distance of its top-left corner from the top-left corner of its container object. Hey, wait a minute! Container? What's a container? A form's container is always the Screen object (which

I'll get to in a moment). A control's container is always the form it is on *unless* the control is placed in a Picture Box or Frame, in which case the Picture Box or Frame is the container. The only other possible container is the Printer object, which is used for (you guessed it!) printing. We'll deal with the Printer object later in the chapter.

Visual Basic's coordinate system works like the Cartesian coordinate graphing system you learned school. Any given point is represented by two numbers. One of these numbers, traditionally called X, indicates the point's horizontal position. While the other number, Y, indicates the point's vertical position. Of course, a coordinate system must have a zero point, or *origin*, the point where both X and Y are 0. It also must have a *scale*, which relates the coordinate units to real measurement units. Does an X value of 2 mean 2 inches or 2 yards?

In all Visual Basic coordinate systems, the default origin is located at the top-left corner of the container. Positive X values move to the right, and positive Y values move down. Negative coordinates are possible, representing positions above or to the left of the container. You'll note that I said "default" origin, implying that the origin can be positioned elsewhere. This is indeed true, at least for some container objects, but let's not worry about that for now.

There are several different scales that you can use in Visual Basic coordinates. While many Visual Basic programs are written using only the default scale, you need to know the options that are available, particularly if you will be doing a lot of graphics programming. The available scale settings are shown in Table 7.1.

Table 7.1 *Visual Basic Scale Settings*

ScaleMode Value	Scale Units
0	Custom
1	Twip (default); there are 1440 twips per logical inch and 567 twips per logical centimeter
2	Point; there are 72 points per logical inch
3	Pixel; this is the smallest unit of monitor or printer resolution
4	Character; one character unit equals120 twips horizontally and 240 twips vertically
5	Inch
6	Millimeter
7	Centimeter

I bet you're probably wondering what *logical* means. When a unit is described as logical, it will measure that unit when printed. For example, a logical inch will measure one inch when printed. You set a container object's scale by using the **ScaleMode** property; however, the only objects that have a **ScaleMode** property are Form, Picture Box, and Printer. The other objects that can be containers, the Screen object and the Frame control, always use twips for measurement.

Before we look at the various object properties that are related to the coordinate system, let's look at the Big Daddy of all containers, the Screen object.

The Screen Object

The Screen object is Visual Basic's logical representation of the entire display screen. Screen coordinates are always measured in twips, and the top-left corner is always located at (0,0). The physical size of the screen varies from system to system, and you will find it helpful to know the screen size to make the best use of available screen real estate. You wouldn't want your forms to extend off the edge of the screen. You can query two of the Screen object's properties to obtain the screen size:

```
ScreenWidthInTwips = Screen.Width
ScreenHeightInTwips = Screen.Height
```

Although you can't change these properties, they will help you to determine where you want to position your form.

The Screen object has some other properties that you need to know about.

The **TwipsPerPixelX** and **TwipsPerPixelY** properties return the number of twips per screen pixel. A *pixel* is the smallest dot of light that can be displayed on the screen, and the physical resolution of a particular display system is expressed in terms of horizontal and vertical pixels. When a program is running, the number of twips per pixel will depend on the system's hardware configuration, as well as the settings of the Windows display driver. You can use these properties to match your program's graphics to the screen characteristics. For example, to draw the thinnest possible horizontal line you would set the line thickness equal to **Screen.TwipsPerPixelY** twips.

The **MousePointer** property specifies the appearance of the mouse pointer while it is over a Visual Basic screen element. With the default setting of 0, the pointer is controlled by the **MousePointer** property of the individual objects in the program (form, control, etc.)—that is, the object the mouse is over at the moment. Other possible settings for the Screen object's **MousePointer** property are given in Table 7.2.

A **MousePointer** property setting of 99 lets you define your own cursor using the **MouseIcon** property. In the statement

```
Screen.MouseIcon = picture
```

picture specifies the name and path of the icon or cursor file that should be used as the mouse cursor while the **MousePointer** property is set to 99.

The **ActiveForm** property returns the form that is currently active. You will find this property very useful in a multiple-form program when you want to write one section of code that will always reference the active form. For example, the line

```
Screen.ActiveForm.MousePointer = 4
```

Table 7.2 *MousePointer Property Settings*

Setting	Description
0	Shape determined by the object (default)
1	Arrow
2	Cross (cross-hair pointer)
3	I-Beam
4	Icon (small square within a square)
5	Size (four-pointed arrow pointing North, South, East, and West)
6	Size NE SW (double arrow pointing Northeast and Southwest)
7	Size N S (double arrow pointing North and South)
8	Size NW SE (double arrow pointing Northwest and Southeast)
9	Size W E (double arrow pointing West and East)
10	Up arrow
11	Hourglass (wait)
12	No Drop
13	Arrow and hourglass
14	Arrow and question mark
15	Size all (customizable under Microsoft Windows NT 3.51)
99	Custom icon specified by the MouseIcon property

will change the **MousePointer** property of whatever form happens to be active at the time the code is executed.

There are a few other Screen properties, but we will leave those until we need them.

Position and Size Properties

Any Visual Basic object displayed on the screen has properties that determine its position and its size. The **Top** and **Left** properties specify the position of the object's top-left corner within its container, and the **Height** and **Width** properties specify its size. All four of these properties use the coordinate units specified by the container's **ScaleMode** property. If you change a container's **ScaleMode** property, either during program design or program execution, the properties of any objects in the container automatically change to the new units.

Two other properties, **ScaleHeight** and **ScaleWidth**, apply only to the Form, Picture Box, and Printer objects. These properties indicate the size of the object's interior, which is the area available for graphics operations. These specifications are different from the specifications provided by **Height** and **Width** properties, which indicate the object's overall size, including borders, title bar, and other object components. The most common use for the **ScaleHeight** and **ScaleWidth** properties is at runtime, when the program reads them to determine the container object's interior size and then uses the values to position objects within the container. You will see how to accomplish this in our first demonstration program, presented later in this chapter.

Take a moment to look at Figure 7.1, which shows the relationships between objects and their containers. Note that there are three levels of "containerness:" a Command Button has been placed in a Frame; the Frame is on a Form; and the Form is on the Screen.

All Visual Basic controls have a **Container** property. This property returns the identity of the control's container object. You can also set this property, which would have the effect of moving a control from one container to another. To be honest, I have never seen this technique used in a program, although I suppose there might be a use for it somewhere!

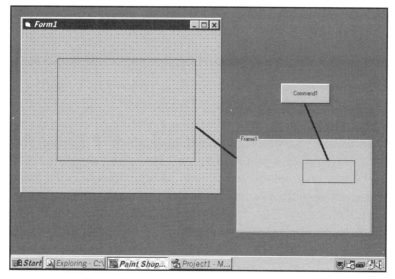

Figure 7.1   *Every Visual Basic object is contained within another object, with the Screen being the top-level container.*

Using Controls as Containers

Two controls, the Picture Box and the Frame, can serve as containers for other controls. Why would you want to use this feature? For Option Buttons, it's a necessity. Two or more Option Buttons placed in a Frame are treated as a group, and only one of the options can be selected at a time. For other control types, however, it is mostly a matter of design convenience. Controls that are drawn on a Frame or Picture Box move as their container is moved, so once you create a group of related controls on a Frame or Picture Box you can move them together.

To place controls on a Frame or Picture Box, draw the container control on the form first, then draw the controls on the container. If you use another method, such as dragging an existing control onto a Frame, it will *look* like it is on the Frame, but it will not move with the Frame or be positioned with respect to the Frame's origin.

Now let's take a moment to look at a demonstration program that shows some techniques you can use to improve your program's screen display. We want the program to do two things:

- Display the form at a specified size and position when the program starts

- Maintain the relative sizes and positions of the form's controls when the form is resized by the user

At startup, this program's form always displays in the center of the screen, with a size equal to half the screen size. For this we use the form's **Load** event procedure. The **Load** event occurs just before a form is displayed. For a single-form program, this is when the program starts. The **Load** event procedure is the ideal place to perform various initialization steps, such as setting a form's size and position. Here's what we'll do:

- To set the form size to half the screen size, we will set the Form **Width** and **Height** properties equal to half of the Screen object's **Width** and **Height** properties.

- To center the form left-to-right we subtract the Form object's **Width** from the Screen **Width**, divide the result by 2, and place the result in the Form's **Left** property.

- To center the form top-to-bottom we subtract the Form **Height** from the Screen **Height**, divide the result by 2, and place the result in the Form's **Top** property.

Begin this project by placing a Picture Box and a Command Button on the form. Don't worry about their exact position or size; we'll take care of these specificiations in code. Leave all the control properties at their default values except for the Command Button's **Caption** property, which should be set to *E&xit.* Place the single statement **End** in the Command Button's **Click** procedure. Save the project and the form (I used the name CENTER for both the form and the project). Next, display the **Form_Load()** event procedure and add the code shown in Listing 7.1.

Listing 7.1   The Form_Load() Event Procedure

```
Private Sub Form_Load()

' Make the form width and height equal to
' half the screen dimensions.
Form1.Width = Screen.Width / 2
Form1.Height = Screen.Height / 2

' Center the form on the screen.
Form1.Left = (Screen.Width - Form1.Width) / 2
Form1.TOP = (Screen.Height - Form1.Height) / 2

End Sub
```

You can run the program now, and you'll see that when you start the program the form displays centered on the screen, with width and height equal to half the screen dimensions. The controls, however, remain in the positions they were given during program design. That's our next task.

To set the size and positions of the controls, we'll use an approach like the one used used for the form—specify each control's size and position in terms of its container's size. Where should we place this code? We want the controls to be positioned whenever the form size changes, and also when the form is first displayed. The ideal place for this code, then, is the **Resize()** event procedure, which is called when the form first displays and any time its size is changed (either by the user or in code). I won't bother explaining the code in this procedure, which is shown in Listing 7.2; I'm sure you'll be able to understand how it works from the comments.

Listing 7.2 The Resize() Event Procedure

```
Private Sub Form_Resize()

' Make the Picture Box size equal to 90% of the form
' width and 70% of its height.
Picture1.Width = Form1.ScaleWidth * 0.9
Picture1.Height = Form1.ScaleHeight * 0.7

' Center the Picture Box left-to-right.
Picture1.Left = (Form1.ScaleWidth - Picture1.Width) / 2

' Make the distance between the top of the Picture Box and
' the form the same as the distance at the sides.
Picture1.TOP = Picture1.Left

' Make the Command Button width 20% of the form width.
Command1.Width = Form1.ScaleWidth * 0.2

' Make the Command Button height one third of the distance between the
' bottom of the Picture Box and the edge of the form.
Command1.Height = (Form1.ScaleHeight - Picture1.ScaleHeight) / 3

' Center the Command Button left-to-right.
Command1.Left = (Form1.ScaleWidth - Command1.Width) / 2

' Center the Command Button vertically in the space between the
' Picture Box and the edge of the form.
Command1.TOP = Form1.ScaleHeight - 0.66 * (Form1.ScaleHeight - (Picture1.TOP +
Picture1.Height))

End Sub
```

Once the **Form_Resize()** procedure is complete, run the program again. You'll see that the Picture Box and Command Button are precisely positioned in the form, as shown in Figure 7.2. If you change the window size, by dragging a border, you'll see that the controls maintain their relative sizes and positions.

Using Fixed-Sized Controls

Not all windows need to be resizable. In fact, for dialog boxes that contain an array of Text Boxes, Option Buttons, and other controls, it is best to leave them at a fixed size. This is accomplished by setting the Form's **BorderStyle** property to *1 - Fixed Single* or *3 - Fixed Dialog*. Then you can design the form, placing the various controls precisely to get the result you want, without having to worry that the user will mess things up by resizing the dialog box! You could use the techniques presented here to adapt each control's size and position when the dialog box is resized, but in my experience it's a lot more work than it's worth.

Who's on First?

Before continuing with our discussion of Visual Basic's coordinate system, I think it's wise to take a brief aside to explain the various events that occur when a form is being loaded and displayed. This is an area that confuses many programmers, but if we get it straight now we won't have to worry about it later.

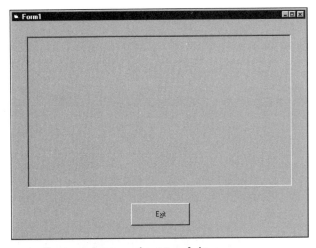

Figure 7.2 *Automatically setting the size and position of objects.*

Each form in a Visual Basic project exists in its own disk file. Showing a form on-screen requires two steps: loading the form from disk into memory, and displaying the form. In a single-form project, the form is loaded and displayed when the program starts. For a multiple-form project, the form that has been designated the *startup* form is loaded and displayed when the program starts. Other forms are loaded and displayed under program control.

You can load a form without displaying it with the **Load** statement:

```
Load form
```

A form will also be loaded if the program makes reference to any of its properties. The **Show** method, shown here

```
form.Show
```

is used to display a loaded form or load the specified form, if it is not already loaded. You will find there is rarely a need to use the **Load** statement. However, I have found two instances in which **Load** is useful:

- If you want the form's **Load()** event procedure to execute without displaying the form, use the **Load** statement.

- If the form is complex (has many controls and/or complex processing in its **Load()** event procedure), use the **Load** statement to load the form before you need to display it. Complex forms display more quickly if they've been loaded ahead of time.

Unload a form you no longer need to free memory or to reset all of its properties to their original values. To unload a form, use the **Unload** statement:

```
Unload form
```

If you want to remove a form from the screen without unloading it, use the **Hide** method:

```
form.Hide
```

If you execute the **Hide** method on a form that isn't loaded, the form is loaded but not displayed.

Figure 7.3 summarizes the relationships between the various methods, statements, and user actions that act on forms and the events that are triggered as a result. You'll see how the **Paint** event is used later in this chapter.

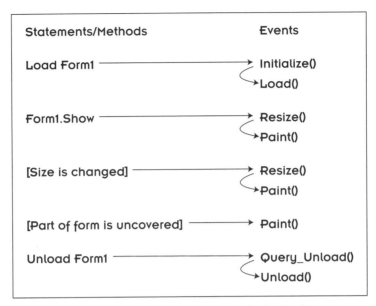

Figure 7.3 *Events associated with loading, showing, sizing, and unloading forms.*

Understanding the Paint Event and the AutoRedraw Property

The **Paint** event is related to the **AutoRedraw** property. Both Form and Picture Box objects have an **AutoRedraw** property. If **AutoRedraw** is set to *Off* (the default), graphics and text are written only to the screen and the **Paint** event occurs, as indicated in Figure 7.3. The graphics and text *are not persistent—* they must be redrawn (using the **Paint()** event procedure) if the object is uncovered or restored. If **AutoRedraw** is set to *On*, the graphics and text are saved in memory as well as being written to the screen, and the display *is persistent—*automatically refreshed from this memory image if the object is restored or uncovered. In this case, the **Paint** event does not occur. **AutoRedraw** applies only to graphics and text created with the **Line**, **Circle**, **Pset**, and **Text** methods—bitmaps and metafiles are persistent regardless of the **AutoRedraw** setting.

Setting **AutoRedraw** to *On* slows down screen display of graphics and consumes extra memory. Both of these effects are particularly noticeable with large objects.

Defining Custom Coordinates

If Visual Basic's assortment of coordinate units don't suit you, then you can define your own. You can also move the origin to another location. This technique can be very useful for certain applications. For example, a program that draws maps could set the graphical coordinate units to a meaningful value, such as miles. You can also "flip" the Y axis so that positive values move upward, which makes it easier to use the Cartesian coordinates that are commonly used in graphs. A custom coordinate system affects not only graphics operations but also the placement of controls.

To define a custom coordinate system, which is possible only for Form, Picture Box, and Printer objects, use the **Scale** method. The syntax is

```
object.Scale (left, top)-(right, bottom)
```

where (left, top) are the new coordinates of the left and top of the object, and (right, bottom) are the new coordinates for the right and bottom of the object. For example

```
Form1.Scale (0, 0)-(100, 200)
```

sets a coordinate system where the top-left corner of the object has coordinates (0, 0) and the lower-right corner has coordinates (100, 200). This example does not move the origin, but only changes the measurement unit to be 1/100 of the object dimension. In contrast, the statement

```
Form1.Scale (0, 200)-(100, 0)
```

sets the same measurement unit and also moves the origin to the lower-left corner of the object and inverts the Y axis so that positive values move upward. Using **Scale** to set custom coordinates also changes the **ScaleMode** property to 0 which, as you saw earlier in Table 7.1, indicates that a custom coordinate system is in effect.

Applying the **Scale** method changes the object's **ScaleWidth**, **ScaleHeight**, **ScaleLeft**, and **ScaleTop** properties to reflect the new coordinates. For instance, after executing the previous **Scale** method the object's **ScaleWidth** property would be 100 and its **ScaleHeight** property would be 200. You can set these properties individually if you want to modify only part of the object's coordinate system. Thus, the statement

```
object.ScaleWidth = 100
```

results in the object's horizontal measurement unit being set to 1/100 of its width, while the location of the origin and the vertical measurement unit would remain unchanged. Executing the **Scale** method with no arguments, like this:

```
object.Scale
```

will reset the coordinate system to the default (twips with the 0, 0 point at the top left).

You must be aware that the **Scale** method defines its units based on the object's size at the time the method is executed. Subsequent changes to the object's size are not automatically taken into account. We'll see how this works in the custom coordinate demonstration program shown in Listing 7.3.

This program uses the **Circle** method in a **For...Next** loop to draw a series of circles on a form. You'll learn the details of the **Circle** method later in the chapter—you needn't worry about it for now. The program consists of a form without controls. Leave all of the form's properties at their default values, and save your work calling both the form and the project SCALE. Next, place the code shown in Listing 7.3 in the form's **Paint()** event procedure.

Listing 7.3   The Paint() Event Procedure

```
Private Sub Form_Paint()

Dim i As Integer

Cls

For i = 1 To 5
    Circle (150 * i, 100 * i), 50 * i
Next i

End Sub
```

The **Circle** method draws a circle with its center at the specified coordinates (the values in the parentheses) and with the specified radius. When you execute the program, it will look more or less like Figure 7.4. I say "more or less" because the appearance may vary slightly if you made your form a different size than I did, or if your display hardware is different from mine.

After running the program, add the following statement to the form's **Load()** event procedure:

```
Scale (0, 1000)-(1000, 0)
```

Run the program again and you'll see a quite different display, as shown in Figure 7.5.

Figure 7.4 *The circles drawn using the default coordinate system.*

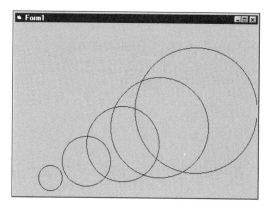

Figure 7.5 *The circle display after changing the coordinate system.*

 **Automatic Object References**

Why is it that we can sometimes refer to properties and methods without specifying an object? For example, in this code we write simply **Scale (0, 1000)-(1000, 0)** rather than **Form1.Scale (0, 1000)-(1000, 0)**. This is because in an event procedure, a reference to a property or method automatically refers to the object that received the event unless another object is specified.

Not only are the circles larger (because the coordinate unit we specified is much larger than a twip), but the circles climb from the bottom of the form rather than descending from the top (because we inverted the Y axis). If you change the size of the form while the program is running, you'll see that the circles stay the same size—they do not grow or shrink along with the form.

Now let's try one more thing. Copy the **Scale (0, 1000)-(1000, 0)** statement and paste it in the **Paint()** event procedure, just after the **Cls** statement. Now when you run the program and increase the size of the form by dragging its border, the circles are redrawn to keep the same size relative to the form. By resetting the form's coordinate system each time it is painted, we ensure that the coordinate system units are always defined relative to the form's current size, and do not remain defined according to its original size.

Try decreasing the form size, however—you'll notice the circles are not re-drawn. Why is this? The **Paint** event is triggered when an object's size is in-creased or when it is uncovered; it is *not* triggered when an object's size decreases.

THE PICTURE BOX CONTROL

Now it's time to look at Visual Basic's most versatile graphics control: the Picture Box. The capabilities of this control fall into three areas:

- Displaying pictures that were created elsewhere and exist in disk files, such as scanned photographs or drawings created with Corel Draw

- Displaying graphics and that were created with program statements, such as the **Circle** method

- Serving as a container for grouping other controls

The third category doesn't relate to graphics, so we won't discuss it further. The other two, while easy to describe, provide a wealth of graphical capabili-ties that are limited only by your imagination. Note that most of the graph-ics actions that apply to the Picture Box control can also be used with the Form object, which we'll cover later in the chapter. Let's see how the Picture Box works.

eXPLORER TIP

Image Controls vs. Picture Box Controls

For displaying existing images, you may want to use an Image control in preference to a Picture Box. Image con-trols have only a subset of the capabilities of Picture Box controls, and as a result they are faster and consume fewer system resources.

Loading a Picture During Program Design

You can load a picture into a Picture Box during program design, which, in effect, embeds the picture in to the project's exectuable file. (Pictures are often stored as .FRX files.) This method is appropriate if a Picture Box will always display the same picture, or if you don't want the separate picture file to be distributed with the program. However, loading a picture during program design does not prevent you from loading another image into the Picture Box while the program is running. You can load a bitmap (*.BMP, *.DIB), a Windows metafile (*.WMF), or an icon (*.ICO) file into a Picture Box. To do so, select the Picture Box's **Picture** property. Visual Basic displays an Open dialog box, which allows you to select the picture file. The picture you select is displayed in the control during design as well as when the program runs.

A picture is loaded into a Picture Box control with the top-left corner of the picture positioned in the top-left corner of the Picture Box. If the image is smaller than the Picture Box, the area outside the image displays the color specified by the control's **BackColor** property. If the image is bigger than the control, the portion outside the Picture Box is clipped if the **AutoSize** property is set to *False* (the default). You can set the Picture Box's **AutoSize** property to *True*, which causes the Picture Box to automatically grow or shrink to fit the image exactly.

You can also load a picture into a Picture Box from the Windows Clipboard. Open the image in the application in which you created or edited it, then copy the image to the Clipboard using the Edit|Copy command. Switch back to Visual Basic, select the Picture Box control, and select Edit|Paste.

Loading a Picture During Program Execution

There are several methods you can use to display a picture in a Picture Box at runtime. One method is to set the control's **Picture** property. You cannot do it directly, as you might expect:

```
Pbox.Picture = filename    ' Does not work!
```

Rather, you must use the **LoadPicture()** function

```
Pbox.Picture = LoadPicture(filename)
```

in which *filename* is the name of a bitmap, Windows metafile, or icon picture file, including the full path, if necessary. The position of the picture, and the effect of the control's **AutoSize** property, are the same as when you load a picture at design time. You can erase a Picture Box by using **LoadPicture** with no argument:

```
Pbox.Picture = LoadPicture()
```

You can also copy a picture from one Picture Box to another by accessing the source control's **Picture** property:

```
Pbox1.Picture = Pbox2.Picture
```

Loading an image into a Picture Box with these methods is fine for most situations, but it does have a few limitations:

- The image is always placed in the upper-left corner of the Picture Box.

- The image size cannot be changed. That is, the image is always displayed with its original size.

- Only one image at a time can be displayed in a given control.

Fear not, you do have alternatives. And the **PaintPicture** method, which we'll discuss next, is one of them.

The PaintPicture Method

The **PaintPicture** method allows you to circumvent the limitations of the previous methods used to load a picture during program execution. Think of **PaintPicture** as a sophisticated cut-and-paste tool. You must start with a source picture, which can be an image in either a Picture Box control or on a form. Then, you can take all or part of that picture—any rectangular region, in fact—and place it anywhere you want on another Picture Box or form or on the source Picture Box or form, if desired. You have numerous options as to how the copied image is combined with any image that already exists in the destination. In addition, you can stretch or shrink the "copied" picture.

Yes, I know that this sounds complicated! Let's take a look at the syntax of the **PaintPicture** method, then I'll explain the arguments (I'll use this format throughout the remainder of the book):

```
object.PaintPicture source, x1, y1, w1, h1, x2, y2, w2, h2, opcode
```

object The name of the Picture Box, Form, or Printer object where the picture is to be placed. This argument is optional. If omitted, the Form with the focus is assumed.

source The source of the graphic. Must be the **Picture** property of a Form or Picture Box object.

x1, y1 Single-precision values indicating the destination coordinates—in other words, the location on the destination object where the top-left corner of the image is to be drawn. The **ScaleMode** property of the object determines the unit of measure used.

w1, h1 Single-precision values indicating the destination width and height of the picture, using units specified by the **ScaleMode** property of the destination object. If the destination width and/or height is larger or smaller than the source width (*w2*) or height (*h2*), the picture is stretched or compressed to fit. These arguments are optional; if omitted, the source width (*w1*) and height (*h1*) are used and there is no stretching or compression.

x2, y2 Single-precision values indicating the source coordinates of the region in the source object that is to be copied (in units specified by the source object's **ScaleMode** property). These arguments are optional; if omitted, 0 is assumed (indicating the top-left corner of the source image).

w2, h2 Single-precision values indicating the width and height of the region within the source that is to be copied (in units specified by the source object's **ScaleMode** property). These arguments are optional; if omitted, the entire source width and height are used.

opcode A type **Long** value that defines the bit-wise operation that is performed between the pixels of the source picture and the pixels of any existing image on the destination (explained shortly). This argument, which is optional, is useful only with bitmaps; if omitted, the source is copied onto the destination, replacing anything that is there.

Think of it as if the source picture were printed on a rubber sheet. You can cut out any rectangular part of the picture you want, stretch it vertically and/or horizontally, and stick it down anywhere you want on the destination picture. Sound useful? You bet it is! The operation of **PaintPicture** is illustrated in Figure 7.6.

object.PaintPicture source, x1, y1, w1, h1, x2, y2, w2, h2, opcode

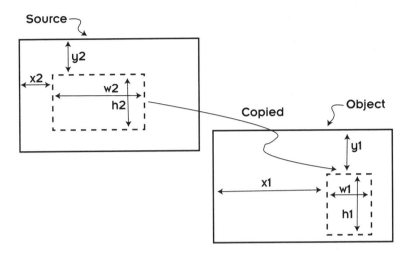

Figure 7.6 *The PaintPicture method's arguments.*

The **opcode** argument can be a bit confusing—and with good reason! How many ways can you copy a picture from one location to another? Well, you would be surprised—dozens, at least! Here's how it works. In the destination object, where the copied picture is going to be placed, there already exists an image. There may be a bitmap picture displayed there already, but even if the destination is blank there's something there, even if it's just white pixels. Over the extent of the copied region, therefore, for each pixel in the copied image there is another pixel at the same location in the destination. How will these pixels be combined? This is what the **opcode** argument controls.

The simplest, and perhaps most common operation, is to have each new pixel replace the original pixel. The **opcode** argument for this is the predefined constant **vbSrcCopy**. Two other useful **opcode** arguments are **vbBlackness** and **vbWhiteness**, which turn the destination rectangle all black or all white. This really isn't a copy of the source picture at all, of course; you still have to specify a source in the **PaintPicture** statement. Other **opcode** arguments perform a variety of logical combinations of the source picture with the destination picture. These can be used to create certain types of visual effects, but I won't go into them here. You can explore the topic further in the Visual Basic Help system.

Hiding the Picture Box

Don't forget that you can set a Picture Box's **Visible** property to *False* so it does not display on screen. It is still a valid source for the **PaintPicture** method, and you can still load pictures into it by setting its **Picture** property or by using the **LoadPicture** statement.

The best way to get a feel for how **PaintPicture** works is to see it in action. The example program PAINTPIC demonstrates three common uses for this statement: enlarging a picture, shrinking a picture, and painting areas with black or white. To start the project, place two Picture Box controls on a form. For the first one, Picture1, set its **AutoSize** property to *True*, then load the picture HOUSROCK.BMP (provided on the companion CD-ROM) into its **Picture** property. All of the properties for Picture2 should be left at their default values. Change the form's **Caption** property to *"Picture magnifier"*.

The program requires three constants, which are placed in the General Declarations section of the form's code. Two of the constants specify the vertical and horizontal magnification, expressed as the portion of the original picture that will be blown up. I used 0.3 for both the vertical and horizontal values; you can experiment with other values if you like. The third constant is the opcode **vbWhiteness**, which unfortunately, is not predefined by Visual Basic and we must do it ourselves. The declarations code is shown here:

```
Option Explicit
Const vbWhiteness = &HFF0062
Const WIDE = 0.3
Const HIGH = 0.3
```

We adjust the form and control sizes in the **Form_Load()** event procedure. Picture1 will already be the size of the loaded picture, since we set its **AutoSize** property to *True*. The following code makes the form size a bit higher, and a bit more than twice as wide, as this Picture Box. Then it makes Picture2 the same size as Picture1, and positions them both on the form.

```
Form1.Width = 2.1 * Picture1.Width
Form1.Height = 1.1 * Picture1.Height

Picture1.Left = 0
Picture1.Top = 0

Picture2.Width = Picture1.Width
Picture2.Height = Picture1.Height
```

```
Picture2.Top = 0
Picture2.Left = Form1.ScaleWidth - Picture2.Width
```

The real action will be triggered by the user clicking on the source picture. A left-button click will trigger the display, in the second Picture Box, of a magnified portion of the picture centered on the location where the mouse was clicked. A right-button click will display nine small copies of the entire picture, each with black and white border surrounding it.

Let's deal with detecting the click first. While the **Click()** event procedure might seem like the way to go, a quick examination reveals that it provides no way to tell which button was clicked or where the mouse pointer was located. Clearly we need something else. Scanning through the list of events that the Picture Box control supports, we notice **MouseDown** and **MouseUp** events. The **MouseUp()** event procedure declaration looks like this:

```
Sub Picture1_MouseUp(Button As Integer, Shift As Integer, X As Single, Y As Single)
```

The **MouseDown()** event procedure is the same. Let's go over the arguments:

Button   Indicates which button was pressed; left button = 1, right button = 2, center button = 4.

Shift   Indicates the state of the keyboard when the event occurred—whether the Shift, Ctrl, and/or Alt keys were depressed; Shift = 1, Ctrl = 2, Alt = 4. If more than one of these keys is depressed the values are summed. For example, if Ctrl + Shift is pressed then *Shift* is equal to 3.

X and *Y*   Indicates the position where the mouse pointer was located in the object's coordinate system when the event occurred.

When testing for buttons and/or Shift keys, you can use the predefined constants shown in Table 7.3.

As you can see, the **MouseUp()** and **MouseDown()** event procedures haves everything we need; we can determine not only which button was clicked, but at what location.

eXPLORER TIP   **Mouse-Related Events**

Visual Basic has four events related to clicking the mouse. If you're not clear on how they relate to each other, you may end up with some subtle and hard-to-find bugs in your programs. We wouldn't want that.

Table 7.3 *Constants Used to Test for Buttons and Shift Keys*

Constant	Value	Description
vbLeftButton	1	Left button is pressed
vbRightButton	2	Right button is pressed
vbMiddleButton	4	Middle button is pressed
vbShiftMask	1	Shift key is pressed
vbCtrlMask	2	Ctrl key is pressed
vbAltMask	4	Alt key is pressed

The **MouseDown** event occurs when the user depresses a mouse button. The object that the mouse pointer is over then *captures* the mouse. This means that the object will receive all mouse events up to and including the **MouseUp** event when the mouse button is released, even if the mouse has been moved off the object while the button was down. However, the **Click** event is generated only if both the **MouseDown** and **MouseUp** events occur on the object; if the mouse is moved off the object before releasing the button, the object receives a **MouseDown** and a **MouseUp** event, but no **Click** event. If the button is released on the object, then the events occur in the order **MouseDown**, **MouseUp**, **Click**. If you double-click an object, the event order is **MouseDown**, **MouseUp**, **DblClick**, **MouseUp**.

Now we can get to the code that does the actual work. If we detect a left-button click, we'll want to perform the following steps:

1. Calculate the coordinates of a rectangle centered on the click location using the magnification constants defined in the declarations section of the program.

2. Check that the rectangle does not extend past the edges of the source picture. If it does, adjust it.

3. Call **PaintPicture** to copy the contents of this rectangle to the entire Picture2 Picture Box, thus magnifying it.

If it's a right-button click, we'll follow these steps instead:

1. Use **PaintPicture** with the **vbBlackness** opcode to paint the entire destination Picture Box black.

2. Set up a nested loop. The outer loop will loop once for each of three rows, and the inner loop once for each of three columns.

3. In the inner loop, use **PaintPicture** with the **vbWhiteness** opcode to create nine white rectangles over the destination Picture Box, so that each one is slightly smaller than one-third of the Picture Box dimension.

4. Still in the inner loop, use **PaintPicture** with the **vbSrcCopy** opcode to put a small copy of the source picture on each of the white rectangles.

The code for these actions is in the **MouseUp()** event procedure, which is shown in Listing 7.4 along with the rest of the form's code. Figure 7.7 shows the program after the user perfoms a left-button click on the source image, and Figure 7.8 shows the effects of a right-button click.

Figure 7.7 *Using PAINTPIC to magnify part of a picture.*

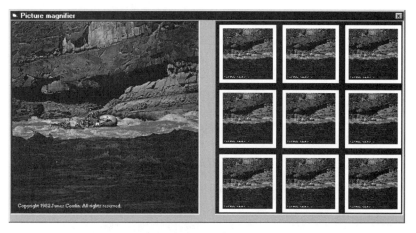

Figure 7.8 *Using PAINTPIC to create nine duplicates of the source picture, each placed on a white rectangle.*

Listing 7.4 PAINTPIC.FRM

```
Option Explicit

' This constant should be predefined by VB, like vbBlackness
' and vbSrcCopy, but it is not so we must do it ourselves.
Const vbWhiteness = &HFF0062

' Use smaller values for greater magnification.
Const WIDE = 0.3
Const HIGH = 0.3

Private Sub Form_Load()

' Make the form the same height and a bit more
' than twice the width of the Picture Box.
Form1.Width = 2.1 * Picture1.Width
Form1.Height = 1.1 * Picture1.Height

' Put the first Picture Box on the left side of the form.
Picture1.Left = 0
Picture1.Top = 0

' Make the second Picture Box the same size
' as the first one (which is the size of the loaded picture
' because its AutoSize property is True).
Picture2.Width = Picture1.Width
Picture2.Height = Picture1.Height

' Put the second Picture Box on the right side of the form.
Picture2.Top = 0
Picture2.Left = Form1.ScaleWidth - Picture2.Width

End Sub


Private Sub Picture1_MouseUp(Button As Integer, Shift As Integer, X As Single, Y
As Single)

Dim XSrc As Single, YSrc As Single
Dim X1 As Single, Y1 As Single, W1 As Single, H1 As Single
Dim row As Integer, col As Integer

If Button = vbLeftButton Then        ' Left button

    ' Calculate the source rectangle X coordinate. Be sure the
    ' resulting rectangle does not extend past the Picture Box
    ' edge on either the left or the right.
    XSrc = X - ((Picture1.Width * WIDE) / 2)
    If XSrc < 0 Then XSrc = 0
    If (XSrc + (WIDE * Picture1.Width)) > Picture1.Width Then
        XSrc = Picture1.Width * (1 - WIDE)
    End If
```

```
        ' Do the same for the Y coordinate.
        YSrc = Y - ((Picture1.Height * HIGH) / 2)
        If YSrc < 0 Then YSrc = 0
        If (YSrc + (HIGH * Picture1.Height) > Picture1.Height) Then
            YSrc = Picture1.Height * (1 - HIGH)
        End If

        ' Paint the contents of the rectangle to the destination Picture Box.
        Picture2.PaintPicture Picture1.picture, 0, 0, Picture2.WIDTH, _
            Picture2.HEIGHT, XSrc, YSrc, Picture1.Width * WIDE, _
            Picture1.Height * HIGH, vbSrcCopy
End If

If Button = vbRightButton Then        ' Right button.
    W1 = Picture2.Width / 3
    H1 = Picture2.Height / 3
    ' The black background.
    Picture2.PaintPicture Picture1.Picture, 0, 0, Picture2.Width, _
Picture2.Height, 0, 0, , , vbBlackness
    For row = 1 To 3
        For col = 1 To 3
        X1 = (row - 0.95) * W1
        Y1 = (col - 0.95) * H1
            ' The white border.
            Picture2.PaintPicture , (row - 0.95) * W1, (col - 0.95) * H1, _
                W1 * 0.9, H1 * 0.9, , , , , vbWhiteness
            ' The picture.
            Picture2.PaintPicture Picture1.Picture, (row - 0.9) * W1, _
                (col - 0.9) * H1, W1 * 0.8, H1 * 0.8, 0, 0, _
                Picture1.Width, Picture1.Height, vbSrcCopy
        Next col
    Next row
End If

End Sub
```

USING THE IMAGE CONTROL

The Image control is another way to display images on your forms. When it comes to displaying bitmaps and metafiles, it behaves very much like a Picture Box control. However, it has only some of the Picture Box's capabilities, which means that an Image control is faster and takes up less of your precious system resources. Image controls are your best bet for displaying pictures; use a Picture Box only when you need its extra features.

Take a look at Table 7.4 to get an idea of the differences between the two controls. You can see that the Image control is specialized for displaying pictures, and that's about it. Note, however, that there's one capability the

Table 7.4   *The Picture Box Control vs. the Image Control*

Feature	Picture Box	Image
Load bitmap and metafile pictures at design- or runtime by setting Picture property	Yes	Yes
Load bitmap and metafile pictures with LoadPicture statement	Yes	Yes
Use as source/destination of PaintPicture method	Yes	No
Display graphics output created with Line, Circle, and Pset methods	Yes	No
Display text created with the Print method	Yes	No
Used to group other controls	Yes	No
Can optionally adjust control size to fit loaded image	Yes	No
Can optionally adjust image size to fit control size	No	Yes
AutoRedraw available	Yes	No

Image control has that the Picture Box does not—the ability to stretch or shrink an image to fit the Image control's dimensions. This is controlled by the Image control's **Stretch** property, which can be set to *True* or *False*.

PUTTING PICTURES ON FORMS

Bitmap and metafile pictures can be displayed directly on a form—without the use of any control. A picture on a form is always located "behind" the controls on the form, so you can use the picture as a background. There are two ways you can display a picture on a form:

- Set its **Picture** property at design-time or at runtime; you must use the **LoadPicture** function at runtime.

- Make it the destination of the **PaintPicture** method (it can also serve as the source)

These techniques work in the same way as they do for a Picture Box control.

DRAWING IN PICTURE BOXES AND FORMS

So far we have seen how to display and manipulate existing images in Picture Boxes and on forms. What if you want to create an image from scratch? Visual Basic has several statements that let you draw just about anything you can think of. When drawing in a Picture Box or on a form, there is always a *current position* that marks the location where the most recent drawing operation finished. The current position is defined by the object's **CurrentX** and **CurrentY** properties. If there have been no draw operations, or if the object's graphics have been erased with the **Cls** method, these properties default to 0.

The Line Method

When you want to draw lines and rectangles on Form, Picture Box, and Printer objects, use the **Line** method.

```
object.Line (X1, Y1)-(X2,Y2), color, mode
```

> *X1, Y1*   The coordinates of the start of the line. If omitted, the object's current position (**CurrentX** and **CurrentY** properties) is used.
>
> *X2, Y2*   The coordinates of the end of the line.
>
> *color*   This optional argument specifies the line color. If omitted, the object's **ForeColor** property is used.
>
> *Mode* (optional)   If set to B, this argument specifies that a rectangle is drawn with diagonally opposite corners, at the given coordinates. The rectangle is filled with color and pattern as specified by the object's **FillColor** and **FillStyle** properties. If set to BF, the rectangle is filled with the same color used to draw the border, and the object's **FillColor** and **FillStyle** properties are ignored.

There are two ways that you can specify **color**. The **RGB()** function lets you specify a color in terms of the relative intensities of the red, green, and blue components. Here's the syntax:

```
RGB(red, green, blue)
```

Each of the three arguments is a number in the range 0 through 255 specifying the relative intensity of the color. For example, the statement

```
Form1.Line (0,0)-(500,500), RGB(0,0,255), BF
```

will draw a rectangle that is completely blue, both its border and interior. You can also specify color with the **QBColor()** function. Its syntax is:

```
QBColor(color)
```

Here, the **color** argument is a number in the range 0 through 15, which corresponds to one of the colors in Table 7.5.

The **QBColor()** function is provided to give you easy access to the 16 colors that were available in the old Quick Basic programming language.

eXPLORER TIP

Red and Green Make...Yellow?

Some readers may wonder why the **RGB()** function uses red, green, and blue. Aren't the primary colors red, blue, and yellow? Yes, but those are the *subtractive* primaries, applicable when the color in question is the result of one color absorbing another color, as in mixing paints. For example, red paint looks red because it absorbs, or *subtracts*, the blue and yellow colors. With a computer screen we are dealing with *additive* colors, in which a color is created by adding different color lights together. If you've ever been in a school play, you've probably noticed, that the stage lights are composed of red, green, and blue bulbs. For example, adding red light to green light makes yellow—hardly what you would expect, but try it for yourself with the demonstration program if you don't believe me!

Color Mixing Demonstration

Now let's try a simple demonstration program. While its main purpose is to show you how the **Line** method and the **RGB()** function work, you'll also

Table 7.5 *QBColor() Colors*

Number	Color	Number	Color
0	Black	8	Gray
1	Blue	9	Light Blue
2	Green	10	Light Green
3	Cyan	11	Light Cyan
4	Red	12	Light Red
5	Magenta	13	Light Magenta
6	Yellow	14	Light Yellow
7	White	15	Bright White

gain some experience in using control arrays and Scroll Bar controls. The program's single form contains a Scroll Bar and Text Box for each of the three primary colors. The Text Boxes display numerical values—from 0 to 255—that you change by using the Scroll Bar. The values, of course, represent the color intensity. A rectangle displaying the selected color is drawn on the form whenever the user changes one of the Scroll Bar values. The final program is shown in Figure 7.9.

To create the program, start a new project and place a control array of three VScrollBar controls and another array of three Text Box controls on the form. Add three Label controls with the **Caption** properties set to *"Red"*, *"Green"*, and *"Blue"*, respectively. Position the controls on the form as shown in Figure 7.9. Be sure that the Scroll Bar and Text Box with Index 0 are under the *"Red"* label, that the Scroll Bar and Text Box with Index 1 under the *"Green"* label, and that the Scroll Bar and Text Box with Index 2 under the *"Blue"* label.

Now we can turn to the code, which is shown in Listing 7.5. Initialization steps are performed in the **Form_Load()** event procedure, as usual. This consists mainly of setting the Scroll Bar properties. Because the three Scroll Bars are all part of a control array, we can use a **For...Next** loop to loop through them (another advantage of control arrays!). The Scroll Bar's **Value** property returns its current setting. There are several properties you can set to customize each Scroll Bar to your current needs:

Max and **Min**   Values corresponding to the Scroll Bar's maximum and minimum positions.

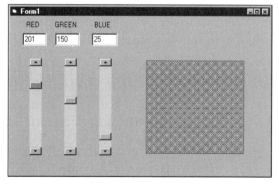

Figure 7.9   *Using the COLORS program to explore the RGB() function.*

> **SmallChange** Amount the Scroll Bar changes when the user clicks on one of the scroll arrows.

> **LargeChange** Amount the Scroll Bar changes when the user clicks between the thumb (the small, moveable box) and one of the scroll arrows.

Since the input arguments to the **RGB()** function fall in the range 0 through 255, that's how we'll set the Scroll Bars' **Min** and **Max** properties. We will also set **SmallChange** to *1* and **LargeChange** to *25*. The final initialization step is to display each Scroll Bar's value in the corresponding Text Box. Since Visual Basic's vertical Scroll Bars have their maximum value when the thumb is at the bottom of the bar, which is somewhat counter-intuitive, we will effectively "flip" the scroll bar by subtracting its **Value** property from 255, which gives us the maximum value when the thumb is at the top.

We will place the actual drawing code in its own sub procedure. Use the Insert Procedure command to create a sub procedure called **DrawRect**, then add the code shown in Listing 7.5. This procedure has only two lines of code. The first one generates a color value by plugging the values of the three Scroll Bars into the **RGB()** function. The second statement uses the **Line** method to draw a filled rectangle on the form using this color. You may need to adjust the rectangle's coordinates to get it placed properly.

As I mentioned earlier, the rectangle is drawn whenever the user changes one of the Scroll Bars. If you haven't guessed, we'll be using Scroll Bar's **Change()** event procedure to signal the change in value. Open this procedure and add the code shown in Listing 7.5. Using the procedure's **Index** argument, which identifies the control in the array that was changed, we update the corresponding Text Box with the new color value and call the **DrawRect** sub procedure to redraw the rectangle. Note here another advantage of using control arrays. Think of how much more code would be required if the three scroll bars were not in an array but rather were independent controls!

Finally, we want the rectangle drawn when the form is first displayed and also if it is hidden on-screen and then uncovered. This is the job of the **Paint()** event procedure, so we place a call to **DrawRect** there.

The program is complete. Start it up and you can experiment with color mixing. Try a setting of Red = 255, Green = 255, and Blue = 0. See! I told you it was yellow!

Listing 7.5 Code in COLORS.FRM

```
Option Explicit

Private Sub Form_Load()

Dim i As Integer

' Set the Scroll Bars for a 0-255 range, with a small
' step of 1 and a large step of 25.
For i = 0 To 2
    VScroll1(i).MIN = 0
    VScroll1(i).MAX = 255
    VScroll1(i).SmallChange = 1
    VScroll1(i).LargeChange = 25
    VScroll1(i).VALUE = 255
    ' Initialize the Text Boxes.
    Text1(i).TEXT = 255 - VScroll1(i).VALUE
Next i

End Sub


Private Sub Form_Paint()

' Draw the rectangle.
DrawRect

End Sub


Private Sub VScroll1_Change(Index As Integer)

' When a Scroll Bar changes, put the new value in
' the Text Box and call the drawing procedure.
Text1(Index).TEXT = 255 - VScroll1(Index).VALUE
DrawRect

End Sub


Public Sub DrawRect()

Dim color As Long

' Generate the color from the Scroll Bar settings.
color = RGB(255 - VScroll1(0).VALUE, 255 - VScroll1(1).VALUE, _
  255 - VScroll1(2).VALUE)

' Draw the rectangle.
Form1.Line (3500, 1100)-(6000, 3400), color, BF

End Sub
```

Dithering Colors

You may find that some of the colors generated by the program COLORS are not smooth, but instead display a pattern that (if you have good eyesight) appears to be made up of different colors. No, your hardware is not broken. This effect is called *dithering*, and is used when your hardware/display driver combination cannot create the exact color called for. Visual Basic then combines two or more colors in a dithered pattern to approximate the color.

The Circle Method

You'll use the **Circle** method to draw circles, ellipses, and arcs. The syntax for this method is:

```
object.Circle (x, y), radius, color, start, end, aspect
```

object   The object on which the circle is to be drawn. If omitted, the current form is used.

x, y   Single-precision values specifying the coordinates of the center point of the circle, ellipse, or arc. The object's current coordinate system is used.

radius   Single-precision value specifying the radius of the circle, ellipse, or arc.

color   Long integer value indicating the color of the circle's outline. If omitted, the value of the object's **ForeColor** property is used. Use the **RGB()** or **QBColor()** function to specify the color.

start, end   Single-precision values used only when drawing an arc (partial circle or ellipse). These arguments specify (in radians) the beginning and end positions of the arc. The range for both is -2 pi radians to 2 pi radians. The default value for start is 0 radians; the default for end is 2 * pi radians, giving a complete circle or ellipse.

aspect   Single-precision value indicating the aspect ratio of the circle, which is the ratio of its horizontal diameter to its vertical diameter. Use values greater than or less than 1.0 to draw ellipses. The default value of 1.0 will draw a perfect circle.

To get a feel for using the **Circle** method, create a new project and place the code from Listing 7.6 in the **Form_Paint()** event procedure, and put this one line

```
Call Form_Paint
```

in the **Form_Resize()** event procedure. Run the program and try moving the window around the screen and changing its size. I called both the form and the project for this demonstration CIRCLES.

Listing 7.6   The Form_Paint Event() Procedure in CIRCLES.FRM

```
Private Sub Form_Paint()

Dim color As Integer, i As Integer
Dim aspect As Single

' Create custom coordinates on the form with (0,0)
' in the center with width and height both 1000 units.
ScaleLeft = -500
ScaleWidth = 1000
ScaleTop = -500
ScaleHeight = 1000
color = 0

' Make the aspect ration the same as the form's proportions.
aspect = Height / Width

Cls

For i = 1 To 500 Step 2
    color = color + 1
    If color = 16 Then color = 0
    Circle (0, 0), i, QBColor(color), , , aspect
Next i

End Sub
```

The Pset Method

You can use the **Pset** method to draw individual points on an object. The syntax for this method is:

```
object.PSet (x, y), color
```

>   *object*   The object where the point is to be drawn. If omitted, the current form is used.

>   *(x, y)*   Single-precision values indicating the coordinates of the point to set in the object's coordinate system.

color   Long integer value specifying the color of the point. If omitted, the object's current **ForeColor** property setting is used. Use the **RGB()** or **QBColor()** function to specify the color.

The size of the point is controlled by the object's **DrawWidth** property. If **DrawWidth** is *1* then the point is a single pixel. For larger values of **DrawWidth**, the point is centered on the specified coordinates. To "erase" a single pixel with the **Pset** method, draw a point using the object's **BackColor** property setting as the color argument.

You can use **Pset** to implement a simple drawing program with only a few lines of code, as illustrated by the relatively few lines of code shown in Listing 7.7. We declare a type Boolean variable that will serve as the drawing flag. This flag is set to True when the user presses the mouse button, and cleared (that is, set equal to False) when the mouse button is released. Then, in the **MouseMove()** event procedure, we test this flag and, if it is True, use **Pset** to draw a single point at the mouse location. The program is extremely basic, and if you try it, you'll see that the drawing cannot keep up with rapid mouse movements.

Listing 7.7   Code in DRAWING.FRM

```
Option Explicit

Dim Drawing as Boolean

Private Sub Form_MouseDown(Button As Integer, Shift As Integer, X As Single, _
  Y As Single)

Drawing = True

End Sub


Private Sub Form_MouseMove(Button As Integer, Shift As Integer, X As Single, _
  Y As Single)

If Drawing Then PSet (X, Y)

End Sub

Private Sub Form_MouseUp(Button As Integer, Shift As Integer, X As Single, _
  Y As Single)

Drawing = False

End Sub
```

Other Drawing Considerations

In this section, I will explain some additional properties and keywords that are relevant when drawing graphics objects.

Using Relative Coordinates

I mentioned earlier that all objects on which graphics can be drawn have a *current position* that is defined by its **CurrentX** and **CurrentY** properties. All drawing methods (including the **Print** method, covered in the next section) update the current position—that is, after the method is executed, the current position points to the location where the drawing ended. In my explanations of the drawing methods, I provided the syntax that uses *absolute* coordinates—coordinates that do not reference the current position—to specify where the drawing is to take place. You can also specify drawing coordinates that are based on the current position. For the **Line** method, you simply omit the first set of coordinates. For example, the statement

```
object.Line -(X,Y)
```

draws a line from the current position to coordinates X,Y. You can also use the **Step** keyword with either or both of the starting and ending coordinates to specify that the current position be treated as the origin. Here are two examples:

```
object.Line Step(10,10)-Step(100,100)
object.Line Step(50,50)-(100,100)
```

The first statement draws a line that begins 10 units below and 10 units to the right of the current position, and ends 100 points below and 100 points to the right of the current position. The second statement draws a line that begins 50 units below and 50 units to the right of the current position, and ends 100 points below and 100 points to the right of the object's origin.

To use relative coordinates with the **Circle** method, include the **Step** keyword before the coordinates. The statement

```
object.Circle Step (0,0), 250
```

draws a circle centered on the current position. **Step** can be used with **Pset** also. The following loop will print a row of 10 dots, starting at the current position with each dot 10 units below the previous dot:

```
For I = 1 to 10
   Form1.Pset Step (0,10)
Next I
```

Without the **Step** keyword, this loop would print all 10 dots at the same location, 10 units below the form's origin.

Remember that an object's current position is defined by its **CurrentX** and **CurrentY** properties. You can set these properties directly to change the current position. The current position can be outside the visible area of the object, and graphical objects can be drawn there, but, of course, they won't be visible.

The DrawStyle and DrawMode Properties

The **DrawStyle** property affects objects drawn with the **Line** and **Circle** methods. It controls whether the line drawn (as a line, border of a rectangle, or edge of a circle) is solid or a combination of dots and dashes. The default is a solid line.

All drawing operations on an object, including the **Print** method, are affected by the object's **DrawMode** property. **DrawMode** governs the interaction between the drawn object and the background of the object. There are 16 different **DrawMode** settings, most of which are of interest only for specialized graphics effects. The default setting, *Copy Pen* (value = 13) does not produce any special effects, simply drawing the graphical object over the background in the specified color. The other 15 settings create various kinds of logical combinations between the background color and the drawing color. I will explain only the most useful one, Invert. Feel free to explore the remaining settings in the Visual Basic Help system.

Setting **DrawMode** to *Invert* (value = 6) causes the background color to be inverted where the graphical object is drawn. The specified color of the drawn object is ignored. The value of the *Invert* setting is twofold. First, the drawn object is guaranteed to be visible no matter what he background, since the existing colors are inverted. Second, you can erase an object drawn in Invert mode simply by drawing it again at the same location—the pixels are "re-inverted" back to their original values, and the object, in effect, disappears.

DISPLAYING TEXT

To display text on a Form, Picture Box, or Printer object, you need to use the **Print** method. The output is created using the font specified by the object's

Font property. The output is placed at the location specified by the object's current graphics location (**CurrentX** and **CurrentY** properties). The **Print** method can also be used with the Debug object to display text in Visual Basic's debug window while a program is executing in the Visual Basic development environment (font and current position are meaningless for the Debug object). The **Print** method's syntax is:

```
object.Print outputlist
```

object   The object to print on. If omitted, the current form is used.

outputlist   A list of one or more expressions to print. If omitted, a blank line is printed.

The **outputlist** argument can contain the following parts, all of which are optional:

expression   Any numeric or string expression.

Spc(n)   Inserts *n* space characters in the output.

Tab(n)   Positions the insertion point at absolute column number *n*. If n is omitted, Tab positions the insertion point at the beginning of the next print zone.

If there is more than one item in **outputlist**, they can be separated either with a space or a semicolon. After the **Print** method is executed, the default is for the output of the next **Print** method to be placed on the next line. You can modify the default by placing one of the following arguments at the end of **outputlist**:

; (semicolon)   Subsequent output follows immediately on the same line.

Tab(n)   Subsequent output follows at the specified column number on the same line.

Tab()   Subsequent output follows at the next print zone on the same line.

Most of the fonts you will use in Visual Basic use proportionally spaced characters, where a wide letter, such as a *W,* occupies more horizontal space a narrow letter, such as an *i.* Therefore, there is no correlation between the number of characters printed and the amount of horizontal space used. You can avoid this problem by using a fixed-pitch font, such as Courier, in which all characters occupy the same amount of horizontal space. Proportional fonts are nicer looking, however, so you'll usually want to use them. How, then, if you use proportional fonts, do you know when the output of the **Print** method is going to reach the right edge of the object being printed on, and it's necessary to start a new line?

Remember that the **Print** method outputs text at the object's current position. If we know the width of the next chunk of text to be printed, we can do the following (as expressed in pseudocode):

```
If ((current X position) + (Width of text)) > (width of object) then
   it won't fit; advance to beginning of next line
else
   it will fit; output on current line
end if
```

You can obtain the width of a unit of text using the **TextWidth** method. All objects to which the **Print** method apply support this method. Passed the text as an argument, **TextWidth** returns the width of the text in the object's current horizontal coordinate units. The value takes into account the object's current **Font** property setting.

How do you "advance" a line? The best way is to manipulate the object's **CurrentY** property directly. First, obtain the height of a line of text using the **TextHeight** method. **TextHeight** works just like **TextWidth**, returning the height, in object units, of the specified text in the current font. The value returned by **TextHeight** includes the *leading*, or space between lines of text. Assume that the variable **S$** contains the next unit of text to be printed on Form1. Assume also that the variables **LMargin** and **RMargin** contain the desired left and right margins, respectively. The following code will wrap to the next line if needed:

```
If ((Form1.CurrentX + Form1.TextWidth(S$)) > (Form1.ScaleWidth - RMargin) Then
   Form1.CurrentX = LMargin
   Form1.CurrentY = Form1.CurrentY + Form1.TextHeight(S$)
End If

Form1.Print S$;
```

THE LINE AND SHAPE CONTROLS

If you need to draw permanent lines and shapes on a form, the Line and Shape controls are your best bet. By "permanent" I mean that you do not need to modify the drawn objects during program execution—what you draw during program design is what will be displayed during program execution. Thus, they are most often used for decorative purposes, such as providing interesting borders for controls or dividing a form into sections. Neither of these controls has any associated events. Figure 7.10 shows a Picture Box with a border that was created with several Shape controls, each slightly larger than the next.

To use the Line or Shape control, simply place it on your form like any other control. You have the following properties to use in order to change the Line control's appearance:

BorderColor   The line color.

BorderWidth   The width of the line, in arbitrary units from 1 to 8192.

BorderStyle   Indicates whether the line is solid, dotted, dashed, etc.

DrawMode   Determines the appearance of the line. The default setting gives a line in the color specified by the **BorderColor** property. Other settings are explained in Visual Basic Help.

The Shape control has these four properties plus some additional ones:

Shape   The type of shape. Choices are rectangle, square, rounded rectangle, rounded square, circle, and oval.

BackStyle   Indicates whether the interior of the shape is transparent or opaque.

Figure 7.10   *Using the Shape control to create borders.*

BackColor   The color of the shape's interior. Ignored if **BackStyle** is set to its default value, *Transparent*.

FillColor and *FillStyle*   These properties do the same thing as **BackColor** and **BackStyle**. If both **BackStyle** and **FillStyle** are set to *Opaque*, then the setting of **FillColor** takes precedence over the setting of **BackColor**. You can therefore toggle a shape's interior color between two values by toggling **FillStyle** between *Transparent* and *Opaque*.

Exploring Visual Basic Help

Don't forget to make regular visits to Visual Basic's online Help system. It's loaded with all the little details that I can't include in the book, and by browsing the Help information and looking at the sample code that is provided, you'll learn a lot of useful things.

PRINTING WITH THE PRINTER OBJECT

So far we have limited ourselves to displaying graphics and text on the screen. Often you'll need to send graphics and text to the printer as well. Visual Basic makes this easy with the Printer object. The Printer object has the same properties and methods as the Form and Picture Box objects (those properties and methods related to graphics, at least). Therefore, if you want to print text to the printer, you write

```
Printer.Print message
```

The same goes for the **Line**, **Circle**, and **Pset** methods. Just like the Form or Picture Box objects, the Printer object has a current position defined by the **CurrentX** and **CurrentY** properties, the ability to report the width and height of text with the **TextHeight** and **TextWidth** methods, the ability to act as the destination (but not the source) for the **PrintPicture** method, and so on. For the most part you can just do the same things with the Printer object or a Form object depending on whether you want the output displayed on the screen or sent to the printer.

There are a few things unique to the Printer object. Table 7.6 lists some Printer object-specific methods.

You should be aware that your printer will not support the same fonts as your screen display. There will be some fonts in common, of course, but you cannot be sure that a font available for the screen will also be available for the Printer object. To determine which fonts your Printer object has available, use the **FontCount** property to determine how many fonts there are, then extract their names from the **Fonts** property. The following code, placed in a form's **Click()** event procedure, will load a List Box control with the names of all the Printer object's fonts:

```
Private Sub Form_Click ()

Dim i As Integer

For i = 0 To Printer.FontCount -1  ' Determine number of fonts.
    List1.AddItem Printer.Fonts(i)  ' Put each font into List Box.
Next I

End Sub
```

You can use this technique to provide a way for the user to select a font. Remember that the Screen object also has **FontCount** and **Fonts** properties, which can be used to get a list of the Screen fonts. One technique that I often use is to obtain lists of both the Screen and Printer object fonts, then compare them and generate a list containing only the fonts common to both.

Given that you can use the same methods and properties for displaying graphics and text on the screen and on the printer, does this mean that you must write two complete sets of program statements, one directing output to the Printer object and the other to a Form? Not necessarily. Visual Basic procedures have the ability to take an argument of type **Object**. In other words, you pass an object to the procedure. This enables you to write a procedure that performs the graphics and text output, and then pass it the Form or the Printer object, depending on where you want the output to go. For example, here's an output procedure that will display a message on either a form or the printer:

```
Public Sub Output(Dest As Object, Msg as String)
```

Table 7.6   *Printer Object Methods*

Method	Description
Printer.NewPage	Ejects the current page and starts a new one
Printer.EndDoc	Aborts printing of a long document; however, the portion already sent to the Windows Print Manager will still be printed
Printer.KillDoc	terminates a print job immediately

```
Dest.Print Msg

End Sub
```

To display the message "Hello" on the form named Form1 use this statement:

```
Call Output (Form1, "Hello")
```

To print the same message on the printer use this statement:

```
Call Output(Printer, "Hello")
```

This technique is demonstrated in the program PRINT1. The program's form contains a control array of three Command Buttons. The button with Index 0 has the caption "&Display", Index 1 has the caption "&Print", and Index 2 has the caption "E&xit". The program's code is presented in Listing 7.8. When you click on the Display button, the form displays the text and graphics shown in Figure 7.11. If you click on the Print button the same output is produced on your printer.

Listing 7.8 Code in PRINT1.FRM

```
Option Explicit

Public Sub Output(Dest As Object)

' Set the font name and size.
Dest.FontName = "Times Roman"
Dest.FontSize = 36

' Display a message.
Dest.Print "Hello world!"

' Print a rectangle to fill the page.
Dest.Line (10, 10)-(Dest.ScaleWidth - 10, Dest.ScaleHeight - 10), , B

' Put an X in the rectangle.
Dest.Line (10, 10)-(Dest.ScaleWidth - 10, Dest.ScaleHeight - 10)
Dest.Line (10, Dest.ScaleHeight - 10)-(Dest.ScaleWidth - 10, 10)

End Sub

Private Sub Command1_Click(Index As Integer)

Select Case Index
    Case 0
        Call Output(Form1)
    Case 1
```

```
        Call Output(Printer)
    Case 2
        End
End Select

End Sub
```

The PrintForm Method

The **PrintForm** method, applicable only to Form objects, sends a copy of the Form to the current printer. Everything on the Form—controls, graphics, text, and bitmaps—will be printed (although **AutoRedraw** must be *On* for graphics created with **Line**, **Circle**, and **Pset** to print). The border and title bar of the form are included in the printout. For the most part, this method is intended as a programmer aid, permitting you to create hard copy records of your program's appearance. For end-user printing you are almost always better off using the Printer object described previously.

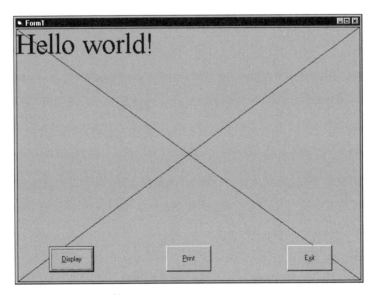

Figure 7.11   *The form displayed by PRINT1.*

File Access
and Management

It's hard to imagine a program that doesn't work with disk files in one form or another. Visual Basic provides a full set of tools for accessing and managing files on your disks.

Files here, files there, files everywhere! The only thing that's been growing faster than hard disk sizes, it seems, is the number of files we need to place on them. Almost every program you write will need to deal with files, and the way your program deals with this challenge has a big impact on its overall quality. Poor design and implementation of file access and management can have a variety of deleterious effects on your program, ranging from slow performance to that ultimate no-no, loss of data.

Note that I draw a distinction between file *access* and file *management*. File access encompasses all the procedures for reading and writing file data; while file management refers to other types of file and disk manipulation, such as creating directories, moving and deleting files, and so on. We'll look at these two topics, and also the Visual Basic controls that are designed for file-related tasks.

READING AND WRITING FILES

If we want to save data until the next time we use our computer, we have to store it in a disk file. If we want to transfer data to another computer, we must store it in a disk file. If we want to use data created by another program, we must read it from a disk file. Yes, a few exceptions to these rules exist, but the general message is clear: Knowing how to use disk files is essential! The Basic language provides a variety of statements and functions that provide us with complete flexibility in file access. While these program statements and functions are part of the Basic language, they are not directly related to the Visual Basic user interface or to its objects and events. The file manipulation statements will be located in general procedures, or very rarely in event procedures.

All Visual Basic file access consists of three steps:

1. Open the file.

2. Read data from or write data to the file.

3. Close the file.

Sounds relatively simple, but within these three steps lies a multitude of options and pitfalls. Let's start by looking at the three different kinds of file access offered by Visual Basic.

Types of File Access

All file data, no matter what its source or contents, is stored as a sequence of bytes in the file. Depending on the type of data and the needs of the program, you will choose from one of three different ways of accessing those bytes. The type of file access your program utilizes ultimately determines the methods it can use to read and write data, as well as the way the data is interpreted. Each of the three access methods is appropriate for certain types of data. This section describes each type briefly with full details given later in the chapter.

Sequential Access Files

A sequential access file stores data as a series of variable length records. The term *record* simply means a unit of data. For example, if we store the value of a type Integer variable in a file, that's one record. Likewise, the contents of a string variable would be another record. The records are *variable length* because each record's length is determined by its contents and not by some overall property of the file.

The data in a sequential file is assumed to be text, meaning that each byte in the file represents a character. The name sequential derives from the fact that this type of file must always be read from the beginning. To read data in the middle of the file, we must first read all the preceding data in sequence. There is no easy way to jump directly to the data in the middle of the file. In a sequential file, numeric data is stored as its corresponding characters and string data is stored in quotation marks. For example, the value 123 is stored as the string "123."

In a sequential file, each record is a line of text that is terminated with a carriage return-line feed (CR-LF) character. Each record can contain zero or more characters, and the records in a given file can be of different lengths. We treat each record as a single line of text, which is appropriate for manipulating plain text files. Sequential file records can also be treated as groups of one or more fields that are separated from each other by delimiters. This approach is useful for working with data that is divided into units that differ in length.

Random Access Files

A random access file stores data as a series of fixed size records. The records in a random access file are numbered sequentially starting at 1. Random access files allow a program to directly access each record by its number, without having to first access previous records. In a 2000 record file, for example, we could access record 1199 without first having to read records 1-1198. We can store both text and numbers in a random access file. Text is stored as characters, but numbers are stored in a special binary format.

Each record in a random access file consists of a fixed number of bytes, or characters. Each record contains one or more fields, each of which also has a fixed length. It follows that the record size is equal to the sum of the field sizes. The sizes of a file's records and fields are defined by the program when the file is created. Unlike sequential files, random files do not use delimiters to separate fields and records. The fixed lengths of the fields and records are used to determine where each field and record begins and ends.

Binary Access Files

Binary access files store data as an unformatted sequence of bytes. No record lengths or delimiter characters are needed to provide structure to the file data. Binary access allows us to manipulate the individual bytes of a file without any assumptions about what the bytes represent. Unlike random access and sequential access files, binary files are not limited to ASCII text or Basic variables. Binary access can be used to read and modify any kind of disk file, as well as to store program data. However, because a binary file has no records or other structure, the program is completely responsible for keeping track of what is stored where.

Opening Files

A program must open a disk file before it can read or write file data. Files are opened with the **Open** statement, which has the following syntax:

```
Open filename [For mode] [Access access] [lock] As [#]filenum [LEN=reclen]
```

filename is a string expression specifying the name of the file to be opened. If filename does not include a drive and path specifier, the file is opened in the current folder.

mode is a keyword that specifies the file access mode, as shown in Table 8.1.

access is an optional keyword that specifies the operations permitted on the open file, as shown in Table 8.2.

Table 8.1 *Mode Types*

Mode	File Access
APPEND	Sequential access; if filename already exists, new data is added at the end of existing data in the file. If filename does not exist, it is created.
BINARY	Binary access; reading and writing. If filename does not exist, it is created.
INPUT	Sequential access; file opened for reading. If filename does not exist, an error occurs.
OUTPUT	Sequential access; file opened for writing. If filename exists, it is deleted and a new file created. If filename does not exist, it is created.
RANDOM	Random access; reading and writing. If filename does not exist, it is created. This is the default if the mode argument is omitted.

Table 8.2 *Access Types*

Access	Result
READ	File opened for reading only
WRITE	File opened for writing only
READ WRITE	File opened for reading and writing. This mode is valid only for random mode files, binary mode files, and sequential mode files opened for APPEND.

Table 8.3 *Lock Types*

Lock	Effect
SHARED	Any process may read or write the file.
LOCK READ	No other process may read the file. A program can open a file in LOCK READ mode only if no other process has read access to the file.
LOCK WRITE	No other process may write to the file. A program can open a file in LOCK WRITE mode only if no other process has write access to the file.
LOCK READ WRITE	No other process may read or write the file. A program can open a file in LOCK READ WRITE mode only if no other process has read or write access to the file, and a LOCK READ or LOCK WRITE is not already in place.

lock is an optional keyword that controls access to a file by other processes. Valid values for lock are shown in Table 8.3.

filenum is an integer expression with a value between 1 and 511. See the next section for more information on file numbers.

reclen is an integer expression that specifies the record length, in bytes, for random access files, and the buffer size for sequential access files (maximum = 32,767; default = 128 for both). The buffer is an internal memory area that is used by Visual Basic programs to temporarily store data before it is written to disk. A larger buffer size can sometimes speed disk operations but decreases memory available for other purposes. Note that reclen is not applicable to binary mode files.

File Numbers

Each file that is opened by a Visual Basic program has a unique file number associated with it. This number is specified by the filenum argument that we pass to the **Open** statement. After the file is open, the program uses the file number to refer to the file when reading and writing the file, and when closing it. The file number must be in the range 1-511, and only one open file can be associated with a given number at a time. When the file is later closed, the file number is freed for use with another file.

Before opening a file, use the **FreeFile()** function to obtain the lowest unused file number. In a multitasking environment like Windows, other programs may have opened files that have used some of the available file numbers. Here's how to use **FreeFile()**:

```
filenum = FreeFile
OPEN "c:\documents\sales.lst" FOR RANDOM AS filenum
```

When called with no argument or an argument of 0, **FreeFile()** returns an unused file number in the range 1-255. An argument of 1 results in a number in the range 256-511:

```
filenum = FreeFile    ' 1-255
filenum = FreeFile(0)' 1-255
filenum = FreeFile(1)' 256-511
```

Closing Files

A file should be closed when the program is finished using it. Closing a file flushes the file's buffer (a temporary storage area in memory), ensuring that all data has been physically written to disk. Closing a file also frees up the file number that was associated with the file, allowing it to be used for another file, as well as freeing the memory that was assigned to the file's buffer. To close a specific file or files, execute the **CLOSE** statement with the file numbers as arguments. To close all open files, execute **CLOSE** with no arguments:

```
CLOSE #1
CLOSE #3, #5, #6
CLOSE
```

All open files are automatically closed when a Visual Basic program terminates. Even so, develop the habit of closing individual files as soon as the program is finished with the file. This technique avoids the possibility of data loss in the event of a system crash or power failure.

USING SEQUENTIAL FILES

As explained earlier, a sequential file stores data in a series of records where each record is a line of text with a carriage return-line feed (CR-LF) combination at the end. We can use a sequential file to store data in two ways: Each record is a single line of text, or each record is a group of fields separated by delimiters. Both methods are covered in this section. Remember that a sequential file can be opened for only one type of operation at a time: to read data from the file (mode = INPUT), to write data to a new file (mode = OUTPUT), or to write data to the end of an existing file (mode = APPEND). To switch from one operation to another—from writing to reading, for example—we must close the file, then reopen it in the new mode.

Fields in Sequential Files

We can use fields in a sequential file when the information to be stored consists of discrete units that all have the same structure. For instance, imagine that we are writing a program to keep a catalog of our books. For each book, we want to store the author's name, the title, and an index number that specifies the book's location on our shelf. If we create a sequential file for this data, it will have the following structure:

- The file will contain one record for each book.

- Each record will contain three fields: one for author, one for title, and one for index number.

Let's say that the first entry in the file is *The Aspern Papers*, by Henry James, index number 12. The record for that entry will be stored in the file as shown here:

> "Henry James, The Aspern Papers,"12

If the second entry is for Dostoyevsky's *Crime and Punishment*, index number 23, it will be stored as follows:

> "Dostoyevsky, Crime and Punishment,"123

Each record would be stored on its own line. If we opened the file in a text editor such as the Visual Basic editor or Window's NotePad, we would see the records just as they are shown here. From these examples, we can see that a sequential file uses commas and double quotation marks to delimit the fields. Fields are separated by commas, and text data is enclosed in quotation marks.

We use the **Write #** statement to write a single record of field-delimited data to a sequential file. Its syntax is:

```
Write #filenum [, list]
```

filenum is the number that was associated with the file when it was opened (as you recall, it had to be in OUTPUT or APPEND mode).

list is a list of one or more Basic expressions to be written to the file. If list contains more than one item, separate them by commas. If list is omitted from the **Write #** statement, an empty record (a blank line) is written to the file.

Here are some examples. This line of code would write one record to the sequential file of book information:

```
Write #1, "Henry James","The Aspern Papers",12
```

Of course, in a real program we would use variables in the **Write #** statement:

```
book.name = "Henry James"
book.title = "The Aspern Papers"
book.index = 12
Write #1, book.name, book.title, book.index
```

Each Write # statement writes one record to the file, and automatically inserts any necessary comma and quotation mark delimiters. Double quotation marks cannot be included in data written with the **Write #** statement.

To read field delimited data from a sequential file, use the **Input #** statement. Input # reads one or more fields from the input file and assigns them to program variables. Its syntax is:

```
Input #filenum, list
```

filenum is the number that was associated with the file when it was opened (in INPUT mode).

list is a list of one or more program variables to be assigned data that will be read from the file. If list contains more than one variable name, separate them by commas.

Input # reads one field from the file for each variable in its argument list, and assigns the fields to the variables in order. Remember that sequential files must be read sequentially, starting with the first field in the first record and proceeding from that point. Here's a brief example:

```
FileNum = FreeFile
```

```
OPEN "BOOKLIST.DAT" FOR OUTPUT AS #FileNum
WRITE #FileNum, "Henry James","The Aspern Papers",12
WRITE #FileNum, "Dostoyevsky","Crime and Punishment",123
CLOSE #FileNum
```

Then, in another part of the program:

```
Dim A As String, B As String, C As String, D As String
Dim x As Integer, y As Integer
FileNum = FreeFile
Open "BOOKLIST.DAT" For INPUT As #FileNum
Input # FileNum, A, B, x
Input # FileNum, C, D, y
Close #FileNum
```

After this code executes, A = "Henry James", B = "The Aspern Papers", x = 12, C = "Dostoyevsky", D = "Crime and Punishment", and y = 123.

The Input # statement reads data from the file on a field-by-field basis, and assigns fields read from the file in the order in which variables appear in the file's argument list. If we replaced the two **Input #** statements in the above example with the single statement

```
Input #FileNum, A, B, x, C, D, y
```

or with the multiple statements

```
Input #FileNum, A, B
Input # FileNum, x, C
Input # FileNum, D, y
```

the results would be exactly the same. The way that **Input #** breaks file data into fields depends on the type of the variable in the **Input #** statement's argument list. If **Input #** is reading data into a string variable, the end of a field is marked by one of the following:

- A double quotation mark if the field begins with a double quotation mark.

- A comma if the field does not begin with a double quotation mark.

- A carriage return-line feed (CR-LF).

If **Input #** is reading data into a numeric variable, the end of the field is marked by:

- A comma.

- One or more spaces.

- CR-LF

When we are using a sequential file to store data, the program is responsible for keeping **Write #** and **Input #** statements synchronized in terms of the type, order, and number of fields in each record. In other words, data items must be read from the file in the same order they were written to it. If this synchrony is disrupted, two kinds of problems can result:

- The program might use **Input #** to read a field from a file into a variable of a different type (for example, reading string data into a numeric variable). No error happens when this occurs, but it can produce unexpected results. When reading a numeric field into a string variable, the variable is assigned the string representation of the number. When reading a string field into a numeric variable, the result depends on the string. If the string starts with a non-numeric character, the variable is assigned the value of 0. If the string starts with one or more numeric characters, the variable is assigned the numeric value of those characters.

- If the number of fields is wrong, the program may lose track of where it is. Remember that the **Input #** statement counts fields, not records, when it reads data from the file. After one **Input #** statement executes, the next **Input #** statement starts with the next field in the file, which may not be the beginning of the next record.

One common use for sequential access files is to store an array of variable length strings. This code fragment demonstrates how to write the array data to a disk file:

```
Dim notes(100) As String, count As Integer, FileNum As Integer
...
FileNum = FreeFile
Open "NOTES.TXT" For OUTPUT As #FileNum

For count = 0 TO 100
   WRITE #1, notes(count)
Next count

Close #FileNum
```

Then, to retrieve the data from the disk file and place it in a string array:

```
Open "NOTES.TXT" For INPUT As #FileNum
```

```
For count = 0 To 100
   Input #1, notes(count)
Next count

Close #FileNum
```

We can also use a sequential file to store arrays of numbers; but as you'll see later in the chapter, another file access mode is actually better suited for this task.

Text in Sequential Files

One common use for sequential files to store text that is not divided into fields—text such as a document or READ.ME file. Each line, or record, in the file is simply treated as a line of text, with no delimiters or other special characters.

To write lines of text to a sequential file, use the **Print #** statement. **Print #** does not delimit fields with commas or enclose strings in double quotes. Rather, it writes data to the file with the exact same format as if the data had been displayed on the screen with the Print statement. You saw **Print #** used in Chapter 6 in the "baby editor" project. The syntax for this statement is:

```
Print #filenum [, list] [,|;]
```

> *filenum* is the number that was associated with the file when it was opened (in OUTPUT or APPEND mode).

> *list* contains one or more string expressions to be written to the file. Multiple expressions in list should be separated by a comma or semicolon. If list is omitted, **Print #** writes a blank line to the file.

The optional comma or semicolon at the end of the **Print #** statement determines the location of subsequent output to the file (that is, the next Print statement):

- No comma or semicolon: subsequent output is placed on a new line.

- Semicolon: subsequent output is placed on the same line immediately following the previous output.

- Comma: subsequent output is placed on the same line at the next print zone.

Looking back to Chapter 6, you will see that we output multiple lines to a file with a single **Print #** statement, which is a useful feature. If the text that is being output (in Chapter 6, the **Text** property of a Text Box control) contains carriage return-line feed (CR-LF) characters, they serve to break the output into multiple lines in the sequential file, just as if each line of the text had been written to the file with a separate **Print #** statement. So you can see that Print # is quite flexible, having the ability to output part of a line of text (if terminated with ; or ,) or multiple lines of text (if the text contains its own CR-LF characters). If neither of these conditions is met, **Print #** outputs one entire line of text to the file.

Let's look at some other examples. The first examples illustrate what happens when we place a comma or semicolon at the end of the **Print #** statement.

Statements:

```
Print #1, "Visual"
Print #1, "Basic"
```

Written to file:

> Visual
>
> Basic

Statements:

```
Print #1, "Visual";
Print #1, "Basic"
```

Written to file:

> VisualBasic

Statements:

```
Print #1, "Visual",
Print #1, "Basic"
```

Written to file:

> Visual Basic

Next, let's take a look at the difference between using a comma or a semicolon as a separator between expressions.

Statements:

```
Print #1, "Visual";"Basic"
```

Written to file:

VisualBasic

Statements:

```
Print #1, "Visual","Basic"
```

Written to file:

Visual Basic

To read lines of text one at a time from a sequential file, use the Line Input # statement. Line Input # reads an entire line of text from the file, without regard for field delimiters, and assigns it to a string variable. The syntax is:

```
Line Input [#]filenum, var
```

> *filenum*   is the number assigned to the file when it was opened (for INPUT).

> *var*   is the type String variable to receive the line of text.

Detecting the End of the File

When reading data from a sequential file, we use the **EOF()** function to detect when we have reached the end of the file. The syntax is

```
EOF(filenum)
```

where *filenum* is the number associated with an open file. **EOF()** returns True if the last record in the file has been read, and returns False if it has not yet been read. If we try to read past the end of a sequential file, an error is generated. The following code shows how to use **EOF()** in a loop to read an entire sequential file, a line at a time, into an array:

```
Dim info(1000) As String
Dim count As Integer
...
Open "MYFILE.DAT" For Input As #1
```

```
count = 0

While Not EOF(1)
   Line Input #1, info(count)
   count = count + 1
Wend
```

USING RANDOM ACCESS FILES

A random file is like a sequential file in that both consist of records. The difference is that random file records must all be the same size, and the program differentiates one record from the next by its position in the file. No special character is used to separate records. For example, if a file's records are each 100 bytes long, bytes 1-100 contain the first record (byte positions in a file always start at position 1), and record 4 is at positions 301-400. The records in a random file are numbered sequentially starting at 1, with a maximum of 2,147,483,647 (if that's not big enough for you, too bad!). Each record is divided into one or more fields. The fields, too, are defined by their length. Each record in a random file contains the same field structure—the same number of fields and the same field sizes. Before we can create or use a random file, we must define its record structure.

Defining Random File Record Structure

The structure of a random file's records is defined in the same manner as the user-defined data type created with the **Type...End Type** statements that were covered in Chapter 4. The first step is to actually create a user-defined data type that has the structure desired for the random file. This method works well, since almost all programs that use random files require the same user-defined data type to manipulate the data in the program. Continuing our earlier example of a filing system for books, we could write:

```
TYPE Book_Data
   Author As String * 20
   Title As String * 25
   Index As Integer
END TYPE

DIM Books(100) As Book_Data
```

Now we have a user-defined type that will serve to manipulate the book data in the program, as well as to define the record structure for the random access file. When opening a file for random access, one of the required parameters is the length of the file's records (we saw this earlier in the chapter in the discussion of the Open statement). This task is easily done using the **Len()** function, which returns the length, in bytes, of a data type. The Open statement would read

```
filenum = FreeFile
Open "BOOKFILE.DAT" FOR RANDOM AS #filenum Len = Len(Books(1))
```

Note that we passed the **Len()** function one array element, not the entire array. This statement opens the random file with a record length equal to the size of the user-defined data structure.

Reading and Writing Random Files

To write data to a random file, use the Put statement. The syntax is:

```
Put [#]filenum,[recnum],usertype
```

>*filenum* is the number associated with the random file when it was opened.

>*recnum* is the record number in the file where the data is to be placed. If recnum is omitted, the next record (the one following the position of the last Get or Put) is used. If no Get or Put has been executed since the file was opened, record 1 is used.

>*usertype* is a structure of the user-defined type that contains the data to be written.

Continuing with the above example, to write data to the first record in the file, we would write:

```
Books(1).Author = "Henry James"
Books(1).Title = "The Aspern Papers"
Books(1).Index = 20
Put #FileNum,1, Books(1)
```

When first creating a random access file, we can start writing data at record 1, then increase the record number by 1 for each successive Put statement. We could also omit the recnum argument in the Put statement and let Visual Basic automatically keep track of record numbers for us. However, if we are adding records to an existing file, we must control recnum to insure that the data is placed where we want it. If we write new data to a record number that is already in use in the file, the new data will replace the old data. If we don't want to overwrite existing data, we must add new records at the end of the file. In other words, for a file that already has *n* records, start adding new records at record *n + 1*.

How do we determine the number of records in a file? We use the **Lof()** function, which returns the file length, or size, in bytes. Its syntax is

```
Lof(filenum)
```

where *filenum* is the number associated with the open file whose length we want to know. And what is the benefit of knowing the file's total size? We already know that the **Len()** function returns the size of each record in bytes. It follows that the total bytes in a file divided by the bytes per record will give us the number of records in the file. Therefore, we would write

```
nextrec = (Lof(1) \ Len(usertype)) + 1
Put #FileNum, nextrec, usertype
```

To obtain the number of the next record to be read or written, use the **Seek()** function. Similarly, the **Loc()** function returns the number of the last record that was read or written.

To read data from a random access file, use the Get statement. Data is read from a specified record in the file and placed in a user-defined structure of the type that was used to create the file. The syntax of the Get statement is:

```
Get [#]filenum,[recnum],usertype
```

filenum is the number associated with the random file when it was opened.

recnum is the number of the record to be read. If recnum is omitted, data is read from the next record (the one after the last Get or Put). If no Get or Put has been executed since the file was opened, record 1 is read.

usertype is a variable of the user-defined type where the data is to be placed.

Again using the book filing system example, to read the first record of a random file, you would write:

```
GET #FileNum, 1, Books(1)
```

To read all records from a random file, use a loop that starts with the first record and reads sequential records until the end of the file is reached, placing them in the elements of an array of the appropriate user-defined type. To detect the end of file, use the **EOF()** function as shown earlier in this chapter for sequential files. We can also calculate the number of the last record in the file by dividing the file length by the record length, as shown previously.

Visual Basic maintains a file pointer for each open random access file. This pointer specifies the record number that will be read or written by the GET or PUT statement if the recnum argument is omitted. When a random access file is first opened, whether it's a new file or an existing file, the file pointer initially points at record 1. As you read and write random file data, the file pointer is maintained as follows:

1. A call to Get or Put without a recnum argument increments the file pointer by 1.

2. A call to GET or PUT with a recnum argument sets the file pointer to (recnum + 1).

To determine the current file pointer position, you can use the **Seek()** and **Loc()** functions. **Seek()** returns the position of the file pointer (the next record to be read or written). **Loc()** returns the position of the last record that was read or written. The syntax is:

```
Seek(filenum)
Loc(filenum)
```

where *filenum* is the number associated with an open random access file. The value returned by **Loc()** is one less than the value returned by **Seek()**. When a file has just been opened, **Loc()** returns 0 and **Seek()** returns 1.

USING BINARY FILES

A binary file stores data as an unformatted sequence of bytes. There is no record/field structure in the file (unless we impose one in code). Binary files provide a great deal of flexibility in storing data, but because of their structure-less nature, it is our job to keep track of what is stored in the file. To do so, we need to keep track of where we are in the file.

File Position

Every open binary file has its own *file pointer*. The file pointer is a numeric value that points at the position in the file where read and write operations will occur. Each "position" in a binary file corresponds to one byte of data; therefore, a file that contains *n* bytes has positions numbered from *1* through *n*. To change the file pointer and determine its value, we use the Seek statement and the **Seek()** and **Loc()** functions. These are the same statements we use when working with random access files. With random access files, the file pointer points at records, not bytes. Visual Basic knows the access mode in which a given file was opened, and interprets Seek or Loc correctly when we use them—as bytes for a BINARY file and records for a RANDOM file. The syntax of the Seek and Loc statements is:

```
Seek [#]filenum, newpos
[pos =] Seek(filenum)
[pos =] LOC(filenum)
```

filenum   is the number associated with the file when it was opened in BINARY mode.

The Seek() statement sets the file pointer to newpos.

The **Seek()** function returns the current position of the file pointer (the next byte to be read or written).

The **Loc()** function returns the position of the last byte that was read or written. Unless we explicitly move the pointer, **Loc()** is 1 less than Seek().

Reading and Writing Binary File Data

To read data from a binary file, use the Get statement. To write data to a binary file, use the Put statement. Again, these are the same statements that are used for random files; they are interpreted differently depending on the mode of the file being read or written. The syntax is:

```
GET [#]filenum, [pos] , var
PUT [#]filenum, [pos] , var
```

filenum   is the number associated with the file when it was opened in BINARY mode.

pos   specifies the byte position where the read or write operation is to take place. If pos is omitted, the current file pointer position is used.

var   is any Basic variable. Get reads data from the file into the var; Put writes data from the var to the file. The statements automatically read or write the number of bytes contained in var. If var is a variable length string, the number of bytes transferred is equal to the number of characters currently in var.

When a binary mode file is first opened, the file pointer is at position 1. Any Get or Put operation automatically increments the file pointer by the number of bytes transferred.

To determine the length of a binary file, use the **Lof()** function

```
[length =] Lof(filenum)
```

where *filenum* is the number associated with the file when it was opened in BINARY mode. The value returned by **Lof()** is equal to the file pointer position of the file's last byte. A program can quickly read an entire binary file, using **Lof()** and a loop. The following code shows how to use binary file access to make a copy of a file. It is assumed that ORIGINAL.DAT is an existing file, and that COPY.DAT does not exist. By using a 1-character fixed length string, the program reads and writes one byte at a time. While this code would certainly work, it is inefficient due to the byte-at-a-time approach.

```
Dim ch As String * 1, count As Integer

Open "ORIGINAL.DAT" For BINARY AS #1
Open "COPY.DAT" For BINARY AS #2

For count = 1 TO Lof(1)
   Get #1, , ch
   Put #2, , ch
Next count

Close #1, #2
```

The **Eof()** function, described earlier in the chapter, can be used to detect the end of a binary file. For example, the loop in the above code could also have been written as follows:

```
While Not Eof(1)
   Get #1, , ch
   Put #2, , ch
Wend
```

The flexibility of binary files makes them an excellent choice for storing program data, particularly when the data format does not lend itself to a random access or sequential access file. Remember that the unstructured nature of binary files makes it necessary for our program to keep track of the data storage format. Here's an example. A program that uses an array of 1000 double precision values could store the entire array in a binary file as follows:

```
Dim data(999) As Double, count As Integer

Open "ARRAY.DAT" For BINARY As #1

For count = 0 To 999
   Put #1, , data(count)
Next count

Close #1
```

The data could later be retrieved from the disk file back into the array as follows:

```
Open "ARRAY.DAT" For BINARY As #1

For count = 0 To 999
   Get #1, , data(count)
Next count

Close #1
```

Nothing prevents us from retrieving the data into an array of type Integer or any other Basic data type, but the results would be meaningless.

Here are a few hints for working with binary files:

- To add new data at the end of an existing file, move the file pointer to the end of the file by executing Seek filenum, Lof(filenum)+1.

- If you Put data in an existing file at a position before the end of the file, the new data will overwrite existing data.

- If you Put data at a file pointer position that is past the end of a file (for example, at position Lof(filenum) + 10), the file will be extended as needed. However, the intervening byte positions will contain garbage (that is, un-defined values).

- If you Get data at a file pointer position that is beyond the end of a file, no error occurs but the returned data will be garbage.

Which File Type Should You Use?

If you are a bit confused by Visual Basic's different file access modes, you are not alone. It's not always clear which type of file is best for a particular application. The following guidelines will help you choose:

1. For data that consists of lines of text, whether generated by a Visual Basic program or another application, use sequential access mode.

2. To manipulate non-text files generated by other applications, use binary mode.

3. To store numerical arrays, use either sequential mode or binary mode. Binary mode is preferred because it is faster and results in significantly smaller data file sizes.

4. To store arrays of variable length strings, use sequential mode. To store arrays of fixed length strings, use either sequential or binary mode. Binary mode has a size and speed advantage, although not as significant as it is with numerical arrays.

5. To store data that is organized in a record and field format, use either sequential or random mode. The final choice depends on the specific needs of the program.

6. Random access mode provides faster access to individual records in the disk file. However, it wastes space for string data because string fields are padded with spaces to fill the allocated field size.

7. Sequential mode is slower at accessing specific records in the file. It uses space more efficiently because strings are not padded with spaces.

The above are just guidelines, and are not meant to be interpreted as hard and fast rules. It's important to understand that a file's access mode does not affect the physical file on disk, but only affects the way a program reads and writes the file data. In other words, any file—no matter which mode was used to create it—is simply a sequence of bytes stored on the disk. For example, we could create a file using random access mode, then later open and read it in binary access mode. As your programming skills develop, you will sometimes find that mixing file access modes is the preferred approach to your data storage needs. Until you are quite familiar with all three file access modes, however, I suggest you follow the above guidelines and limit yourself to one access mode per file.

FILE MANAGEMENT

This section demonstrates how to use a number of other file and disk related commands that are related to file management tasks.

Deleting Files

To delete a file, use the Kill statement

```
Kill filename
```

where *filename* is a string expression specifying the file or files to delete. It can contain a drive and path name, and can also contain the wild card characters * and ?. Trying to Kill a file that does not exist, a file that's open, or a file for which we do not have the needed access privileges generates an error. As you may know, the so-called *wildcard* characters * and ? can be used to specify groups of files. The * character stands for any sequence of 0 or more characters, while ? stands for any single character. Some examples are shown in Table 8.4.

Deleting and Creating Folders

To delete a folder (or subdirectory), use the RmDir statement:

```
RmDir path
```

path is a string expression that specifies the folder to delete, and can include a drive specification. If you try to delete a folder that does not exist or that is not empty (contains one or more files or folders), an error is generated.

Table 8.4   *Wildcard Characters*

File Specification	Matches	Does Not Match
DATA*.*	DATA.DAT	MYDATA.DAT
	DATASEPT.DAT	DATES.TXT
	DATASUMMARY.TXT	
DATA?.A*	DATA1.ASC	DATA.ASC
	DATA2.A	DATASEPT.ASC
	DATAX.ARG	DATAX.DAT
.	All files	-

To create a new folder, use the MkDir statement

```
MkDir path
```

where *path* specifies the name of the folder to create, and can include a full path and drive specification. If only a name is specified, the new folder is created in the current folder on the current drive.

Changing to Another Folder or Drive

To make another folder current, use the ChDir statement

```
ChDir path
```

where *path* specifies the new folder, and can include a drive specification. ChDir does not change the current drive. If the current drive is C: and you execute ChDir "D:\DATA," the current directory on drive D: is changed but C: remains the current drive.

To make another drive current, use the ChDrive statement

```
ChDrive drive
```

where *drive* specifies the new drive to make current. Only the first character of drive is significant. If we attempt to make an invalid drive current, an error is generated.

Getting Path and Folder Information

To determine the current path on a specified drive, use the **CurDir()** function

```
[path =] CurDir[(drive)]
```

where *drive* specifies the drive of interest. Only the first character of drive is significant, and it must refer to a valid drive, or an error will be generated. If the drive argument is omitted, **CurDir()** returns the current path on the current drive.

You can obtain the path of the current Visual Basic application by reading the **App** object's **Path** property:

```
CurrentPath = App.Path
```

This property returns the path where the project file (.VBP) is located if the application is running in the Visual Basic environment, and the path where the executable file (.EXE) is located when running the program as an executable file. This property is extremely useful when we want to be sure that a program's data or configuration files are stored in the same directory as the .EXE file. Be aware that the value returned by this property does not include a trailing backslash, so we must add it. The following code opens a file named CONFIG.DAT in the program's EXE directory:

```
Filename = App.Path
Filename = Filename & "\CONFIG.DAT"
Open Filename For Input as #1
```

 ## Current Path versus Application's Path

What's the difference between the current path on a drive and an application's path? An application's path is simply the path to the folder containing the program's executable file. It has no special status except that each application may want to keep certain files in this folder. A drive's current path points at the current default folder on that drive. Each drive in our system can have only one default path at a time, and this information is maintained by the operating system (although it can be changed by programs). The default path is the location where file operations will take place if a specific path is not specified. For example, the statement

```
Open "C:DATA.TXT" For Output As #1
```

will open a file in the folder pointed to by drive C:'s current path. A drive letter followed by only a colon always refers to the drive's current path. The operating system also maintains track of the default drive, which is the disk where file operations will occur if a specific disk is not requested. Thus,

```
Open "DATA.TXT" For Output As #1
```

would open the file on the default drive, in the folder indicated by that drive's default path. Likewise,

```
Open "\SALES\DATA.TXT" For Output As #1
```

would open the file in the \SALES folder on the default drive.

Finding Files

To obtain the name of the first file that matches a template, use the **Dir()** function:

```
[filename = ] Dir[(template)]
```

template is the file template to match. It can contain a drive specifier, path, and wildcard characters (as explained earlier in the chapter). The first time a program calls **Dir()**, it must pass a template argument. **Dir()** returns the name of the first file in the specified or current folder directory that matches template. If there is no match, an empty string is returned. If **Dir()** is called again one or more times with the template argument omitted, it returns the next file that matches the original template, or a null string if no other match exists.

The **Dir** function is typically used to see if a particular file exists. It's done by calling **Dir()** with the file name as argument, then seeing if a null string is returned:

```
If Dir "MYFILE.TXT" = "" Then
   ' File does not exist.
Else
   'File exists
End If
```

Dir can also be used to get a list of all files that match a template that includes wildcards. For example, the following code would load the List Box List1 with the names of all files with the .DAT extension in the specified directory:

```
Dim s As String
s = Dir "C:\DATA\*.DAT"
Do While s <> ""
   List1.AddItem s
   s = Dir
Wend
```

To change the name of a file or folder, or to move a file to a different folder on the same drive, use the **Name** statement:

```
Name oldfilespec As newfilespec
```

oldfilespec gives the name of the existing file or folder, and can include a drive and path. *newfilespec* gives the new file or folder name, and must refer to the same drive as *oldfilespec*. We cannot use **Name** with an open file.

To obtain the handle or mode of an open file, use the **FileAttr()** function:

```
[result =] FileAttr(filenum, flag)
```

filenum is the number associated with the file when it was opened.

flag specifies the type of information returned by the function. If flag = 1, **FileAttr()** returns a code indicating the mode in which the file was opened:

Return Value	File Mode
1	INPUT
2	OUTPUT
4	RANDOM
8	APPEND
32	BINARY

If flag = 2, **FileAttr()** returns the file's operating system handle.

FILE-RELATED CONTROLS

Most of what we do with files in Visual Basic will involve the Basic statements and functions presented so far. Other types of file access, such as loading a picture into a Picture Box control, are handled more or less automatically by the associated control. However, a few Visual Basic controls have been designed specifically to work with files. These controls are the topic of this section.

The three file-related controls are designed to help us navigate our system's disk drives. Think of how things are arranged on the disk. Each disk, or drive, is identified by a letter followed by a colon. On each drive are one or more folders, or subdirectories, arranged in a hierarchical structure. In each folder are one or more files, each with its own name. Thus, locating any file is a three-tiered process: drive, folder, file name. One control is designed to deal with each of these three levels.

File List Box

The FileListBox control displays a list of all or selected files in a specified folder for our selection. The folder whose files are listed is determined by the control's **Path** property. Thus, to list the files in the folder \DATA on drive C:, you would write:

```
File1.Path = "c:\data"
```

Often, the property for a FileListBox is obtained from a Directory List Box control, as we'll see later. The FileListBox control has several other properties you need to know about.

The **Pattern** property specifies the template for file names to be displayed. The default Pattern in "*.*" and it displays all files. To display, for example, only files with the .DAT extension, you would write:

```
File1.Pattern = "*.DAT"
```

We can use multiple templates separated by semicolons. Thus, the following code

```
File1.Pattern = "*.DAT;*.TXT;*.BAT"
```

would display only those files with the .DAT, .TXT, or .BAT extensions.

The **FileName** property returns the name of the file that is currently selected in the list. If no file is selected, this property returns a zero-length string. If we are using a FileListBox to permit the user to select a file, we retrieve the file name from this property. The path of the selected file is obtained separately, from the **Path** property. For example, if File1 is the name of a FileListBox control, the following code would open the file selected by the user.

```
Dim MyFile As String
...
MyFile = File1.Path & "\" & File1.Filename
If File1.Filename <> "" Then Open MyFile For Output As #1
...
```

We can set the **Filename()** property in code, which results in the specified file becoming selected (highlighted) in the control on-screen.

A number of events are associated with the FileListBox control. Several of them are the standard events supported by most Visual Basic controls, such as click. A couple of them, however, are special for this control. The **PathChange** event is triggered if the control's **Path** or **Filename** properties are changed in code. The **PatternChange** property is triggered if the **Pattern** property is changed. These events are used to synchronize the operation of a FileListBox with other parts of the program.

Directory List Box

The Directory List Box, or DirListBox, displays a list of directories, or folders. The user can utilize this list to navigate the folder structure of a drive. Selecting a folder in a DirListBox actually changes the current active path. By synchronizing a DirListBox with a FileListBox, we can easily provide a display of files in a user-selected folder.

The **Path** property sets and returns a DirListBox's current path. The control will display the name of the current folder with an open folder icon next to it. Above will be a heirarchical display of parent folders (if any), up to and including the root folder on the current drive. Below will be a list of any subfolders located in the current folder. This hierarchy is illustrated in Figure 8.1. In this figure the current folder is SAMPLES. Its parent folder is MSVC20, which is located in the root folder on drive D:, indicated by the backslash. Within the SAMPLES folder are five subfolders: MFC, OLE2, and so on. To make any visible folder current, the user must double-click it.

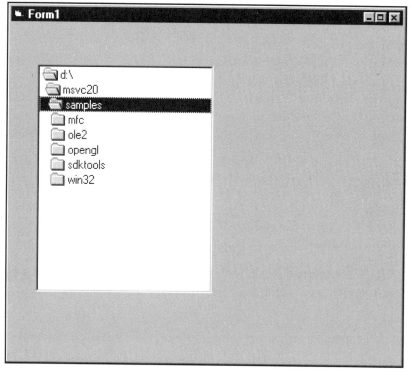

Figure 8.1 *A Directory list box.*

The DirListBox's **Change()** event is executed when the control's **Path** property changes, either by the user double-clicking a folder in the list or in code. You can use this event to synchronize a FileListBox with the DirListBox. The code shown here will result in the FileListBox's display updating to show files in any new folder that is selected in the DirListBox:

```
Private Sub Dir1_Change()

File1.Path = Dir1.Path

End Sub
```

Drive List Box

The Drive List Box control (DriveListBox) displays a list of available drives at run time. It takes the form of a dropdown list. When closed, it displays the letter of the current drive. We can pull down the list and select another drive; doing so not only changes the display in the control, but actually changes the system's current drive. The control's **Drive** property returns or sets the current drive. By assigning a DriveListBox's **Drive** property to a DirListBox's **Path** property, we can synchronize the two so that the DirListBox will display folders on the drive selected in the DriveListBox. This step is done in the DriveListBox's **Change()** event procedure, which is triggered any time the **Drive** property changes (in code or by the user). Here's the code:

```
Private Sub Drive1_Change()

Dir1.Path = Drive1.Drive

End Sub
```

If the DirListBox is synchronized with a FileListBox as described earlier, the three controls can be combined to provide a dialog box where the user can select a drive, select a folder, and then select a file. This combination is at the heart of implementing a File Open dialog.

Demonstrating the File-Related Controls

To demonstrate using the file-related controls, I first considered showing you how to create your own File Open or File Save dialog box. However, the Common Dialog control provides us with perfectly good Open and Save dialogs, so I wanted to come up with something that might actually be useful!

A file finding utility seemed like a good choice. Since I often have use for this program, other people are likely to need it, too.

A file finding utility is simple in concept. The user specifies a drive, a starting folder, and a file template. The program searches the specified folder and all subfolders for matching files, and displays them in a list. But how do we implement this in code? On the surface it sounds rather complicated. If you approached the problem from a brute force perspective, your solution might well end up being complicated, too! With some inside knowledge of how the DirListBox (directory list box) control works, however, the solution suddenly becomes greatly simplified. This is an excellent example of how an intimate knowledge of Visual Basic and all its parts is essential to solving programming problems with maximum efficiency.

Let's look at the problem again. We already know how to search a specific folder for files that match a template—just use the **Dir** function that was covered earlier in the chapter. The problem is extending the search to the subfolders of the starting folder, to their subfolders, and onward until the entire tree has been searched. If we closely examine the characteristics of the DirListBox control, we'll find the solution.

At run time, a DirListBox displays the drive's hierarchical folder structure. Above the current folder, the parent folder, its parent, and so on are listed—back to the drive's root directory. Below the current folder, its subfolders are listed. Each item in this list has an index number, as follows:

- The current folder's index is -1.

- Folders above the current folder have negative indexes.

- The number of subfolders in the current folder is indicated by the control's **ListCount** property. These subfolders have indexes starting at 0 and running to ListCount -1.

This last characteristic of the DirListBox is the one we will use. It enables us to obtain the names of the current folder's subfolders. We then apply a recursive algorithm as follows:

1. Start in the directory specified by the user.

2. Use the **Dir** function to search the current directory for files that match the template. If any files are found, add them to the list of matching files.

3. Check for any subfolders in this folder. If none exists, we are finished with this folder, and can move "up" one level to the parent folder. If we have returned to the starting folder, we are finished. If we have subfolders, use the **List** and **ListCount** properties to obtain the subfolder names and create a list of them.

4. Make the first folder in this list current.

5. Return to step 2.

This general type of algorithm is called *recursion*. The same procedures are applied over and over to the data until there is no more data to process. In this case the "data" consists of folders. As you'll see in the demonstration program, the code required to implement the file search is actually quite simple. As is often the case in computer programming, having the proper algorithm is an important step in designing code.

Creating the Form

One important Visual Basic technique illustrated by this project is the use of hidden controls. Just because a control is hidden (**Visible** property = *False*) does not mean it is nonfunctional. Of course the user cannot interact with it, but it can be used by code. In this project we will use a hidden DirListBox control to implement the file search algorithm.

Start a new project. Add a DriveListBox and two DirListBox controls, setting the **Visible** property of one of the DirListBoxes to *False*. Next, add a CheckBox, a ListBox, and a control array of three Command Buttons. Finally, add one Text Box and three labels to identify the text Box, visible DirListBox, and DriveList Box. Our form now looks more or less like Figure 8.2. The DirListBox superimposed on the ListBox is the one that will be hidden. Set control and form properties as shown in Listing 8.1.

Listing 8.1   Objects and Properties in FINDFILE.FRM

```
Begin VB.Form Form1
   Appearance      =    0  '3D
BorderStyle     =    1  'Fixed Single
   Caption         =    "File Finding Utility"
   Begin VB.ListBox lstFiles
      BeginProperty Font
         name            =    "Courier New"
         size            =    9.75
```

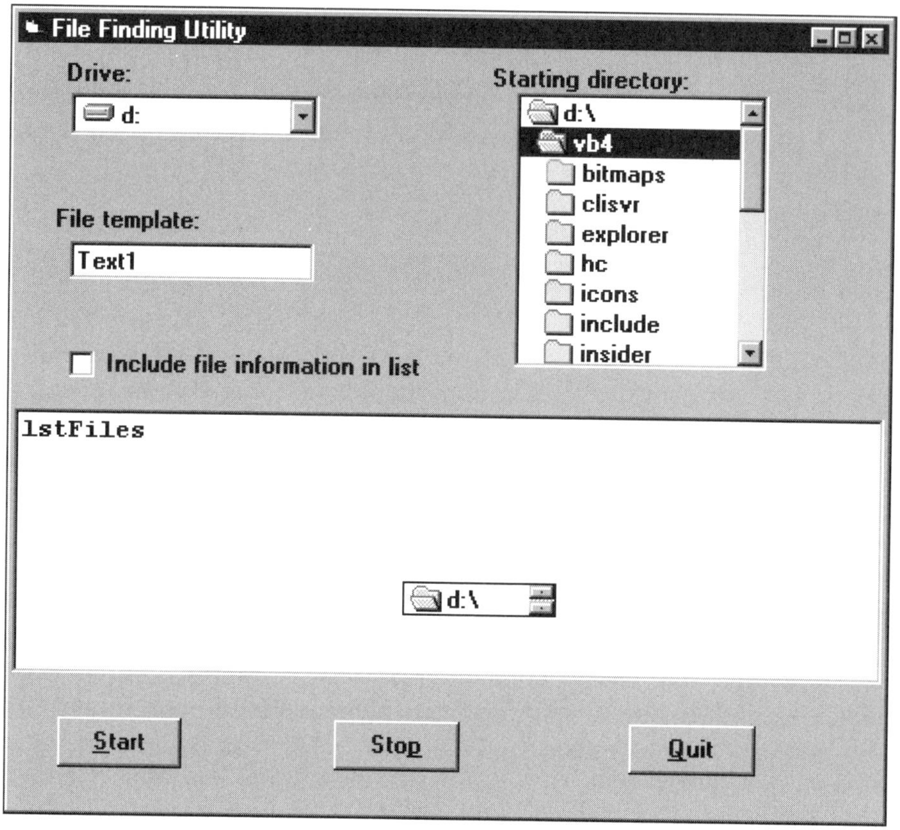

Figure 8.2   *The File Finding Utility form during design.*

```
    EndProperty
End
Begin VB.CheckBox chkFileInfo
    Caption        =   "Include file information in list"
End
Begin VB.DirListBox dirHidden
Visible        =   False
End
Begin VB.DirListBox dirStart
End
Begin VB.DriveListBox Drive1
    Appearance     =   1  '3D
End
Begin VB.CommandButton Command1
    Caption        =   "&Quit"
    Index          =   2
End
Begin VB.CommandButton Command1
    Appearance     =   0  'Flat
    Caption        =   "Sto&p"
```

```
      Index          =    1
   End
   Begin VB.CommandButton Command1
      Appearance     =    0  'Flat
      Caption        =    "&Start"
      Index          =    0
   End
   Begin VB.TextBox txtPattern
      Text           =    "Text1"
   End
   Begin VB.Label Label3
      Alignment      =    1  'Right Justify
      Caption        =    "File template:"
   End
   Begin VB.Label Label2
      Alignment      =    1  'Right Justify
      Caption        =    "Starting directory:"
   End
   Begin VB.Label Label1
      Alignment      =    1  'Right Justify
      Caption        =    "Drive:"
   End
End
```

Now for the code. The program requires two global variables, one a type Boolean flag that signals whether the user has canceled the search; the other a type Integer that keeps track of the depth of the search—in other words, how many folders "deep" are we. These variables should be declared in the General Declarations section of code:

Listing 8.2   General Declarations in FINDFILE.FRM

```
Option Explicit

' Global flag to abort search.

Dim Halt As Boolean
Dim Depth As Integer
```

The program actions are triggered by the **Click()** event procedure for the Command Button control array. It's quite simple, as you can see in Listing 8.3. To start the search, it calls the procedure **StartSearch()**. To terminate an ongoing search, it sets the flag variable Halt to *True*. And to exit the program, it executes the End statement.

Listing 8.3   The Command Button Click() Event Procedure

```
Private Sub Command1_Click(Index As Integer)
```

```
Select Case Index
    Case 0 'Start button
        Call StartSearch
    Case 1 'Stop button
        Halt = True
    Case 2       ' Exit button
        End
End Select

End Sub
```

The **StartSearch()** procedure is where the action begins. This is a general procedure that we add to the module with the **Insert()** Procedure command. Its code is shown in Listing 8.4. First, code in this procedure clears the List Box where the search results will be displayed and sets the Halt flag to *False*. It then disables all of the controls that should not be available during a search.

Next we turn our attention to the hidden DirListBox control. It is this control's **Change()** event procedure that triggers the actual search action. We need to set this control's **Path** property to the folder that the user specified as the start folder for the search, obtained from the **Path** property of the visible DirListBox. This property change will normally trigger the control's **Change()** event. But what if the hidden DirListBox control's **Path** property is already pointing at the desired start directory? No **Change()** event will be generated, so we must generate one ourselves (remember that event procedures can be called in code just like non-event procedures). Here is the code:

```
If dirHidden.Path = dirStart.Path Then
    dirHidden_Change
Else
    dirHidden.Path = dirStart.Path
End If
```

Note that we display the hourglass mouse pointer while the search is in progress. Once that **Change()** event is triggered for the hidden DirListBox control, execution recurses within event procedures until the search is completed, at which time it returns to the same location in the **StartSearch()** procedure. The final lines of code in this procedure re-enable the form's controls that were disabled when the search began, and return the normal mouse pointer.

Listing 8.4   The StartSearch() Procedure

```
Private Sub StartSearch()

' We come here to start a search.
```

```
' Empty the List Box.
lstFiles.Clear

' Clear the Halt flag.
Halt = False

' Disable all controls except the Stop Button.
Command1(0).Enabled = False
Command1(1).Enabled = True
Command1(2).Enabled = False
Drive1.Enabled = False
dirStart.Enabled = False
txtPattern.Enabled = False

' If the invisible Dir list is already pointing to
' the same directory as the visible Dir list, we must
' trigger a Change event. If not, change its Path property,
' which will automatically trigger a Change event.

' It is the dirHidden.Change event that triggers the search process.

' Display the hourglass mouse pointer.
Screen.MousePointer = 11

If dirHidden.Path = dirStart.Path Then
    dirHidden_Change
Else
    dirHidden.Path = dirStart.Path
End If

' We reach here after the search is complete.
' Re-enable all controls except the Stop button.
Screen.MousePointer = 0
Command1(0).Enabled = True
Command1(1).Enabled = False
Command1(2).Enabled = True
Drive1.Enabled = True
dirStart.Enabled = True
txtPattern.Enabled = True

End Sub
```

As noted earlier, the search begins when the hidden DirListBox's **Change()** event procedure is triggered. The code in that procedure is shown in Listing 8.5. The code here is really simpler than it looks. The first step is searching the current folder (the one we just changed to) for files that match the search template entered by the user. The path is placed in the List Box, then a loop obtains the names of all matching files by calling the **Dir$** function repeatedly. These names are also added to the List Box, along with file information if the FileInfo option is selected. Note that there are Visual Basic functions called **FileDateTime()** and **FileLen()** that we use to obtain the desired information about the file.

Once all of the files in the current folder have been processed, it's time to turn to any subfolders. Remember, the DirListBox's **ListCount** property will tell us the number of subfolders. By using that value, plus the control's **List()** indexed property, we can loop through the list of subfolders and place them in an array.

When this array is loaded with the names of any subfolders in the current folder, the rest is easy. We set up a loop that goes through the array, assigning each subfolder name (which includes the full path) to the hidden DirListBox's **Path** property. And guess what? Each time we do this, we trigger another **Change()** event procedure and the entire process I have just described is repeated.

Listing 8.5 The Hidden DirListBox's Change() Event Procedure

```
Private Sub dirHidden_Change()

' Triggered when the hidden directory list changes. It is here
' that the actual search is performed.

Dim Path As String, FileName As String
Dim FileName1 As String, Path1 As String, Entry As String
Dim NumDirs As Integer, X As Integer, Y As Integer
Dim DirAdded As Boolean, Spaces As Integer

Depth = Depth + 1

' For testing as described in text, uncomment the next line.
debug.Print "Depth = ", Depth

' Get the current path and add a backslash if necessary.
Path = dirHidden.Path
If Right(Path, 1) <> "\" Then
    Path = Path & "\"
End If

' Create the full search pattern by combining the current path
' with the file pattern from the txtPattern Text Box.
Path1 = Path & txtPattern.TEXT

' The Dir function returns an empty string if
' a matching file is not found, and the file name if
' a matching file is found.
FileName = Dir(Path1)
DirAdded = False
```

```
' Loop as long as a matching file is found.
Do Until FileName = ""

    ' If the directory name has not already been added to the
    ' List Box, add it now.
    If (DirAdded = False) Then
        lstFiles.AddItem "[ " & dirHidden.Path & " ]"
        DirAdded = True
    End If

    ' Start building the next List Box entry.
    Entry = "    " & FileName

    ' If the FileInfo check box is checked, add the
    ' file's date, time, and length to the entry.
    If chkFileInfo.VALUE Then
        FileName1 = Path & FileName
        Spaces = 16-Len(FileName)
        Entry = Entry & Space(Spaces) & FileDateTime(FileName1)
        Spaces = 20-Len(FileDateTime(FileName1))
        Entry = Entry & Space(Spaces) & FileLen(FileName1)
    End If

    ' Add the entry to the List Box.
    lstFiles.AddItem Entry

    ' Look for the next matching file.
    FileName = Dir$
Loop

' How many subdirectories are in the current directory?
NumDirs = dirHidden.ListCount

' Put the subdirectory names in an array.
ReDim DirList(NumDirs) As String

For X = 0 To NumDirs-1
    DirList(X) = dirHidden.List(X)
Next X

' For each subfolder, repeat the search process. Call DoEvents
' to enable user to abort the search by clicking the Stop
' Command button.
For X = 0 To NumDirs-1
    dirHidden.Path = DirList(X)
    Y = DoEvents()
    If Halt Then
        Exit Sub
    End If
Next X

Depth = Depth-1

End Sub
```

When considering how this recursion works, it is essential to understand that when a function calls itself—which is what the **Change()** event procedure does by changing the control's **Path** property—each call results in a completely new and separate copy of the procedure being executed. And each of these copies has its own independent array of subfolder names, and its own set of other local variables. Each copy of the **Change()** event procedure sits waiting until the "lower" copies of the procedure have completed (by running out of subfolders to process). Then execution returns to the specific copy of the procedure and continues there until its array of subfolders is exhausted, at which time execution passes "up" one more level. Only when each and every subfolder off the starting subfolder has been processed does execution return to the **StartSearch()** procedure.

To get a feel for what's happening, use the debug.Print statement to display the value of the Depth variable by uncommenting the line of code near the start of the **Change()** event procedure. You'll see a sequence of values displayed in the Debug window similar to this:

```
1
2
3
3
2
3
3
4
4
3
2
```

At each iteration, the value displayed gives us a feeling for how many "layers" of **Change()** event procedures exist, each with its own array of subfolders. Once you understand the basic principle behind iterative algorithms, you'll probably find other programming challenges to which they can be applied.

There's a bit more code in this project, as shown in Listing 8.6. Nothing here is too complicated—you should be able to figure out how it works from the comments in the listing. The final code is shown after the example of performing a Find in Figure 8.3.

I have found this to be a handy little utility. Actually, I don't use it as a stand-alone program very often, but I have incorporated its algorithm and code into other projects. For example, we can use the three file-related controls plus the

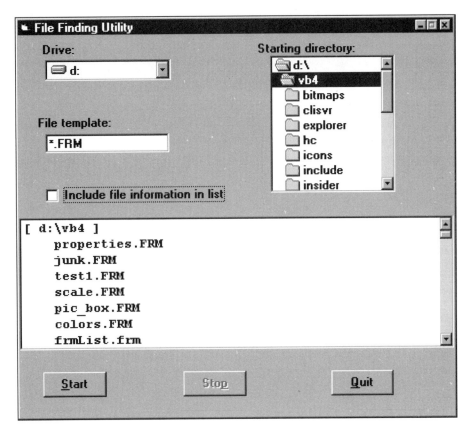

Figure 8.3 *The File Finding Utility in action.*

file finding techniques presented here to create a File Open dialog box that permits the user to find files anywhere on the disk.

Finally, I want to mention that this project is an excellent example of using creative thinking to find a use for a Visual Basic control that its creators probably never envisioned. There are many other possibilities in the Visual Basic toolbox, but remember—a working knowledge of the tools is a prerequisite for getting the most out of them!

Listing 8.6   Remaining Code in FINDFILE.FRM

```
Private Sub Drive1_Change()

' If the user changes drives, pass the new path
' to the Dir list control.

dirStart.Path = Drive1.Drive
```

```
End Sub


Private Sub Form_Load()

Halt = False
txtPattern.TEXT = "*.EXE"
lstFiles.Clear
depth = 0

End Sub


Private Sub Text1_GotFocus()

' Highlight entire contents of Text Box.

txtPattern.SelStart = 0
txtPattern.SelLength = Len(txtPattern.TEXT)

End Sub

Private Sub txtPattern_GotFocus()

' Highlight Text Box contents when it gets the focus.

txtPattern.SelStart = 0
txtPattern.SelLength = Len(txtPattern.TEXT)

End Sub
```

Serial Communication

CHAPTER 9

Serial
communication
is the most
popular method
for computers to
exchange data.
With the
Visual Basic
Comm control,
adding serial
capabilities to
your program
is easy.

It's a rare computer that operates in total isolation these days. Even computers that are not a part of a local area network frequently communicate with other computers to exchange data files, programs, and electronic mail. Most people who access CompuServe, America Online, or the Internet do so with serial communications (via a modem). And if you need to transfer that 15 megabyte data file from one computer to another, you'll find that setting up a serial link is much easier than shuffling floppy diskettes for an hour!

SERIAL COMMUNICATION FUNDAMENTALS

Serial communication is called *serial* because the individual bits of data follow each other over the same electrical connection. It contrasts with parallel communication where multiple connections enable the link to carry more than one bit at a time (for example, your printer port). Serial com-

229

munication is bidirectional, meaning that data flows in both directions: from computer A to computer B and also from B to A.

Serial communication is carried out by means of a *serial port* on your computer. Serial ports have many names, including comm port, RS-232 port, and asynchronous communications port. Whatever the moniker, it refers to the same thing. In theory, a serial link requires only three wires: one wire for the data going out, one for the data coming in, and a ground wire. If you look at the serial ports on the back of your computer, however, you will find that the physical connection is either a 9-pin D shell on newer models or a 25-pin D shell on older systems. Why all the extra connections? Many of the pins remain unused in the 25-pin serial connection, however, many more than three lines are employed. These "extra" lines do not carry data but are used for *handshaking* signals. Handshaking signals are used by the computers on the two ends of the serial link to coordinate their actions.

Of course, serial communication links can be used for much more than linking one computer to another. They are also used to link a computer to modems, mice, plotters, and printers, to mention just a few. No matter what two devices are involved in a serial link, however, certain things remain constant. Serial communication standards ensure that all serial ports follow the same rules. Within this set of rules, however, there is some flexibility. You can control how fast data is sent over the serial link, and you can also control certain aspects of the data format. These settings are called *communication parameters*. For serial communication to operate properly, the devices at both ends of the link must be using the same parameters.

Serial Communication Parameters

Perhaps the most important parameter is the *baud rate*, which determines the speed at which data is transmitted. The baud rate is approximately equal to the number of bits per second. Serial port hardware supports a variety of standard baud rates:

110	14400
300	19200
600	38400
1200	56000
2400	128000
9600	256000

Another parameter is the *word length*, which specifies the number of bits that make up each unit of data transmitted. While serial hardware can support word lengths of 5 to 8 bits, PCs always work with word lengths of 7 or 8 bits.

The *parity* parameter determines whether a parity bit is added to each word. When used, a parity bit enables the serial port hardware to detect certain kinds of errors in transmission. Parity can be set to None, Odd, or Even. A setting of None does not add a parity bit. When Odd parity is used, the parity bit is set to 0 or 1 so that the total number of bits set to 1 in the data word/parity bit combination is odd. Even parity works the same way, but the total number of set bits will be even. At the receiving end, the hardware looks at each data word/parity bit set to see if the proper number of bits is set (even or odd). If a single bit has flipped due to a transmission error, the receiving hardware will detect the error and request that the word be resent.

The *stop bit* parameter specifies how many stop bits are used. In serial communication, start and stop bits delineate the beginning and end of each data word. One start bit is always used, and one or two stop bits can be used. Most PC communications use one stop bit.

 **Serial Ports and Modems**

One of the most common uses for serial ports is to connect a modem (even if your modem is internal, it is still logically connected to one of the system's serial ports). Do you need to worry about that alphabet soup of modem protocols when programming a serial port? In a word, no. The various protocols that adorn modem advertisements (such as V.32bis and MNP5) have to do with various transmission speeds, error correction protocols, and data compression standards. When you use a modem attached to a serial port (as we'll do later in the chapter), you may send it commands specifying which of these protocols to use. However, the serial port is still just a serial port and is treated no differently whether there is a modem, a printer, or a plotter on the other end.

USING THE COMM CONTROL

While serial communication is simple in principle, in practice you will understand what people mean when they say "the devil is in the details." Serial communication is filled with details, including the various handshake lines that may or may not be used in a specific situation, the importance of setting the serial parameters properly, and so on. Fortunately, Microsoft has extended the practice of software components to this problem, providing us with the Communications control, or Comm control, which greatly simplifies the job of supporting serial communication in your Visual Basic programs.

The Comm control is not visible during program execution, since its sole job is to act as an intermediary between your program and a serial port. You can have two or more Comm controls in a program, each one linked to a different serial port. Data to be transmitted is placed in one of the control's properties; data received by the serial port is retrieved from another of the control's properties. Additional properties are used to set and read serial port parameters. Before we look at these properties in detail, we first need to understand the two basic methods of using the Comm control.

Polling versus Event-Driven Communications

One of the more difficult aspects of serial port programming is dealing with incoming data. To be more precise, the problem lies in knowing when data has been received by the port and is available to be read by the program. The Comm control offers two approaches to this problem.

- *Polling* is the traditional method by which Basic programs handled serial communication before the advent of the Comm control. It is still supported by the Comm control and is perfectly suitable for some applications. This method requires the program code to check the status of the serial port on a regular basis to see if data has been received, if an error has occurred, or if there has been a change in the status of the handshaking lines.

- *Event-driven communications* is a more powerful technique in which the Comm control generates an event whenever data is received. Your program does not have to sit idly waiting for data. It can busy itself with other tasks and still respond immediately whenever the serial port has data to be read. The same event is also triggered if a communications error occurs, or if one of the handshaking lines changes status.

Polling may be perfectly suitable for relatively simple applications like a phone dialer, where the program only has to keep an eye on the serial port. For more demanding applications, however, you will find that the event-driven approach is superior.

Comm Control Properties

The Comm control has a long list of properties, many of which are unique to this control. A number of these properties are related to the various handshaking protocols and signal lines that serial ports support. We won't discuss these advanced properties here, since they are rarely involved in basic serial communication. Rather, we will concentrate on the more fundamental properties that are always associated with the Comm control.

Setting Serial Port Parameters

You set serial port parameters by means of the **CommPort** and **Settings** properties. **CommPort** specifies the serial port to which the control is linked. It can be set to any value between 1 (the default) and 99, but an error will occur if you specify a port that does not actually exist on the system in use. The **CommPort** property must be set before the port can be opened.

Communications parameters such as baud rate and parity are designated using the **Settings** property. You place a string with the following format in the **Settings** property:

```
"BBBB,P,D,S"
```

In this **Settings** string, *BBBB* is the baud rate, *P* is the parity, *D* is the number of data bits, and *S* is the number of stop bits. If you do not explicitly change a Comm control's parameters, the default settings are 9600 baud, no parity , 8 bit data word, and 1 stop bit. The valid baud rates are 110, 300, 600, 1200, 2400, 9600, 14400, 19200, 38400, 56000, 128000, and 256000. Note that the four highest rates are listed in the Visual Basic Help system as being "reserved," although there is no explanation of what this means.

The valid parity values are shown in Table 9.1.

Table 9.1 *Parity Settings*

Setting	Description
E	Even
M	Mark
N	None (default)
O	Odd
S	Space

The valid data bit values are 4, 5, 6, 7, and the default 8. Valid stop bit values are 1 (the default), 1.5, and 2.

Here is an example. The following code would set the Comm control named Comm1 to link with serial port 1 using 2400 baud, no parity, 8 bit data word, and 1 stop bit:

```
Comm1.CommPort = 1
Comm1.Settings = "2400,N,8,1"
```

Sending and Receiving Data

Before reviewing the details of how the Comm control sends and receives data, you need to understand the concept of a *buffer*. A buffer is a temporary storage location where data is held before processing. The Comm control has two buffers, an input buffer and an output buffer. Proper use of these buffers simplifies serial port programming and results in more reliable communications.

When your program sends data to the Comm control for transmission, it is placed in the output buffer. The Comm control reads data from the buffer and transmits it. Likewise, when the Comm control receives data, it is placed in the input buffer where your program can read it. Reading the Input property removes the data from the buffer, so there is no danger of reading the same data twice. These buffers make it possible for your program to operate without being perfectly synchronized with the serial port. If your program sends data to the Comm control faster than the serial port can transmit it, no problem. The extra data will remain in the output buffer until it can be transmitted. Similarly, if your program is reading data from the Comm control more slowly that the serial port is receiving it, the input buffer will hold the data until the program catches up. Without these buffers, your program would have to utilize the various handshaking signals to ensure that its activities are synchronized with the serial port—a difficult programming task to be sure!

The output buffer's default size is 512 bytes. To set a different buffer size or determine the current size, use the **OutBufferSize** property. The default setting is usually sufficient, but you will need to increase it if an overflow error occurs (see Error Handling later in the chapter). Setting the output buffer size too large will not improve performance; it will only reduce the amount of memory available to the application.

To determine how many characters are currently in the output buffer, read the **OutBufferCount** property. To clear the buffer and erase its current contents without transmitting them, set the **OutBufferCount** property to 0.

The size of the input buffer is set with the **InBufferSize** property, whose default value is 1024. As with the output buffer, too small a value can result in overflow errors, while too large a value simply wastes memory. The number of characters currently in the input buffer is specified by the **InBufferCount** property. Setting this property to 0 clears the input buffer.

To transmit data over the serial line—or, more precisely, to place the data in the output buffer—put the data in the Comm control's **Output** property. To read data that was received by the serial port, use the **Input** property. By default, reading the **Input** property obtains all the characters currently in the input buffer. To read a specified number of characters, set the **InputLen** property to the desired number of characters before reading the **Input** property. If the input buffer contains fewer characters than specified by **InputLen**, **Input** returns a null string. You can use the **InBufferCount** property to be sure that the buffer contains enough characters before reading it. Reset **InputLen** to its default value of 0 to return to reading all characters from the input buffer.

Here is an output example. The following code sends each character typed on a form to the Comm control.

```
Private Sub Form_KeyPress (KeyAscii As Integer)
   MSComm1.Output = Chr$(KeyAscii)
End Sub
```

As an input example, this code checks to see that there is input data available; if so, it uses the Print method to display it on the form:

```
If MSComm1.InBufferCount Then
   Form1.Print MSComm1.Input
End If
```

Determining Port Status

How can you determine the status of the serial port? The **CommEvent** property returns a code that represents the most recent change in port status. These changes include error conditions as well as communications events. Values between 1001 and 1010 represent error codes; you can refer to the Visual Basic Help system for details on what the various codes represent and on the defined constants available for your programs. Values between 1 and 7 represent communication events—that is, normal things that occur during error-free serial communication. It's important to realize that the value of the **CommEvent** property reflects the most recent event or change in the Comm control. If the most recent occurrence was reception of data, the property value will be 2. If the most recent occurrence was an error, the property value will be the code for that error. How do we know when something of importance has happened? The answer to this question is our next topic.

The OnComm Event

Central to most uses of the Comm control is the **OnComm** event. This event is triggered by a change in the status of the Comm control (with some limitations, as explained below). Expressed another way, this event is triggered any time the **CommEvent** property changes. We now have the answer to the previous question, "How can we know when the Comm control's status has changed?" The answer is simple: by using the **OnComm** event procedure. In this event procedure, we place code that tests the value of the **CommEvent** property, which branches accordingly. The most important use for this event procedure is to read data from the **Input** property after it has been received. It can also be used to react to error conditions. The essential communications events are listed in Table 9.2.

The **SThreshold** property specifies the number of characters in the output buffer that trigger the **CommEvent** procedure. The settings for this property are shown on the next page.

Table 9.2 *Communication Events*

Constant	Value of CommEvent	Description
comEvSend	1	There are fewer than SThreshold number of characters in the transmit buffer.
comEvReceive	2	Received RThreshold number of characters. This event is generated continuously until you use the Input property to remove the data from the receive buffer.
comEvRing	6	Ring detected. Some UARTs (universal asynchronous receiver-transmitters) may not support this event.
comEvEOF	7	End Of File (ASCII character 26) character received.

0   OnComm is never triggered for data transmission.

1   OnComm is triggered when the output buffer is empty.

n   OnComm is triggered when the number of unsent characters in the output buffer falls below *n*.

You can use this event to pace data transmission from your program to the Output property. When transmitting large quantities of data—for example, a text file—your program may write data to the Comm control's **Output** property faster than it can be sent, running the risk of an overflow error. You can eliminate this problem by using use the **ComEvSend** event, which only allows the program to send another block of data to the **Output** property when the contents of the output buffer fall below a certain level.

The **RThreshold** property specifies how many characters must be received before triggering an **OnComm** event. If you want the program to respond each time a single character is received, set this property to 1. If you set **RThreshold** to 0, **OnComm** will not be triggered, regardless of how many characters are received.

A Demonstration

To demonstrate the use of the Comm control, I have created a very simple program implementing a *dumb terminal.* By definition, a dumb terminal does nothing more than send what you type to the serial port and display on-screen any text received by the serial port. Text is displayed in a Text Box control. I could have used the Print method to display the text directly on a form, but the Text Box's built-in scrolling capabilities are useful when the text exceeds the form length. The form has only two controls, the Text Box and one MSComm control. Set the Text Box's **Multiline** property to *True* and its **ScrollBars** property to *Both.* The form's objects and properties are given in Listing 9.1, and the operating program is shown in Figure 9.1.

Listing 9.1   Objects and Properties in COMMDEMO.FRM

```
Begin VB.Form Form1
    Caption        =    "Terminal"
    Begin VB.TextBox Text1
        MultiLine      =    -1   'True
        ScrollBars     =    3    'Both
    End
    Begin MSCommLib.MSComm MSComm1
    End
End
```

Figure 9.1 *The dumb terminal program.*

The code for this program is shown in Listing 9.2. In the **Form_Load** event procedure, we initialize the Comm control and open the port. I selected the communications parameters of 14000,E,7,1 because they are required by my CompuServe connection to test the program. You will need to set these parameters according to your own requirements. Note that I also set the **RThreshold** property to 1 to trigger the **OnComm** event each time a single character is received.

The Text Box control's **KeyPress** event procedure links the user's input to the Comm control. Rather than sending each individual character as it is typed, this procedure saves the input in a buffer and sends it all at once when the user presses the Enter key.

Received data is handled in the **OnComm()** event procedure. After checking the **CommEvent** property to see that the event was indeed triggered by receipt of data, the code adds the received character to the end of the Text Box's **Text** property, then moves the insertion point to the end of the text.

Listing 9.2   Code in COMMDEMO.FRM

```
Option Explicit

Dim Buf1 As String

Private Sub Text1_KeyPress(KeyAscii As Integer)

' Add the key to the buffer.
Buf1 = Buf1 & Chr$(KeyAscii)
```

```
' If it was a carriage return send the
' buffer contents to the Comm control and empty the buffer.
If KeyAscii = 13 Then
    MSComm1.Output = Buf1
    Buf1 = ""
End If

End Sub

Private Sub Form_Load()

' Initialize the Comm control.
MSComm1.CommPort = 1
MSComm1.Settings = "14400,E,7,1"

' Comm event will be triggered when
' a single character is received.
MSComm1.RThreshold = 1

' Open the port.
MSComm1.PortOpen = True

End Sub


Private Sub Form_Resize()

' Set Text Box to fill the form.
Text1.Width = Form1.ScaleWidth
Text1.Height = Form1.ScaleHeight
Text1.Left = 0
Text1.TOP = 0

End Sub

Private Sub Form_Unload(Cancel As Integer)

' Close the port.
MSComm1.PortOpen = False

End Sub

Private Sub MSComm1_OnComm()

' When a comm event occurs.

' Was it a "receive" event? If so, add the received character
' to the Text Box and set the insertion point at the end of
' the text. Other events are ignored.

Select Case MSComm1.CommEvent
    Case comEvReceive
        Text1.TEXT = Text1.TEXT & MSComm1.Input
```

```
        Text1.SelStart = Len(Text1.TEXT)
End Select

End Sub
```

If you use this program with a modem, you'll have to type the modem commands yourself (the commands are usually sent automatically by a communications program). Most modems adhere to the AT command set, originally developed by Hayes for their modems. The first command you should send is ATZ, which resets and initializes the modem. The model will respond "OK." There are a few other commands in Table 9.3; refer to your modem documentation for more information.

This very basic demonstration program is intended to show you only the fundamentals of using the Comm control. It includes no error handling and is vulnerable to many problems in use. Even with the Comm control, writing a full-featured and reliable serial communications program is a major task. Whenever I need anything but the most basic communications capabilities in a Visual Basic program, I always investigate the third party market for a custom control rather than trying to do the job myself using the Comm control.

Table 9.3 *Modem Commands*

Command	Description
ATDT	Dial the following number using tone dialing. For example, ATDT5551212 would cause the modem to dial 555-1212.
ATE	Disable echoing of input. Use this command if the program is displaying everything you type twice.
ATH	Hang up the phone.

Multimedia Magic

Some say that multimedia is the wave of the future. If this is true, Visual Basic can be your surfboard.

It seems that everyone is going multimedia crazy. You can't open a daily newspaper without seeing ads for "multimedia PCs" on sale at the local lawn and garden store or gas station. An exaggeration perhaps, but you know what I'm saying. Lots of people have heard about multimedia, and more and more of them are expecting to see multimedia when they fire up their PCs.

What does this mean for you, Joe or Jane Programmer? When programming for fun, multimedia projects can be very enjoyable and rewarding. If you program for a living, knowing multimedia is a necessity. You can bet your competition does! Whatever the reasons, you'll be pleasantly surprised at how easy multimedia programming is, since all of the essential capabilities are built into Visual Basic and Windows.

I won't pretend that this chapter provides complete coverage of Visual Basic's multimedia capabilities. The subject would require an entire book, and in fact a book—and a very good one at that—

has been written by Scott Jarol: *Visual Basic 4 Multimedia Adventure Set*, published by Coriolis Group Books. For an in-depth treatment, I suggest you turn to Scott's book. My goal in this chapter is simply to show you how to perform the basic, common multimedia operations, namely playing sound and video.

WHAT IS MULTIMEDIA?

If we try to pin down the meaning of the word *multimedia*, I think you'll find it more elusive than it appears at first glance. *Media* is the plural of *medium*, a means or method of communication. Multimedia, then, literally means *more than one method of communication*. When your kid sister is screaming at you and whacking you on the head at the same time, that's multimedia!

Of course, this is a far cry from computer multimedia! When you experience a computer playing stereo sound through a pair of high-tech speakers while showing a video on-screen, that's multimedia. But what about a hypertext presentation that combines text and pictures—is that multimedia? How about an animated icon? It can be difficult to determine the exact boundaries. Even more importantly, it doesn't matter! Whether you call it multimedia, interface enhancement, or chopped liver, the bottom line is still the same: You need to know how to program this stuff. Thanks to Windows and Visual Basic, it's not too great a challenge.

THE MULTIMEDIA PC STANDARD

While not all multimedia requires special hardware, much of it does. In order to reduce confusion and give developers a target platform, Microsoft developed the *Multimedia PC (MPC) standard*, a specification of the minimum hardware required for a computer to be considered MPC compatible. Here's the list:

- A 386SX or better microprocessor

- A minimum of 2 megabytes of memory

- A VGA display system

- An MPC-compatible sound card supporting PCM playback of WAVE files, MIDI playback through a synthesizer, and an internal audio mixer

- A CD-ROM drive with a seek time under one second and a data transfer rate of at least 150 kilobytes per second

By today's hardware standards, such a system seems almost quaint. In fact, it's doubtful that you could buy a system with exactly those specifications without heading for the flea market in Last Chance, Nevada. With a CD-ROM built into almost every PC sold today, the only necessary addition is the sound card. If your system is not MPC ready, I recommend investigating the various available multimedia kits, including a sound card, speakers, CD-ROM drive, and software. This route is probably the easiest and most economical way to upgrade.

Note that the equipment on an MPC compatible PC does not encompass all the possible multimedia hardware. Various kinds of specialized devices, such as video disk players and image scanners, are supported under Windows' multimedia capabilities. The MPC standard simply defines the minimum level of hardware that a developer can assume the end user will have.

THE WINDOWS MEDIA CONTROL INTERFACE

Programs use the *Windows Media Control Interface*, or MCI, to interact with multimedia hardware. Hardware can consist of any media devices that Windows supports—audio CD players, audio boards, MIDI sequencers, video disc players, and videotape players and recorders. At the program end is a standardized command syntax. Your program issues standard commands and the MCI, working with the specific drivers for the device in use, translates your commands to the exact signals required to carry out the requested action. Thus, the Play command starts playback whether it's an audio CD, a MIDI file, or a video clip. Figure 10.1 illustrates the relationship between your program, the MCI, and multimedia devices. Table 10.1 lists the multimedia devices supported by Windows. New devices are added as they become popular, so this list may have expanded already by the time you read this.

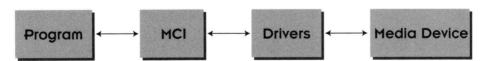

Figure 10.1 *The Media Control Interface mediates interactions between your program and multimedia hardware devices.*

Table 10.1   *Multimedia Devices Supported by Windows*

Device ID	Description
AVIVideo	Digital video
CDAudio	Standard audio CD
DAT	Digital audio tape
DigitalVideo	Digital video
MMMovie	Multimedia movie
Other	Undefined device
Overlay	Analog video
Scanner	Image scanner
Sequencer	MIDI sequencer
VCR	Video cassette recorder
Videodisc	Videodisc player
WaveAudio	Digital audio

Note that the term *device* does not refer to a discrete physical component such as a sound card or a CD-ROM drive. It's more accurate to think of a device as one format of multimedia data that Windows is capable of playing. For example, CDAudio and WaveAudio are two distinct multimedia devices that use the computer's sound card to play digital music. They differ in the source of the digital data—an audio CD in the CD-ROM drive in the case of CDAudio and a file on disk in the case of WaveAudio. AVIVideo requires no special hardware at all, playing digital video images on standard video display hardware (although a sound card, if present, will be used to play the accompanying soundtrack).

How Multimedia Sound Works

With digital sound, the original audio waveform is sampled digitally and the resulting digital samples, or numerical values, are saved. During playback those digital values are retrieved and sent to a digital-to-analog converter (DAC) on the sound card, which converts them back into a reasonable approximation of the original waveform. The source of the digital data can be either a WAVE file (*.WAV) on disk or a standard audio CD in the computer's CD-ROM drive.

Musical Instrument Digital Interface (MIDI) sound stores a series of commands. The commands specify the length, loudness, pitch, and other characteristics of each note. During playback the commands are sent to the MIDI synthesizer of the sound card, which converts them into the corresponding sounds.

MCI Commands

A program controls multimedia devices by means of MCI commands. The MCI command set is a remarkably simple set of commands applicable to all multimedia devices. Of course, some commands are specific for certain devices; but generally speaking, the basic sequence of steps for using a multimedia device is:

1. Open the device. For some devices, this step includes specifying the file where the data is stored—for example, a .WAV file on disk. For other devices, such as playing audio from a CD or video from a videodisk, the data is part of the device so there is no file to open.

2. Play the device (or, in some cases, record). This step may include pausing, seeking to a new location in the data, and so on.

3. Close the device.

Let's take a look at some simple MCI commands. To play a WAVE file, perhaps the CHIMES.WAV that comes with Windows, here is the first command:

```
Open c:\media\chimes.wav type waveaudio alias chime
```

This command opens the desired WAVE file, specifies its type (from Table 10.1 so Windows knows which driver to use), and assigns an *alias*, a name we can use in subsequent commands to refer to this device. Opening the device does not actually play the sound. The command for that is:

```
Play chime
```

We use the Play command with the alias assigned to the device. The sound will start playing, and control will pass back to our program. Although CHIMES.WAV is a short sound, we can play long sounds where the sound will continue to play to the end while our program does other things. When we finish with the device, we close it as follows:

```
Close chime
```

The Close command terminates play, so we must delay executing it until the sound has completed playing. We'll see how to do this later.

The basic MCI commands are listed in Table 10.2, although we will not be exploring them all here. Rather, my goal is to show you how to perform the

Table 10.2 *The Basic MCI Commands*

Command	Action
capability	Requests information about a device's capabilities
close	Closes a device
info	Requests specific information about a device (such as its driver name)
open	Opens and initializes a device
pause	Suspends playback or recording
play	Starts playback
record	Begins recording
resume	Resumes play or recording on a paused device
save	Saves recorded data
seek	Moves to a specific position on the media
set	Changes a device's control settings
status	Obtains device status information
stop	Stops playback or recording

most common multimedia tasks in your Visual Basic program. For more details of multimedia, refer to one of the books published on the topic.

Note that we cannot simply type these commands into our Basic code; we have to send them to the MCI. How? Examining the two available methods is the topic for the remainder of this chapter.

Sending MCI Commands with MCISendString()

One way to send commands to the MCI is to use the function **mciSendString()**. Not a part of Visual Basic, this function is part of the Windows API (Applications Programming Interface), the huge collection of functions that provides most of Windows capabilities. When a Visual Basic program—or one written in any other language, for that matter—performs any operating system related task, it is actually calling Windows API functions to do the job. When we open a file by writing code in Basic, Visual Basic translates it into the necessary Windows API call to perform the task. Not all API capabilities are included in Visual Basic; but fortunately, when we run into this situation, we can call the API function directly. Which is exactly what we will do here.

Before our program can use a Windows API function, we must declare it. The declaration provides the program with certain information about the function, such as its name, the library it is in, and the number and types of its arguments. We can save time by copying API function declarations from the API Text Viewer application that is typically installed along with the Professional Edition of Visual Basic, and pasting them into our code. Here's the declaration for the **mciSendString()** function:

```
Declare Function mciSendString Lib "winmm" Alias "mciSendStringA" _
    (ByVal lpstrCommand As String, ByVal lpstrReturnString As String, _
    ByVal uReturnLength As Long, ByVal hwndCallback As Long) As Long
```

This declaration tells us the following:

The function is named **mciSendString.**

- It is located in the library named WINMM (a library is a disk file where Windows keeps its functions).

- Its alias—the name it goes under in the library—is "mciSendStringA" (while this sort of alias is essential for the function declaration, it has no other relevance to your program).

- It takes four arguments, two strings and two Longs.

- It returns a type Long value.

The declaration must be placed in one of two locations. For calling the function only from within one form module, place the declaration in the General Declarations section of the module's code. Remember to place the Private keyword at the beginning of the declaration, since Public declarations (the default) are not permitted in form modules. When calling the function from more than one module, place it in a Basic module that is part of the project.

Let's take a look now at the function's argument. The first one, **lpstrCommand**, is a string containing the command that we want to send to the MCI (these are the commands shown previously). The second argument, **lpstrReturnString**, is used by the MCI to return a message to the calling program. Not all commands result in a return message. The third argument, **uReturnLength**, specifies the length of the returned string. The final argument is used only in C and C++ programming, so we can ignore it. The function returns 0 if it is successful in carrying out the requested action, and a non-zero error code otherwise.

Now for a real example. Once we have declared the function, we play a MIDI file as follows:

Table 10.3 *Status Parameters for Sound and Video Devices*

Parameter	Meaning
length	Length of the file in frames (video) or samples (sound)
mode	Returns the device's current mode: "not ready", "paused", "playing", "seeking", or "stopped"
position	Current position in the file; sample for sound, frame for video
ready	Returns True if the device is ready
window handle	Returns the handle of the window being used for video playback

```
cmd = "Open C:\win95\media\canyon.mid type sequencer alias canyon"
retval = mciSendString(cmd, reply, 0, 0)
cmd = "play canyon"
retval = mciSendString(cmd, reply, 0, 0)
' In a real program we would have to wait
' for play to finish before closing the device.
cmd = "close canyon"
retval = mciSendString(cmd, reply, 0, 0)
```

If we executed this code as is, with the Close command sent immediately after the Play command, we would hear nothing. The device would be closed immediately. We need some way to pause until the playback—whether sound or video—is complete. There are two methods for doing this.

One method uses the Wait parameter to the Play command. Wait instructs the MCI not to accept any other commands, such as Close, until the current playback is completed:

```
cmd = "play canyon wait"
retval = mciSendString(cmd, reply, 0, 0)
cmd = "close canyon"
retval = mciSendString(cmd, reply, 0, 0)
```

With this code, the full CANYON.MID file will play. However, since our program is frozen during playback, the user cannot continue with other tasks. Thus, Wait is a good solution for short sounds where a "frozen program"is not a problem; but for longer playback, it clearly will not suffice. For this we can use the Status command, which has the following syntax:

```
Status device parameter
```

The *device* argument specifies which device's status we are requesting; this is the name we assigned with the Alias keyword when we opened the device.

The *parameter* argument specifies which status we are requesting. Table 10.3 lists the status parameters that are commonly needed for sound and video devices.

Using the Status command, here is a method to delay issuing the Close command until the music file is finished playing:

```
cmd = "Open C:\win95\media\canyon.mid type sequencer alias canyon"
retval = mciSendString(cmd, reply, 0, 0)
cmd = "play canyon"
retval = mciSendString(cmd, reply, 0, 0)

' Wait for play to finish before closing.
cmd = "status canyon mode"
do
    retval = mciSendString(cmd, reply, 0, 0)
until reply <> "playing"

cmd = "close canyon"
retval = mciSendString(cmd, reply, 0, 0)
```

Did you notice a problem with this approach? The program is not technically frozen as the sound plays, but it is effectively frozen while it mindlessly executes a loop over and over. We'll see a way to use Visual Basic's Timer control to get around this problem later in the program. First, let's look at some of the other MCI commands.

The Seek Command

The Seek command repositions the pointer in a device. The pointer indicates the current playing position. Play stops when we use Seek, and any subsequent Play command resumes playing from the new position. The syntax of this command is:

Seek to *position*

The most common use for Seek is to reset the file pointer to the beginning of the file, which is accomplished by using a value of 0 for the *position* argument. If we want to seek to any location other than the beginning, we must specify the *position* argument in the device's current TimeFormat (discussed later in the chapter).

The Set Command

Set allows us to control certain aspects of playback such as controlling individual speakers for sound playback, and controlling display of video playback. The syntax is:

Set *device setting*

The *device* argument is the alias established for the device when it was opened. The *setting* argument is one of the following, which should be self-explanatory:

- audio all on   (or off)

- audio left on   (or off)

- audio right on   (or off)

- video on   (or off)

The Capability Command

Use the Capability command to determine if an opened device has a specified capability. Initiating this command sends a capability name as argument:

Capability *CapabilityName*

In this case, the **mciSendString()** function returns *True* in the ReturnStrung argument if the device has the capability, *False* if not. Note that these return values are the strings "True" and "False" and not the usual logical values. The most essential capabilities are listed here:

- can eject

- can save

- can play

- can stretch

- can record

- can reverse

- has audio

- has video

- uses files

- uses palettes

Dealing with Errors

Like all other aspects of programming, the MCI has the potential for errors. A CD not inserted in the drive, a corrupt AVI file, or a malfunctioning sound card are examples of the many things that can conspire to interfere with smooth multimedia presentations. Errors of this nature are not trappable using Visual Basic's standard error handling mechanisms (which I will cover in a later chapter). Even so, a well-designed program must detect multimedia errors and handle them gracefully, reporting needed corrective action to the user when possible. Fortunately, the MCI provides us with the necessary capabilities.

As you may recall, the return value of the **mciSendString** function is zero on success, and a non-zero error code if an error occurred. Central to MCI error trapping, then, is checking the return value of **mciSendCommand** every time a command is issued. If the return value is 0, everything is fine. If not ... well, to be honest, a numerical error code is not a great deal of help. Sure, we could whip out our reference books and look it up, but is there a better way?

Definitely. The "better way" is the **mciGetErrorString** function. Passing the numerical error code to this API function returns a string that describes the exact nature of the error. Since this is not a Visual Basic function, but rather is part of the Windows API, we must declare it as follows:

```
Declare Function mciGetErrorString Lib "winmm" Alias "mciGetErrorStringA" _
    (ByVal dwError As Long, ByVal lpstrBuffer As String, _
    ByVal uLength As Long) As Long
```

The *dwError* argument is the error code returned by **mciSendString**. The *lpstrBuffer* argument is a string variable where the descriptive error message will be placed. This should be a fixed-length string at least 255 characters long. The final argument *uLength* specifies the length of *lpstrBuffer*, in characters. Assuming that the variable Cmd contains an MCI command, the code to handle an MCI error would look like this:

```
Dim ErrorMessage As String * 255, ReturnString As String * 255
...
x = mciSendString(Cmd, ReturnString, 255, 0)
if x <> 0 then
    r = mciGetErrorString(x, ErrorMessage, 255)
    MsgBox(ErrorMessage)
End If
```

Demonstrating the MCI Commands

The project SOUND1 presents a relatively simple demonstration of the multimedia techniques discussed so far. The program displays a blank form with a single menu command, File Open. We can open a video file (*.AVI), a WAVE file (*.WAV), or a MIDI sequencer file (*.MID). The program will play it through to the end and close the file. We can then open another file and play it.

What's unusual about this program is the method used to determine when playback is complete. As mentioned above, this is a shortcoming of using the MCI commands with Visual Basic: MCI has no way to notify the Visual Basic program when a command has been completed (unless we use the Multimedia control, covered next). There is one alternative, however. If we use **mciSendCommand** to send the command

```
status alias mode
```

to the device, the return value argument to the **mciSendString** function will contain a string giving the device's current mode. While the device is playing, the return string will be "playing." If we can check the device mode repeatedly, we know it's safe to close the device as soon as the returned value is not "playing." How can we do this?

The answer lies in Visual Basic's Timer control. Set the timer interval, start the timer, and it will repeatedly count down to zero, reset itself to the specified interval, then start counting down again. Each time the Timer counts to 0, its **Timer** event procedure is triggered. Code in this procedure can obtain the MCI device mode and close it once playback is completed.

To specify the Timer control's countdown interval, set its **Interval** property. The unit used is milliseconds, or thousandths of a second. Next, set its **Enabled** property to *True* to begin timing, and set **Enabled** to *False* to terminate timing. The Timer control is never visible on screen (except during program design). It just works in the background. We can have more than one Timer control on the same form.

Now let's get to work on the demonstration project. Start with a blank form and add one Timer control and one CommonDialog control. Leave the properties of both at their default settings. Create a File menu with the two commands, Open and Exit. The form's objects and properties are given in Listing 10.1.

Listing 10.1 Objects and Properties in SOUND1.FRM

```
Begin VB.Form Form1
   Caption         =   "MCI Demonstration"
   Begin VB.Timer Timer1
   End
   Begin MSComDlg.CommonDialog CommonDialog1
   End
   Begin VB.Menu mnuFile
      Caption         =   "&File"
      Begin VB.Menu mnuFileOpen
         Caption         =   "&Open"
         Shortcut        =   ^O
      End
      Begin VB.Menu mnuSeparator
         Caption         =   "-"
      End
      Begin VB.Menu mnuFileExit
         Caption         =   "E&xit"
      End
   End
End
```

The program code is presented in Listing 10.2. From what you have learned in the text and the comments in the code, you should be able to figure out how the code works. Remember that the two API function declarations must be placed in the General Declarations section of the form's code. It is possible to eliminate typing by copying the declarations from the API text viewer application provided with Visual Basic.

Listing 10.2 Code in SOUND1.FRM

```
Option Explicit

Private Declare Function mciSendString Lib "winmm" Alias "mciSendStringA" _
  (ByVal lpstrCommand As String, ByVal lpstrReturnString As String, _
  ByVal uReturnLength As Long, ByVal hwndCallback As Long) As Long

Private Declare Function mciGetErrorString Lib "winmm" Alias "mciGetErrorStringA" _
  (ByVal dwError As Long, ByVal lpstrBuffer As String, ByVal uLength As Long) _
  As Long

' Constant for the MCI alias since we'll only
' have one device open at a time

Const ALIAS = "MyDevice"


Private Sub Form_Load()
```

```vb
' Set up the Open dialog's filter.

CommonDialog1.Filter = "WAVE (*.WAV)|*.wav|MIDI (*.MID)|*.mid|Video (*.AVI)|*.avi"

End Sub


Private Sub Form_Unload(Cancel As Integer)

Dim cmd As String, ret As String * 255, x As Long

' When the form unloads be sure the device is closed.

cmd = "close " & ALIAS
x = mciSendString(cmd, ret, 255, 0)

End Sub


Private Sub mnuFileExit_Click()

End

End Sub


Private Sub mnuFileOpen_Click()

Dim cmd As String, devicetype As String, ret As String * 255
Dim rv As Long, rv1 As Long

' DIsplay the Open dialog.
CommonDialog1.ShowOpen

' Exit if user canceled.
If CommonDialog1.filename = "" Then Exit Sub

' Get the selected file name extension.
cmd = UCase$(Right$(CommonDialog1.filename, 3))

' Set the "type" argument depending on the
' extension of the file selected.

Select Case cmd
    Case "AVI"
        devicetype = "avivideo"
    Case "MID"
        devicetype = "sequencer"
    Case "WAV"
        devicetype = "waveaudio"
    Case Else
        MsgBox ("Invalid file format")
        Exit Sub
End Select
```

```
' Set up the MCI command and send it.
cmd = "open " & CommonDialog1.filename & " type " & devicetype
cmd = cmd & " alias " & ALIAS
rv = mciSendString(cmd, ret, 255, 0)

' On error.
If rv <> 0 Then
    rv1 = mciGetErrorString(rv, ret, 255)
    MsgBox ("Error opening device: " & ret)
    Exit Sub
End If

' Send the "play" command.
cmd = "play " & ALIAS
rv = mciSendString(cmd, ret, 255, 0)

If rv <> 0 Then
    rv1 = mciGetErrorString(rv, ret, 255)
    MsgBox ("Error playing device: " & ret)
    Exit Sub
End If

' Play command successful. Enable the timer and set a 1000
' msec interval. Disable the File menu.
Timer1.Interval = 1000
Timer1.Enabled = True
mnuFile.Enabled = False

End Sub


Private Sub Timer1_Timer()

Dim cmd As String, ret As String * 255, rv As Long

' Each time the timer counts down, check the
' MCI device to see if it is still playing.

' Set up the MCI command and send it.
cmd = "status " & ALIAS & " mode"
rv = mciSendString(cmd, ret, 255, 0)

' If the mode is not "playing" then we are done and can close
' the device, disable the timer, and enable the File menu.
If Left$(ret, 7) <> "playing" Then
    cmd = "close " & ALIAS
    rv = mciSendString(cmd, ret, 255, 0)
    Timer1.Enabled = False
    mnuFile.Enabled = True
End If

End Sub
```

Using the Visual Basic Multimedia Control

The second method for sending MCI commands is Visual Basic's Multimedia control. When displayed on a form, this control provides an array of buttons that can be used to control a multimedia device. The control is shown in Figure 10.2. The buttons are defined, from left to right, as Prev(ious), Next, Play, Pause, Back, Step, Stop, Record, and Eject.

The first step in using the Multimedia control is to set its **FileName** property or its **DeviceType** property. Set the **FileName** property when the data to be played is in a file that specifies the type of device to be opened; WAVE, MIDI, and AVI video files are examples. Set the **DeviceType** property when the device does not use files, such as CD Audio, or with a compound device where the associated file's extension does not specify the type of device.

Next, open the device by setting the Multimedia control's **Command** property to "Open." The control takes care of the details of sending the command to the MCI and obtaining the necessary information about the device. When it comes to actually manipulating the device, we have two choices:

- Have the control visible on-screen (Visible property = *True*). When the user clicks the buttons on the control, the appropriate commands are sent to the device.

- Hide the control (Visible property = *False*). To execute commands, place them in the control's **Command** property.

Of course, these two methods can be used in conjunction with each other. If the control is visible, we can still send commands by placing them in the Command property. Likewise, if the control is hidden, it can be made visible if needed.

Much of the appeal of the Multimedia control is the simplification of tasks that could be accomplished with more difficulty by directly accessing the MCI, as shown earlier in this chapter. The control has many properties that correspond to information about the open multimedia device, such as the informa-

Figure 10.2   *The multimedia control.*

tion accessible with the **Capabilities** command. For example, simply read the Multimedia control's **CanEject** property to determine if the open device can eject its media, and read the **Mode** property to determine the current state of the device. Let's take a closer look at some of these properties (refer to Visual Basic Help for details on all Multimedia control properties).

Multimedia Control Properties

The **Mode** property returns one of the following values (as a type Long), indicating the current mode of the open device in Table 10.4.

The **CanEject**, **CanPlay**, **CanStep**, and **CanRecord** properties return *True* or *False*, depending on whether the open device has the indicated capability.

The **AutoEnable** property determines if the individual buttons on the Multimedia control are automatically enabled and disabled to reflect the capabilities of the open device (**AutoEnable** = *True*), or whether the program must enable and disable individual buttons by setting the corresponding *Button***Enabled** property (**AutoEnable** = *False*), where *Button* is one of Back, Eject, Next, Pause, Play, Prev, Record, Step, or Stop.

The **Enabled** property controls user access to the entire Multimedia control. If **Enabled** is set to *False,* the user cannot select any of the control's buttons.

The **Command** property mentioned earlier is used to send commands to an MCI device. Set the Multimedia control's **Command** property to a valid MCI command string, and the command is sent to the open MCI device associated with the control. The valid commands are Open, Close, Play, Pause, Stop, Back, Step, Prev, Next, Seek, Record, Eject, Sound, or Save. The command is executed immediately, and the error code is stored in the **Error** property (see below).

Table 10.4   *Mode Property Values*

Value	Constant	Meaning
524	mciNotOpen	Device is not open
525	mciStop	Device is stopped
526	mciPlay	Device is playing
527	mciRecord	Device is recording
528	mciSeek	Device is seeking
529	mciPause	Device is paused
530	mciReady	Device is ready

The **TimeFormat** property sets the format that the device uses to measure time. Several different time formats are available, and detailed information is available in the Visual Basic Help system. Knowing the current time format is essential, because the **From**, **To**, **Length**, **TrackLength**, **Position**, **TrackPosition**, and **Start** properties all use the current time format. Each type of device has a default time format that can be changed if desired. Note, however, that certain devices do not support all the available time formats. If we attempt to set the **TimeFormat** property to an unsupported value, the setting is ignored and the old setting is retained. The default time format settings for the most common devices are shown in Table 10.5.

Upon examining this table, you may wonder why the time format used for CDAudio includes frames. To tell you the truth, I wondered that too! If you insert an audio CD in your CD ROM drive and open the device, that is the TimeFormat value returned by the Multimedia control. I don't see what use the Frame value plays in this format, but we can't argue with Microsoft!

The **Orientation** property determines whether the Multimedia control is displayed horizontally (the default) or vertically. Set this property to the constant *mciOrientHorz* (value = 0) for a horizontal control, or to *mciOrientVert* (value = 1) for a vertical control.

The **Wait** property works just like the Wait argument in a command sent directly to the MCI. Set **Wait** to *True* to have execution return to your program only after the MCI has completed the current operation. If **Wait** is *False* (the default), execution returns immediately.

Table 10.5 *Default Time Format Settings for Common Devices*

Constant	Value	Default for	Description
mciFormatMilliseconds	0	WAVE and MIDI	Time is expressed in milliseconds
mciFormatMfs	2	CDAudio	Minutes, seconds, and frames are packed into a 4-byte type Long. The least significant byte holds the Minutes value, the next byte holds seconds, the next byte holds frames, and the most significant byte is not used.
mciFormatFrames	3	AVI (digital video)	Time is expressed in frames

Multimedia Control Events

The Multimedia control supports only eight events. Two of these, **DragOver** and **DragDrop**, operate like events of the same name associated with many other Visual Basic controls. The other six events are unique to the Multimedia control. Some of these events are what make the Multimedia control so useful, allowing us to do things that would not be possible by sending commands directly to the MCI.

Four of the events are related to the individual buttons on the control. Each of the buttons – Back, Eject, Next, Pause, Play, Prev, Record, Step, and Stop – has its own discrete event procedures. They are as follows:

The **ButtonClick** event occurs when the button is clicked. The default is for each button, when clicked, to send the corresponding command to the MCI. These commands are shown in Table 10.6.

We can specify additional code to be executed with or instead of the button's command when it is clicked. The skeleton of each button click procedure looks like this:

```
Sub MMControl_ButtonClick (Cancel As Integer)

End Sub
```

Table 10.6   *MCI Button Commands*

Button	Command sent to MCI
Back	MCI_STEP
Step	MCI_STEP
Play	MCI_PLAY
Pause	MCI_PAUSE
Prev	MCI_SEEK
Next	MCI_SEEK
Stop	MCI_STOP
Record	MCI_RECORD
Eject	MCI_SET with the MCI_SET_DOOR_OPEN parameter

MMControl is the name of the Multimedia control, and *Button* is the name of the button (Back, Eject, and so on.). When the button is clicked, code placed in the event procedure is executed. If the Cancel argument is left at its default value of *False*, the button's command is sent to the MCI after the code in the procedure is executed. If Cancel is set to *True*, the command is not sent (but the code in the procedure is still executed). It's easy to see how flexible this arrangement can be: When a button is clicked, we can execute our own code, the default command, or both.

The ***Button*GotFocus** event procedure executes when the button gets the focus, and the ***Button*LostFocus** procedure executes when the button loses the focus. No special features are attached to these event procedures.

The ***Button*Completed** event is triggered when the MCI operation started by a Multimedia control button click is complete. For example, if the user clicked the Play button, the **PlayCompleted()** event procedure will be executed when the play is completed. The ***Button*Completed** event procedure looks like this:

```
Sub MMControl_ButtonCompleted (Errorcode As Long)

End Sub
```

The Errorcode argument will be 0 if the operation completed without an error. It will be set to a non-zero value if the operation did not complete successfully. When an error is detected, we can use the **Error** and **ErrorMessage** properties (discussed soon) to determine the nature of the error.

The **Done** event procedure is executed when an MCI command finishes executing. This event procedure is not automatically executed, but rather is controlled by the Multimedia control's **Notify** property. **Notify** is normally *False*, which means that the **Done** event will not be triggered. If we set **Notify** to *True*, however, the **Done** event will be triggered at the completion of the next MCI command executed. This is true both for MCI commands that result from clicking one of the control buttons, as well as for commands executed by means of the control's **Command** property.

The **Done** event procedure is passed a type Integer argument named NotifyCode. The value in this argument indicates the result of the MCI operation that just completed. This value is the same as that in the **NotifyValue** property as shown in Table 10.7.

Table 10.7 *Values for the Done Event Procedure*

Value	Constant	Result
1	mciSuccessful	Command completed successfully
2	mciSuperseded	Command was superseded by another command
4	mciAborted	Command was aborted by the user
8	mciFailure	Command failed

Remember that setting **Notify** to *True* affects only the next MCI command to be issued, and does not affect subsequent commands or the command currently being executed (if any). We must set **Notify** to *True* before each and every MCI command for which we want the **Done** event procedure triggered.

Perhaps you have already seen how the **Done** event and the **ButtonCompleted** events allow us to solve a problem that we had to kludge around earlier when sending commands directly to the MCI—namely, knowing when the play operation is complete so we can close the device or perform whatever other actions we need to take. Remember that fourth argument to the **mciSendCommand()** function? I said that it was used in C and C++ programming and that we need not worry about it. This argument is used to pass to MCI the address of a program function that would be called when the MCI command was complete, a *callback function*. Since Visual Basic does not support callback functions, we could safely ignore this argument. We may need it, but we couldn't use it. Using the Multimedia control allows us to avoid this limitation and use the **Done** and **ButtonCompleted** events to respond appropriately when an MCI process is completed.

The **StatusUpdate** event occurs each time the Multimedia control checks the status of the device associated with it. The interval at which this checking occurs is specified by the **UpdateInterval** property. The default value of 1000 milliseconds results in status checks every second. Code in the **StatusUpdate** event procedure can be used to provide the user with information about the current operation, obtained from Multimedia control properties such as Mode, Length, and Position.

Handling Multimedia Control Errors

As I mentioned earlier, using the Multimedia control has the potential for errors. A CD not inserted in the drive, a corrupt AVI file, or a malfunctioning sound card are examples of the many things that can conspire to interfere with smooth multimedia presentations. Errors of this nature are not trappable using Visual Basic's standard error handling mechanisms (which I will cover in a later chapter). Even so, a well-designed program must detect multimedia errors and handle them gracefully, reporting needed corrective action to the user when possible. Fortunately, the Multimedia control provides us with the needed capabilities.

Most important are the **Error** and **ErrorMessage** properties. The **Error** property contains the error code returned by the last MCI command, and the **ErrorMessage** property provides a string description of the error. When everything works okay, the error code is 0 and the string in **ErrorMessage** is "The specified command was carried out." It is possible to check these properties in the **StatusUpdate** event procedure to keep a constant eye on the progress of the MCI command.

The second tool for dealing with errors is the NotifyCode argument passed to the **Done** event procedure. If this argument is equal to mciFailure (value = 8), the command failed and we can look in the **Error** and **ErrorMessage** properties for details.

The third tool is the ErrorCode argument passed to the **ButtonCompleted** event procedures. If Error code is not 0, an error occurred. Once again, check the **Error** and **ErrorMessage** properties for details on the error.

A Multimedia Control Demonstration

Now that we have explored the more important details of the Multimedia control, let's see just how easy it is to use it. The project SOUND2 uses the Multimedia control to implement a simple media player. We can open a media file—MIDI, WAVE, or AVI—or the CD Audio device (assuming an audio CD is in the drive). Then we can use the Multimedia control's buttons to play the device. There's no error handling in the program, which is something you might want to add. In fact there are many enhancements you could add to the program. The Multimedia control has enough power to serve as the heart of a full-featured media player. A good project to tackle on your own would be modifying this program so that the Multimedia control is hidden but still used as the program's interface to the MCI.

The program, shown operating in Figure 10.3, has a single form with two controls: one Mutlimedia control and one CommonDialog control. There's also a File menu with three commands: Open, Play CD, and Exit. The form's objects and properties are shown in Listing 10.3 and its code in Listing 10.4.

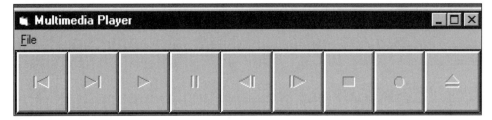

Figure 10.3 *The SOUND2 media player.*

Listing 10.3   Objects and Properties in SOUND2.FRM

```
Begin VB.Form Form1
    Caption         =   "Multimedia Player"
    Begin MSComDlg.CommonDialog CommonDialog1
    End
    Begin MCI.MMControl MMControl1
    End
    Begin VB.Menu mnuFile
        Caption         =   "&File"
        Begin VB.Menu mnuFileOpen
            Caption         =   "&Open"
        End
        Begin VB.Menu mnyFilePlayCD
            Caption         =   "&Play CD"
        End
        Begin VB.Menu nmuSeparator
            Caption         =   "-"
        End
        Begin VB.Menu mnuFileExit
            Caption         =   "E&xit"
        End
    End
End
```

Listing 10.4   Code in SOUND2.FRM

```
Option Explicit

Dim DeviceOpen As Boolean

Private Sub Form_Load()

Dim x As Integer, y As Integer

' Initialize flag.
DeviceOpen = False

' Set form size and control position.
x = Form1.Width - Form1.ScaleWidth
y = Form1.Height - Form1.ScaleHeight
```

```
Form1.Width = MMControl1.Width + x
Form1.Height = MMControl1.Height + y

MMControl1.Left = 0
MMControl1.TOP = 0

CommonDialog1.Filter = _
  "Wave (*.WAV)|*.wav|MIDI (*.MID)|*.mid|Video (*.AVI)|*.avi"

End Sub

Private Sub Form_Unload(Cancel As Integer)

' Close the device

MMControl1.Command = "Close"

End Sub


Private Sub MMControl1_Done(NotifyCode As Integer)

End Sub

Private Sub MMControl1_PlayClick(Cancel As Integer)

' Since the program has nothing else to do, there's
' no harm in setting Wait to True.
MMControl1.Wait = True

' Disable the menu while play is in progress.
mnuFile.Enabled = False

End Sub


Private Sub MMControl1_StopClick(Cancel As Integer)

' Enable the menu.
mnuFile.Enabled = True

End Sub


Private Sub mnuFileExit_Click()

End

End Sub

Private Sub mnuFileOpen_Click()
```

```
' If the device is open, close it.
If DeviceOpen Then
    MMControl1.Command = "Close"
    DeviceOpen = False
End If

' Show the Open dialog.
CommonDialog1.ShowOpen

' If user cancels, exit sub.
If CommonDialog1.filename = "" Then Exit Sub

' Set MM control properties.
MMControl1.filename = CommonDialog1.filename
MMControl1.DeviceType = ""
MMControl1.Command = "Open"
DeviceOpen = True

End Sub


Private Sub mnuFilePlayCD_Click()

' Open the CD Audio device. The CD should already be
' inserted in the drive.
MMControl1.DeviceType = "CDAudio"
MMControl1.Command = "Open"
DeviceOpen = True


End Sub
```

DATABASE BASICS

One of the most outstanding things about Visual Basic is the powerful assortment of database tools that it provides. In this chapter we'll start examining these tools.

If we surveyed all the computers in the world, what kind of program would be running most often? Not games, not word processors, but database programs. When another long distance company calls to pitch its service, the agent uses a database program. When someone sends an order for elk-lined pajamas to L.L. Bean, the order goes into a database program. When the clerk at the auto parts store checks to see whether they have a left-handed cam inverter for your 1971 Ford Falcon, he or she uses a database program. Wherever information needs to be managed, we find a database program at work.

What's more, a large percentage of those programs were created with Visual Basic. Recognizing that database programming is in great demand, Microsoft wisely included a whole slew of powerful database tools in Visual Basic. The Basic language itself has all the features needed to create a database program, which is the first thing we'll look at in this chapter. Visual Basic also includes the Jet database engine. In conjunction with some

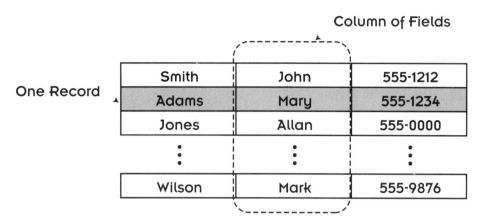

Figure 11.1 *A database is organized in row and column format.*

specialized controls, it provides a great deal of database support and requires very little programming. We'll look at Jet later in the chapter. First, we need to get some basics under our belt.

SO, WHAT'S A DATABASE?

A *database* is a collection of information, or data, that is arranged in a particular manner. The basic unit of information in a database is called a *record*. Each record in a database contains two or more *fields* that hold specific types of information; for example, a database designed to hold an address list. Each entry in the database constitutes one record. Each record in the database contains fields that hold separate items of information—first name, last name, address, city, and so on. These fields are the same for every record, and they are assigned names identifying the data they contain.

A database is sometimes organized and displayed in row and column format. Each row contains one record, and each column contains one field, as illustrated in Figure 11.1. In this case, records are referred to as a row, and fields are referred to as a column. The entire collection of records is called a *table*. Some databases contain more than one table, with the records in each table having a different field structure. We can deal with multiple table databases in later chapters; for now we'll stick with single table databases.

A database program is designed to let us work with the information in a database. Some capabilities are required in any application and common to any database program—adding, finding, and deleting records, for example. Many other capabilities are customized to fit a specific program. In an address list database, for example, we may want the ability to print envelopes and to sort the records by ZIP code. A graphics database might need the ability to input and store images from a scanner. The possibilities are endless. If you write database programs as part of your job, you never know what someone might ask you to do next. Here's one of the advantages of Visual Basic. Being a full-featured programming language, it offers the flexibility to build any capabilities right into the database program. Thanks to its database tools, most of the fundamental database tasks are simple to accomplish.

DOING IT THE OLD WAY

Before Visual Basic had specialized database tools, we had no choice but to program all of the program's functionality using Visual Basic's standard controls and the Basic language. This approach is still possible, and many database programs were created this way. But these days, specialized database tools provide so many advantages (as well as speeding up the programming process) that "doing it yourself" is rarely desirable. Still, there are a couple of reasons why you should know the process. For certain relatively simple database tasks, the old methods are more than adequate and provide a smaller, faster program that avoids the overhead associated with the specialized data access tools. Later in the chapter, when I cover the Jet database engine, I'll explain some of the factors to consider when deciding upon the best approach.

The program we'll develop in this section is a bare-bones address list. It's not something we would actually use to keep track of names and addresses, since it's lacking a number of features that most people would consider essential. However, it demonstrates the fundamentals of roll-your-own database programming, as well as several other Visual Basic techniques.

Planning the Database

What features do we want in the address list program? Keeping track of people's address information, of course. We'll define a data structure to hold the required information, as shown here:

```
Type Address
    FName As String * 20
    LName As String * 20
    Address As String * 40
    City As String * 15
    State As String * 2
    Zip As String * 5
End Type
```

The user-defined Address type gives us a place to store address information while the program is running. It will also define the structure of the random access file utilized for disk storage of the database information. We reviewed the relationship between a user-defined type and random access files in Chapter 8; now we'll see them in action.

The program should have the basic features of viewing records, adding new records, deleting records that are no longer needed, and editing existing records. We'll also add the ability to display an alphabetical list of all records. A number of other features are possible, but let's stop here. We want the project to be manageable! Later I'll describe some additional features we might want to add.

Designing the Form

The address form needs one Text Box for each of the six pieces of information, or fields, that every address record will contain. Each Text Box requires an identification label, as well. Command Buttons arranged in two control arrays of four buttons each will serve as our user commands. The completed form, which is saved as ADDRESS.FRM, is shown in Figure 11.2. The upper row of Command Buttons is assigned the Name property of **cmdAction**, with Index properties 0-3 from left to right. The lower set of Command Buttons is

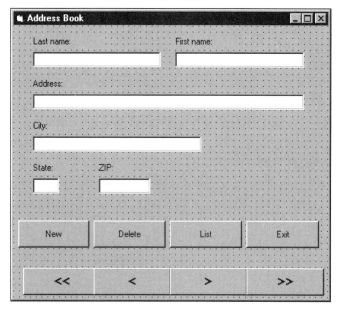

Figure 11.2 *The address database form.*

named **cmdMove**, and also has Index properties 0-3 from left to right. The full description of this form's objects and properties is given in Listing 11.1. Save the project under the name ADDRESS.

Listing 11.1 Objects and Properties in ADDRESS.FRM

```
Begin VB.Form Form1
   BorderStyle     =   1  'Fixed Single
   Caption         =   "Address Book"
   MaxButton       =   0   'False
   MinButton       =   0   'False
   Begin VB.CommandButton cmdAction
      Caption         =   "List"
      Index           =   2
   End
   Begin VB.CommandButton cmdAction
      Caption         =   "Exit"
      Index           =   3
   End
   Begin VB.CommandButton cmdAction
      Caption         =   "Delete"
      Index           =   1
   End
   Begin VB.CommandButton cmdAction
      Caption         =   "New"
      Index           =   0
   End
   Begin VB.CommandButton cmdMove
      Caption         =   ">>"
      Index           =   3
   End
   Begin VB.CommandButton cmdMove
      Caption         =   ">"
      Index           =   2
   End
   Begin VB.CommandButton cmdMove
      Caption         =   "<"
      Index           =   1
   End
   Begin VB.CommandButton cmdMove
      Caption         =   "<<"
      Index           =   0
   End
   Begin VB.TextBox txtZip
   End
   Begin VB.TextBox txtState
   End
   Begin VB.TextBox txtCity
   End
   Begin VB.TextBox txtAddress
   End
   Begin VB.TextBox txtFName
```

```
       End
       Begin VB.TextBox txtLName
       End
       Begin VB.Label Label6
          Caption         =    "ZIP:"
       End
       Begin VB.Label Label5
          Caption         =    "State:"
       End
       Begin VB.Label Label4
          Caption         =    "City:"
       End
       Begin VB.Label Label3
          Caption         =    "Address:"
       End
       Begin VB.Label Label2
          Caption         =    "First name:"
       End
       Begin VB.Label Label1
          Caption         =    "Last name:"
       End
End
```

Adding a Basic Module

Rather than placing all of the program code in the form module, a Basic module will hold the Type definition and the global variable declarations. A Basic module contains no visual elements, only code. Why bother with a separate module? Why not just place all the code in the form module? We use a Basic Module for several reasons:

- Procedures in a Basic module can be called from all parts of the program —from all modules, both form and Basic. In contrast, a procedure in a form module can be called only from within that form. If we want a procedure to be available in different modules, we must put it in a Basic module. Although this reason does not apply to the current project, it is the most important one for using a Basic module.

- Basic modules can be reused, serving as software components. When writing procedures that have general utility, place them in a Basic module. To use those procedures in another Visual Basic project, we just add the Basic module to the project (using the Add File command on the File menu).

- A Basic module is the best place to declare variables that are global to two or more modules.

Notice that the Basic module in this project contains no procedures, only variable declarations. Strictly speaking, we could have finished this project without a Basic module, but I believe that it is preferred programming practice to place global variable declarations in a Basic module rather than scattering them around the various form modules (we will be adding a second form to this project in a bit). Bottom line: You need to learn how to use Basic modules, and now is as good a time as any!

To add a Basic module to the project, pull down the Insert menu and select Module. A code editing window will open with a default name in its title bar. Enter the code shown in Listing 11.2. When the code has all been entered, select Save from the File menu and assign the name ADDRESS.BAS to the code module file.

Listing 11.2   Code in ADDRESS.BAS

```
Option Explicit

Type Address
    FName As String * 20
    LName As String * 20
    Address As String * 40
    City As String * 15
    State As String * 2
    Zip As String * 5
End Type

Public CR As Address
Public EnteringNew As Boolean
Public CurrentRecord As Integer
Public NumberOfRecords As Integer
Public OldRecord As Integer
Public FullFileName As String
Public FileNum As Integer
Public Const FILENAME = "ADDRESS.DAT"
```

Look at the code in Listing 11.2. First, we have the Type statement defining the Address user-defined data structure. This structure contains six fixed-length string elements to hold the six fields of the address record. Next are declarations of the program's global variables. Note the use of the **Public** keyword in place of the usual **Dim** keyword. By using **Public**, we specify that the variable is global to all modules in the program, not just to the module where it is declared. If we had used **Dim** instead, the scope of these variables would be limited to the Basic module.

The first variable, CR, is an instance of the **Address** type. The program will use CR to hold the current record. Don't we need an array of type **Address** to hold the entire database? That's one solution, but I've used a different method. The database itself will remain stored on disk. Only the current record—the one being viewed, modified, or added—will be read into memory. Changes to the database will immediately and automatically be written to disk.

Note that we define a constant to hold the name of the database file. The program always works with the same database file, on the assumption that most people need only a single address list. We could modify the program to let the user specify the database file if that feature would be valuable.

The other variables should be self-explanatory. You'll see how they are applied in subsequent code listings.

Using Multiple Forms

In the address database's design specification, we said that the program should have the ability to list all entries in the database in alphabetical order. Rather than trying to squeeze this list onto our existing form, we'll use a separate form. The ListBox control is ideal for displaying our list, since it has a Sorted property that causes items in the ListBox to automatically sort alphabetically when it is set to True.

To add a second form to the project, select Form from the Insert menu. A new, blank form will be displayed. Place a ListBox control on the form; the size and position do not matter since they will be set in code when the form is displayed. Set the ListBox's Sorted property to True, and the form's Caption property to Address List. Select Save File from the File menu, and save the form as FRMLIST.FRM. The form's objects and properties are given in Listing 11.3.

Listing 11.3   Objects and Properties in FRMLIST.FRM

```
Begin VB.Form frmList
   Caption         =   "Address List"
   Begin VB.ListBox List1
     Sorted        =   -1  'True
   End
End
```

When a project contains more than one form, how does it know where to start when the program executes? Every multiple form project has a *startup form,* which is displayed first. The display of other forms is then controlled by program code. By default, the first form we create in a project is the startup form. To change the startup form, select Options from the Tools menu, then click the Project tab in the displayed dialog box. Pull down the Startup Form list and select the desired startup form. We have no need to change the startup form for this project, however.

We can also specify that a Basic module be executed first when the program runs. This technique is not commonly used, but it can be valuable when initialization code in the Basic module must be executed before any forms are loaded. Once the initialization is complete, code in the Basic module displays the program's first form.

Chameleon Command Buttons

Let's take a few minutes to think about the program's Command Buttons. Four of them navigate among the records: forward or back one record, and to the first or last record. What other commands might the user need to enter? An Exit button is necessary, of course, and also a List button for displaying the alphabetical list. These two buttons will be available at all times. What else? The program will always be in one of two states: browsing and editing records, or entering a new record (indicated by the EnteringNew Boolean variable). If the user is entering a new record, Save and Cancel commands are needed. If the program is in the browsing state, New (to enter a new record) and Delete (to delete the current record) commands are needed. We now have four commands but only two remaining Command Buttons. Do we need to add two more Command Buttons?

No. We can use a neat programming trick that allows a single Command Button to serve two or more purposes. By changing the button's **Caption** property, and by using a flag variable to determine what the program does when the button is clicked, two of the Command Buttons can serve double duty. Here's how it works:

- When the program starts, the buttons will display the default "New" and "Delete" captions that we assigned during form design. The EnteringNew flag variable is set to *False*. The button's Click event procedure tests the value of EnteringNew and directs execution accordingly.

- If the user clicks the New button, EnteringNew is set to *True* and the button captions are changed to "Save" and "Cancel." Code in the **Click()** event procedure can now direct execution differently because EnteringNew has a different value.

- When the user clicks Save or Cancel, the process is reversed: EnteringNew is set to False again and the button captions are set back to "New" and "Delete."

Some of this action goes on in the **Click()** event procedure for the array of Command Buttons. This code is shown in Listing 11.4.

Listing 11.4   The Action Buttons' Click() Event Procedure

```
Private Sub cmdAction_Click(Index As Integer)

' For the control array of four "action" buttons.

Dim Reply As Integer

If EnteringNew Then      ' If we're entering a new record, the first two
    Select Case Index    ' buttons have different meanings.
        Case 0        ' Save.
            Call SaveCurrentRecord
            EnteringNew = False
            cmdAction(0).Caption = "New"
            cmdAction(1).Caption = "Delete"
        Case 1        ' Cancel
            CurrentRecord = OldRecord
            EnteringNew = False
            cmdAction(0).Caption = "New"
            cmdAction(1).Caption = "Delete"
            Call DisplayRecord(CurrentRecord)
        Case 2        ' List
            frmList.Show
        Case 3        ' Exit
            Call ByeBye
    End Select
Else                  ' If we're not entering a record.
    Select Case Index
        Case 0        ' New
            EnteringNew = True
            Call AddNewAddress
        Case 1        ' Delete
            Reply = MsgBox("Delete this address?", vbYesNo + vbQuestion)
            If Reply = vbYes Then
                txtFName.TEXT = ""
                txtLName.TEXT = ""
                txtAddress.TEXT = ""
                txtCity.TEXT = ""
                txtState.TEXT = ""
                txtZip.TEXT = ""
                Call SaveCurrentRecord
            End If
        Case 2        ' List
            frmList.Show
```

```
        Case 3      ' Exit
             Call ByeBye
    End Select
End If

End Sub
```

Two other things in Listing 11.4 require mention. If the user selects the List button, this line of code is executed:

```
frmList.Show
```

The first part, frmList, is the name of the form where the records will be listed. The Show method does just what it implies—shows the form. What happens next is determined by code in that form module, which we will deal with soon.

If the Exit button is selected, the program calls the **ByeBye()** procedure, which closes the file and uses the Unload statement to unload the program's main form (see Listing 11.5).

Listing 11.5   The ByeBye() Procedure Ends the Program

```
Public Sub ByeBye()

' Close the data file and end the program.

Close #FileNum
Unload Form1

End Sub
```

Why not execute the **End** statement to end the program? We would like to let the user confirm, just in case the Exit button was clicked by accident. End does not permit this, since it terminates the program immediately. In contrast, unloading a form triggers its **QueryUnload()** event procedure. Code in this procedure can query the user to confirm the desire to end the program. The skeleton of this procedure is shown here:

```
Private Sub Form_QueryUnload(Cancel As Integer, UnloadMode As Integer)

End Sub
```

The UnloadMode argument specifies how the unload event was triggered. The possible values are shown in Table 11.1.

Table 11.1   Possible Values for UnloadMode

Constant	Value	Meaning
vbFormControlMenu	0	The user chose the Close command from the form's Control menu.
vbFormCode	1	The Unload statement is invoked from code.
vbAppWindows	2	The current Windows session is ending.
vbAppTaskManager	3	The Windows Task Manager is closing the application.
vbFormMDIForm	4	An MDI child form is closing because the MDI form is closing.

In our case, the UnloadMode argument will have the value 1; but since we don't really care why the form is being unloaded, we will just ignore this argument. The Cancel argument, on the other hand, is central to the purpose of this procedure. If code in the procedure sets Cancel to any non-zero value, the unload event is canceled and the program does not terminate. If Cancel is left at its initial zero value, the program terminates. In our program, we'll display a message box with Yes and No buttons asking if the user really wants to exit, then set the value of Cancel accordingly. This procedure is shown in Listing 11.6.

Listing 11.6   The QueryUnload() Event Procedure

```
Private Sub Form_QueryUnload(Cancel As Integer, UnloadMode As Integer)

' If the user tries to exit, confirm.

Dim Reply As Integer

Reply = MsgBox("Exit—are you sure?", vbYesNo + vbQuestion)

If Reply = vbYes Then
    Call ByeBye
Else
    Cancel = True   ' Setting Cancel to a non-zero value
End If              ' cancels the exit.

End Sub
```

Initializing the Program

Program initialization steps are carried out in the **Form_Load()** event procedure, which is shown in Listing 11.7. The first step is to generate the full path of the data file, using the Path property of the App object to obtain the program directory. We then add a backslash and the data file name, which is contained in the constant FILENAME. Next, the file is opened specifying RANDOM mode and a record length equal to the length of the user defined type Address, obtained by passing an instance of type Address to the Len function. The number of records in the file is obtained by dividing the file length by the record length.

If there are no records in the file—in other words, if we are starting a new database—a message box is displayed asking whether the user wants to start entering addresses. If the reply is No, the program terminates. Otherwise, the EnteringNew flag is set, the form is displayed, and the **AddNewAddress()** procedure is called to permit entry of the first record. If the file is not empty, the form is displayed and the first record's data displayed.

Listing 11.7   The Form_Load() Event Procedure

```
Private Sub Form_Load()

Dim Reply As Integer

' Generate the full data file path and name.
' We store it in the application directory.
FullFileName = App.Path & "\" & FILENAME
FileNum = FreeFile

' Open the data file and calculate the number of records in it.
Open FullFileName For Random As #FileNum Len = Len(CR)
NumberOfRecords = (LOF(FileNum) / Len(CR))

' If the file is empty (just created).
If NumberOfRecords = 0 Then
    Reply = MsgBox("New file—start entering addresses?", vbYesNo, _
        "New file")
    If Reply = vbYes Then
        EnteringNew = True
        Form1.Show
        Call AddNewAddress
    Else
        Close (FileNum)
        End
    End If
Else            ' If the file is not empty, display the first record.
    CurrentRecord = 1
    EnteringNew = False
    Call DisplayRecord(CurrentRecord)
End If

End Sub
```

Adding an address involves calling the **AddNewAddress()** procedure, which is shown in Listing 11.8. New records are always added at the end of the file. The procedure starts by incrementing the **NumberOfRecords** by 1, then setting **CurrentRecord** to point at this new, blank record. The previous **CurrentRecord** is saved so we can revert to it should the user cancel entry of the new address. The two CommandButton captions are changed (as discussed earlier), the six Text Boxes are cleared, and the focus is set to the LastName text box in preparation for data entry.

Listing 11.8   The AddNewAddress() Procedure

```
Public Sub AddNewAddress()

' Add a new address to the database.

' Add new record at the end of the file.
NumberOfRecords = NumberOfRecords + 1

' Remember the previous current record number.
OldRecord = CurrentRecord

' Set current record pointer to slot for new record.
CurrentRecord = NumberOfRecords

' Change captions on two of the command buttons.
cmdAction(0).Caption = "Save"
cmdAction(1).Caption = "Cancel"

' Erase contents of the text boxes.
txtFName.TEXT = ""
txtLName.TEXT = ""
txtAddress.TEXT = ""
txtCity.TEXT = ""
txtState.TEXT = ""
txtZip.TEXT = ""

' Set the focus to the Last Name text box.
txtLName.SetFocus

End Sub
```

After entering the address data in the Text Boxes, the user can click Save to save the new address, or Cancel to delete. Clicking on Save calls the procedure **SaveCurrentRecord()** to save the new record, then resets the Command Button captions and **EnteringNew** flag. The code for the **SaveCurrentRecord()** procedure is shown in Listing 11.9. The code in this procedure copies the data from the Text Boxes to the CR structure, then uses the **Put** statement to save CR to the file. Remember, the variable **CurrentRecord** has already been set to point at the new record at the end of the file.

Listing 11.9   The SaveCurrentRecord() Procedure

```
Public Sub SaveCurrentRecord()

' Saves the current record.

CR.LName = txtLName.TEXT
CR.FName = txtFName.TEXT
CR.Address = txtAddress.TEXT
CR.City = txtCity.TEXT
CR.State = txtState.TEXT
CR.Zip = txtZip.TEXT

Put #FileNum, CurrentRecord, CR

End Sub
```

Displaying a record is handled by the procedure **DisplayRecord()**. Passed the desired record number as its one argument, this procedure reads the specified record from the file into the structure CR, then copies the individual fields from CR into the six Text Boxes on the form. This code is shown in Listing 11.10.

Listing 11.10   The DisplayRecord() Procedure

```
Public Sub DisplayRecord(Record As Integer)

' Reads the specified record from the file and displays it.
Get #FileNum, Record, CR

txtLName.TEXT = CR.LName
txtFName.TEXT = CR.FName
txtAddress.TEXT = CR.Address
txtCity.TEXT = CR.City
txtState.TEXT = CR.State
txtZip.TEXT = CR.Zip

End Sub
```

The last procedure in the program's main form is concerned with navigating through the address records in response to clicks of the lower set of Command Buttons. The **Click()** event procedure for this control array is presented in Listing 11.11. The code should be easy to understand; it sets the **CurrentRecord** variable to point at the desired record, then calls **DisplayRecord()** to load and display that record.

Listing 11.11   The Navigation Button's Click() Event Procedure

```
Private Sub cmdMove_Click(Index As Integer)

' For the control array of "movement" buttons.
```

```
' If we're entering a new record we don't want these
' buttons to work
If EnteringNew Then Exit Sub

' Save the current record in case it has been edited.
Call SaveCurrentRecord

Select Case Index
    Case 0       'First record.
        CurrentRecord = 1
    Case 1       ' Previous record.
        CurrentRecord = CurrentRecord-1
        If CurrentRecord < 1 Then
            CurrentRecord = 1
            MsgBox ("Already at first record!")
        End If
    Case 2       ' Next record.
        CurrentRecord = CurrentRecord + 1
        If CurrentRecord > NumberOfRecords Then
            CurrentRecord = NumberOfRecords
            MsgBox ("Already at last record!")
        End If
    Case 3       ' Last record.
        CurrentRecord = NumberOfRecords
End Select

Call DisplayRecord(CurrentRecord)

End Sub
```

The List Form

We've already designed the form that will display the alphabetical list of addresses. What about its code? When the form is activated by the **Show** method, it is loaded and displayed just like a program's startup form at the beginning of program execution. We'll use its **Load()** event procedure to perform the form's main task, that of reading all of the address records from the disk file and placing them in the List Box. This procedure will be executed when the Show method is used in the program's main form to display the list form. This simple code is shown in Listing 11.12. We set up a loop that will start at record 1 and progress to the last record. Each record is read into the CR structure; then the various parts of the address, starting with the last name, are concentrated into a temporary string variable before being loaded into the List Box with the **AddItem** method. Since we set the List Box's **Sorted** property to *True*, the List Box will automatically sort the items.

The final item is the **Resize()** event procedure, shown in Listing 11.13. Code in this procedure sets the size of the List Box to fill the form, a familiar technique.

Listing 11.12   The List Form's Load() Event Procedure

```
Private Sub Form_Load()

Dim i As Integer, buf As String

' When the form loads, go through the entire database
' file reading each record and adding it to the list box.

For i = 1 To NumberOfRecords
    Get #FileNum, i, CR
    buf = RTrim$(CR.LName)
    buf = buf & ", " & RTrim$(CR.FName)
    buf = buf & "    " & RTrim$(CR.Address)
    buf = buf & ", " & RTrim$(CR.City)
    buf = buf & " " & RTrim$(CR.State)
    buf = buf & " " & RTrim$(CR.Zip)
    List1.AddItem buf
Next i

End Sub
```

Listing 11.13   The List Form's Resize() Event Procedure

```
Private Sub Form_Resize()

' Make the list box the same size as the form.

List1.Left = 0
List1.TOP = 0
List1.Width = frmList.ScaleWidth
List1.Height = frmList.ScaleHeight

End Sub
```

Additional Features for the Address Database

Our address database works pretty well. We can enter addresses, type in new ones, and so on. After using it for a short time, however, the shortcomings will become apparent. The most important feature it lacks, at least in my mind, is the ability to search for records based on a person's name. You certainly don't want to scroll through several hundred addresses just to find one! The ability to print envelopes would be nice, too, as would the addition of fields for such information as phone numbers.

A more serious drawback is the way the program handles deleted records. When we delete a record, the program does not actually remove that record from the file. Rather, as shown in Listing 11.4, it simply erases the contents of the record's fields. The blank record still takes up space in the file, and will still display as we scroll through the database. There are several approaches we can take to this problem:

- Add code that will skip over blank records during the scrolling process or when the records are listed. The blank records will still take up disk space, but at least they won't be displayed.

- Change the code—instead of always adding new records at the end of the file, it will look through the file for an empty record and place the new one there, moving to the end only if there are no empty spaces.

- Compact the database file on a regular basis— for example, each time the program starts. Compacting consists of going through the file looking for empty records and filling them, usually by moving data from the last record in the file to the blank record.

This concludes our tour of the old-fashioned way of writing database programs in Visual Basic. Please remember, I am not using "old-fashioned" in a pejorative sense. Just because it is the old way does not make it automatically inferior to the new way.

USING VISUAL BASIC'S JET DATABASE ENGINE

The "new way" is to use the Jet database engine that is provided with Visual Basic. In this context, the term *engine* is not used to mean a source of power, as in an automobile engine, but rather a mechanism or device. The engine sits between your Visual Basic program and the database file that contains the records. Our program pulls levers and pushes buttons at its side of the engine, and the gears, cams, and springs in the engine go to work and perform the requested action on the database. The result, if requested, pops out of a slot ready for program use.

Of course, "pulling levers and pushing buttons" means sending commands, but the basic idea is the same. We tell the engine *what* we want to accomplish, and the engine worries about *how* to do it. Part of the beauty of this system is the ability of the database engine to work with several different kinds of databases, as shown here:

- Microsoft Access

- Paradox 3.X and 4.X

- dBASE III and IV

- FoxPro 2.0 and 2.5

- Btrieve

- ODBC

We can write a Visual Basic program to manipulate data in any of these database formats. Of course, all types of databases use the same file-record-field format, but each type of database file uses its own proprietary method of storing the data and its related information. The Jet database engine that Visual Basic uses is actually the same engine used by Microsoft's Access database program.

There are two levels at which a Visual Basic program can interact with a database. The most common is to connect the Visual Basic program to an existing database. The program can add, delete, and otherwise manipulate the data in the database, but it cannot change the structure of the database. In other words, it cannot create a new database, add or delete tables in an existing database, or change the field structure of records in a table. The second level permits all these activities—the user of the Visual Basic program can create a database from scratch, specifying the tables and fields it is to contain. This second level is considerably more complicated to program, and we will not pursue it further in this book. The first approach, where the database structure is fixed, is by far the most useful and the one we encounter most often in our programming.

The database that our Visual Basic program will manipulate must already exist. It may be a client's database that already contains thousands of records, or it might be a brand new database created as part of the program development process. A new database can be empty—contain no data—but its table and record structure is defined, and this is what's important.

An important tool for database programming is Visual Basic's Data Manager, which we start from the Add-Ins menu. The Data Manager has four main functions:

- Create a new database from scratch, defining its table and record structure. New databases can be created only in the Microsoft Access file format.

- Open an existing database and examine its table and record structure.

- Open an existing database and add, delete, or edit records.

- Create indexes for a database.

The Ups and Downs of Indexes

A database table can have one or more indexes associated with it. Each index is based on one or more of the fields in the table. In effect, an index sorts the records based on the data in the associated field. The physical order of the records is not actually changed; rather, the index provides a look-up table into the database table. Once you define an index, it is maintained automatically by the database engine. If you have two or more indexes, you can "sort" the database two or more ways and instantly change the effective sort order by using a different index. For certain database operations, the current index determines the order in which records are returned from the table.

Defining indexes for your database tables requires a trade-off. Defining an index on a particular field greatly speeds up queries, or searches, that involve that field. At the same time, it slows down data entry and updates because of the time required for the Jet engine to update the index.

Data Manager is a programmer's tool that is part of Visual Basic—it is not something you distribute with your applications.

The Database – Program Link

A complex chain of links exists between the database table and what the user sees and does in the program. The complexity lies in the details that go on behind the scenes. The parts handled by the programmer are actually relatively simple.

The first link, the one closest to the database, is the Jet database engine. The programmer rarely has to be concerned with the engine—it's just there, doing its job.

The next link is the data control. This control is placed on a form similar to any other control. It displays as a horizontal bar with arrows at either end, as shown in Figure 11.3. To use a data control, we must attach it to a database file and to a specific table within that file. Then the Data control will allow us to browse through the records in the table using its arrows, and to manipulate the table data using its methods.

The third link in the chain between user and database is *data aware controls* (sometimes called *data bound controls*). A data aware control can either be linked to a specific Data control or to a specific field in the table to which the Data control is linked. Once the link is in place, data is automatically trans-

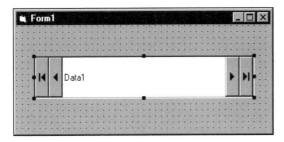

Figure 11.3 *The Data control.*

ferred back and forth between the database and the control. If we move to a certain record in the database, that record's data is automatically displayed in the control. If the user enters new data in the control, the new data is automatically saved in the database. All this is handled automatically with little or no need for programming. The links between a data aware control and a database table are diagrammed in Figure 11.4.

Several of Visual Basic's controls are data aware. The CheckBox, TextBox, Label, Picture, Image, ListBox, and ComboBox controls can be bound to a single field of a table linked to the Data control. The MaskedEdit and 3DCheckBox controls, available in the Professional Edition, are also data aware. These controls all deal with a single record at a time. The DBList, DBCombo, and DBGrid controls are also data aware, and are used to display or manipulate several records at once.

Except for the last three controls mentioned previously, the data aware controls do not have to be used in conjunction with a Data control. In other words, their data-awareness is an option.

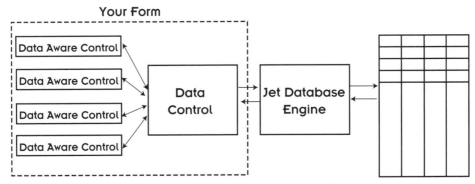

Figure 11.4 *The links between a data aware control and a database table.*

Designing the Database

In order to demonstrate the Jet database engine and the associated controls, I wanted to design a database similar to the address list database that we created earlier in the chapter using traditional Basic programming methods. Rather than creating another address list, however, I thought we would try something different—but what? Looking around my living room, the answer became clear. My scattered collection of over 1000 LPs and CDs is in serious need of organization. A database to keep track of my recordings and their shelf locations would be a good start. So that's what we'll develop here, a musical recording database. While different in detail from the address database developed earlier, the recordings database will be similar enough in basic structure and functionality to provide a good comparison.

Using the Data Manager to Create the Database

Select Data Manager from the Add-Ins menu. The Data manager will start and display a blank window.

Select New Database from the Data Manager's File menu. The New Database dialog is displayed. Select the folder where you want the database located; for our purposes this should be the folder where the Visual Basic project will be placed. Type the database name Music in the File name box and click the Save button.

The Data Manager will now display the list of tables in our database, as shown in Figure 11.5. Since we have not designed any tables yet, this list is empty. To create the database's only table, click the New button to display the Add Table dialog box, which is shown in Figure 11.6.

In the Name box, type the table name. We'll call ours Recordings. Next, use this same dialog box to define the fields that will be in this table. Follow these steps for each field:

1. Type the field name in the Field Name box.

2. Pull down the Type list and select the data type of the field. You have all of Visual Basic's data types available, plus a couple of new ones (we won't worry about these just yet).

3. For the **String** data types, specify the length of field (the maximum number of characters it can contain).

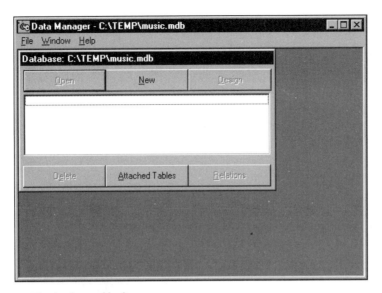

Figure 11.5   *The database tables list.*

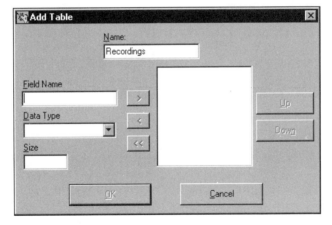

Figure 11.6   *The Add Table dialog box.*

4. Once the field is defined, click the right arrow to add it to the list of fields.

For our database, add the following Text fields. The number following the field name indicates the field length in Table 11.2.

To change the order of fields, click the field name in the list, then click the Up or Down button to move it. The dialog box after the Recordings table is defined is shown in Figure 11.7. Once the table's field definitions are finished, click OK.

Table 11.2   *Text Fields*

Field	Length
Composer/Group	40
Title	40
Media	4
Publisher	12
Location	6
Notes	50

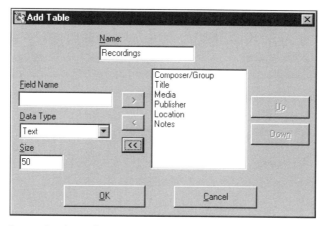

Figure 11.7   *The completed recordings table definition.*

The next step is to define an index for our table. A table does not have to have an index, but the advantages of an index include faster queries and automatic sorting of records. Each index is linked to one field in the table, and is used to sort the table, based on the data in that field, and also to speed queries on that field. While a table can have more than one index, we will create only one, linked to the Title field. Since we want the database sorted on this field and since the database's search capabilities will be limited to the Title field, this index will suit our needs perfectly.

Modifying Database Tables

We can use the Data Manager to open an existing database and change the field structure of a table. Most of these changes—modifying the data type of a field or changing its length—will result in data loss. This is one reason to plan carefully before designing the database tables and entering data. When changing the table structure is a necessity, we are almost always better off creating a brand new table with the desired structure than writing a Visual Basic program to transfer existing data from the old table to the new. Doing this is easier than it might seem. Simply place two Data controls on a form, one linked to each table, and each with the required number of Text Box controls linked to it. Use the techniques covered later in this chapter to read each record from the old table into one set of Text Boxes, transfer it to the other set, then save it in the new table.

After completing the table definition, the Data Manager window should look like Figure 11.8. To create an index, click Recordings in the tables list, then click the Design button. The Table Editor dialog box, shown in Figure 11.9, opens.

This window displays the structure of our table and the characteristics of the various fields in the table. We can click a field, then click the Edit button to modify a field definition, or click Add or Delete to add a new field or remove an existing one. Any of these actions, however, will delete existing data in the table. Sometimes we only need to add an index. To do so, click the Indexes button. A small dialog box opens listing the table's current indexes; in this case, we have none. Click the Add button to display the Add Index dialog box, shown in Figure 11.10.

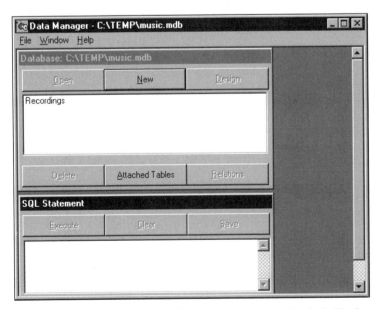

Figure 11.8 *After defining the Recordings table, the Data Manager window looks like this.*

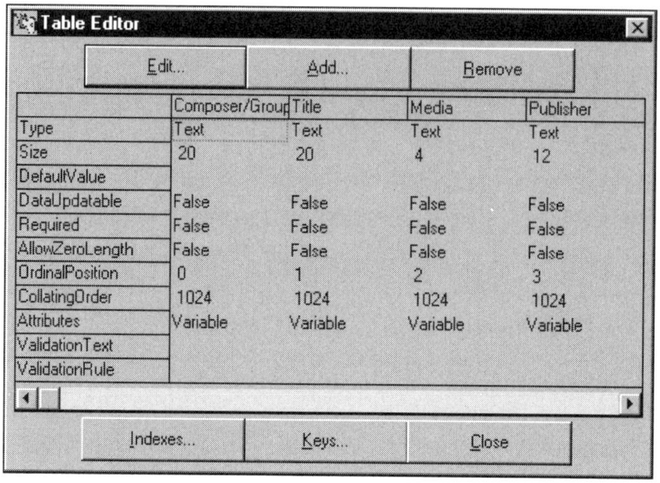

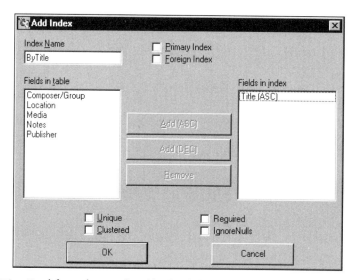

Figure 11.9 *The Table Editor window.*

Figure 11.10 *You define indexes in the Add Index dialog box.*

Type the index name in the corresponding box. It should be descriptive, so I used the name ByTitle for the index for the Recordings table. Then, in the list of table fields, click the name of the field on which the index is to be based, then click the Add (ASC) button to add the field to the index definition. This creates an index based on the specified field in ascending order (A-Z, 0-9). If we wanted a reverse-order index, we would use the Add (DEC) button.

We could add additional fields to the index definition. In the case of identical data in the first field, the data in these additional fields would be used to determine the index order. We only need the one field, however, so you can click OK to close the Add Index dialog box, then click Close to close the Indexes dialog box. Finally, click Close to close the Table Editor dialog box. The database definition is now complete.

Only more more step is required before closing the Data Manager. While we have defined the structure of our database table, it is empty—that is, it contains no data. This is OK, because you can place code in your Visual Basic program that will deal with an empty database table. We can skip adding this special code to our program, however, if we add at least a single record to the database table using Data Manager. Real data is fine, although we can add a dummy record and instruct our users to delete it when they enter real data.

To add a record to the table we just defined, highlight the table name in the Tables/Query Defs dialog box and click the Open button. The dialog box shown in Figure 11.11 will open, providing a text box for each of the fields in the table. Type the dummy record's data into the dialog box, then click the Update button followed by the Close button. Our table now has one record in it, and we can close the Data Manager and return to Visual Basic.

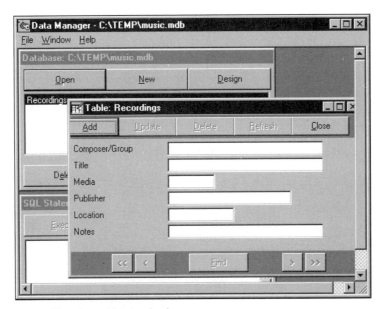

Figure 11.11   Adding data to the new database.

Designing the Main Form

The main form needs Text Box controls to display the database fields. It also requires labels to identify those Text Boxes, and Command Buttons for the program commands. Last but not least, it needs a Data control to interface with the database. The form is shown in Figure 11.12, and its objects and properties are presented in Listing 11.14. Rather than hold your hand through every step of creating this form, I'll refer you to the figure and the listing, which provide all the information necessary to create the form. I will point out that the Command Buttons are in a control array, so it's important to match the **Caption** and **Index** properties as indicated.

Binding Controls to the Data Table

Once the form has been designed, the next step is to bind the controls to the data. There are two steps to this: (1) Bind the Data control to a specific database file and to a specific table within that file, and (2) Bind each data aware control to the Data control and to a specific field in the table to which the Data control is bound. As you might expect, we do this with the control properties. For the Data control, set its **DatabaseName** property to the database you just created and set its **RecordSource** property to *Recordings*. (Since a database can have more than one table, specify the exact table to which the Data control is linked.) Also, set the Data control's **RecordsetType** property to *1 -Dynaset* (more on Recordsets and Dynasets soon). For the six Text Box

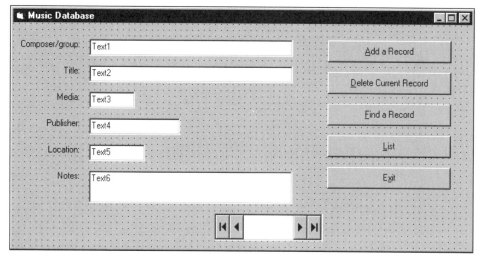

Figure 11.12 *The music database program's main form.*

controls, set the **DataSource** property of each one to *Data1,* pointing at the Data control. Then, set the **DataField** property of each control to the name of its associated field: *"Composer/Group"* for the first Text Box, *"Title"* for the second, and so on.

While the program is not complete, we can run it and see the power of data-aware controls in action. The "dummy" record that we entered in the database from the Data Manager will be displayed in the Text Box controls. Had we entered multiple records, we would be able to move between them by clicking the arrows on the Data control. All this without a single line of code! We do need some code, although surprisingly little, to complete the database program's functionality.

Listing 11.14 Objects and Properties in MUSIC.FRM

```
Begin VB.Form Form1
    Caption         =   "Music Database"
    Begin VB.CommandButton Command1
        Caption     =   "E&xit"
        Index       =   4
    End
    Begin VB.CommandButton Command1
        Caption     =   "&List"
        Index       =   3
    End
    Begin VB.CommandButton Command1
        Caption     =   "&Find a Record"
        Index       =   2
    End
    Begin VB.CommandButton Command1
        Caption     =   "&Delete Current Record"
        Index       =   1
    End
    Begin VB.CommandButton Command1
        Caption     =   "&Add a Record"
        Index       =   0
    End
    Begin VB.TextBox Text6
        DataField   =   "Notes"
        DataSource  =   "Data1"
    End
    Begin VB.TextBox Text5
        DataField   =   "Location"
        DataSource  =   "Data1"
    End
    Begin VB.TextBox Text4
        DataField   =   "Publisher"
        DataSource  =   "Data1"
    End
```

```
Begin VB.TextBox Text3
   DataField      =    "Media"
   DataSource     =    "Data1"
End
Begin VB.TextBox Text2
   DataField      =    "Title"
   DataSource     =    "Data1"
End
Begin VB.TextBox Text1
   DataField      =    "Composer/Group"
   DataSource     =    "Data1"
End
Begin VB.Data Data1
   Connect        =    "Access"
   DatabaseName   =    "D:\VB4\EXPLORER\music.mdb"
   Exclusive      =    0     'False
   Options        =    0
   RecordsetType  =    1     'Dynaset
   RecordSource   =    "Recordings"
End
Begin VB.Label Label6
   Alignment      =    1     'Right Justify
   Caption        =    "Notes:"
End
Begin VB.Label Label5
   Alignment      =    1     'Right Justify
   Caption        =    "Location:"
End
Begin VB.Label Label4
   Alignment      =    1     'Right Justify
   Caption        =    "Publisher:"
End
Begin VB.Label Label3
   Alignment      =    1     'Right Justify
   Caption        =    "Media:"
End
Begin VB.Label Label2
   Alignment      =    1     'Right Justify
   Caption        =    "Title:"
End
Begin VB.Label Label1
   Alignment      =    1     'Right Justify
   Caption        =    "Composer/group:"
End
End
```

Adding the Remaining Code

The code for the array of Command Buttons is remarkably simple, largely due to the power of the database engine. This code is shown in Listing 11.15. If we want to add a new record, we just call the **AddNew** method of the Recordset object that is associated with the Data control. Other than the convenient touch of setting the focus to the first Text Box, that's all there is to it! The method takes care of clearing the Text Boxes in preparation for entry of new data, as well as saving the new data once it has been entered. Compare this with the code for adding a new record in this chapter's first program—what a difference!

Deleting a record is equally easy. Executing the Recordset object's **Delete** method is all that is required. We follow this with the **MoveNext** method, which displays the next record so the form's Text Boxes do not remain blank.

Finding a particular record requires a call to the **FindRecord()** procedure, which we'll explore soon. Likewise for listing all records, where we rely on the **Show** method to display a separate form.

Listing 11.15   The Command Button Click() Event Code

```
Private Sub Command1_Click(Index As Integer)

Select Case Index
    Case 0        ' Add
        Text1.SetFocus
        Data1.Recordset.AddNew
    Case 1        ' Delete
        Data1.Recordset.DELETE
        Data1.Recordset.MoveNext
    Case 2        ' Find
        Call FindRecord
    Case 3        ' List
        1stForm.Show
    Case 4        ' Exit
        End
End Select

End Sub
```

Recordsets

But what is a Recordset? It's a type of Visual Basic object that acts as an abstract representation of an actual database table on disk. Your program accesses and manipulates the data in the table by means of the Recordset object, which has its own properties and methods. When a form containing a Data control is loaded, and if that Data control is validly linked to a table in a database, a Recordset is automatically created and is available for use by means of the Data control's **Recordset** property. A Recordset can also be created in code, independent of a Data control, but this is a technique we will not explore in this chapter. For a complete look at the many properties and methods of the Recordset object, please refer to the Visual Basic Help system.

The Recordset object is not only very powerful, it is also complex. To complicate matters further, we can choose from three types of Recordsets: Table, Dynaset, and Snapshot. How do these Recordset types vary? Each type of Recordset uses basically the same commands, but they interact differently with their underlying table (called the *base* table) or tables.

- A **Snapshot** type Recordset provides a static, read-only copy of the base table. The records in the base table cannot be deleted or modified (although new records can be inserted). Changes to the base table—in a multiuser environment, for example, when another user adds data to the table—are not reflected in the Snapshot. Technically speaking, a **Snapshot** type Recordset contains the results of an SQL query operation on the base table. In other words, the Snapshot contains selected records from the base table. When attached to a Data control, a Snapshot's initial condition is to contain all the records from the base table—in other words, the results of a "select all records" query. **Snapshot** type Recordsets are intended for situations where your program will be reading but not modifying the table data, such as in report generation.

- A **Dynaset** type Recordset provides dynamic access to a table's records. Records can be added, deleted, and edited. Also, changes to the table made by others are reflected in the Dynaset. Otherwise, a **Dynaset** type Recordset is very much like a Snapshot type Recordset.

- A **Table** type Recordset provides the most direct access to all of the base table's records. No SQL query is implicit in a **Table** type Recordset, so it always includes all of the table's records. This type of Recordset provides very quick access to all of the table's records, but extracting particular sets of records can require some complicated programming.

Of course, my descriptions of the three types of Recordsets are rather oversimplified. Other differences exist among them that only come into play in the most complicated and demanding types of database applications where tables contain hundreds of thousands of records. With a few exceptions, such as the **Snapshot** type Recordset's inability to update records in the base table, the three types can all do the same things. The difference between them is primarily in database performance (speed). Further discussion in this area is beyond the scope of an introductory book, but the amount of published information is abundant if you are interested. When in doubt, use a **Dynaset**.

 **Recordset Hints**

If you have used earlier versions of Visual Basic to write database programs, you may be familiar with the Snapshot object and the Dynaset object. The Dynaset object is no longer supported, but is replaced by the Dynaset type Recordset. The Snapshot object is supported only for reasons of backward compatibility. It is recommended that you use the Snapshot type Recordset in preference to a Snapshot object.

Finding a Record

Finding a particular record in the database table is also simplified by the Recordset object's methods. Our database program will be limited to searching the Title field, but the same methods apply to searches, or *queries*, on other fields. While a Recordset method performs the actual search, some additional programming is required to prepare for the search and respond to its result. This step is accomplished in the **FindRecord()** procedure, shown in Listing 11.16.

The procedure first uses the **InputBox()** function to ask the user what to search for. **InputBox()** displays a dialog box with a prompt, a Text Box where the user types a response, and OK and Cancel buttons. If the user selects OK, the string entered in the Text Box is returned by the function. If the user selects Cancel, an empty string is returned, in which case we exit the procedure.

The next step is incorporating the desired search template into a command string that can be passed to the Recordset object's **FindFirst** method. This string consists of the name of the field we are querying, in brackets, followed by an equal sign and the string we are searching for in single or double quotes. For example, to find records where the Title field contains "Rubber Soul" (the title of a Beatles album, for those of you too young to know), we would use this command string:

```
[Title] = "Rubber Soul"
```

While either single or double quotes will work to enclose the search string, I prefer using double quotes because it permits the search string itself to contain a single quote, letting you search for other Beatles titles such as *Hard Day's Night*. Since you cannot enter a double quote directly into a Basic string, use the **Chr$()** function to return the double quote character, passing the argument of 34 (the ASCII code for the double quote). You can see how this is done in the listing.

The **FindRecord()** procedure makes use of the Recordset object's **Bookmark** property to keep track of the record that is current before the search is performed. This step is necessary; if the **FindFirst** method finds no match, it makes the first record in the table current. If we want the record that was displayed when the search was initiated to remain displayed if the search fails, we must make a note of it and explicitly return there. The **Bookmark** property returns a string value that identifies the current record. Understanding the nature of this string is not necessary. Just save it. If the search fails, assign it back to the Recordset's **Bookmark** property to make that record current again.

How do you know if the search has failed? The Recordset object's **NoMatch** property is *False* unless a search has failed, so by testing this property we know the search outcome. If the search is successful, the matching record automatically becomes current and is displayed in the bound controls. The **FindFirst** method looks for the first record that exactly matches the search template. There is also a **FindLast** method that finds the last matching record, in effect searching from the end of the table. If you have used **FindFirst** to locate the first match, you can use the **FindNext** method one or more times to locate subsequent matching records.

Fine-Tuning the Search

What if you don't want the search restricted to exact matches? For example, if you enter the search string "Hard," you would like the search to locate titles such as "A Hard Day's Night" and "Hard Times." To accomplish this, you must use the **Like** keyword in the command string that you pass to the **FindFirst** or **FindNext** methods. You can use the * wildcard to represent any zero or more characters. For example, the command string

```
[Title] Like "*Hard*"
```

will find any record whose Title field contains the word "Hard." The Like keyword is a Structured Query Language (SQL) keyword, and the Jet database engine understands SQL. In other words, you can pass SQL statements to the FindNext and related Recordset object methods. SQL is a very complex and powerful database language for which I will not attempt to provide any systematic coverage. If you want to learn more about SQL, you can look at the Visual Basic Help system or refer to one of the many books published on the topic.

Listing 11.16   The FindRecord() Procedure

```
Public Sub FindRecord()

Dim Template As String
Dim Previous As String

Template = InputBox("Find what?", "Find a Title")

' If user selects Cancel a blank string is returned.
If Template = "" Then Exit Sub

' Save the current position.
Previous = Data1.Recordset.Bookmark

' Set up the search template and use the FindFirst
' method to perform the search.
Template = "[Title]= " & Chr$(34) & Template & Chr$(34)
Data1.Recordset.FindFirst Template

' If no match, return to original record and
' display a message.
If Data1.Recordset.NoMatch Then
    Data1.Recordset.Bookmark = Previous
    MsgBox ("No match found")
End If

End Sub
```

Listing All Records

As with the earlier address list database program, we would like the capability to display an alphabetical list of all the records in the database. As before, we'll use a separate form with a List Box control, adding a Command Button to close the list window. As an added feature, we'll add code so that when the user clicks a title in the list, the program's main form will display the entire record for that title.

To create the form, select Form from the Insert menu. Set the form's **Name** property to *lstForm*, and its **Caption** property to *List All Recordings*. Save the form with the name FRMLIST2. Add a ListBox and a CommandButton control. Set the Command Button's **Caption** property to *&Close*, and be sure that the List Box's **Sort** property is set to *True*. Don't worry about the size and position of these controls, as they will be set in code.

Listing 11.17 Objects and Properties in FRMLIST2.FRM

```
Begin VB.Form 1stForm
   Caption         =   "List All Recordings"
   Begin VB.CommandButton cmdClose
     Caption         =   "&Close"
   End
   Begin VB.ListBox List1
   End
End
```

The code in FRMLIST2.FRM contains only four event procedures. The **Click()** procedure for the Command Button is simple, using only the Unload statement to unload the form and return the focus to the program's main form.

Somewhat more complex is the **Form_Load()** procedure. Here we need to extract the Title field data from all of the records in the Recordings table, and load them into the List Box (which automatically sorts them). We start by saving the current record's bookmark so we can return to it when we are finished:

```
Bookmark = Form1.Data1.Recordset.Bookmark
```

Next, we want to move to the first record in the Recordset and then loop one at a time through all of them. To do this, we need to know how many records exist. This information is obtained from the Recordset object's **RecordCount** property. Before we read this property, however, we must move to the end of the Recordset with the **MoveLast** method. Why is this? A **Dynaset** type Recordset does not necessarily read all of the table's records into memory at once; and until it has actually read the entire table, it will not have an accurate record count. We therefore force a read to the end of the table with the **MoveLast** method. Now the **RecordCount** property will contain an accurate count of the records; and after storing that value, we can use **MoveFirst** to move to the first record:

```
Form1.Data1.Recordset.MoveLast
NumRecs = Form1.Data1.Recordset.RecordCount
Form1.Data1.Recordset.MoveFirst
```

We are now ready to load the List Box. Using the **Clear** method first to be sure it's empty, we loop through the table reading the Tile field from each record and load it into the List Box with the **AddItem** method. Finally, we return to the original record that was saved:

```
List1.Clear
```

```
For i = 0 To NumRecs-1
    x = Form1.Data1.Recordset.Fields("Title").VALUE
    If IsNull(x) Then x = ""
    Form1.Data1.Recordset.MoveNext
    List1.AddItem x
Next i

Form1.Data1.Recordset.Bookmark = Bookmark
```

Note the complex line of code that actually retrieves the Title data from the current record and stores it in the string variable x. It may be easier to read this line from right to left: "The Value of the Field named Title in the Recordset that is associated with the Data control named Data1 on the form named Form1."

 **Control Names and Forms**

Note the syntax that you use to refer to a control on another form. A control name by itself automatically refers to the current form—that is, the form whose module contains the code. To refer to a control on a different form, precede the control name with the form name and a period. If the form referred to has not yet been loaded, it will be loaded (but not displayed).

How do we go about displaying a record in the main form when the user clicks its title in the list? My approach is to use the **FindFirst** method to search for the record. Since we retrieved the title directly from the database table, we know a match will occur when we search for that title. We place the required code in the List Box's **Click()** event procedure. When the user selects an item in a List Box, either by clicking or using the keyboard, the **Click()** event is generated. Obviously the program will permit either mouse or keyboard input. The numerical position of the selected item in the list is returned by the **ListIndex** property. To get the item itself, we use the **ListIndex** property as the index to the List Box's **List** property. Here's the code, which places the title from the List Box in a query string:

```
Template = "[Title] = " & Chr$(34) & List1.List(List1.ListIndex) & Chr$(34)
Form1.Data1.Recordset.FindFirst Template
```

Lastly, we have the form's **Resize()** event procedure, which sets the ListBox and Command Button sizes to fill the form. We have already reviewed this procedure, so I won't go into details. The complete code in FRMLIST2.FRM is presented in Listing 11.18.

Listing 11.18   Code in LSTFORM2.FRM

```
Option Explicit

Private Sub cmdClose_Click()

Unload lstForm

End Sub

Private Sub Form_Load()

Dim x As Variant, NumRecs As Integer
Dim i As Integer, Bookmark As String

Bookmark = Form1.Data1.Recordset.Bookmark
Form1.Data1.Recordset.MoveLast
NumRecs = Form1.Data1.Recordset.RecordCount
Form1.Data1.Recordset.MoveFirst

List1.Clear

For i = 0 To NumRecs-1
    x = Form1.Data1.Recordset.Fields("Title").VALUE
    If IsNull(x) Then x = ""
    Form1.Data1.Recordset.MoveNext
    List1.AddItem x
Next i

Form1.Data1.Recordset.Bookmark = Bookmark

End Sub

Private Sub Form_Resize()

List1.Left = 0
List1.TOP = 0
List1.Width = lstForm.ScaleWidth
List1.Height = lstForm.ScaleHeight * 0.9
cmdClose.TOP = List1.Height + 1
cmdClose.Left = 0
cmdClose.Width = lstForm.ScaleWidth
cmdClose.Height = lstForm.ScaleHeight * 0.1

End Sub


Private Sub List1_Click()

Dim Template As String
```

```
' Set up the template and perform the search. Since
' we know that there must be a matching title we do not
' have to provide for the possibility of no match.

' We use Chr$(34) to enclose the search template in double
' quotes. This permits the template to contain single quotes, which
' is not possible if the template itself is enclosed in double quotes.

Template = "[Title] = " & Chr$(34) & List1.List(List1.ListIndex) & Chr$(34)
Form1.Data1.Recordset.FindFirst Template

End Sub
```

This completes our music database program. If you try it out, you'll see that it provides all the functionality of the address list program, but with fewer lines of code. The executing program, with both forms displayed, is shown in Figure 11.13. The ease with which we created this program reflects the power of Visual Basic's Data control and the data aware controls that can be linked to it. Several things that would be desirable in even a simple database program are missing. No error trapping exists, which is perhaps the most serious omission. Error trapping permits a program to deal gracefully with errors such as a corrupt database file, disk problems, and the like. Likewise we have no data validation, ensuring that the user does not enter invalid data—for example, a title that is longer than the maximum 40 characters permitted by the table definition. We will delve into these and other important database topics in the following chapters.

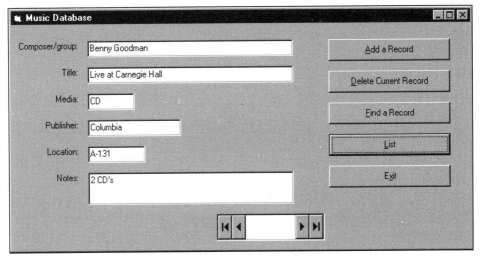

Figure 11.13   *The music database in action.*

Of course, this is a simple database program that requires none of the sophisticated and complex features of many commercial database applications. Visual Basic's database tools provide for these as well, and we'll see in the next several chapters how to approach the design of a database program with a variety of features that would be required in a project you create for a paying client.

PRELIMINARY CONSIDERATIONS

CHAPTER 12

So you want to play with the database big-boys? Visual Basic is the key, but picking up some basics first will be a big boost.

Database programming is unlike any other kind of programming you've ever approached. Sure, a simple database such as the one we tackled in the previous chapter can be slapped together pretty easily with a little common sense and a few fundamental programming skills. But quite honestly, that's greasy kid stuff. The database applications that paying customers desire are many times more complex, and correspondingly more difficult to program.

SOME BASICS IN TERMINOLOGY

When doing serious database development, you will be working almost exclusively with *relational* databases. So the first step is knowing exactly what a relational database is and familiarizing yourself with the specialized terminology thrown around by database developers.

Relational Databases

With rare exceptions, all serious database development involves *relational* databases, as opposed to the *flat file* database that we developed in the earlier chapter. A flat file database contains only a single table, from which it derives its name—it is two-dimensional, or flat. One dimension is represented by the fields, or columns, and the other dimension is represented by the records, or rows. Flat file databases are perfectly suitable for tasks such as address lists. But as the user's demands grow more complex, the flat file structure soon reveals its weaknesses.

This contrast will be clearer if we look at an example. In the case of a database that is intended to keep track of inventory for an electronics store, each record will contain the fields necessary to hold the information about a single stock item:

Stock Number

Description

Type

Wholesale Cost

Retail Price

Quantity on Hand

Manufacturer Name

Manufacturer Order Number

Manufacturer Street Address

Manufacturer City

Manufacturer State

Manufacturer Zip

Manufacturer Telephone

At first glance this may seem OK, but imagine what would happen if the store had many items from one manufacturer. For each stock item, the manufacturer's name and other information would have to be entered, even though this information is the same for each item. This system is highly inefficient, not only because of the wasted operator time and the increased chance of errors, but because valuable disk space is consumed just storing all the duplicate information. The solution? A *relational* database. Instead of a single table that contains all of the needed information, the database contains multiple tables with the information spread among them. For this example, the structure of the two tables might be as follows:

The "Stock Items" table:

Stock Number

Description

Type

Wholesale Cost

Retail Price

Quantity on Hand

Manufacturer Name

The "Manufacturers" table:

Manufacturer Name

Manufacturer Street Address

Manufacturer City

Manufacturer State

Manufacturer Zip

Manufacturer Telephone

As you can see, information is not duplicated within this structure. One record exists for each manufacturer, and one record exists for each stock item. The two tables are linked by the one field they have in common, Manufacturer Name. A relational database manager—the application program—will have the ability to relate or *join* the tables in various ways as required by the user. For example, in this application the user would probably want the following capabilities (among others):

• When creating a new entry in the Stock Items table, prompt for the manufacturer's address information if the manufacturer is not already entered in the Manufacturers table.

- Print or display the manufacturer's address for a particular part.

- List all parts that come from a particular manufacturer.

With two or more tables, the database is no longer flat—the third dimension is provided by the multiple tables. The tables are designed to hold all of the needed information. The relational database program can *relate* the information in one table to information in other tables in a variety of ways, such as the three listed above. This capability is where the term *relational* is derived.

The Table's the Thing

A table in a relational database is really the same as a table in a flat file database. Each column, or field, holds an individual piece of information; while each record, or row, holds all the information about an individual item. Note that in almost all cases, each table in a database represents something that exists in the real world—people, invoices, orders, and so on.

In the world of database programming, some additional terminology has come into use. A table is sometimes referred to as an *entity* or an *entity class.* Rows (records) are sometimes called *tuples* or *entity occurrences.* Columns (fields) can be called *attribute classes.* Note that an attribute class or field represents the most granular level of data—the smallest unit of information. The intersection of a row and column—a single field in a specific record—is an *attribute.* An attribute represents one unit of information about a real-world object, such as a specific individual's last name or specific company's ZIP code.

Tables have one requirement in a relational database that is not required for flat file databases, strictly speaking. Each table must have a *primary key,* a field that uniquely identifies each record in a table. In other words, the data in the primary key field must be unique for each record in the table. In our example database, Stock Number is the primary key for the Stock Items table, and Manufacturer Name is the primary key field for the Manufacturers table. Most relational database applications provide for *compound* primary keys, where the primary key consists of data from more than one field. Compound keys can be used when the combined data from two or more fields uniquely identifies each record, as opposed to the data from a single field.

We must be alert for situations in which the data being placed in the table does not include a primary key. In a table that contains name and address information, for example, we cannot be sure that first name, last name, or even telephone number will not be duplicated between two or more records;

although it may be extremely unlikely. If Social Security number is one of the table's fields, it could be used as the primary key. Lacking such a unique field, however, we can create our own primary key by adding a field to the table that will contain data we know is unique, such as a sequential number that is incremented as new records are added. Note that the primary key field need not contain meaningful data (although it is preferred), but only unique data.

While we are on the subject of keys, let me introduce you to the concept of a foreign key. A *foreign key* is a field whose data serves to link the records in the table with the primary key in another table. The data in a foreign key field does not have to be unique for each record, and rarely is. In the Stock Items table, Manufacturer Name is the foreign key. The Manufacturers table does not have a foreign key.

Tables are sometimes referred to as *primary* and *dependent*. A dependent table is one in which the records depend on information in another table for completion. The records in a primary table have no such dependency, being complete in and of themselves. In our example, the Stock Items table is dependent, requiring information from the Manufacturers table to provide complete data for one stock item. The Manufacturers table is a primary table, since it does not depend on another table to provide complete information (address, telephone, and so on). about a manufacturer. Generally speaking, primary tables are created to avoid the need to place duplicate information in another table.

That's an Order

In a relational database, the records in each table do not exist in any meaningful order. In most cases, the physical order of records in the disk file is the order in which the records were entered; and this rarely, if ever, has any meaning. Of course, the structure of the disk files is something that should never be our concern. Any decent relational database application should completely isolate the user from any worries about disk files, file structure, and the like.

Does this mean that we can't sort the records in our tables? Of course not—sorting is an important aspect of using databases. Rather than physically sorting the records, however, a database application utilizes *logical* sorting based on *indexes*.

Used in this context, *index* does not mean the same thing as the index in the back of a book. The meaning is similar, however, in that a database index also indicates where to find things. Each index is based on one or more fields in the table. The index itself is sorted based on the data in that field, and each entry in the index contains a *pointer* that specifies the physical location of the corresponding record in the table. This is format illustrated in Figure 12.1.

When you want the records to be "sorted" on a particular field, simply tell the database program to use the index that is based on that field. During display, printing, and so on, the table records will appear in the order specified by the index. We can quickly change to another "sort" order by using another index.

In addition to ordering the records in a table, an index greatly speeds up searches, or queries, based on the data in the indexed field. If we are searching for data in a non-indexed field, the database application has no choice but to look through all the records one at a time for a match. If the field has been indexed, however, a binary search algorithm can be used, greatly increasing the speed of the process. Here's how a binary search works:

1. Look at the record in the middle of the index.

2. Is it a match? If so, you're finished. If not, continue with step 3.

3. Is the item you are searching for "less than" the data in the current record? If yes, the matching record (if any) must be in the first half of the index. If not, the matching record must be in the second half of the index.

4. Discard the half of the index where you know the match is *not* located, and return to step 1.

Database file		Index file	
Physical Location	**Data**	**Pointer**	**Data**
1	98163	2	05312
2	05312	4	27715
3	41390	3	41390
4	27715	5	70911
5	70911	1	98163

Figure 12.1   How an index "sorts" records in a table.

When designing a database, the question arises as to which fields a table should be indexed by. More indexes increase flexibility but slow things down, since all indexes must be updated whenever new records are entered. A table should be indexed on its primary key field, which some database applications do automatically. It should also be indexed on any foreign indexes it may contain. Other indexes depend on the details of the application, and are usually restricted to fields that are used as the basis for queries.

Joins

One of the most common tasks that database users need to perform is extracting information from the database tables. When the operation involves two or more tables, it is called a multi-table select, or, more commonly, a *join*. When joining two tables, three possibilities exist:

- A one-to-one join occurs when only one record in a dependent table relates to a record in a primary table. One-to-one relationships are rare in relational databases. When two tables stand in a one-to-one relationship, it is usually better to combine their fields into a single table. The fact that a one-to-one relationship exists indicates that there would be no duplication of data if the tables were combined.

- A one-to-many join occurs when multiple records in the dependent table relate to a single record in the primary table. This join is the most common and most useful type of join used in relational database programs. In our example, a many-to-one relationship exists between the Stock Items table and the Manufacturers table—multiple stock items relate to each manufacturer.

- A many-to-many join occurs when multiple records in the dependent database relate to multiple records in the primary table. For example, if each stock item could be obtained from several manufacturers, and each manufacturer made several stock items, you would have a many-to-many join. Obviously, this kind of join could not be based on a primary key field in either table. Strictly speaking, a many-to-many join is not a true join because it requires an intervening table, the *relation table*, to hold the values of the foreign keys; and relational database theory only defines joins between two tables. The relation table stands in a one-to-many relationship with each of the other tables.

DATABASE FRONT END APPLICATIONS

When we work with Visual Basic to create a database application, we are actually generating a database *front end*. Now, your car has a front end, and your boat has a front end, but what the devil is a database front end? And if it has a front end, does it also have a back end?

A database front end is an application that can be used to view and manipulate the data in a database. The back end is the set of related database tables, and, in some cases, the database engine that serves as the interface between the front end and the tables. Why bother with this separation between the front and back ends of a database? Why not just combine all database functionality into a single application?

The answer to this question will become clear if you think for a moment about how most organizations use a database. The information contained in the database covers a wide range—personnel records, salary information, sales data, inventory information, and so on. The various users, however, need to access selected subsets of this information in specific ways. The personnel department, for example, requires access to the personnel data and needs to look at information such as Social Security contributions and medical insurance payments. The shipping department has no use for personnel information (and may even be denied access to it), but does need to view sales and inventory data.

If the front and back ends of the database were combined in a single application, a single application would have to cover the needs of all potential users. It would be unavoidably large, complex, and cumbersome, not to mention difficult to customize for new or changed needs of a specific group of users. In addition, and perhaps even more importantly, maintaining database integrity and validity would become a nightmare.

The front end/back end approach avoids most of these problems. Each group of users can be given its own specialized software that is designed to do just what they want, and nothing more. With a single program—the back end's database engine—coordinating all access to the actual database files, matters of integrity and validity can be dealt with more easily, and controlling access to different parts of the database becomes feasible.

Database front ends fall into two categories:

- Decision support applications permit the user to view and query information in the database, but not to add or modify information.

- Transaction processing applications include the capability to add, delete, and edit data in the database.

Decision support applications are the most common type of database front end and vary widely in scope. This type of program can be extremely specialized and limited, as in an application designed for sales personnel that only displays their clients and sales information. These programs can also be extremely flexible, as in complex management information systems (MIS) that provide summary data on all of the information in a company's database. Decision support applications generally have read-only access to the database files—that is, they can read the data but cannot change it.

Two approaches, often combined, can be taken toward the design of decision support applications. You can provide the user with one or more fixed, non-modifiable ways of examining the data; or you can provide for the design of individual queries and reports. The former method has the advantage of requiring less training on the part of the final user, but productivity will suffer unless the program's predefined capabilities are closely matched with the user's needs.

Transaction processing applications provide the capability to add new data to a database and to edit or delete existing data. Because a transaction processing application can change the actual table data, some additional programming considerations come into play. The application has the responsibility for preserving the integrity, or accuracy, of the data in the tables.

Multiuser Database Considerations

Most databases are designed for use by more than one person at a time. In multiuser environments, transaction processing front ends must be concerned with the *concurrency* and the *consistency* of the database tables. Let me explain these terms briefly. Concurrency problems can happen if two or more users attempt to update the same record simultaneously. The outcome of the simultaneous update requests may not be predictable—one update or the other may prevail. Consistency problems can occur when one user updates a set of records, and another user attempts to view those records while that transaction is in progress. The data seen by the second user may be incorrect, reflecting only part of the update transaction.

The solution to both of these problems involves *locking* the record during an update, preventing any other user from accessing the record until the update is completed. In the first case, concurrency problems are prevented by the fact that one update is forced to wait until the other one is completed, ensuring that both updates will be reflected in the record. In the second case, consistency problems are avoided because the second user will not be able to access the records for viewing until the first user's update transaction is completed.

SHOULD VISUAL BASIC BE YOUR DATABASE DEVELOPMENT TOOL?

Before moving to our main subject, which is how to use Visual Basic to create relational database front end applications, we must address an important question: Should you use Visual Basic at all? I know this may sound like heresy coming from an avowed Visual Basic fan, but I would be amiss in my duties if I skipped it. The simple fact is that Visual Basic is *not* the preferred choice in all circumstances. This statement is no slur on Visual Basic—no other tool brings such a combination of ease of use and power to database development —but it is unrealistic to expect any one tool, no matter how terrific, to be the best choice for all jobs. In this section we'll take a brief look at some of the factors to consider when deciding whether to use Visual Basic.

Programmer, Know Thyself

One of the most important factors when deciding on a database development tool is to assess your own experience and knowledge. Obviously, you are interested in Visual Basic or you wouldn't be reading this book. But are you a complete novice at Basic, or do you have many years of Basic programming experience (with, for example, Quick Basic) and are new only to the "Visual" part. Perhaps you are an expert in xBase programming (this is the language used by the dBase family of database products and a number of clones, such as FoxPro) and are investigating Visual Basic as a possible alternate tool. If the programming project is a "rush" job with strict deadlines, you may be wise to go with the development tool you know best and leave Visual Basic on the shelf until next time. If the timetable is more relaxed, however, it may be a good opportunity to hone your Visual Basic skills while working on a real-world project.

Is It a Legacy Database?

If you are being asked to write new front end applications for an existing, or *legacy*, database, the nature of the existing database may place restrictions on your choice of development tools. Clearly, the existing data will have to be retained, so the new application must be able to access it. Many old database systems run on mainframes or minicomputers and utilize obscure or antiquated database file formats. If you are completely revamping the entire system, the possibility exists for you to convert existing data files to a different format. If parts of the existing system will remain in use, you cannot modify the data file format but rather must select a development tool that supports that format. In the next chapter I will provide information about the database formats supported by Visual Basic.

The Visual Basic Fan Club

As you can see, a number of considerations might steer you away from using Visual Basic for a specific database application development project. In the absence of such particular negatives, however, the selection of a development tool is still an important decision. I cannot claim to be completely objective, if only because I have more extensive extensive knowledge of Visual Basic than any other database development tool. All this aside, here are some of the reasons why I think that Visual Basic leads the pack when it comes to Windows database development.

- **Cost**   With a Visual Basic application, you can distribute as many copies as you like without paying royalties. Many other development tools require payment of a license fee for each distributed copy of the final application. Furthermore, Visual Basic's purchase price is considerably lower than many other database development tools.

- **Flexibility**   Being a full-featured programming language, Visual Basic provides much more flexibility than development tools that are designed solely for database development.

- **Software components**   Visual Basic's support for custom OCX controls means that we'll have dozens of functional modules that we can drop into our application, providing sophisticated capabilities with little programming on our part.

- **OLE and OLE Automation**   With full support for OLE 2.0 and OLE Automation (as we will cover in a later chapter), a Visual Basic application has the capability to interact and integrate with other OLE applications.

- **Visual Basic for Applications**   Microsoft is actively pushing Visual Basic for Applications (VBA) as the common control and macro language for all

Windows applications. VBA has a great deal in common with Visual Basic, and programmers who learn Visual Basic will have have a leg up on using VBA to integrate their applications with other Windows programs.

Structured Query Language

Before finishing this chapter there's one more topic I need to mention—structured query language, or SQL (pronounced ess-cue-ell, not "sequel," as it is more commonly but incorrectly pronounced). SQL is a language designed specifically for accessing and manipulating databases, and it has become the *de facto* standard for database programming. I am not aware of any relational database back end that does not support SQL (although they may support other proprietary languages as well).

SQL had its origin in 1974 at an IBM research lab in something called Structured English Query Language, or SEQUEL. Since then, the language has evolved to today's SQL. Unfortunately, one should use the plural, SQLs, as there is no single accepted SQL standard. Not only are there several SQL "standards," but many vendors have added product-specific extensions (extra features) to SQL for their database programs. The Access SQL supported by the Access database engine is a good example. While the bulk of the language is common to all of the different implementations, you need to be aware of the differences.

Unlike Basic and most other programming languages, SQL is a *non-procedural* language. This means that SQL contains no statements or constructs to control the sequence, or order, of program execution. Thus, SQL does not have the equivalents of Basic's **If...Then...Else** or **Select Case** statements, nor does it support named procedures. SQL statements are limited to expressing *what* you want to do; the program that carries out the SQL instructions interprets the statement and returns the result.

Before going any further, let's take a look at a couple of SQL statements for the purpose of familiarity. For these examples we work with a table named Clients that has fields named FirstName, LastName, Address, City, State, ZIP, and Telephone. To obtain a list of all records for individuals in New York, the SQL statement is:

```
SELECT * FROM Client WHERE State = 'NY'
```

Can you see why SQL is described as "English like"! The meaning of this command is clear: Select all fields from the table named Clients where the State field contains 'NY'. What if you don't need all of the fields in the result?

Here's the SQL statement to display only the FirstName, LastName, and Telephone fields from those records where the State field contains 'NY':

```
SELECT FirstName, LastName, Telephone FROM Client WHERE State = 'NY'
```

To go one step further and sort the result list by Last Name:

```
SELECT FirstName, LastName, Telephone FROM Client WHERE State = 'NY' ORDER BY
LastName
```

As we work through the database project in the next few chapters, I will be demonstrating how to perform a variety of database manipulations using SQL. No attempt will be made to cover the entire SQL language, as that's a topic large enough for its own book. Generally, it isn't a good idea to try to learn a great deal of SQL right off the bat. Just get started by working through the next few chapters. When venturing out on your own database projects, you can turn to an SQL reference as needed to accomplish specific tasks.

FOR MORE INFORMATION

Visual Basic database programming is a large and complex subject. The next few chapters will give you a good start, but that's about all. When you're finished, you should have a firm grasp of the techniques needed to create a single user relational database front end, for both a decision support application and a transaction processing application. Using Visual Basic for professional database development, however, will require some real in-depth understanding! The two books that I have found most useful are *Visual Basic Database Programming* by Karen Watterson (Addison-Wesley, 1994) and *Database Developer's Guide With Visual Basic 3* by Roger Jennings (Sams, 1994). These books cover the previous version of Visual Basic (version 3), but they will most likely be updated for Visual Basic 4.0. Even without an update, most of the information they contain is still relevant.

BEYOND THE BASICS: TOOLS FOR DEVELOPING DATABASE APPLICATIONS

Before we begin our relational database project, we need to take a closer look at the tools that Visual Basic provides for database development.

Visual Basic offers a powerful and flexible array of tools for database development. We'll be using some of these tools in the relational database that we'll develop in the next few chapters, but there are many that we won't need. This chapter offers a brief overview of some of the more important components of the Visual Basic database toolbox, just to give you a good idea of what's available.

THE DATA OBJECT MODEL

The Microsoft and Visual Basic approach to databases is based on something I call, for lack of an official name, the *data object* model. Why that name? Because to a large extent, all of the components that make up a database are objects. And what is an object? It's a type of software component, just like the software components you use in Visual Basic every day. Objects contain variables (properties) and subprograms (methods), and data objects usually contain members that are also objects, such as records.

The data object model is hierarchical. At the top level is the *database object*, which represents a physical database file with its contained tables and other components. The file associated with a database object can be any one of several formats (detailed later in the chapter), and while the specific capabilities of each type of file may differ, the general treatment is the same.

A database object contains other objects. Since the data in a database is contained in tables, you might expect that objects are related to tables. There is a TableDef object, which contains the definition of a database table (but not the actual data). There is one TableDef object for each table in the database. Each TableDef object contains one or more Field objects; each Field object contains the definition of a single field in a table. Each TableDef object also contains one or more Index objects, and each Index object contains the definition of an index for the associated table.

You might also expect a Table object that would contain each table's data. You are right—and wrong. Visual Basic indeed supports Table objects, but only for purposes of backward compatibility with earlier versions of Visual Basic. The Table object indeed represents a single table's data. Using a table-type Recordset object in place of the old Table object is recommended.

A Recordset object provides a logical representation of the records in a table —the table's data. There are three types of Recordset objects:

- A **Table** type Recordset replaces the old Table object. This type of Recordset provides access to all of the records in a specified table. The records are returned in the order specified by the current index, which is set using the Recordset object's **Index** property.

- A **Dynaset** type Recordset object provides access to a selected subset of the records in one of more tables. The records and fields contained in a Dynaset type Recordset are specified by a query.

- A **Snapshot** type Recordset is similar to a **Dynaset** type Recordset except that it is a read-only copy of the data specified by the query. In other words, you cannot use a Snapshot to modify (add, delete, or edit) the records in the underlying tables. In addition, since the Snapshot represents a "picture" of the data at the time the Snapshot was created, subsequent changes to the underlying data—for example, by other users in a multiuser environment—will not be reflected in the Snapshot.

Instead of accessing the records in a table directly, we create the appropriate type of Recordset object and work with it. Each of the three types of Recordset objects is appropriate for different types of tasks. The **Table** type is used when we need to view and manipulate all of the records in a table. The **Dynaset** type is appropriate for viewing and manipulating subsets of records and fields from one or more sets. In other words, a **Dynaset** type Recordset can be the result of a join between two tables. A **Snapshot** type Recordset is appropriate when we need to view but not manipulate data, such as for report preparation.

QueryDef objects are unique to Access databases. A Querydef object contains a representation of an SQL statement used to create a **Dynaset** or **Snapshot** type Recordset.

A Relations object contains the definitions of all the relationships in a database—for example, the relationship between one table's primary key and another table's foreign key.

A Database object can also contain *object collections*. A collection is a group of same-type objects. The name of a collection is the plural of the object type it contains. Thus, the TableDefs object contains all of the TableDef objects in the database. Likewise, an Indexes collection contains all of the Index objects for a TableDef object. The Fields collection contains all of the Field objects for a TableDef, QueryDef, Recordset, or Relation object.

Now that you are thoroughly confused, let me clarify things with some examples of how we access these various objects. This description is not a complete lesson on accessing and manipulating data access objects, but simply a demonstration showing how the objects are related and how you can access and use their properties and methods.

A Database object can be represented in code in two different ways: as the **Database** property of a Data control or as a type Database variable. In either case the Database object must be linked to a physical database file on disk. For a Data control named MyData, for example:

```
MyData.Database = "c:\data\orders.mdb"
MyData.Refresh   ' Necessary to open the database.
```

If you are not using a Data control, you could write:

```
Dim MyDatabase as Database
Set MyDatabase = OpenDatabase("c:\data\orders.mdb")
```

Now, let's say you want to load a ListBox with all the tables in this database. The TableDefs object has a **Count** property that gives the zero-based number of tables in the database. It also has an indexed **Name** property that returns the name of each table. You would write it as follows (if using a Data control):

```
For I = 0 To MyData.Database.TableDefs.Count - 1
   List1 AddItem MyData.Database.TableDefs(I).Name
Next I
```

If you are not using a Data control, it would look like this:

```
For I = 0 To MyDatabase.TableDefs.Count - 1
   List1 AddItem MyDatabase.TableDefs(I).Name
Next I
```

Here's another example. If the above database contains a table named "Customers" and you want to load a List Box with the names of the fields in that table, you would write (if using a Data control):

```
For I = 0 To MyData.Database.TableDefs("Customers").Fields.Count - 1
   List1 AddItem MyData.Database.TableDefs("Customers").Fields(I).Name
Next I
```

Let's dissect one of these statements so we can see the relationships between the various parts. Review the statement above that adds a field name to the List Box. Reading from right to left:

1. Name is an indexed property of the Fields object collection.

2. Fields(I) specifies the Ith Field in the collection.

3. The Fields object collection is a member of the TableDefs collection.

4. TableDefs("Customers") specifies the Table in the collection named "Customers."

5. The TableDefs object collection is a member of the Database object.

6. Database is a property of the Data control that identifies the associated Database object.

You can see that a great deal of our work with the data object model consists of "burrowing down" through the hierarchy of objects to find the property or data of interest. It's important to understand the relationships of the various objects in the model.

Accessing Other Database Formats

The fact that Visual Basic supports a wide range of database file formats is one of the major reasons it is so attractive to database developers. If you are going to limit yourself to mastery of one database front end development tool, Visual Basic is an excellent choice because of this breadth of support. Visual Basic does not have a native database format *per se*, because all file formats are treated more or less the same way. Access is Visual Basic's default file format, and unless you have specific reasons to use another file format— for example, supporting a legacy database in another format—there is no reason to change from the default.

Some file formats are supported directly through the Jet database engine. Others are supported through Open Database Connectivity, or ODBC, a Microsoft-initiated standard for database access. To access an ODBC database, a driver is needed to interface the front end program with the data source or database files. ODBC configuration is performed using the "32 bit ODBC" selection in the Windows Control Panel. Some ODBC drivers are supplied by Microsoft and others come from third-party vendors. The data source format supported by the Jet database engine, Microsoft ODBC drivers, and third-party drivers are listed in Table 13.1. The table was current as of this writing, when both Windows 95 and Visual Basic 4.0 were still in beta testing. Support for additional file formats may well be available by the time you read this.

We will be limiting ourselves to Access databases, but it's good to know that Visual Basic supports all these other file formats when programming needs require it.

Creating Databases at Runtime

So far we have dealt only with situations where the database already exists on disk, created using Data Manager. An existing database created any other way, say with the Access or Paradox database programs, is handled the same way. But what if the database doesn't exist? Can we create one from scratch using Visual Basic? The answer is "yes, but..."

Why the qualification? Indeed, you can create new databases in Visual Basic code, defining the table and record structure as well as adding new data. In that sense, you could use Visual Basic to write a program that permits users to define their own databases from scratch rather than being limited to databases that already exist. Here comes the catch: This approach is not one that I would generally advise. Designing a database from scratch requires a lot of

Table 13.1   *Data Source Formats*

Jet Database Engine	Microsoft ODBC Drivers	Third-Party Drivers
Access	Access	Digital Rdb
Btrieve	Btrieve	Gupta SQLBase
dBase III and IV	dBase III and IV	HP Allbase/SQL
FoxPro	Excel	HP Image SQL
Paradox	FoxPro	IBM DB2, DB2/2
	Microsoft SQL Server	IBM OS/2 DBM
	Oracle 6	IBM SQL/DS
	Paradox	Informix
	Sybase SQL Server	Ingres
	Text	NCR Teradata
		Netware SQL
		Progress
		Tandem Nonstop SQL
		Watcom SQL
		XDB

complicated and difficult programming. Not only would you have to accept user specifications regarding table structure, field names, data types, and the like, and then convert this information into the necessary commands to create the database; you also have to provide the capability to design forms and reports if the data is to be of value to the user.

While this type of program can and has been written successfully in Visual Basic, it's not for the faint of heart. Even if you find a custom control that provides much of the required functionality, it's still a daunting project with a lot of potential pitfalls. A much better approach is to use a dedicated database front end generator such as Microsoft Access or Borland Paradox. The functionality for creating new databases and designing forms is built into these applications. Then your job is using the application's internal programming language (Access Basic for Access, PAL for Paradox) to create the customized interfaces and queries that the client requires. As an alternative approach, you can combine a commercial program (Access or Paradox) for database design and creation with a custom Visual Basic program for decision support and transaction processing, once the database has been created.

Accessing Databases without the Data Control

In spite of the Data control's convenience, it does have limitations. For one, only a subset of Visual Basic controls can be bound to the Data control. This is less of a problem with Visual Basic 4.0, which includes have data-aware Grid and List controls, something that was lacking in Visual Basic 3.0 (third-party custom controls excepted). We presented some examples of accessing a database without using a Data control earlier in the chapter.

There's no doubt that using the Data control simplifies our programming tasks. My approach is to make use of it whenever possible. After all, that's one of the main reasons I use Visual Basic in the first place—to make use of the many software components it offers. If I wanted to do everything myself, I would program in C++! When we develop the demonstration relational database in the following chapters, we may encounter some situations where we will avoid using the Data control.

DATA-AWARE CONTROLS

Although you were introduced to data-aware controls earlier in the book, now is the time to look at the full complement of available data-aware controls. Data-aware controls work in conjunction with a Data control. A data-aware control can be *bound* to a specific field in the table that is represented by a Data control's associated Recordset. This is done with the control's **DataSource** property, which is set to the name of the Data control, and its **DataField** property, set to the name of the desired field in the Recordset. There are ten data-aware controls provided with the Professional Edition of Visual Basic. Here's a brief review of the seven standard data-aware controls:

Label   Used for static display of text data. The user cannot edit or otherwise modify data displayed in a Label control.

Text Box   Used for dynamic display of text data. The user can edit or enter data in a Text Box control

Check Box   Used for dynamic display of boolean (Yes/No, True/False) data.

Combo Box   The Text Box portion of the Combo Box displays the data in the linked field. The List Box portion contains items that have been added specifically with the **AddItem** method. If the user selects an item from the list, it replaces the original field data. Can be used for data entry/editing when the user must select from a predefined list of possibilities.

List Box　　Similar to a Combo Box.

Picture Box　Can display a graphical image from a bitmap, icon, or metafile that is stored in a linked image/binary data field.

Image　　Similar to a Picture Box, but uses fewer resources and offers less capability.

As useful as these controls are, they are all limited to displaying data from *one* field in *one* record at a time. For certain applications, this is not enough. There are three custom data-aware controls that provide additional capabilities.

The dbGrid Control

The dbGrid control provides a grid, or matrix, of cells. Each column in the grid displays data from one field in the linked table, and each row displays data from one record. A dbGrid control is shown in Figure 13.1 displaying data from the Music database we developed in an earlier chapter.

By default, a dbGrid control displays all of the table's fields and records, with vertical and/or horizontal scroll bars if the data is too wide or too tall to display completely. The user can move from cell to cell, viewing and editing data. The bottom row on the control, marked by an asterisk in the left column, can be used to enter new data. Column widths can be changed, fonts can be specified, and many other aspects of the control's appearance and behavior can be manipulated by means of control properties.

Composer/Group	Title	Media	Publisher	Location	Notes
Handel	4 Organ Concertos	CD	LaserLight	G-12	Poor sound quality
Schubert	Death and the	LP	RCA Victor	H-12	Very clean recordin
Jim Brock	Hard Day's Night	LP	Capitol	D-11	Scratchy!
Michael Newman	Italian Pleasures	LP	Sheffield	A-141	
Haydn	Keyboard Sonatas	LP	VOX	B-97	
Benny Goodman	Live at Carnegie Hall	CD	Columbia	A-131	2 CD's
McCoy Tyner	New York Reunion	CD	Chesky	B-78	
Mozart	Piano Music	CD	EMI	B-98	Includes Bach,
Berlioz	Requiem	CD	Telarc	J-16	Very fine recording
Jim Brock	Tropic Affair	LP	Reference	C-7	Top quality sound
Handel	Water Music	LP	Phillps	C-21	Tempo slower than

Figure 13.1　*The dbGrid control.*

The dbGrid control consists of a collection of columns, each with an indeterminate number of rows. A dbGrid control can contain a maximum of approximately 1700 columns; the number of rows is limited only by the system resources. Each column is a partially independent object with its own properties. Thus, some properties belong to the dbGrid control itself and affect operation and appearance of the entire control, but there is also a set of properties for each column. The Columns (note the plural) collection has properties that relate to all columns, such as Count, which returns the number of columns in the control.

We'll see more of the dbGrid control's features in the demonstration program. Refer to the Visual Basic Help system for complete details on its properties, methods, and events.

The dbList and dbCombo Controls

The dbList and dbCombo controls are similar to each other: They both provide a list of items from which the user can choose. The dbCombo control adds a TextBox that displays the currently selected item and also permits entry/editing by the user. In many ways these controls are similar to the standard ComboBox and ListBox controls; however, they are data-aware, and can be automatically loaded with values from the Recordset field to which they are linked.

These controls can be extremely useful, both in speeding the task of data entry and reducing the chance of errors. For example, when entering a new Invoice record, both the Customer and each Item are likely to come from existing tables in the database. Rather than require the operator to manually enter the customer name or the item's stock number, we can display a dbListBox for each field that shows all the currently available values for that entry. We'll see how these controls are used in the demonstration project.

Back to the Beginning: Designing the Database

Hindsight may be 20-20, but it's generally worthless unless we can "plan behind." So that means we have to plan ahead!

Before writing a single line of code, we need to do some planning. How careful and thorough we are during the planning stages will have a major impact on our speed and efficiency in completing the project, as well as on the quality of the finished product. This chapter will cover some general considerations related to database design, walking you through the first steps of designing the demonstration database program. The discussion will be limited to designing a new database from scratch, where we have no existing tables or applications to consider. If your own project involves a legacy database, the design process will be different, and although you probably won't have the option of changing table structure, the other considerations will still apply.

FUNDAMENTAL DESIGN CONSIDERATIONS

Database design remains as much an art as a science. While there are some rules and guidelines to follow, no defined design method regularly produces properly designed databases. The knowledge and skills of the programmer come into play in a way that could almost be called intuition. Ask an experienced database programmer why he or she designed a table in a certain way, and you may hear an answer like "I don't know—it just seemed the obvious way to do it."

The demonstration database covered here is a fairly simple project, and the reasons behind design decisions will most likely be clear. With more complex projects—and some databases involve dozens of tables—the table design may be much less obvious. It's true that alternate designs might work, but not as well as the optimal design.

The Design Process

It's impossible to lay out a fixed sequence of steps in designing a database. It's a fluid process with lots of interactions between the various stages. We often have to go back and change something that we decided on earlier, such as a table structure or a key field, because of unforeseen problems that arise later. Of course, minimizing those setbacks is important, since every time we have to go back and change something, we waste time and effort. By paying attention to the basic principles discussed in this chapter, as well as gaining more and more experience, we can minimize mistakes—but don't count on ever being able to eliminate them entirely!

Here, then, are the most important steps to follow in designing a Visual Basic database application. Remember that this sequence is not fixed, although it is generally best to follow a similar order. In spite of any other variations, the first step should always be Gathering Information.

Gathering Information

In many respects, this is the single most important step in database design. No matter how skilled you are as a programmer, you can't create an application for a certain task unless you know exactly what that task is! Generally, there will be a formal specification for the database, whether provided by the client or noted as a result of conversations with the client. This specification will include information such as lists of the items (entities) that need to be tracked, the individual pieces of information about each item (attributes) that must be recorded, and the types of forms and reports that must be generated. While this information is essential, don't stop here! Ask to see all of the paper data forms that are currently in use. Find out which data-related tasks are performed frequently, and which ones are rarely, if ever, necessary. When re-placing a legacy system, talk to the operators to discover what they like and don't like about the current software. The more information at our command, the easier our job will be.

Designing the Tables

Designing the database tables is usually the next step when we have all of the necessary information. Because the tables are the foundation of the database, this makes perfect sense. Table design is a paper-and-pencil process, since visual representations of tables and the relationships between them can be a big help. Create tables based on important entities in the assortment of data that the database will hold—people, orders, invoices, and so on. Be sure that the data type of each field is appropriate for the data it will hold, and that the length of text fields is matched to the information that will be placed there. When the data lends itself to being divided into tables in two or more ways, make a decision based on how the data will be used and also on the availability of keys and links.

Plan the Links

Sketch out the links between tables. In order to be useful, every table in a relational database must be linked to at least one other table. In most cases, links should be of the one-to-many (1:M) variety. A table structure with 1:1 links will usually benefit from redesign, while M:M links require special treatment.

Decide on Primary Keys, Foreign Keys, and Indexes

Every table should have a primary key, even if it is a surrogate key that you generate. Every table on the "many" side of a 1:M link also needs a foreign key, usually the same data item as the primary key in the table to which it is linked. Choose the fields that will be used for indexes. Each table should be indexed on its primary key field, and also on any fields that will regularly be used for searching or sorting the table records.

Sketch Out the Forms

Once the tables have been designed, we can start sketching out the Visual Basic forms that the program will use. Form design is based on the table structure, and also depends heavily on how the users need to view and edit the information. It's a good idea to test your preliminary form designs by incorporating them into a dummy program and allowing the people who will be using the database try them. Form designs are easier to change now than at a later stage of program development! Once this stage of design is completed, we should have a preliminary idea of how many forms the program will have and what controls each one will need.

Plan the Flow of Execution

Once we have a clear idea of the program's forms, we can begin thinking about program execution. What will the user see when the program starts? How will the user select program functions—menus, toolbar, command buttons? How do the forms relate to each other? For example, can the user move from a data entry form to a query form directly, or is it necessary to close the data entry form and return to the opening screen first? This stage of design should also be influenced by the needs of the users. Will a single operator be responsible for taking orders and entering inventory, switching from one to the other task frequently? Or will these two tasks be performed by different operators, with no need to quickly switch between them?

Gotcha's

Rarely has a programmer completed a database design project without looking back and wishing that he or she had done something differently. In my own experience, there are no sure guarantees to avoid this! It is possible to lessen the number and severity of these problems, however, by keeping in mind a relatively small number of database design boo-boos that are easy to make. Here's a list of "dos" and "don'ts":

Keep Your Data Atomic

No, that doesn't mean your database should be radioactive! Data that is *atomic* cannot be broken down any further into smaller chunks of data — at least not meaningful chunks. This relates to the field structure of your tables. An Address table with a single Name field that holds each person's full name does not have atomic data, since it could be further subdivided into first name and last name. Problems arise later when we need to perform manipulations based on only part of the field data, such as sorting the records by last name. The solution of writing code to extract the last name from each Name field is unnecessarily cumbersome. Separating your data into the smallest meaningful pieces at the beginning is the best approach, since combining data is always easier than extracting it.

Of course, this rule must be applied in combination with some common sense. If we need to break peoples' names into First Name and Last Name fields, shouldn't we have a separate field for Middle Initial? The answer is no, because the isolated middle initial is not meaningful in any sense — to my knowledge, no one has ever wanted to sort a database by middle initials! It is standard practice to include the middle initial in the First Name field.

Use a Primary Key Field

Although this has been mentioned before, it bears repeating. Every table should have a primary key, a field whose data uniquely identifies each record. For many tables this is not a problem, since one of the required data fields provides a primary key. Other tables, usually the "many" table in a one to many relationship, will have no field whose data uniquely identifies each record. We then have two methods for creating a primary key.

Most databases have the capability to use *compound* keys, where the data in two or more fields combine to provide a unique identifier. For example, in a database of musical recordings, combining the Performer field with the Title field could provide a unique value for each record. This method has the advantage that no extraneous field additions to the table are necessary to provide a key, and also that the key consists of meaningful data. A possible disadvantage is that the resulting keys may be rather long, such as "The Chicago Symphony Orchestra—Beethoven's Sixth Symphony." Any processing that utilizes such a lengthy key will be correspondingly slow.

The second approach is to create a new field whose sole purpose is to hold an arbitrary key generated by the application, such as a sequential number or a letter-number combination. This is sometimes called a *surrogate key*. The disadvantage lies in adding meaningless data to the table, data that takes up space but has no purpose other than serving as the primary key. Such keys are likely to be concise, however, which speeds processing. One compromise is to generate a unique value for the primary key field that consists of part of the record's "real" data combined with a generated number. Using the musical recordings database as an example once again, we could create a unique key field that consists of the first five letters of the Title field, followed by a sequential number, such as Beeth001.

Avoid Bad Keys

There's no precise definition of a "bad" primary key, but we do have some definite guidelines to follow. Avoid using a big field—one that contains a sizable chunk of data—since the processing overhead required to maintain and use such a key will slow the application down. This is particularly true when the primary key is used to index the table, which is common practice. Don't use a field where data is likely to change, such as telephone number. When a primary key's data changes, all associated indexes must be updated. Even more problematic, the data in all linked foreign keys must be updated as well.

It's essential, of course, that the data in the primary key be unique for each record. Even if the data "should" be unique, such as Social Security Number, we have no guarantee that a typing error during data entry won't result in a duplicate number. Most database applications give us the option of designating a field as a primary key, and will then check each new entry against existing entries to ensure that no duplicates exist. This does not solve the problem of typographical errors, of course, but at least it guarantees that our primary key field remains unique.

Use Descriptive Table and Field Names

This one might seem like a no-brainer, but you would be surprised at how many people ignore it. Assign names to your tables and fields that describe the data they contain. Of course, some trade-off exists between clarity and brevity, but the names should be such that anyone who has some familiarity with the database data will be able to tell from the field and table names exactly what is being stored where. For a field that will hold Part Number, for example, "PN" is too cryptic, while "Part Number" is probably unnecessarily long. "PartNo" would be a good compromise.

Do Not Use Duplicate Field Names

With one exception, you should never use the same field name in different tables in the same database. To do so is just asking for confusion. For example, a database might contain a "Suppliers" table and a "Customers" table, each of which has a field for telephone number. You should not call that field "TelNo" in both tables, even though it might seem perfectly logical to do so. Rather, create two field names such as "CustTelNo" and "SuppTelNo". Not only does this avoid the possible confusion of duplicate field names, but it follows the previous suggestion to use descriptive field names.

Be Aware of International Issues

Many databases need to accommodate international information that is expressed or formatted differently than in the U.S., such as addresses, currencies, and phone numbers. Even if a database is intended for use only with domestic data, it may be a good idea to include the required flexibility. Windows itself provides some features to help you deal with different number and time formats and other related issues. Look in Windows Help under Regional Settings.

THE JOB

In this and the next few chapters, we are going to develop a complete relational database system for an imaginary client. We'll start from scratch with the client's wishes and specifications, working though all the design and development stages until we have a complete, tested, and functioning product. Approaching the task this way should be much more informative (and interesting!) than simply presenting you with the finished program and trying to explain how it works.

Before describing the project, I want to mention a dilemma that computer book authors often face. When creating a demonstration program, we have to find a good balance between two extremes. On the one hand, we could create a complete program that has all the details, capabilities, and safety features needed for use in a real-world setting without any further additions. On the other hand, we could create a program that contains only the bare essentials needed to illustrate the principles and techniques under discussion, with no concern for how this knowledge is applied in a real, functioning program.

In the first approach, the programming techniques that the author is trying to communicate may be obscured by details that might be necessary to the final program but are irrelevant to the topic under discussion. The second approach is flawed by the fact that the reader learns the techniques in isolation and never sees how they are integrated into a complete program. My approach is to try to walk a middle line between these two extremes. In the database project that we will develop, you will receive enough real-world detail to understand how these things are done, but not so much that the main topic—relational database design—is obscured. As you examine the project, you may see a number of places where the program is lacking a feature that would be necessary for a real commercial application. Don't fret —I'm aware of them too.

The Client

Our imaginary client is the GrapeVine Distributing Company, a firm that distributes wine to local restaurants, liquor stores, and hotels. An old family-run firm, they have been using an antiquated paper-based system for keeping track of customers, inventories, and invoices. While old wine may be good, they realize that old business methods are not. They want to computerize their system, and we are the lucky programmers selected for the job. The basic specifications of the project have already been sketched out by the client:

- We need to keep a customer list, including their company name, address, and phone number, as well as the name of the wine buyer. This list will be used to generate shipping labels and invoices, and for promotional mailings and similar tasks.

- We also need to keep track of our inventory. For each wine, we need to record a description, its type, vintage year, the quantity on hand, and the wine's quality rating as assigned by a popular wine magazine. We also need the wine's cost (the price we pay), its wholesale price (what we charge our customers), and the suggested retail price.

- Finally, we need a method for entering and keeping track of orders. Some orders come by mail, others over the phone. In some cases the customers know exactly what they want; other times they ask us to suggest something: "I want a French or Czechoslavakian red that I can sell for under $15.00."

We now have sufficient information to start designing the database. The first step is to design the tables.

Designing the Tables

The preferred database design is one in which tables represent actual objects, at least as closely as possible. With this in mind, we quickly see that our database naturally divides itself into three tables—one for customers, one for wines, and one for invoices. Each is a physical object that exists in the real world, and each is a unit of information that is of interest to the client. Starting with the customers table (which we will cleverly call "Customers"), we can plan for the following fields:

Field Name	Description
CompanyName	Name of customer firm
Address	Customer's street address
City	Customer's city
State	Customer's state
ZIP	Customer's ZIP code
Contact	Name of contact person
Phone	Contact's phone number

At first glance this looks OK, but two potential problems already exist. First, by placing the contact person's entire name in one field, aren't we violating the principle of atomicity that was covered earlier? Strictly speaking...yes, we are. Should we split the contact person's name into FirstName and LastName fields? In this case, it would be unnecessary. The function of this table is such that the contact name is not a central piece of information—we will never need to sort the table records by contact name—so placing the entire name in one field will not cause any problems.

The second problem with this table design is—you got it!—no primary key field. You cannot be sure that any of these fields, even CompanyName, will always be unique for each record. And even if you feel sure that CompanyName will always be unique, there is a chance that an existing company will change its name. As I explained earlier, we should not select any field as a primary key if its data is changeable. Therefore, we will have to add a surrogate key field named CustID (for Customer Identification) to hold a unique identifier for each customer. We'll worry about generating this unique identifier later.

Next let's turn to the table that will hold information about the wines. Here's the preliminary specification for this table:

Field name	Description
StockNo	Stock number
Description	Description from wine's label
Country	Country of origin
Year	Vintage year
Rating	Wine's rating
OurCost	What we pay per unit
WholesaleCost	What we charge per unit
RetailPrice	Suggested retail price per unit
QOH	Quantity on hand

This table may seem adequate at first glance, but then we begin thinking about some conversations we overheard down at the GrapeVine offices. Things like "Hey Charlie, the Downtown Hotel wants a case of fancy white Burgundy for the mayor's reception. Got any ideas?" or "The fraternity guys want a case of the cheapest red we've got—what shall we send them?" It seems that some characteristics of wines do not fit in this preliminary table design. A quick phone call to the folks at GrapeVine confirms your suspicions. Every wine has a color—red, white, or rosé—as well as a type that specifies its region of origin and/or the grape varieties used in making it. This can be important information in making a sale, so it should be included in the database. Therefore you add two more fields, Color and Type.

The last table we need to design is the Invoices table. Each Invoice record will have a unique invoice number, the order date, the customer's purchase order number, and the customer identification number. In addition, we need to make room for the items that were ordered—for each item, the stock number and the quantity. But wait . . . how many items should we allow on each invoice? Some invoices may include only a couple of items, while others will have dozens. How can we handle this? We have just run into . . .

The Problem of Repeating Fields

Many database designs run into the problem of repeating fields. To illustrate just exactly what this problem means, consider the Invoices table that we are working on, designed to hold information about invoices. A basic table design might look something like this:

Field Name	Description
CustID	Customer identification number
Date	Date of invoice
InvNo	Invoice number (primary key field)
CustPO	Customer's purchase order number
StockNo	Your stock number for the item ordered
Quantity	Quantity ordered

"But wait," you say. "This permits only one type of item to be recorded per invoice record." You are absolutely right, so let's add some more fields to the table:

CustID
Date
InvNo

CustPO
StockNo1
Quantity1
StockNo2
Quantity2
StockNo3
Quantity3

Now we have what are called *repeating fields*—the StockNo and Quantity fields repeat to permit the entry of more than one item. In certain situations, where you know that the number of items—or whatever it might be that is being repeated—will be strictly limited to a small number, this type of table structure may be satisfactory. Generally, however, it should be avoided. No matter how many times you repeat the field or fields, there's always the chance that it won't be enough for some records. And for most records, where the majority of the repeated fields go unfilled, you are wasting disk space. Remember, all fields, even empty ones, take up space.

The solution is to split the data into two tables. One table holds the information that is unique to each invoice. The other table holds the individual line items. This relationship is illustrated in Figure 14.1.

The link between these two tables is provided by the InvNo (Invoice Number) field. InvNo is the primary key for the Invoices Table and a foreign key for the Items table.

You may have noticed that the Items table does not have a primary key. InvNo, StockNo, and Quantity will not be unique for each record in the table. In terms of the information this table needs to hold, a primary key field is not

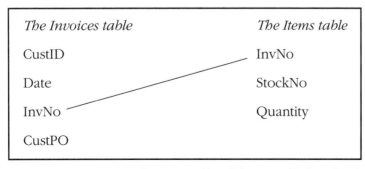

Figure 14.1 *The relationship between the Invoices table and the Items table that solves the problem of repeating fields.*

necessary. In terms of database design, however, providing every table with a primary key is a good idea. If no meaningful data is available to serve as a primary key, we can add an additional field to the table structure and have the database program generate unique sequential numbers to serve as the primary key.

Our table definitions are complete—at least for now. Figure 14.2 shows the table structure, the primary keys in each, and the links between them.

Carefully examine this database design. No problems are apparent. No data is duplicated, each table has a primary key field, and each table is linked to at least one other table. Let's look at the type of links we have:

Link	Type
CUSTOMERS:INVOICES	1:M (one to many)
WINES:ITEMS	1:M
INVOICES:ITEMS	1:M

There are no 1:1 links that might suggest a need for redesigning the table. Nor are there any of the M:M (many to many) links that would require special treatment. It's safe to conclude that we have a good database table design. If we're lucky, this design will remain unchanged throughout the remainder of the project.

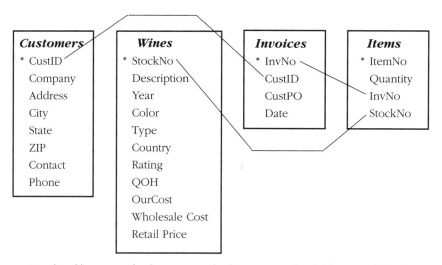

Figure 14.2 *The table structure for the GRAPEVIN database. Primary key fields are marked with an asterisk, and links are indicated by lines.*

Creating the Database

Now that we have our table design, we can use Data Manager to create the database and its tables. We need to place some data in the tables, otherwise we will have nothing to use when testing forms and other parts of the program. Ideally, this should be real data provided by our client. If that is not available, we can create "dummy" data that will be deleted from the database later.

It's time to use Data manager to create the database and its tables. We covered the basics of using Data Manager in Chapter 11, so please refer to that section if your memory needs jogging. Create a database named GRAPEVIN with the following four tables:

The CUSTOMERS table:

Field name	Date type/length
CustID	Long Integer
Company	text 24
Address	text 30
City	text 15
State	text 2
ZIP	text 5
Contact	text 24
Phone	text 12

Next, the WINES table:

Field name	Data type, length
StockNo	text, 10
Description	text, 40
Year	text, 4
Color	text, 5
Type	text, 15
Country	text, 15
Rating	Integer
QOH	Integer
OurCost	Currency
WholesaleCost	Currency
RetailPrice	Currency

The INVOICES table:

Field name	Data type, length
InvNo	Long Integer
CustID	text, 8
CustPO	text, 12
Date	Date/Time

And finally, the ITEMS table:

Field name	Data type, length
ItemNo	Long Integer
Quantity	Integer
InvNo	Long
StockNo	text, 10

You may have some questions about the data type I selected for some of these fields. It may even seem that a different data type would have been more appropriate for some of these fields. Let me explain.

- ZIP in the CUSTOMERS table. Since ZIP code is a number, why not use a numeric data type? Some ZIP codes begin with 0, and if the data type were numeric, we would have to write special code to display or print the leading 0. By using a text field, we avoid this problem.

- Phone in the CUSTOMERS table. Why not use a length 10 text field, since a phone number contains only 10 digits (including area code)? The separators could be added later when the number is displayed. This argument is valid, but we're talking about only two extra characters, or bytes, per phone number for the separators (the dashes in a phone number such as 919-555-1212). By storing the phone number fully formatted, we not only save programming hassles but take up a trivial amount of extra space.

- InvNo in the INVOICES table. Why not make this a text field so the invoice identifiers can include letters as well as numbers? We have no reason to do this beyond meeting client desires, such as wanting to continue with the existing system that uses an alphanumeric code for invoices. Using a numeric variable type makes it easy to generate sequential, unique values for this field.

- ItemNo in the ITEMS table. The reasoning explained in the previous paragraph applies here as well.

Once the table definitions are complete, we can close the Data Manager. We're not finished with it, by any means. We still need to enter the initial data in the tables. In addition, you will see that Data Manager provides many other tools for defining various characteristics of the tables; for example: Is a field allowed to be blank or must some data be entered in it? These are subjects for later chapters.

Forms and Fields, Fields and Forms

To avoid certain pesky problems, we can use field properties to match the tables to the data. We also need to design forms for viewing and manipulating the data.

A field in an Access database is not just a simple container in which we can toss a chunk of data. Fields have a number of properties that we can set so that the characteristics of the field match the needs of the database. Once this is complete, we can move on to a very important—and I think fun—part of the project, designing the forms.

FIELD PROPERTIES

Each field in a table definition has a set of properties. Three of these properties were evident when we designed the structure of the database tables back in Chapter 14: the **Name** property, which specifies the field name; the **Type** property, which specifies its data type; and (for Text fields only) the **Size** property that specifies the field size, or maximum number of characters it can hold. Fields have several other properties, and using them judiciously can be an important part of database design. Let's look at the properties first, then I'll describe how to set them for the demonstration project.

Validation Properties

The term *validation* refers to the process of ensuring that the data entered in a field meets certain criteria. Some validation rules are quite simple, such as requiring the field to contain some data and not be left empty. Others can be much more involved, such as requiring that the entry in a Part Number field consist of two letters followed by a 4-digit number. Visual Basic provides several properties that determine how (and if) a field's data is validated.

ValidationRule   An SQL statement used to validate the data entered into a field. When the SQL statement is applied to the data in the field, it must evaluate to True; otherwise, an error message is displayed (see the **ValidationText** property). The **ValidationRule** property takes the form of an SQL WHERE clause minus the WHERE keyword.

ValidationText   The error text that is displayed when the conditions specified by the **ValidationRule** property are not met.

ValidateOnSet   If this property is True, the validation rule (if any) associated with the field is applied as soon as the field's value is set or changed. If set to False, validation occurs only when the entire record is updated (along with validation for other fields).

Required   Determines whether the field can contain a Null value. Null is a special Visual Basic value used to indicate missing or unknown data, and it is designated by the Null keyword. A Null value in a field is not the same as a blank field, a zero-length string, or a 0 value. Some fields, particularly those defined as the primary key, cannot contain Null values.

AllowZeroLength   Specifies whether a zero-length string ("") is permitted in a type Text or Memo field.

While these validation properties can be very useful, the **Validate** event is often preferred. This event will be covered later in the chapter.

Other Field Properties

You should also know about several miscellaneous field properties:

OrdinalPosition   Specifies the relative position of the field in the table, with 0 being the first position. When fields are displayed, for example in a dbGrid control, the default display order is determined by the ordinal positions of the fields. The default ordinal positions of fields are determined by the order in which they were added to the table during database design.

DefaultValue   A string or a Basic expression that evaluates to the appropriate data type for the field. When a record is created, this value is automatically entered in the field, and can be changed by the user if desired.

CollatingOrder   Specifies the order used when sorting records based on text data in the field. This property is an integer value that indicates the language rules to be used for sorting. The default is dbSortGeneral (value = 1033), which uses the general sort order appropriate for English, French, German, Portuguese, Italian, and Modern Spanish. Specialized collating orders are available for Dutch, Greek, Hebrew, and a number of other languages (see Visual Basic Help for details).

Fixed/Variable Length   Defines whether the field length is fixed (the default for numeric fields) or variable (the default for text fields). You should not change these properties.

Counter   Specifies that the field is automatically filled with a unique type Long integer that cannot be changed. Useful for creating a unique surrogate key field for a table.

DataUpdatable   Specifies whether the data in the field can be changed.

Note: *The three preceding properties—**Fixed/Variable Length**, **Counter**, and**DataUpdatable**—are actually all combined in the single **Attributes** property of a field object. In the field editing dialog box, which we will discuss in a moment, they are broken out so you can view and set each one separately.*

Setting Field Properties for the Demonstration Database

Now that we know what the various field properties do, it's time to set them for the GRAPEVIN database. The procedure for setting field properties is as follows:

1. In Visual Basic, select Data Manager from the Add-Ins menu.

2. In Data Manager, use the File Open command to open the GRAPEVIN.MDB database.

3. Click the name of the table you want to work with, then click the Design button. The Table Editor dialog box will open, displaying one column for each field in the table, with the field's properties listed. This is shown in Figure 15.1 for the CUSTOMERS table.

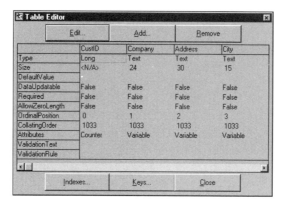

Figure 15.1 *Editing fields in the CUSTOMERS table.*

4. Click the column of the field you want to edit, then click the Edit button. The Edit Field dialog box opens, as shown in Figure 15.2 for the CustID field.

5. Set and enter field properties as desired, then click the OK button to return to the Table Editor dialog box.

6. Repeat steps 3-5 to edit the properties of other fields as needed.

7. Back in the Table Editor dialog box, click the Close button.

8. If necessary, repeat steps 3-7 to edit fields in another table.

9. Click the Close button.

For our database, relatively minor changes will be required to the default property settings. We will do all of our data validation in code, using the

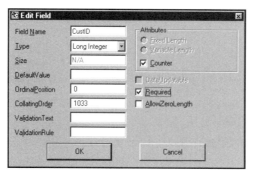

Figure 15.2 *The Edit Field dialog box showing data for the CustID field.*

Validate event, so there's no need for any entries to the **ValidationRule** or **ValidationText** properties. Using the above procedures, make these changes:

In the CUSTOMERS table:

> CustID, Company, Address, City, State, and ZIP are all required fields, so **AllowZeroLength** should be *False* and **Required** should be *True*. Since we cannot be sure each firm has a specific contact person and phone number, these fields may be left blank with settings of **AllowZeroLength** = *True* and **Required** = *False*. Set the CustID attribute to counter I so the database engine will automatically generate uniquely sequential values for this field.

In the WINES table:

> All fields in this table are required entries except for RetailPrice. **AllowZeroLength** should be *False* and **Required** should be *True* for all fields except RetailPrice, where the values are reversed.

In the INVOICES table:

> We want the InvNo field to be an automatically generated sequential number, so set its **Counter** property to *True*. For the other three fields in this table, set **Required** to *True* and **AllowZeroLength** to *False*.

In the ITEMS table:

> ItemNo will also be automatically generated, so set its **Counter** property to *True*. The other three fields are required, so set **Required** to *True* and **AllowZeroLength** to *False*.

That's it—all field properties are set as needed. We can now turn our attention to the database's indexes and relationships.

Defining Indexes and Relationships

Along with setting field properties, another capability of the Data Manager is defining indexes and relationships in a database. To briefly review:

- An index is a logical sorting, or ordering, of the records in a table based on the data contained in one or more fields.

- A relationship is a linkage between the primary key in one table and a foreign key in another table. In most cases the relationship is 1:M, or one to many. This means that for each record in the table containing the primary key (the *primary* table), multiple matching records can exist in the table containing the foreign key (the *dependent* table).

To define an index for a table, start the Data Manager, open the database file, then highlight the table name and click the Design button. Then:

1. Click the Indexes button. The Indexes dialog box opens, as shown in Figure 15.3. Any defined indexes in the table will be listed in this dialog box.

2. To add an index, click the Add button to display the Add Index dialog box (Figure 15.4).

3. Type the name for the new index in the Index Name box. I prefer to choose an index name by the field that it will be based on, but you can use other names as well.

4. From the Fields in Table list, click the name of the field on which you want the index to be based.

5. Click the Add (Asc) button to add the field to the index, to sort in ascending order (A-Z, 0-9). Click Add (Dec) for a reverse sort order (Z-A, 9-0). The field name will move to the Fields in Index list.

6. Repeat steps 4 and 5 if you want the index based on more than one field.

7. Click the Primary option if this field (or combination of fields) is the table's primary key. Click the Foreign option if this field is a foreign key.

8. Click the Unique option if the values in the field uniquely identify each record and you want the database engine to check for duplicates during data entry and editing.

9. Click the Required option if the field requires an entry (cannot be NULL) and you want the database engine to verify during data entry.

Figure 15.3 _The Indexes dialog box._

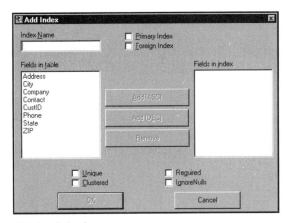

Figure 15.4 *The Add Index dialog box.*

10. Click OK to return to the Indexes dialog box.

11. Repeat steps 2-10 to add additional indexes if required.

12. Click the Close button.

The indexes to be defined for the GRAPEVIN database are shown in Table 15.1. All should be in ascending order.

> **Trade-Offs in Using Indexes**
>
> Selection and design of indexes is, to some extent, a subjective process. Defining an index on a field is not necessary for sorting the records based on that field or searching for data in that field. However, having an index certainly speeds up these operations. Of course, overhead is involved in every index. Each time the user adds a new record or edits an existing record, all of the table's indexes are automatically updated by the Jet engine. This updating takes time. While the time may not be noticeable initially when the database is small, it can become a problem later when the database has grown to thousands of records.

In regard to relationships, we have three to define. These are shown in Table 15.2 and in Figure 14.2 of the previous chapter.

Now is the time to define the above three relationships for the GRAPEVIN database, using these steps:

1. Start Data Manager and open the database.

Table 15.1   *GRAPEVIN Database Fields and Attributes*

Table	Index Name	Field	Primary	Foreign	Unique	Required
CUSTOMERS	CustID	CustID	y	n	y	y
	Company	Company	n	n	n	y
WINES	StockNo	StockNo	y	n	y	y
	Type	Type	n	n	n	n
	RetailPrice	RetailPrice	n	n	n	n
INVOICES	InvNo	InvNo	y	n	y	y
	CustID	CustID	n	y	y	n
ITEMS	ItemNo	ItemNo	y	n	y	y
	StockNo	StockNo	n	y	n	y
	InvNo	InvNo	n	y	n	y

Table 15.2   *GRAPEVIN Database Relationships*

Primary Table/Field	Dependent Table/Field
CUSTOMERS/CustID	INVOICES/CustID
INVOICES/InvNo	ITEMS/InvNo
WINES/StockNo	ITEMS/StockNo

2. In the Table/Query Defs dialog box, click the Relations button. The Relationships dialog box will be displayed, as shown in Figure 15.5.

3. Pull down the Primary Table list and select the primary table. The primary key field will automatically be selected (if there's more than one primary key, you'll be able to choose).

4. Select the dependent table from the Related Table list.

5. Select the related field (the foreign key) from the Select Matching Fields list.

6. Turn on the Enforce Referential Integrity option if desired (explained below).

7. Click Add.

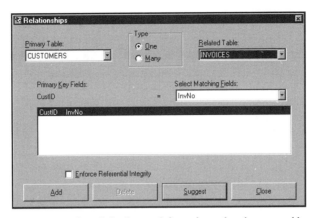

Figure 15.5 *Use the Relationships dialog box to define relationships between tables.*

Maintaining Record Integrity

What is referential integrity? To answer this question, think for a moment about the purpose of a relationship between a dependent and a primary table. In a record in the dependent table, the value of the foreign key indicates or "points" to a record in the primary table that contains related information. For example, in the GRAPEVIN database, in the INVOICES table, the value in the CustID field matches up with a single record in the CUSTOMERS table. As a result, each INVOICE record is linked to the required customer information. When referential integrity is enforced, the database engine checks to see that the primary table contains a matching record whenever a record in the dependent table is entered or edited. If we enforced referential integrity for the CUSTOMERS:INVOICES relationship, the database engine would check for a matching record in the CUSTOMERS table each time we entered or edited a record in the INVOICES table.

For our demonstration we do not require that referential integrity be enforced. As you'll see later, the way we enter data into the foreign key fields ensures the existence of a matching primary key.

THE VALIDATE EVENT

An important part of any good database design is validating the data being entered. Proper validation during data entry and editing can save a lot of headaches down the road. Certain kinds of validation can be accomplished using the field object's validation properties, as discussed earlier in the chapter. Considering the limitations of these properties, I have found the **Validate** event to be much more useful. This event applies only to the Data control. As you may have already guessed, this event is triggered whenever a record is about to be updated. To be more precise, the Data control's **Validate** event occurs:

- Before a different record becomes the current record.

- Before the Update method (but not when data is saved with the UpdateRecord method)

- Before a Delete, Unload, or Close operation.

In the **Validate()** event procedure, we place code that checks the data in the current record against our criteria, and then displays a message and aborts the save operation if necessary. Let's see how this works.

The **Validate()** event procedure has the following structure:

```
Sub CtrlName_Validate ([ index As Integer,] action As Integer, save As Integer)
```

Here's a breakdown of the procedure's arguments:

CtrlName   the **Name** property of the Data control.

index   identifies the Data control when it is in a control array, but is not used if the Data control is not in a control array.

action   indicates the operation that caused the **Validate()** event procedure to be triggered (see below).

save   a Boolean expression specifying whether bound data has changed (see below).

The action argument informs the procedure why the validate event procedure has been triggered. In addition, if code within the procedure sets action to 0, the triggering event will be cancelled when that event procedure terminates. The possible values and the associated constants are listed in Table 15.3.

The save argument is *True* if data in any of the data-aware controls that are bound to this Data control has changed, *False* if it has not. In the procedure, code can change the value of save. If save is *True* when the event procedure terminates (regardless of its initial value), the **Edit** and **UpdateRecord** methods are invoked. If save is *False*, these methods are not invoked.

Table 15.3   *Action Argument's Constants and Values*

Constant	Value	Description
vbDataActionCancel	0	Cancel the operation when the Sub exits
vbDataActionMoveFirst	1	MoveFirst method
vbDataActionMovePrevious	2	MovePrevious method
vbDataActionMoveNext	3	MoveNext method
vbDataActionMoveLast	4	MoveLast method
vbDataActionAddNew	5	AddNew method
vbDataActionUpdate	6	Update operation (not UpdateRecord)
vbDataActionDelete	7	Delete method
vbDataActionFind	8	Find method
vbDataActionBookmark	9	The Bookmark property has been set
vbDataActionClose	10	The Close method
vbDataActionUnload	11	The form is being unloaded

Be aware that the **Validate** event occurs, even if no changes have been made to the data in bound controls. It occurs even if no bound controls exist. Therefore, while checking the validity of changed/new data is a major use of this event procedure, it is not the only possible use. Some clever uses are made possible by the fact that code in the event procedure can change the action argument, thereby changing the action. For example, the **AddNew** method could be changed into any of the **Move** methods. Some limitations exist, however. Attempting to change **AddNew** or one of the **Moves** into any of the other actions will be either ignored or will produce a trappable error. As mentioned above, any action can be stopped by setting action to 0.

To save time when validating data for an edited record, check each bound control's **DataChanged** property and perform the validation only when this property is *True*. This avoids the potential of wasting time to validate data that has not changed (and therefore will already have been validated upon entry). When desirable, it is possible to set a bound control's **DataChanged** property to *False,* and that data will not be saved in the database.

In a **Validate()** event procedure, we cannot use any methods, such as **MoveNext**, on the underlying Recordset object that would trigger another **Validate()** event.

Some Data Validation Hints

What sort of things do you look for when validating data? It depends on the specific situation, of course, but several general criteria are often used:

- Is a number within a certain range? For example, a Quantity on Hand field may be zero or positive, but never negative.

- Is a text entry the proper length or within the acceptable length range? For example, a ZIP code (entered as text) must be five characters long.

- Does a text entry fit the required format? Your firm's Stock Numbers may all follow the format XXXNNNN, where X is a letter and N is a number; any other format of entry should be rejected.

- Is a Date entry within the allowable time span? For example, if an employee's birth date is entered as May 4, 1852, you can be reasonably sure a mistake was made!

- Does the data fit known restrictions for that type of data? For example, all domestic telephone area codes have 0 or 1 as their second digit; any other entry must be an error.

The Basic language provides a full range of tools for validating data. Use of the Variant data type in data validation routines is recommended. The automatic "awareness" of data type that Variant variables are able to provide can eliminate some tedious coding, particularly when it comes to converting strings to numbers and numbers to strings.

Basic Program Structure

Before starting on a project of this complexity, always consider the various options that Visual Basic provides for the overall program structure and appearance. We know that the program will require several "forms" to display the database data in various ways and permit entry and editing of data (why "forms" is in quotes will become clear). The user also needs a way to move from form to form and select the task to be performed.

First, let's look at the available options for display of program elements:

- Use the multiple document interface (MDI) architecture. In an MDI program, one "master" form, the MDI form, serves as a parent or container for all other forms, which are called *child* forms. Any number of child forms can exist; and while multiple child forms can be displayed at one time, only one can be active. Display of child forms is limited to the internal area of the parent form; if the parent form does not occupy the full screen, the child forms cannot be moved outside of it. Each child form can have its own menu; when the form is active, this menu is displayed on the menu bar of the parent form. If you have used a Windows word processor like Microsoft Word, you have seen an MDI program in action.

- Use a collection of non-MDI forms. This configuration also uses multiple forms, but with no parent and no children. Each form is an independent entity that displays its own menu and can be moved and sized independently of the other forms. The Visual Basic development environment uses this approach.

- Use a single form with multiple Picture Box "forms." Remember that a Picture Box control can be used as a container for other controls. In this design the program would consist of a single Visual Basic form with several Picture Box controls on it. Each Picture Box contains the controls required for a particular program function—one for entry of records in the CUSTOMERS table, another for creating new INVOICE records, and so on. Code in the program determines which of the Picture Box controls is visible and active at a given time, permitting the display of multiple "forms" on a single form. In examining the BIBLIO sample project that comes with Visual Basic (in the \VB4\SAMPLES\DATACTRL folder), you'll see an application that uses this approach.

There are also several control options. Of course, it is possible to use these different control methods in combination with each other; but for the sake of simplicity, our demonstration project will be limited to only one. In a real commercial application, we would probably want to use two—for example, a toolbar plus menus. Here are the tasks to be completed:

- Design a menu system with the commands.

- Display Command Buttons for the commands.

- Design a toolbar with buttons for the commands.

For demonstration purposes, we are using an MDI interface with a toolbar. Some other choices might have worked equally well, but this approach gives you the opportunity to learn how to implement an MDI interface and a toolbar, two very important Visual Basic tools.

PRELIMINARY FORM DESIGN

Rather than trying to tackle the entire project at once, we'll start by designing and coding the simpler forms, and creating the MDI interface. For both the CUSTOMERS table and the WINES table, we need a form that permits entry of new records, editing of existing records, and deletion of existing records. These forms should be fairly straightforward, requiring a TextBox and identifying Label for each field and a group of Command Buttons for the various actions. We'd also like a way to list all of the records in the table on a single form, with the option of sorting the list on different fields. Here the dbGrid custom control will come in very handy. But first we need the parent MDI form and its Toolbar.

Creating the MDI Form and Toolbar

Creating the MDI form first is not necessary, but it isn't a bad idea, either. Start a new project and select MDI Form from the Insert menu. Change the form's **Caption** property to "Grapevine Wine Distributors." Click the Toolbar icon in the Toolbox and drag to place a Toolbar on the form. Remember, if the Toolbar icon is not displayed in the Toolbox, you must use the Tools Custom Controls command to load it.

Working with the Toolbar Control

The Toolbar starts out empty, with no buttons. You have the option of using text or images on the Toolbar buttons. For images, bind the Toolbar to an ImageList control, which manages the images (icons or bitmaps) that are displayed on the Toolbar buttons. For the present project we will limit ourselves to text buttons. Please refer to Visual Basic Help for more information on using the ImageList control.

Before starting to work on the Toolbar buttons, set the **Align** property of the Toolbar to *Top*, which causes the Toolbar to automatically position itself at the top of the container form, filling it from side to side. This property must be set in the regular Visual Basic properties window, not in the Toolbar's pop-up property sheet, which we will be using next

The Toolbar is an object with its own properties, and it contains a number of Button objects with their own properties. When a Toolbar control is selected on the Visual Basic design screen, the Properties window displays the Toolbar's properties, which control variables such as the button size and font. To access

Button properties and add or delete buttons, we need to display the Toolbar's property sheet by right-clicking the control and selecting Properties from the menu that is displayed. The Toolbar Control properties sheet—which is just another name for dialog box—is shown in Figure 15.6.

This dialog box has four tabs that deal with the following settings:

General   Toolbar properties (a subset of those available in the Visual Basic Properties window)

Buttons   Button properties, adding and deleting buttons

Pictures   Displaying images on buttons

Fonts   The font used for button text·

We will make use of the General and Buttons tabs (the font is changeable, but I used the default setting). Here are descriptions of the properties on the General tab; the settings needed for the current project are in parentheses:

AllowCustomize   Permits the user to customize the toolbar at runtime (off). Customization includes double-clicking the Toolbar to display the Customize Toolbar dialog box, which permits adding and removing buttons and changing their order.

ShowTips   Displays a ToolTip (programmer defined) if the mouse cursor rests on the button briefly (on).

Enabled   Same as for other Visual Basic controls—activates or deactivates the toolbar (on).

Wrappable   Indicates whether the Toolbar buttons wrap to multiple rows, if needed, when the container window is resized (on).

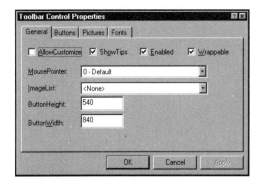

Figure 15.6   *The Toolbar Control Properties sheet.*

MousePointer Displays when the pointer is over the Toolbar (default).

ImageList When displaying images on the buttons, the ImageList controls where the images are stored (none).

ButtonHeight and *ButtonWidth* Shows the size of the buttons, expressed in the ScaleMode units of the toolbar's container. The **ButtonWidth** property is automatically adjusted to match the longest label (**Caption** property) on a button (default settings).

Before getting to the details of adding buttons to the Toolbar, we need to understand the relationship between a Toolbar control and its buttons. As mentioned previously, each button is represented by a Button object, and all of the Button objects on a Toolbar are represented by the Buttons collection. The Buttons collection is a 1-based group of indexed Button objects (1-based means that the first button has index 1 rather than 0, which is more common in some other parts of Visual Basic). In code, therefore, we can access individual buttons and the Buttons collection using standard Visual Basic collection syntax. If our Toolbar is named Toolbar1, for example, we could create a type **Button** variable pointing at a specific button in one of several ways. First, declare the variable:

```
Dim btnX As Button
```

Then we could retrieve a specific button by its index number:

```
Set btnX = Toolbar1.Buttons(2)   'Second button on Toolbar
```

We could also reference a button by a unique key (such as the Button object's Key property):

```
Set btnX = Toolbar1.Buttons("second") ' If Key = "second"
```

We can also use the Item method:

```
Set btnX = Toolbar1.Buttons.Item(2)
```

Once we have retrieved the desired button, we can set its properties; for example:

```
btnX.Caption = "Close"
btnX.Enabled = False
```

The Toolbar control provides a great deal of flexibility, including the ability to add and remove buttons at runtime. (Refer to the Visual Basic Help system for more details.) Note that Toolbar buttons can be used in two basic ways. One is to initiate a process, similar to a Command Button control. The Save Project and Open Project buttons on the toolbar in the Visual Basic development environment operate in this fashion. The second is to turn options on and off, like the Lock Controls button on the toolbar in the Visual Basic development environment. We determine how a Button operates by manipulating its properties.

Back to the project: After setting the Toolbar control's General properties as described above, click the Buttons tab, shown in Figure 15.7. We will be adding three buttons to the Toolbar for now. Here are the basic steps to follow for each button:

1. Click the Insert button and the new button will be inserted to the right of the current button. If no buttons exist, the new button will become the first button at the left of the Toolbar. If necessary, use the left and right arrow buttons to make the appropriate button current before clicking the Insert button.

2. Type the button's caption in the Caption box.

3. Repeat steps 1 and 2 for additional buttons, then click OK.

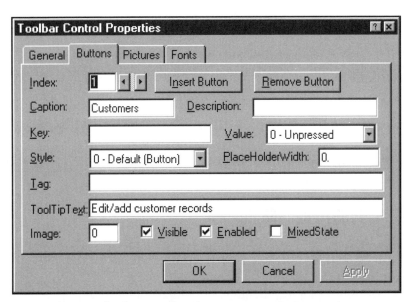

Figure 15.7 *Add new Toolbar buttons and set their properties on the Buttons tab.*

While these are the minimum steps required to add a button to a Toolbar, the Button object has a number of other properties that we can use:

Caption   The text displayed on the button.

Description   The button description displayed at runtime in the Customize Toolbar dialog box.

Key   A unique string that identifies the button.

Value   Whether the button is pressed (Value = *1*) or unpressed (Value = *0*)

Style   The button's style. See Table 15.4.

PlaceholderWidth   The width of a button if its **Style** is set to *PlaceHolder*.

Tag   This property is not used by Visual Basic. It serves as a location for extra data (in string format) that your program can use in any manner it requires (similar to the **Tag** property of other controls).

ToolTipText   The text that is displayed next to the mouse cursor when it is placed on a button briefly (but only if the Toolbar's **ShowTips** property is *True*).

Image   The index of the button's image in the associated ImageList control.

Visible   Whether or not the button is visible. If a button's **Visible** property is *False*, buttons to the right move over to fill in the space where the button would be displayed if **Visible** = *True*.

Enabled   Whether the button is active (can be clicked).

MixedState   Controls whether the button is displayed in the mixed state (grayed out). A mixed state button can still be active (Enabled).

Now, what about this Style property? A Button object can have one of six different styles. Clearly, some Button properties are not relevant for certain styles. The available styles, the defined constants available for setting them, and the descriptions are given in Table 15.4.

Adding Buttons to Our Toolbar

We took a long detour to cover the details of the Toolbar control! Now we're back on track, and it's time to create the three buttons for the Toolbar on our MDI form. Using the techniques explained above, add three buttons, leaving all of their properties at the default setting except as shown in Table 15.5.

Table 15.4 *Available Styles for a Button Object*

Constant	Value	Description
tbrDefault	0	(Default) Button. The button is a regular push button.
tbrCheck	1	Check. The button is a check button, which can be checked or unchecked.
tbrButtonGroup	2	ButtonGroup. All buttons with this style constitute a group. One and only one button in a group can be depressed at a given time; clicking one button automatically "unclicks" the one that was depressed previously. A Toolbar can have only one group.
tbrCheckGroup	3	CheckGroup. All buttons with this style constitute a Check group. Such a group functions similarly to a Button Group except that it is valid when no buttons in a Check Group are depressed. A Check Group functions in a manner similar to a group of Option Button controls.
tbrSeparator	4	Separator. The button functions as a separator with a fixed width of 8 pixels.
tbrPlaceholder	5	Placeholder. The button appears and functions like a separator but has a settable width. A "button" with this style can be used to place another control on a Toolbar. For example, to place a drop-down text box on a toolbar, add a Button with the PlaceHolder style and adjust its width to the desired size. Then place a ComboBox of the same width on the placeholder button.

Table 15.5 *Special Properties for the Three Buttons*

Index	Caption	ToolTipText
1	Customers	Edit/add customers
2	Wines	Edit/add wines
3	Exit	Exit program

After adding these buttons, close the Toolbar's property sheet. Your MDI form should resemble Figure 15.8.

As you might have guessed, responding to Toolbar button clicks is accomplished in an event procedure. The Toolbar object has a **ButtonClick()** event procedure that is called when any of the control's buttons is clicked. This procedure is passed a type Button argument that specifies which button was clicked. We can query the Button argument's properties to identify the button,

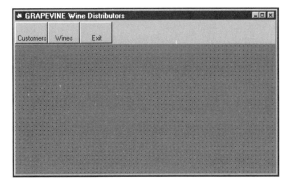

Figure 15.8 *The MDI form and Toolbar after adding the first three toolbar buttons.*

and we can use any of the properties that are unique to each button, such as Index or Caption. To add code to this event procedure, right-click the Toolbar and select View Code from the pop-up menu. A code editing window opens; if necessary, select ButtonClick from the Proc list at the top of the window.

The code for this procedure is shown in Listing 15.1. Notice that we respond to clicks of the "Customers" and "Wines" buttons by displaying the appropriate form. These forms haven't been designed yet, but we can reference them in code as long as we don't try to execute the code (which would, of course, give an error message). Clicking the Exit button first displays a message box confirming that the user wants to exit, then uses End to terminate the program.

Listing 15.1   The Toolbar Control's ButtonClick() Event Procedure

```
Private Sub Toolbar1_ButtonClick(ByVal Button As Button)

Dim Reply As Integer

Select Case Button.Caption
    Case "Customers"
        frmCustomers.Show
    Case "Wines"
        frmWines.Show
    Case "Exit"
        Reply = MsgBox("Quit program - are you sure?", _
                vbYesNo + vbQuestion, "Quit?")
        If Reply = vbYes Then End
End Select

End Sub
```

One last thing before we leave the MDI form: Place the following line of code in the **Form_Load()** event procedure:

```
EnteringRecord = False
```

This line initializes the flag variable to the proper value when the program loads.

Designing the Customers Form

Our next task is designing the form to display Customer information. To add a new form to the project, select Form from the Insert menu. The Customers form will contain the following items:

- A control array of eight TextBox controls, one for each field in the Customers table.

- A control array of eight Label controls, one to identify each TextBox. The Label controls do not have to be in a control array, but using cut-and-paste is easier than dragging each individual control when placing several controls of the same type.

- A control array of four Command Buttons.

- One Data control.

When placing the TextBox controls, add them in the order that a user would desire to move between them—that is, in the same order as the fields are arranged in the database table. By adding the controls in this order, the tab order will be arranged similarly, and the user can tab and shift+tab between Text Boxes in the most efficient order. The completed form is shown in Figure 15.9.

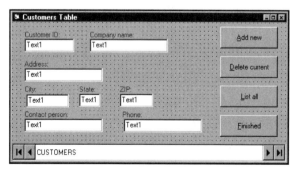

Figure 15.9 *The Customers form.*

The form's objects and properties are given in Listing 15.2. For the most part, the properties are left at their default settings. Here are the most important changes you need to make:

1. Set the **TabStop** property of the first Text Box (the one for the CustID field) to *False* and the **Locked** property to *True*. Because the attribute of this field was set to Counter during database design, the database engine will automatically generate unique values for this field. The user does not need access to this TextBox. Note that setting **Locked** to *True* prevents the user from editing the TextBox, but does not prevent us from changing it in code.

2. For the Data control, set the **DatabaseName** to point at the GRAPEVIN database, and the **RecordSource** property to the CUSTOMERS table. Set the **RecordsetType** property to *Table* and the **Align** property to *Bottom*.

3. For each TextBox, set the **DataSource** property to *Data1* and the **DataField** property to the appropriate field.

4. Set the form's **BorderStyle** property to *Fixed Single* so the user cannot change its size at runtime.

Save the form as CUSTOMER.FRM, and assign a **Name** property of *frmCustomers*. Be sure to set the form's **MDIChild** property to *True* to make it a child of the MDI form we created earlier.

Listing 15.2 Objects and Properties in CUSTOMER.FRM

```
Begin VB.Form frmCustomers
    BorderStyle     =   1  'Fixed Single
    Caption         =   "Customers Table"
    ClientHeight    =   3465
    ClientLeft      =   3900
    ClientTop       =   2955
    ClientWidth     =   7065
    Height          =   3825
    Left            =   3840
    LinkTopic       =   "Form1"
    MaxButton       =   0    'False
    MDIChild        =   -1   'True
    MinButton       =   0    'False
    ScaleHeight     =   3465
    ScaleWidth      =   7065
    Top             =   2655
    Width           =   7185
    Begin VB.CommandButton Command1
        Caption         =   "&Finished"
```

```
   Height           =    540
   Index            =    3
   Left             =    5355
   TabIndex         =    19
   Top              =    2310
   Width            =    1485
End
Begin VB.CommandButton Command1
   Caption          =    "&List all"
   Height           =    540
   Index            =    2
   Left             =    5355
   TabIndex         =    18
   Top              =    1575
   Width            =    1485
End
Begin VB.CommandButton Command1
   Caption          =    "&Delete current"
   Height           =    540
   Index            =    1
   Left             =    5355
   TabIndex         =    17
   Top              =    840
   Width            =    1485
End
Begin VB.CommandButton Command1
   Caption          =    "&Add new"
   Height           =    540
   Index            =    0
   Left             =    5355
   TabIndex         =    16
   Top              =    105
   Width            =    1485
End
Begin VB.Data
   Align            =    2 'Align Bottom
   Caption          =    "CUSTOMERS"
   Connect          =    "Access"
   DatabaseName     =    "D:\VB4\EXPLORER\Grapevin.mdb"
   Exclusive        =    0    'False
   Height           =    435
   Left             =    0
   Options          =    0
   ReadOnly         =    0    'False
   RecordsetType    =    0    'Table
   RecordSource     =    "CUSTOMERS"
   Top              =    3030
   Width            =    7065
End
Begin VB.TextBox Text1
   DataField        =    "Phone"
   DataSource       =    "Data1"
   Height           =    330
```

```
         Index           =    7
         Left            =    2835
         TabIndex        =    7
         Text            =    "Text1"
         Top             =    2415
         Width           =    2010
      End
      Begin VB.TextBox Text1
         DataField       =    "Contact"
         DataSource      =    "Data1"
         Height          =    330
         Index           =    6
         Left            =    315
         TabIndex        =    6
         Text            =    "Text1"
         Top             =    2415
         Width           =    2010
      End
      Begin VB.TextBox Text1
         DataField       =    "ZIP"
         DataSource      =    "Data1"
         Height          =    330
         Index           =    5
         Left            =    2415
         TabIndex        =    5
         Text            =    "Text1"
         Top             =    1785
         Width           =    855
      End
      Begin VB.TextBox Text1
         DataField       =    "State"
         DataSource      =    "Data1"
         Height          =    330
         Index           =    4
         Left            =    1365
         TabIndex        =    4
         Text            =    "Text1"
         Top             =    1785
         Width           =    540
      End
      Begin VB.TextBox Text1
         DataField       =    "City"
         DataSource      =    "Data1"
         Height          =    330
         Index           =    3
         Left            =    315
         TabIndex        =    3
         Text            =    "Text1"
         Top             =    1785
         Width           =    645
      End
      Begin VB.TextBox Text1
         DataField       =    "Address"
         DataSource      =    "Data1"
```

```
      Height          =    330
      Index           =    2
      Left            =    315
      TabIndex        =    2
      Text            =    "Text1"
      Top             =    1155
      Width           =    2010
   End
   Begin VB.TextBox Text1
      DataField       =    "Company"
      DataSource      =    "Data1"
      Height          =    330
      Index           =    1
      Left            =    1995
      TabIndex        =    1
      Text            =    "Text1"
      Top             =    420
      Width           =    2010
   End
   Begin VB.TextBox Text1
      DataField       =    "CustID"
      DataSource      =    "Data1"
      Height          =    330
      Index           =    0
      Left            =    315
      Locked          =    -1   'True
      TabIndex        =    0
      TabStop         =    0    'False
      Text            =    "Text1"
      Top             =    420
      Width           =    1275
   End
   Begin VB.Label Label1
      Caption         =    "Phone:"
      ForeColor       =    &H00FF0000&
      Height          =    225
      Index           =    7
      Left            =    2835
      TabIndex        =    15
      Top             =    2205
      Width           =    960
   End
   Begin VB.Label Label1
      Caption         =    "Contact person:"
      ForeColor       =    &H00FF0000&
      Height          =    225
      Index           =    6
      Left            =    315
      TabIndex        =    14
      Top             =    2205
      Width           =    1380
   End
   Begin VB.Label Label1
      Caption         =    "ZIP:"
```

```
         ForeColor      =    &H00FF0000&
         Height         =    225
         Index          =    5
         Left           =    2415
         TabIndex       =    13
         Top            =    1575
         Width          =    435
      End
      Begin VB.Label Label1
         Caption        =    "State:"
         ForeColor      =    &H00FF0000&
         Height         =    225
         Index          =    4
         Left           =    1365
         TabIndex       =    12
         Top            =    1575
         Width          =    540
      End
      Begin VB.Label Label1
         Caption        =    "City:"
         ForeColor      =    &H00FF0000&
         Height         =    225
         Index          =    3
         Left           =    315
         TabIndex       =    11
         Top            =    1575
         Width          =    435
      End
      Begin VB.Label Label1
         Caption        =    "Address:"
         ForeColor      =    &H00FF0000&
         Height         =    225
         Index          =    2
         Left           =    315
         TabIndex       =    10
         Top            =    945
         Width          =    960
      End
      Begin VB.Label Label1
         Caption        =    "Company name:"
         ForeColor      =    &H00FF0000&
         Height         =    225
         Index          =    1
         Left           =    1995
         TabIndex       =    9
         Top            =    210
         Width          =    1275
      End
      Begin VB.Label Label1
         Caption        =    "Customer ID:"
         ForeColor      =    &H00FF0000&
         Height         =    225
         Index          =    0
         Left           =    315
```

```
        TabIndex      =    8
        Top           =    210
        Width         =    960
    End
End
```

Designing the Wines Form

We can now turn our attention to the Wines form. In general concept, it is quite similar to the Customers form that we just created. We will cover one new technique, using a ComboBox in place of a TextBox for data entry for some of the fields. A ComboBox can be seen as as a combination of a TextBox and ListBox; users can type data into the TextBox part of the control, or they can select from the drop-down list of items. A ComboBox is appropriate when the data entry into a particular field (either usually or always) consists of an item from a predefined list. This is the case for the Color and Type fields in the Wines table. Note that using a ComboBox does not force a selection from the list—users can always type in something else—but it does make the entry of list items faster and error-free.

Select Insert Form to add a new form to the project. The form's **Name** property should be set to *frmWines*, and it should be saved under the name WINES.FRM. This form will contain the following controls:

- A control array of nine TextBox controls, one for each field in the Customers table except for the Color and Type fields

- Two ComboBox controls

- A control array of 11 Label controls, one to identify each TextBox and ComboBox

- A control array of four Command Buttons

- One Data control

After placing the controls, the form should look like Figure 15.10.

1. Add the individual TextBox controls in the proper order so the resulting tab order is correct. You can always modify the **TabIndex** properties later if necessary. Be sure to include the ComboBox controls in the desired position in the tab order.

2. For the Data control, set the **DatabaseName** property to point at the GRAPEVIN database and the **RecordSource** property to the WINES table. Set the **RecordsetType** property to *Table* and the **Align** property to *Bottom*.

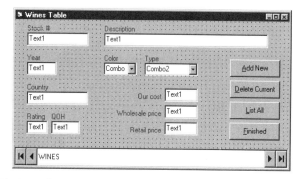

Figure 15.10 The Wines form.

3. For each TextBox and ComboBox, set the **DataSource** property to *Data1* and the **DataField** property to the appropriate field.

4. Set the form's **BorderStyle** property to *Fixed Single* and its **MDIChild** property to *True*.

The complete set of objects and properties on the Wines form is presented in Listing 15.3.

Listing 15.3   Objects and Properties in WINES.FRM

```
Begin VB.Form frmWines
   BorderStyle     =   1  'Fixed Single
   Caption         =   "Wines Table"
   ClientHeight    =   3660
   ClientLeft      =   225
   ClientTop       =   1335
   ClientWidth     =   7065
   Height          =   4065
   Left            =   165
   LinkTopic       =   "Form1"
   MaxButton       =   0   'False
   MDIChild        =   -1  'True
   MinButton       =   0   'False
   ScaleHeight     =   3660
   ScaleWidth      =   7065
   Top             =   990
   Width           =   7185
   Begin VB.CommandButton Command1
      Caption         =   "&Finished"
      Height          =   435
      Index           =   3
      Left            =   5565
      TabIndex        =   26
      Top             =   2520
      Width           =   1275
```

```
End
Begin VB.CommandButton Command1
   Caption         =    "&List All"
   Height          =    435
   Index           =    2
   Left            =    5565
   TabIndex        =    25
   Top             =    1995
   Width           =    1275
End
Begin VB.CommandButton Command1
   Caption         =    "&Delete Current"
   Height          =    435
   Index           =    1
   Left            =    5565
   TabIndex        =    24
   Top             =    1470
   Width           =    1275
End
Begin VB.CommandButton Command1
   Caption         =    "&Add New"
   Height          =    435
   Index           =    0
   Left            =    5565
   TabIndex        =    23
   Top             =    945
   Width           =    1275
End
Begin VB.ComboBox ComboType
   DataField       =    "Type"
   DataSource      =    "Data1"
   Height          =    315
   Left            =    3360
   Sorted          =    -1   'True
   TabIndex        =    22
   Text            =    "Combo2"
   Top             =    1050
   Width           =    1380
End
Begin VB.ComboBox ComboColor
   DataField       =    "Color"
   DataSource      =    "Data1"
   Height          =    315
   Left            =    2310
   Sorted          =    -1   'True
   TabIndex        =    21
   Text            =    "Combo1"
   Top             =    1050
   Width           =    855
End
Begin VB.TextBox Text1
   DataField       =    "RetailPrice"
   DataSource      =    "Data1"
```

```
      Height          =      330
      Index           =      8
      Left            =      3885
      TabIndex        =      8
      Text            =      "Text1"
      Top             =      2520
      Width           =      855
   End
   Begin VB.TextBox Text1
      DataField       =      "WholesaleCost"
      DataSource      =      "Data1"
      Height          =      330
      Index           =      7
      Left            =      3885
      TabIndex        =      7
      Text            =      "Text1"
      Top             =      2100
      Width           =      855
   End
   Begin VB.TextBox Text1
      DataField       =      "OurCost"
      DataSource      =      "Data1"
      Height          =      330
      Index           =      6
      Left            =      3885
      TabIndex        =      6
      Text            =      "Text1"
      Top             =      1680
      Width           =      855
   End
   Begin VB.TextBox Text1
      DataField       =      "QOH"
      DataSource      =      "Data1"
      Height          =      330
      Index           =      5
      Left            =      945
      TabIndex        =      5
      Text            =      "Text1"
      Top             =      2520
      Width           =      750
   End
   Begin VB.TextBox Text1
      DataField       =      "Rating"
      DataSource      =      "Data1"
      Height          =      330
      Index           =      4
      Left            =      315
      TabIndex        =      4
      Text            =      "Text1"
      Top             =      2520
      Width           =      540
   End
   Begin VB.TextBox Text1
      DataField       =      "Country"
```

```
   DataSource       =    "Data1"
   Height           =    330
   Index            =    3
   Left             =    315
   TabIndex         =    3
   Text             =    "Text1"
   Top              =    1785
   Width            =    1590
End
Begin VB.TextBox Text1
   DataField        =    "Year"
   DataSource       =    "Data1"
   Height           =    330
   Index            =    2
   Left             =    315
   TabIndex         =    2
   Text             =    "Text1"
   Top              =    1050
   Width            =    750
End
Begin VB.TextBox Text1
   DataField        =    "Description"
   DataSource       =    "Data1"
   Height           =    330
   Index            =    1
   Left             =    2310
   TabIndex         =    1
   Text             =    "Text1"
   Top              =    315
   Width            =    4215
End
Begin VB.TextBox Text1
   DataField        =    "StockNo"
   DataSource       =    "Data1"
   Height           =    330
   Index            =    0
   Left             =    315
   TabIndex         =    0
   Text             =    "Text1"
   Top              =    315
   Width            =    1590
End
Begin VB.Data Data1
   Align            =    2        'Align Bottom
   Caption          =    "WINES"
   Connect          =    "Access"
   DatabaseName     =    "C:\VB4\EXPLORER\Grapevin.mdb"
   Exclusive        =    0        'False
   Height           =    480
   Left             =    0
   Options          =    0
   ReadOnly         =    0        'False
   RecordsetType    =    0        'Table
   RecordSource     =    "WINES"
```

```
         Top             =    3180
         Width           =    7065
      End
      Begin VB.Label Label1
         Alignment       =    1   'Right Justify
         Caption         =    "Retail price"
         ForeColor       =    &H00FF0000&
         Height          =    225
         Index           =    11
         Left            =    2835
         TabIndex        =    20
         Top             =    2625
         Width           =    960
      End
      Begin VB.Label Label1
         Alignment       =    1   'Right Justify
         Caption         =    "Wholesale price"
         ForeColor       =    &H00FF0000&
         Height          =    225
         Index           =    10
         Left            =    2625
         TabIndex        =    19
         Top             =    2205
         Width           =    1170
      End
      Begin VB.Label Label1
         Alignment       =    1   'Right Justify
         Caption         =    "Our cost"
         ForeColor       =    &H00FF0000&
         Height          =    225
         Index           =    9
         Left            =    3045
         TabIndex        =    18
         Top             =    1785
         Width           =    750
      End
      Begin VB.Label Label1
         Caption         =    "QOH"
         ForeColor       =    &H00FF0000&
         Height          =    225
         Index           =    8
         Left            =    945
         TabIndex        =    17
         Top             =    2310
         Width           =    750
      End
      Begin VB.Label Label1
         Caption         =    "Rating"
         ForeColor       =    &H00FF0000&
         Height          =    225
         Index           =    7
         Left            =    315
         TabIndex        =    16
         Top             =    2310
```

```
         Width          =    750
      End
      Begin VB.Label Label1
         Caption         =    "Stock #"
         ForeColor       =    &H00FF0000&
         Height          =    15
         Index           =    6
         Left            =    0
         TabIndex        =    15
         Top             =    210
         Width           =    750
      End
      Begin VB.Label Label1
         Caption         =    "Country"
         ForeColor       =    &H00FF0000&
         Height          =    225
         Index           =    5
         Left            =    315
         TabIndex        =    14
         Top             =    1575
         Width           =    750
      End
      Begin VB.Label Label1
         Caption         =    "Type"
         ForeColor       =    &H00FF0000&
         Height          =    225
         Index           =    4
         Left            =    3360
         TabIndex        =    13
         Top             =    840
         Width           =    750
      End
      Begin VB.Label Label1
         Caption         =    "Color"
         ForeColor       =    &H00FF0000&
         Height          =    225
         Index           =    3
         Left            =    2310
         TabIndex        =    12
         Top             =    840
         Width           =    750
      End
      Begin VB.Label Label1
         Caption         =    "Year"
         ForeColor       =    &H00FF0000&
         Height          =    225
         Index           =    2
         Left            =    315
         TabIndex        =    11
         Top             =    840
         Width           =    750
      End
      Begin VB.Label Label1
         Caption         =    "Description"
```

```
        ForeColor      =   &H00FF0000&
        Height         =   225
        Index          =   1
        Left           =   2310
        TabIndex       =   10
        Top            =   105
        Width          =   960
     End
     Begin VB.Label Label1
        Caption        =   "Stock #"
        ForeColor      =   &H00FF0000&
        Height         =   225
        Index          =   0
        Left           =   315
        TabIndex       =   9
        Top            =   105
        Width          =   750
     End
  End
End
```

Designing the List Form

Part of our design plan was having the ability to list all of the records in both the Wines and the Customers table. You can see that we included a "List All" button on both the Customers and Wines forms. How can we implement a list of all records? The dbGrid control provides the ideal solution—it was designed for just this kind of task. We will create a single form for listing records, then specify which table's records are to be displayed in code before the form is displayed.

Add a new form to the project. Set its **Name** property to *frmList* and save it as LIST1.FRM. Add one dbGrid control, one Data control, and one Command Button control to the form. Set the dbGrid's **DataSource** property to *Data1* and its **Alignment** property to *Top*. The Data control's **DatabaseName** and **RecordSource** properties do not need to be set, since we will be setting them in code. You should make its **Visible** property *False*, however, as we will not need this control visible on the form. Listing 15-4 gives the complete set of objects and properties for LIST1.FRM.

Listing 15.4   Objects and Properties in LIST1.FRM

```
Begin VB.Form frmList
   Caption        =   "Form1"
   ClientHeight   =   4530
   ClientLeft     =   1725
   ClientTop      =   1350
   ClientWidth    =   5160
   Height         =   4935
```

```
Left               =    1665
LinkTopic          =    "Form1"
ScaleHeight        =    4530
ScaleWidth         =    5160
Top                =    1005
Width              =    5280
Begin VB.CommandButton Command1
    Caption        =    "&Finished"
    Height         =    435
    Left           =    1155
    TabIndex       =    1
    Top            =    4095
    Width          =    3060
End
Begin VB.Data Data1
    Caption        =    "Data1"
    Connect        =    "Access"
    DatabaseName   =    ""
    Exclusive      =    0       'False
    Height         =    435
    Left           =    420
    Options        =    0
    ReadOnly       =    0       'False
    RecordsetType  =    1       'Dynaset
    RecordSource   =    ""
    Top            =    3465
    Visible        =    0       'False
    Width          =    4740
End
Begin MSDBGrid.DBGrid DBGrid1
    Align          =    1 'Align Top
    Height         =    2745
    Left           =    0
    TabIndex       =    0
    Top            =    0
    Width          =    5160
End
End
```

WRITING THE CODE

Now that we have designed the project's first three forms, we can turn our attention to writing the code that will give these forms their functionality. Of course, these three forms are only a part of what the project requires—so why don't we design the remaining forms before starting on Basic code? This is one approach, but my own experience has proven that working on the project one section at a time—both forms and code—reaps better results. This way we have part of the program working properly before moving on to the next part. Coming back and making changes later is to be expected. We already have enough forms designed to provide part of the programs functionality—entering, editing, and listing records in the Customers and Wines table—and we should be sure that this much is working before moving on.

The Basic Module

Complex projects such as this one almost always require a Basic module for declaration of global variables and similar tasks. To add a Basic module, select Module from the Insert menu. Type the following code:

```
' True when entering a record, False otherwise.

Global EnteringRecord As Boolean
```

Save the module under the name GRAPEVIN (Visual Basic will add the .BAS extension).

Coding the Customers Form

Our approach to coding this form is to provide its basic functions, but not necessarily everything we eventually want it to have. We'll write code to permit entry, editing, deleting, and listing of records, but leave the code for data validation until later.

In this form, we will again use the "chameleon Command Button" technique covered in an earlier chapter, permitting the four Command Buttons to do the work of six. When the user is viewing or editing records in the default state, the global variable EnteringRecords will be *False* and the first two Command Buttons will have the captions "Add New" and "Delete Current" When the user clicks the Add New button, EnteringRecords is toggled to *True*, the Add New button's caption is changed to Save, and the Delete Current button's caption is changed to Cancel. When the user clicks Save or Cancel after entering the new record, the process is reversed. While the user is entering a new record, we want the List and Finished Command Buttons and the Data control disabled as well.

As for the database itself, the commands are fairly simple and consist of methods belonging to the Recordset object. Here are the methods we'll use:

AddNew   Clears the bound controls in preparation for entry of new data.

Update   After an AddNew, copies the data entered in the bound controls into a new record in the table.

Delete   Deletes the current record from the table.

CancelUpdate   After an AddNew, cancels the add record operation.

We'll also use two of the Recordset object's properties. The **Bookmark** property returns a unique bookmark identifier for the Recordset's current record. We can save the **Bookmark** property to a type **Variant** at any time to keep track of which record was current at the moment. If we set the **Bookmark** property to a valid bookmark, the corresponding record becomes current. Thus, we can use the **Bookmark** property to keep track of our location and return there later. We can also use the **LastModified** property, which returns the bookmark of the record that was most recently changed or added.

As for the List All command, the capabiliies of the dbGrid control make this a simple one to code. All we have to do is set the properties of the Data control to which the dbGrid is bound so they point at the same database and table as the Customer form's Data control, refresh the Data control, and use the **Show** method to display the form. Here's the code:

```
frmList.Data1.DatabaseName = frmCustomers.Data1.DatabaseName
frmList.Data1.RecordSource = frmCustomers.Data1.RecordSource
frmList.Data1.Refresh
frmList.Show
```

The full **Command1_Click()** event procedure for the Customers form is shown in Listing 15.5.

Listing 15.5   The Command1_Click() Event Procedure in CUSTOMER.FRM

```
Private Sub Command1_Click(Index As Integer)

Dim CurrentRecord As Variant, Reply As Integer

' Save current location.
CurrentRecord = Data1.Recordset.Bookmark

Select Case Index
    Case 0        ' Add New or Save
        If EnteringRecord Then      ' Save command.
            EnteringRecord = False
            ' Change command buttons.
            Command1(0).Caption = "&Add New"
            Command1(1).Caption = "&Delete Current"
            ' Enable the data control.
```

```
                Data1.Enabled = True
                ' Enable List and Finished buttons.
                Command1(2).Enabled = True
                Command1(3).Enabled = True
                ' Save the new record.
                Data1.Recordset.UPDATE
                ' Make the new record current.
                Data1.Recordset.Bookmark = Data1.Recordset.LastModified
            Else                        ' Add New command.
                EnteringRecord = True
                ' Put focus in first text box. This is actually the
                ' second TextBox as the first one (CustID) is locked.
                Text1(1).SetFocus
                ' Disable List and Finished buttons.
                Command1(2).Enabled = False
                Command1(3).Enabled = False
                ' Change command buttons.
                Command1(0).Caption = "&Save"
                Command1(1).Caption = "&Cancel"
                ' Disable the data control.
                Data1.Enabled = False
                ' Add a new record.
                Data1.Recordset.AddNew
            End If
        Case 1      ' Delete current or Cancel
            If EnteringRecord Then       ' Cancel command
                Reply = MsgBox("Discard current entry?", _
                        vbYesNo + vbQuestion, "Cancel Entry")
                If Reply = vbNo Then Exit Sub
                Data1.Recordset.CancelUpdate
                Data1.Recordset.Bookmark = CurrentRecord
                EnteringRecord = False
                ' Enable List and Finished buttons.
                Command1(2).Enabled = True
                Command1(3).Enabled = True
                Command1(0).Caption = "&Add New"
                Command1(1).Caption = "&Delete Current"
            Else                         ' Delete Current command
                Reply = MsgBox("Delete this record?", vbYesNo + vbQuestion, _
                        "Cancel Entry")
                If Reply = vbNo Then Exit Sub
                Data1.Recordset.DELETE
                Data1.Recordset.MoveNext
            End If
        Case 2      ' List all
            frmList.Data1.DatabaseName = frmCustomers.Data1.DatabaseName
            frmList.Data1.RecordSource = frmCustomers.Data1.RecordSource
            frmList.Data1.Refresh
            frmList.Show
        Case 3      ' Finished
            Hide
    End Select

End Sub
```

Coding the Wines Form

The code for the Wines form is a bit more complicated. As for handling the Command Buttons, we follow the exact same procedure as we did for the Customers form, including the use of chameleon Command Buttons. The code for this event procedure is shown in Listing 15.6.

Listing 15.6 The Command1_Click() Event Procedure in WINES.FRM

```
Private Sub Command1_Click(Index As Integer)

Dim CurrentRecord As Variant, Reply As Integer

' Save current location.
CurrentRecord = Data1.Recordset.Bookmark

Select Case Index
    Case 0      ' Add New or Save
        If EnteringRecord Then      ' Save command.
            EnteringRecord = False
            ' Change command buttons.
            Command1(0).Caption = "&Add New"
            Command1(1).Caption = "&Delete Current"
            ' Enable the data control.
            Data1.Enabled = True
            ' Enable List and Finished buttons.
            Command1(2).Enabled = True
            Command1(3).Enabled = True
            ' Save the new record.
            Data1.Recordset.UPDATE
            ' Make the new record current.
            Data1.Recordset.Bookmark = Data1.Recordset.LastModified
        Else                        ' Add New command.
            EnteringRecord = True
            ' Put focus in first text box.
            Text1(0).SetFocus
            ' Disable List and Finished buttons.
            Command1(2).Enabled = False
            Command1(3).Enabled = False
            ' Change command buttons.
            Command1(0).Caption = "&Save"
            Command1(1).Caption = "&Cancel"
            ' Disable the data control.
            Data1.Enabled = False
            ' Add a new record.
            Data1.Recordset.AddNew
        End If
    Case 1      ' Delete current or Cancel
        If EnteringRecord Then      ' Cancel command
            Reply = MsgBox("Discard current entry?", vbYesNo + vbQuestion, _
```

```
                     "Cancel Entry")
           If Reply = vbNo Then Exit Sub
           Data1.Recordset.CancelUpdate
           Data1.Recordset.Bookmark = CurrentRecord
           EnteringRecord = False
           ' Enable List and Finished buttons.
           Command1(2).Enabled = True
           Command1(3).Enabled = True
           ' Reset captions.
           Command1(0).Caption = "&Add New"
           Command1(1).Caption = "&Delete Current"
      Else                          ' Delete Current command
           Reply = MsgBox("Delete this record?", _
                 vbYesNo + vbQuestion, "Cancel Entry")
           If Reply = vbNo Then Exit Sub
           Data1.Recordset.DELETE
           Data1.Recordset.MoveNext
      End If
   Case 2      ' List all
      frmList.Caption = "Wines Table"
      frmList.Data1.DatabaseName = frmWines.Data1.DatabaseName
      frmList.Data1.RecordSource = frmWines.Data1.RecordSource
      frmList.Data1.Refresh
      frmList.Show
   Case 3       ' Finished
      Hide
End Select

End Sub
```

What's different about the Wines form is the ComboBox controls that are used
for entry of the Color and Type data. These controls must be loaded with the
appropriate choices in order to be available when the user displays the form.
Place this code in the **Form_Load()** event procedure, as shown in Listing
15.7. Another method would be to load each ComboBox from a text file that
is kept in the same directory as the database. In fact, this method is preferable
for a commercial program because it permits changes to the Color and Type
lists without modifying the source code and recompiling the program—the
only thing needed would be to edit the text file.

Listing 15.7   The Form_Load() Event Procedure in WINES.FRM

```
Private Sub Form_Load()

' Load the Combo boxes

ComboColor.AddItem "red"
ComboColor.AddItem "white"
```

```
ComboColor.AddItem "rose"
ComboColor.AddItem "dessert"
ComboColor.AddItem "sparkling"

ComboType.AddItem "Chardonnay"
ComboType.AddItem "Pinot noir"
ComboType.AddItem "Burgundy"
ComboType.AddItem "Pinot blanc"
ComboType.AddItem "Barolo"
ComboType.AddItem "Barbaresco"
ComboType.AddItem "Cabernet"
ComboType.AddItem "Semillion"
ComboType.AddItem "Bordeaux"
ComboType.AddItem "Chateauneuf de Pape"
ComboType.AddItem "White zinfandel"
ComboType.AddItem "Champagne"

End Sub
```

Coding the List Form

Coding this form is very simple because most of the form's work is already handled by the dbGrid control—all that functionality is built right in, so you don't have to do a thing. (Aren't software components great?) However, we do need to add a little code. In the **Form_Resize()** event procedure, we need to adjust the control sizes; this code is shown in Listing 15.8. Note that we are only concerned with the height of the dbGrid control—when we set its **Align** property to *True*, it will automatically be positioned at the top of the form and sized to match the form.

Listing 15.8   The Form_Resize() Event Procedure in LIST1.FRM

```
Private Sub Form_Resize()

' Set size and position of controls.

DBGrid1.Height = ScaleHeight - Command1.Height
Command1.TOP = ScaleHeight - Command1.Height
Command1.Left = 0
Command1.Width = ScaleWidth

End Sub
```

The only other code required for the List form is placing the single line of code

```
Hide
```

in the Command Button's **Click()** event procedure. By hiding the List form, we automatically return to the form that called it—the Customers form or the Wines form—which had remained inactive in the background while the List form was displayed.

What Now?

The answer to that one is easy—try it out! Now we have a partially functional database front end to take on a trial run. Watch for error messages; if any appear, check your code to be sure you entered everything properly. As it stands right now, the program gives you the capability to add new records to the Customers and Wines tables, to edit and delete existing records, and to view a list of all records in either table. Note that changes to the table data made in List view are saved, providing another way for the user to edit table data.

We're off to a good start! But clearly, we have a long road ahead before we reach a fully functional program.

CHAPTER 16

WRAPPING IT UP: VALIDATION CODE AND THE INVOICES FORM

The final steps in our database project are to write data validation code and to design the form for creating Invoices.

A well written program does everything it can to prevent errors. Certain types of errors are impossible to prevent—you can't control when a disk drive is going to crash, for example. Other errors can be prevented, particularly errors in data entry. If you know something about the data that belongs in a particular field, you can verify that new or edited data meets the required criteria. Once we've written validation code, we'll turn to a more complicated form for the database program—the Invoice Entry form. We'll then have a functional, if admittedly bare-bones, relational database.

VALIDATION CODE

There are a number of approaches to validation of data. One method simply prevents the entry of inappropriate keystrokes. For example, in a ZIP code field you know that only the 10 numerical digits are permitted, plus a hyphen if 9-digit ZIP codes will be allowed. Filtering input characters is accomplished in the **KeyPress()** event procedure. This procedure receives a type Integer argument containing the ANSI code of the key that was pressed. Code in the procedure can examine this value and determine if it is one of the allowed keys. If it is not, setting the KeyAscii argument to 0 cancels the keystroke, preventing it from reaching the underlying control. For example, the following code will permit entry of the digits 0 through 9 only, beeping if another key is pressed:

```
Private Sub Text1_KeyPress(KeyAscii As Integer)


If KeyAscii < 48 Or KeyAscii > 57 Then
    Beep
    KeyAscii = 0
End If

End Sub
```

ANSI Codes

Keyboard and other characters are represented internally by the ANSI codes, with numeric values in the range of 0 through 255 representing each character. The **KeyPress()** event procedure receives the ANSI code of the pressed key as its argument, so your code must either use these codes for its comparisons or use the **Chr$()** function to convert the code into its corresponding character. Thus, this line of code

```
If KeyAscii = 76
```

and this line

```
If Chr$(KeyAscii) = "L"
```

both test for the uppercase "L" character. See the Character Set topic in Visual Basic Help for a listing of all characters and their ANSI codes. *Note: You should always pass through a KeyAscii value of 8, representing Backspace, or else users will not be able to use the Backspace key to erase characters.*

Another approach to validating data is to use the data entry control's **LostFocus** event, examining the data in the control and verifying that it meets the criteria. Using a ZIP code field as an example again, we could verify that exactly five characters were entered as follows:

```
Private Sub Text1_LostFocus()

If Len(Text1.TEXT) <> 5 Then
    MsgBox ("This field must contain 5 characters")
    Text1.SetFocus
End If

End Sub
```

If some other number of characters was entered, a message box is displayed and then the focus is set back to the TextBox to permit the user to edit it.

Another validation method is to use the database engine's validation capabilities. Based on the properties you have set for each field, and the indexes and keys defined, the database engine will trigger an error that your program can trap. (You'll learn more details about trapping program errors in a later chapter, but I'll present the basics here.) For example, if you defined an index on a particular field and checked the Unique option, the database engine checks to see that a newly entered or edited value in the field is, in fact, unique—is not duplicated in any other record in the table. If a duplicate is found, error number 3022 is generated. Your program can "trap" the error and respond accordingly.

Here's a code example of how this would be done. Assume that the Recordset's **Update** method is executed in this event procedure (because it's the **Update** event that causes the database engine to perform validation). The comments in the code explain what each line of text is doing.

```
Private Sub Command1_Click(Index As Integer)

' Specify that if an error is generated in this event procedure,
' execution is to go to the location identified as "ErrorHandler"
On Local Error GoTo ErrorHandler


...
' Other code here.
...
' Exit Sub statement here so execution does not "fall into"
' the error handling code.
Exit Sub

' A label followed by a colon identifies a location in code.
ErrorHandler:
' Was the error that occurred number 3022? If so, display an explanatory
' message and set the focus back to the text box so the user can edit
' the entry.
If Err = 3022 Then
```

```
    MsgBox ("Duplicate employee numbers are not allowed")
    Text1.SetFocus
End If

End Sub
```

The fourth method of data validation involves the **Validate()** event procedure. I explained the basics of using the **Validate** event in Chapter 15, and you'll see its use in the demonstration program later.

Now that you understand the various methods you can use to validate data, we can turn our attention to data validation in the demonstration database. I will not attempt to include every possible data validation rule that I can think of. Rather, I will include those that are most critical to database integrity and also serve to demonstrate the four methods I've just described.

Validating Customers Data

For the Customers table, we'll make these verifications:

- That the ZIP code field contains 5 characters

- That the Company, Address, City, and State fields all contain data

Let's tackle the ZIP code first. We'll use the **LostFocus** event, which is triggered whenever the control loses the focus. During data entry or editing, this will occur when the user tabs to the next TextBox or, if the focus is on the ZIP Code field, when one of the Command Buttons is clicked. Listing 16.1 shows the code to place in the **Text1_LostFocus()** event procedure.

Listing 16.1   The LostFocus() Event Procedure for the TextBox Array in CUSTOMER.FRM

```
Private Sub Text1_LostFocus(Index As Integer)

' Verify that entry in ZIP field has 5 characters. The index
' of that TextBox is 5.

If Index = 5 Then
    If Len(Text1(5).TEXT) <> 5 Then
        MsgBox ("ZIP code must have 5 characters")
        Text1(5).SetFocus
    End If
End If

End Sub
```

For the next validation task, we'll use the **Validate** event. This will be a bit more complicated because of the way the program is structured. The **Validate** event is triggered when the **Update** method is called in the **Command1_Click()** event procedure, when the user clicks the Save button. That code is shown here:

```
...
If EnteringRecord Then       ' Save command.
        EnteringRecord = False
        ' Change command buttons.
        Command1(0).Caption = "&Add New"
        Command1(1).Caption = "&Delete Current"
        ' Enable the data control.
        Data1.Enabled = True
        ' Enable List and Finished buttons.
        Command1(2).Enabled = True
        Command1(3).Enabled = True
        ' Save the new record.
        Data1.Recordset.UPDATE
        ' Make the new record current.
        Data1.Recordset.Bookmark = Data1.Recordset.LastModified
Else
...
```

By the time **Update** is called and **Validate** is triggered, the Command Buttons have been reset, the Data control has been enabled, and the **EnteringRecord** flag has been cleared—in other words, the form has been switched from "data entry mode" to "data viewing/editing mode." If **Validate** detects a problem with the data, we want to return to data entry mode so the user can correct the problem. We'll do this by moving the **Update** method to the start of this block of code, and by including a flag variable that will cause execution to exit without resetting the form if **Validate** detects a problem.

Here's what we need to do:

1. Add the following declaration to the GRAPEVIN.BAS Basic module:

```
Global Saving As Boolean
```

2. Edit the code in the CUSTOMER.FRM **Command1_Click()** event procedure as follows. Note that the comments on the second through fifth lines are there only to help you identify the changes; you need not enter them in your code:

```
...
If EnteringRecord Then       ' Save command.
        Saving = True        ' New line
```

```
        ' Save the new record.    ' Moved line
        Data1.Recordset.UPDATE    ' Moved line
        If Not Saving Then Exit Sub ' New line
        EnteringRecord = False
        ' Change command buttons.
        Command1(0).Caption = "&Add New"
        Command1(1).Caption = "&Delete Current"
        ' Enable the data control.
        Data1.Enabled = True
        ' Enable List and Finished buttons.
        Command1(2).Enabled = True
        Command1(3).Enabled = True
        ' Make the new record current.
        Data1.Recordset.Bookmark = Data1.Recordset.LastModified
Else                             ' Add New command.
...
```

3. Enter the code from Listing 16.2 in the **Data1_Validate()** event procedure in CUSTOMER.FRM.

Listing 16.2 The Data1 Control's Validate() Event Procedure in CUSTOMER.FRM

```
Private Sub Data1_Validate(Action As Integer, Save As Integer)

Dim i As Integer, Missing As Boolean

Missing = False

' Exit sub if bound data has not changed.
If Not Save Then Exit Sub

' Loop through the TextBox controls for Company,
' Address, City, and State.
For i = 1 To 4
    If Len(Text1(i).TEXT) = 0 Then Missing = True
Next i

If Missing Then
    MsgBox ("Company, Address, City, and State may not be blank.")
    ' Cancel the Update action.
    Action = vbDataActionCancel
    ' Clear Saving flag.
    Saving = False
    ' Set focus to Company Text Box for correction.
    Text1(1).SetFocus
End If

End Sub
```

Validating Wines Data

For the Wines table, we will validate two things:

- That the stock number is not duplicated

- That the entry in each of the price fields contains only numbers and the decimal point

To prevent duplicate stock numbers, we'll use the Jet database engine's verification capabilities. Since we defined an index on the StockNo field and specified that it be a unique index, the database engine will automatically check for duplicated data when you save a new record. We can trap this error by editing the **Command1_Click()** event procedure to include the error-handling code explained earlier in this chapter.

A problem arises, however. The database engine checks for duplicates in the StockNo field not only when a new record is added, but also when an existing record is edited. But there will never be a need to edit the StockNo field— once a stock number is assigned, it will not change. Rather than deal with the possibility of the user creating a duplicate number by editing the StockNo field, we'll lock the StockNo TextBox to prevent editing and unlock it only during entry of a new record.

Display the Wines form and select the TextBox associated with the StockNo field, then change its **Locked** property to *True*. All other changes are made to the code in the **Command1_Click()** event procedure. The edited procedure is shown in Listing 16.3; new and changed lines are marked with comments.

Listing 16.3   The Edited Command1_Click() Event Procedure That Handles Duplicate Stock Number Errors

```
Private Sub Command1_Click(Index As Integer)

On Local Error GoTo ErrorHandler   ' New line

Dim CurrentRecord As Variant, Reply As Integer

' Save current location.
CurrentRecord = Data1.Recordset.Bookmark

Select Case Index
    Case 0       ' Add New or Save
        If EnteringRecord Then      ' Save command.
            ' Save the new record. ' Moved line
```

```
        Data1.Recordset.UPDATE ' Moved line
        EnteringRecord = False
        ' Relock the StockNo TextBox' New line
        Text1(0).Locked = True    ' New line
        ' Change command buttons.
        Command1(0).Caption = "&Add New"
        Command1(1).Caption = "&Delete Current"
        ' Enable the data control.
        Data1.Enabled = True
        ' Enable List and Finished buttons.
        Command1(2).Enabled = True
        Command1(3).Enabled = True
        ' Make the new record current.
        Data1.Recordset.Bookmark = Data1.Recordset.LastModified
    Else                          ' Add New command.
        EnteringRecord = True
        ' Unlock the StockNo Text Box  ' New line
        Text1(0).Locked = False      ' New line
       ' Put focus in first text box.
        Text1(0).SetFocus
        ' Disable List and Finished buttons.
        Command1(2).Enabled = False
        Command1(3).Enabled = False
        ' Change command buttons.
        Command1(0).Caption = "&Save"
        Command1(1).Caption = "&Cancel"
        ' Disable the data control.
        Data1.Enabled = False
        ' Add a new record.
        Data1.Recordset.AddNew
    End If
Case 1     ' Delete current or Cancel
    If EnteringRecord Then      ' Cancel command
        Reply = MsgBox("Discard current entry?", _
                    vbYesNo + vbQuestion, "Cancel Entry")
        If Reply = vbNo Then Exit Sub
        Data1.Recordset.CancelUpdate
        ' Relock the StockNo TextBox' New line
        Text1(0).Locked = True    ' New line
        Data1.Recordset.Bookmark = CurrentRecord
        EnteringRecord = False
        ' Enable List and Finished buttons.
        Command1(2).Enabled = True
        Command1(3).Enabled = True
        ' Reset captions.
        Command1(0).Caption = "&Add New"
        Command1(1).Caption = "&Delete Current"
    Else                        ' Delete Current command
        Reply = MsgBox("Delete this record?", _
                    vbYesNo + vbQuestion, "Cancel Entry")
        If Reply = vbNo Then Exit Sub
        Data1.Recordset.DELETE
        Data1.Recordset.MoveNext
```

```
        End If
    Case 2      ' List all
        frmList.Caption = "Wines Table"
        frmList.Data1.DatabaseName = frmWines.Data1.DatabaseName
        frmList.Data1.RecordSource = frmWines.Data1.RecordSource
        frmList.Data1.Refresh
        frmList.Show
    Case 3      ' Finished
        Hide
End Select

Exit Sub                                        ' New line

ErrorHandler:                                   ' New line
  If Err = 3022 Then                            ' New line
    MsgBox ("Duplicate stock numbers not allowed")  ' New line
    Text1(0).SetFocus                           ' New line
  End If                                         ' New line

End Sub
```

For the second validation task, we'll use the Text Box control's **KeyPress**
event to ensure that only the desired characters—in this case, numbers and
the period or decimal point—can be entered in the WINES form's three price
fields. The **KeyPress()** event procedure for the WINES.FRM Text1 control is
shown in Listing 16.4.

Listing 16.4   The Text1_KeyPress() Event Procedure in WINES.FRM

```
Private Sub Text1_KeyPress(Index As Integer, KeyAscii As Integer)

' Filter only for the 3 price fields, which have indexes 6, 7, and 8.

If Index < 6 Or Index > 8 Then Exit Sub

'  46 = period, 8 = Backspace
If (KeyAscii < 48 Or KeyAscii > 57) And KeyAscii <> 46 And KeyAscii <> 8 Then
    Beep
    KeyAscii = 0
End If

End Sub
```

After entering the validation code presented, you can run the program again.
The functionality of the program will not appear different from before *unless*
you try to enter invalid data that is caught by one of the validation methods
we have added. I'm sure you can come up with other aspects of data entry
that would benefit from validation. Now that you know the validation methods available, you should try to write the code yourself.

ENTERING ORDERS

The last steps in our database development project—at least the last steps that we'll be dealing with here—involve entering of orders and generation of invoices. After all, that's the main job of this database: to permit the entry of order information. Let's take a moment to think about what the program user will need to do for each order:

* Specify the customer who is placing the order. To minimize the chance for errors, we'll design the program so that the customer is selected from a list of names that are already in the Customers table. If it's a new customer, the customer data will have to be entered using the Customers form before the order can be entered.

* Enter the customer's purchase order (PO) number. Since there's no way we can know this ahead of time to generate it in code, this item of information will simply have to be typed in.

* Enter the order date. We can let the computer do this, retrieving the date from its clock and entering it in the proper database field.

* Select one or more wines. For each wine, the quantity being ordered must be specified, too. Again, we'll simplify the operator's task and minimize errors by requiring that each wine be selected from a list of wines already entered in the Wines table.

You can already see that this will be the most complex part of the project. All four of the database tables will be involved: the Customers and Wines tables to permit selection, the Invoices table since we're adding a new invoice record, and the Items table because we're adding one or more new records to it. Juggling all of these tables and keeping things straight is not a trivial task, but we'll see that Visual Basic provides a number of tools that simplify things a great deal.

The Invoices Form

The Invoices form will contain the following visible objects:

• A list of customers from which the user can select, implemented using the dbList control.

• A Text Box for entry of the customer's PO number.

• A TextBox where the date will automatically be entered by code.

- A Text Box where the selected customer's identification (the value of the CustID field in the Customers table) will be entered. You'll see how this is done automatically using the dbList control.

- A list of the wines ordered, implemented as a dbGrid control.

- Three command buttons.

There will also be some hidden controls:

- Three Data controls, one each for the Invoices, Customers, and Items tables.

- Several Text Box controls that serve for data transfer and temporary storage.

Before we get started, let's take a look at how the dbList control works, since we'll be using two of them in this part of the project.

The dbList Control

The dbList control is similar to a regular List control in that it displays a list of items from which the user can select. However, the dbList control can be bound to a Data control so that it automatically displays the contents of a specified field in Recordset associated with the bound Data control. There are two control properties that determine what the dbList control will display:

RowSource   The name of the Data control.

ListField   The name of the field to display in the list. Must be a valid field in the Recordset of the Data control specified by the **RowSource** property.

So far, so good. But wait, there's more. The dbList control has **BoundColumn** and **BoundText** properties that really make it useful. The **BoundColumn** property specifies a field in the bound Recordset—a different field than is specified by the **ListField** property. When the users select an item in the dbList control, they are effectively selecting a record in the associated Recordset. The **BoundText** property then makes available the value of the corresponding field—the field specified by the **BoundColumn** property— in the selected record.

I know this is confusing, so let's look at a specific example. We want the user of our program to be able to select from a list of customers. We'll add a Data control linked to the Customers table, then bind a dbList control to that data control. The **ListField** property will be set to "Company" and the **BoundColumn** property will be set to "CustID". The dbList control will display a list of all companies in the Customers field. When the user selects one by clicking, the selected customer's CustID will become available in the dbList control's **BoundText** property.

Starting the Form

With the database project loaded, use the Insert Form command to add a new form to the project. Change its **BorderStyle** property to *Fixed Single* and its **Caption** property to *New Order*. Add a control array of three Command Buttons, and set their **Caption** properties as follows:

Index 0:	&Save
Index 1:	&Add Wine
Index 2:	&Cancel

Next, add a Data control and set its properties as follows:

Name:	DataCustomers
Caption:	Customers
Visible:	False
DatabaseName:	GRAPEVIN.MDB (be sure to include the path)
RecordSource:	Customers
RecordsetType:	Snapshot

We use a **Snapshot** type recordset because we won't be modifying or adding records to the table—we simply want to access the data that is already there. The **Caption** property is simply a convenience that will allow us to tell this Data control from the others we will be adding (at design time only, of course, since the control will not be visible while the program is running).

Next, add a dbList control. Remember, you may need to use the Tools Custom Controls command to add this custom control to your Toolbox. Set its properties as shown here:

Name:	DBListCustomers
RowSource:	DataCustomers
ListField:	Company
BoundColumn:	CustID

Finally, add a Text Box. Set its **Name** property to *txtCustID* and its **Text** property to *CustID*. There will be more controls for this form, but we'll stop here to see how things work so far. We need code to copy the customer ID from the **BoundText** property of the DBList control into the Text Box. The place for this is in the DBListCustomers control's **Click()** event procedure. Add the three lines of code as shown here:

```
Private Sub DBListCustomers_Click()

txtCustID.TEXT = DBListCustomers.BoundText

End Sub
```

Finally, we need to add a button to the main form's Toolbar to display the Invoices form. Add a button to the Toolbar with the caption "Orders", then add code to the Toolbar's **ButtonClick()** event procedure as shown in Listing 16.5.

Listing 16.5 Modified ButtonClick() EventProcedure for the Toolbar

```
Private Sub Toolbar1_ButtonClick(ByVal Button As Button)

Dim Reply As Integer

Select Case Button.Caption
    Case "Customers"
        frmCustomers.Show
    Case "Wines"
        frmWines.Show
    Case "Orders"          ' New Line
  frmInvoice2.txtCustID = ""     ' New Line
  frmInvoice1.Show     ' New Line
    Case "Exit"
        Reply = MsgBox("Quit program - are you sure?", _
               vbYesNo + vbQuestion, "Quit?")
        If Reply = vbYes Then End
End Select

End Sub
```

There are only two lines of code executed when the user clicks on the Orders button. The first one clears the txtCustID Text Box. The caption we placed there was only to help identify it during program design, and is not needed during program execution. The second line displays the Invoices form that we just designed.

There's plenty more to add to this form, but we've done enough to take it for a spin and see how the dbList control works. Start the program and click the Orders button on the Toolbar. The form that you just created will display, and a list of customers will be displayed in the dbList control. Click on a company name, and its CustID will be displayed in the Text Box, as shown in Figure 16.1. This is how we will obtain the CustID for the Invoices record—remember that CustID is the field that links the Customers and the Invoices tables. Since there's no reason for the user to see the CustID information, we'll later make this Text Box's **Visible** property *False* so that it doesn't display on the form. We'll also see how to sort the list of companies into alphabetical order.

Connecting to the Invoices Table

Since the main purpose of this form is to enter orders, or invoices, clearly it must be connected to the Invoices table in our database. That's the next step we'll take. Add a Data control to the form, and set its properties as follows:

Name:	DataInvoices
DatabaseName:	GRAPEVIN (with path)
RecordsetType:	Table
RecordSource:	Invoices
Visible:	False

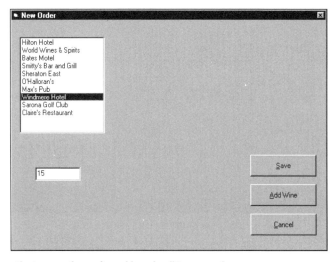

Figure 16.1 *The Invoices form after adding the dbList control.*

We also need one bound Text Box for each of the four fields in the Invoices table, as follows:

CustID   We already have the Text Box for this, which receives the CustID information from the dbList control. Set its **Visible** property to *False* and bind it to the DataInvoices control by setting its **DataSource** property to *DataInvoices* and its **DataField** property to *CustID*.

InvNo   The data in this field will be automatically generated by the database engine because we specified this field to be a Counter that generates unique sequential numbers. However, we still need a Text Box bound to this field so we can get the InvNo for the current Invoice record and transfer it to each new record in the Items table. This Text Box should have its **Name** property set to *txtInvNo1*, its **Text** property to *InvNo1*, and its **Visible** property to *False*. Set its **DataSource** property to *DataInvoices* and its **DataField** property to *InvNo*.

Date   We'll write code to place the current system date in this Text Box. Set its **Name** property to *txtDate*, its **Text** property to *Date*, and leave its **Visible** property set to *True*. Position it on the form adjacent to the dbList control and add a label reading "Date:" to identify it. Bind this control to the Date field of the DataInvoices Data control.

CustPO   The user will manually enter data in this Text Box. Set its **Name** property to *txtCustPO*, its **Text** property to *CustPO*, and bind it to the CustPO field in the DataInvoices Data control. Leave its **Visible** property at *True*, position it above the Date Text Box, and add an identifying Label control that reads "Customer's PO #:".

With these Text Boxes bound to the DataInvoices Data control, we have the means to add a new invoice record to the Invoices table. You've seen these steps before, but to refresh your memory:

1. Execute the **AddNew** method for the DataInvoices Data control's RecordSet object. This step will clear all bound controls in preparation for entry of new data.

2. Place the new record's field values in the bound controls.

3. Execute the **Update** method to save the new record, or the **CancelUpdate** method to cancel it.

Before we get to the code for these steps, there's one more essential ingredient in the process of creating a new invoice: the Items table.

Adding New Items

Think back to the way we designed this database. For each order, or invoice, there will be one record in the Invoices table, identified by a unique value in the Invoice Number (InvNo) field. Then, for each individual wine ordered, there would be a record in the Items table that is linked to the record in the Invoices table by the InvNo field. Once we have started a new Invoice, adding wines to it requires adding records to the Items table. We will need a Data control linked to the Items table, with the following property settings:

Name:	DataItems
DatabaseName:	GRAPEVIN (with path)
Caption:	Items (for visual identification only)
Visible:	False
RecordsetType:	DynaSet
RecordSource	Items

The Items table has four fields. The ItemNo field will not require a bound control since we will simply let the database engine deal with it (as a Counter field). For the other three fields, we'll need the following three Text Box controls:

Quantity Add a Text Box using these property designations: **Name** = *txtQuantity*, **Visible** = *False*, **DataSource** = *DataItems*, and **DataField** = *Quantity*. The value for this field will come from the Select Wine form, which we will design soon.

StockNo Add a Text Box using these property designations: **Name** = *txtStockNo*, **Visible** = *False*, **DataSource** = *DataItems*, and **DataField** = *StockNo*. This value too will come from the Select Wine form.

InvNo Add a Text Box using these property designations: **Name** = *txtInvNo*, **Visible** = *False*, **DataSource** = *DataItems*, and **DataField** = *InvNo*. We'll obtain the data for this Text Box from the Text Box that is bound to the InvNo field in the Invoices table, which we added earlier *(txtInvNo1)*.

Before we move on to the Select Wine form, there's one more control needed on the Invoices form. As the user adds wines to an order, we would like a list of these items displayed on the form. The dbGrid control is ideal for this purpose. Add a dbGrid control and set its properties as follows:

Align:	Bottom
Caption:	Items
DataSource:	DataItems
Name:	DBGrid1
RowDividerStyle:	Dark gray line
ScrollBars:	Automatic

We'll see later how to use an SQL statement so that the DataItems RecordSet contains only those items associated with the current invoice. At this point during program design, your Invoices form should look something like Figure 16.2.

Setting Properties Twice

If you examine this project, you'll see that for some of the Data controls I have set their **DatabaseName** and **RecordSource** properties both at design time and in code. Isn't this redundant? Not really. Setting these properties at design time makes it easier to set certain other properties, such as the **DataField** property of a Text Box that's bound to the Data control, since the property sheet will present a list of the available fields. By again setting these properties in code at runtime, particularly the **DatabaseName** property using the App object's **Path** property, I avoid problems that could be caused if the database file is in a different directory.

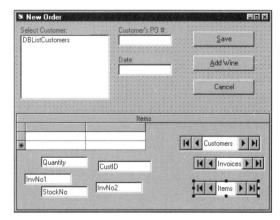

Figure 16.2   *The Invoices form during program design.*

The Select Wine Form

Once the Invoices form is displayed and the user has started a new invoice by selecting a customer, we need a way to select the individual wines that will make up the order. For each wine, we need the quantity and the stock number for insertion into the Items table. (The other two fields in this table are the Item number, which is automatically generated by the database engine, and the invoice number, which is obtained from the Invoices table.) To select a wine, we'll use the same technique used earlier—allow the user to select from a list. We'll again use the dbList control, displaying the Description field from the Wines table and providing the Stock Number of the selected wine.

Use the Insert Form command to add a new form to the project. Set the form's **Caption** property to "Select Wine" and its name to "frmSelectWine." The **BorderStyle** property should be *Fixed Single*. Then add the following controls to the form, and set their properties as indicated:

DBList control

Name:	DBList1
BoundColumn:	StockNo
RowSource:	DataWines

Data control

DatabaseName:	GRAPEVIN (with path)
Name:	DataWines
RecordsetType:	Snapshot
RecordSource:	Wines
Visible:	False

Text Box

Name:	txtQuantity

SpinButton

(all properties at default values)

Command Button (in a control array)

Index:	0
Caption:	&OK

Command Button (in a control array)

> **Index:** 1
>
> **Caption:** &Cancel

Finally, add two label controls to identify the DBList control and the Text Box. When you finish designing this form, it will look something like Figure 16.3.

When the Select Wine form first displays (which will be triggered by the user clicking the Add Wine button on the Invoices form), it needs to set up the Data and DBList controls.

We want the Data control connected to the Wines table, and we also want its Recordset to contain all records in the table, sorted by the Description field. We specify the DatabaseName control using the variable theDatabase, which code elsewhere in the program has initialized to point at the GRAPEVIN.MDB database file in the application's directory. To set the Recordset, we assign the following SQL statement:

```
Select * From Wines Order by Description
```

This is easy enough to understand: It specifies that the Recordset will contain all the fields and all the records in the table, sorted by the Description field.

For the DBList control, we set the ListField property to Description so the control will display the wine descriptions, and we set the **BoundColumn** property to *StockNo* so the **BoundText** property will return the *StockNo* value for the selected wine. The complete **Form_Load()** procedure for this form is shown in Listing 16.6.

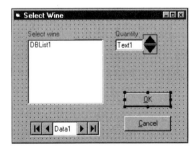

Figure 16.3 *The Select Wine form.*

Listing 16.6   The Select Wine Form's Load() Event Procedure

```
Private Sub Form_Load()

' Assign data source for the data control.
DataWines.DatabaseName = theDatabase
DataWines.RecordSource = "Select * From Wines Order by Description"

' Set up the dbList control.
DBList1.ListField = "Description"
DBList1.BoundColumn = "StockNo"

txtQuantity.TEXT = 1

End Sub
```

When selecting a wine, the user must specify the quantity being ordered. Users can type the value drectly into the Text Box, or they can use the SpinButton control to increment or decrement the value (which we initialize to 1). Programming the SpinButton is easy: It has separate event procedures, called **SpinDown()** and **SpinUp()**, for clicking the down or up arrow. We modify the value in the Text Box as shown in Listing 16.7. Note that in the **SpinDown()** procedure, we add a conditional test to prevent the value in the box from ever going below 1.

Listing 16.7   Event procedures for the SpinButton control

```
Private Sub SpinButton1_SpinDown()

If Text1.TEXT > 1 Then Text1.TEXT = Text1.TEXT - 1

End Sub


Private Sub SpinButton1_SpinUp()

txtQuantity.TEXT = txtQuantity.TEXT + 1

End Sub
```

Finally, this form needs a procedure for the Command Buttons. If the user selects the Cancel button, code sets the value in the Quantity Text Box to 0. This signals the calling function that the user canceled (as we'll see later). If the user selects a wine and then clicks OK, several steps must be performed:

1. Copy the quantity value from the Text Box on the Select Wines form to the appropriate TextBox on the Invoices form.

2. Copy the StockNo value from the DBList control's **BoundText** property to the appropriate Text Box on the Invoices form.

3. Copy the InvNo (invoice number) value from the Text Box that is bound to the InvNo field in the Invoices table to the Text Box that is bound to the InvNo field in the Items table. Both of these Text Boxes are located on the Invoices form.

4. Enable the Save button on the Invoices form. This button was previously disabled, since before any wines were selected, there is nothing to save.

5. Hide the Select Wines form.

The code for the Select Wines form's Command Button's **Click()** event procedure is presented in Listing 16.8.

Listing 16.8   The Event Erocedure for the Select Wine Form's Command Buttons

```
Private Sub Command1_Click(Index As Integer)

Select Case Index
    Case 0        ' OK
        ' Copy the data for the selected wine to
        ' the Invoices form.
        frmInvoice1.txtQuantity.TEXT = txtQuantity.TEXT
        frmInvoice1.txtStockNo.TEXT = DBList1.BoundText
        frmInvoice1.txtInvNo2.TEXT = frmInvoice1.txtInvNo1.TEXT
  ' Enable the "Save" button on the Invoices form.
        frmInvoice1.Command1(0).Enabled = True
        ' Hide the SelectWine form.
        Hide
    Case 1       ' Cancel, as indicated by this Text Box being 0.
        frmInvoice.txtQuantity.TEXT = 0
        Hide
End Select

End Sub
```

Completing the Invoices Form

Now that the Select Wine form is complete, we can put the finishing touches on the Invoices form. We'll start with the one global flag variable that the form requires. Place this line of code in the form's general declarations section:

```
Dim AddingWine As Boolean
```

When the form loads, we need to perform several initialization steps. The three Data controls must be initialized to point at the proper tables in the database. In addition the DBList control that will permit the user to select a customer needs to be initialized. Yes, we did this before by setting the control properties, but as explained in the Tip earlier, it's a good idea to perform this type of data control property setting both during design and in code at runtime. Finally, the DBGrid control is hidden (we'll display it once there's something in it) and the **AddingWine** flag is set to *False*. The code for the Invoices form's **Load()** procedure is presented in Listing 16.9.

Listing 16.9 The Invoices Form's Load() Event Procedure

```
Private Sub Form_Load()

' Assign data sources to the three data controls.
DataCustomers.DatabaseName = theDatabase
DataCustomers.RecordSource = "Select * from Customers Order by Company"

DataInvoices.DatabaseName = theDatabase
DataInvoices.RecordSource = "Invoices"

DataItems.DatabaseName = theDatabase
DataItems.RecordSource = "Items"

' Set up the dbList control.
DBListCustomers.ListField = "Company"
DBListCustomers.BoundColumn = "CustID"

' Hide the grid control.
DBGrid1.Visible = False

AddingWine = False

End Sub
```

Note that we are using the variable *theDatabase* to specify the database file with which the Data controls are to be associated. This variable is initialized when the program first starts, in the main form's **Load()** event procedure, which also initializes a flag that signals whether a record is being entered. Add this code to the project's main form, as shown in Listing 16.10.

Listing 16.10 The Main Form's Load() Event Procedure

```
Private Sub MDIForm_Load()

EnteringRecord = False
theDatabase = App.Path & "\GRAPEVIN.MDB"

End Sub
```

Of course, we need a declaration of *theDatabase*, and it needs to be a global variable. There are a couple of other global variables we need, and their declaration should be placed in a Basic module attached to the project. Use the Insert Module command to create a Basic module, then place the code from Listing 16.11 in the module's General Declarations section. Save the module with the name GRAPEVIN.BAS

Listing 16.11 Global variable declarations in GRAPEVIN.BAS

```
Global EnteringRecord As Boolean
Global Saving As Boolean
Global theDatabase As String
```

Now back to the Invoices form. When this form is displayed (by the user clicking the Orders button on the program's Toolbar), the entire process of starting an invoice is initiated by the user selecting a customer from the list that's displayed in the DBList control. Clearly, then, we can place the required code in the DBList control's **Click()** event procedure. Here are the steps needed:

1. Use the **AddNew** method to add a new record to the Invoices table.

2. Use Visual Basic's **Date** function to retrieve the system date and place it in the txtDate Text Box.

3. Get the CustID (customer ID) from the DBList's **BoundText** property and place it in the Text Box that's bound to the CustID field in the Invoices table.

4. Set the Recordset property of the Data control connected to the Items table to include only those items where the InvNo field is equal to the InvNo value of the newly created record in the Invoices table. This value was created by the database engine and placed in the Text Box that's bound to the InvNo field in the Invoices table when the **AddNew** method was executed for the Invoices table. We use this value in an SQL statement, which is then assigned to the Data control's **Recordset** property. Note: At this time there are no records in the Items table with this InvNo value—they will come later when the user adds wines to the order.

5. Use the **Refresh** method to update the Item's Recordset.

Once this code is executed, we have all the information required to add the new record to the Invoices table—except the CustPO value, which is optional and can be entered by the user if desired. Code for this procedure is shown in Listing 16.12.

Listing 16.12   The DBList control's Click() Event Procedure

```
Private Sub DBListCustomers_Click()

' When the user selects a customer, the procedure
' of creating a new invoice is started.

Dim s As String

' Add a new record.
DataInvoices.Recordset.AddNew

' Set the date.
txtDate.TEXT = Date

' Set flag to indicate a new record has been created.
AddingInvoice = True

' Get the customer ID from the DBlist control.
txtCustID.TEXT = DBListCustomers.BoundText

' Specify the Recordset for the Items data control - it should
' be limited to records where the invoice number is the same as for
' the new invoice we are adding. This number is generated automatically
' because we have specified that the InvNo field in the Invoices
' table is an automatically generated serial number.
s = "Select * from Items where InvNo = " & txtInvNo1.TEXT
DataItems.RecordSource = s
DataItems.Refresh

' Enable the Save button.
Command1(1).Enabled = True

End Sub
```

Much of the Invoice form's action takes place within the event procedure for the array of Command Buttons. Three actions are handled here: Adding a new wine to the invoice, saving the invoice, or canceling the invoice. The code for this procedure is shown in Listing 16.13. You should be able to understand the operation of the code in this procedure from the comments shown in the listing. Note that each time a wine is added, the DataItems Data control is updated and refreshed, then the DBGrid control is also refreshed. This approach ensures that the DBGrid control accurately displays the items that have been entered for the current invoice.

Listing 16.13   The Invoice Form's Command Button Click() Event Procedures

```
Private Sub Command1_Click(Index As Integer)

Select Case Index
    Case 0      ' Save invoice button.
        ' Can UPDATE only if have executed AddNew, which
        ' is indicated by the AddingInvoice flag.
        If AddingInvoice Then
            DataInvoices.Recordset.UPDATE
            AddingInvoice = False
        End If
        ' Hide the grid then hide the form.
        DBGrid.Visible = False
        Hide
    Case 1      ' Add wine to invoice button.
        ' Create new record and set flag.
        DataItems.Recordset.AddNew
        AddingWine = True
        ' Call AddWine function, which returns True if the user
        ' selects a wine, False if they Cancel.
        If AddWine() Then      ' f a wine was selected
            ' update the table and refresh it.
            DataItems.Recordset.UPDATE
            DataItems.Refresh
            ' Make the grid visible and refresh it.
            DBGrid1.Visible = True
            DBGrid1.Refresh
        Else            ' If the user canceled.
            ' Cancel the new record.
            DataItems.Recordset.CancelUpdate
        End If
    Case 2      ' Cancel new invoice.
        If AddingInvoice Then
            DataInvoices.Recordset.CancelUpdate
            AddingInvoice = False
            DBGrid.Visible = False
        End If
        Hide
End Select

End Sub
```

The final procedure that we need is the **AddWine()** function. This function, shown in Listing 16.14, is called by code in the **Command1_Click()** event procedure when the user clicks the Add Wine button. It displays the Select Wine form by executing its **Show** method. The form is displayed modally by passing the argument 1 to the **Show** method, which means that the user cannot interact with any other forms until this form is explicitly removed by code. Remember that, in the Select Wine form, the txtQuantity Text Box is set to 0 if the user selects Cancel; it will be a non-zero value otherwise. The value of this Text Box is used by code in **AddWine()** to determine whether the function should return *True* or *False*. This return value is then used by code in **Command1_Click()**, as was shown in Listing 16.13.

Listing 16.14   The AddWine() Function

```
Public Function AddWine() As Boolean

' Show the wine selection form.
frmSelectWine.Show 1

' If the user selected cancel it is indicated by
' a 0 in the txtQuantity box.
If txtQuantity.TEXT > 0 Then
    AddWine = True
Else
    AddWine = False
End If

End Function
```

Trying It Out

Believe it or not, our database program is finished—at least it is as finished as we are going to make it! You can try it out—there's a sample GRAPEVIN.MDB database on the disk with a small amount of data entered—and see how all the features work together. Figure 16.4 shows the program while a new wine is being added to an invoice.

I will be the first to admit this program needs a lot more before it would be even close to ready for release to a paying customer. We would at least need to add such features as the ability to print invoices and shipping labels, to update the Quantity on Hand field in the Wines table when an order is filled, to permit viewing a list of all invoices—the list could go on and on. The program also needs work in the area of error trapping, a topic we'll get to in Chapter 19.

To bring the project to completion, where the program is ready for commercial release, would require a lot more work and a lot more pages in this book! My goal is to teach you the fundamentals of Visual Basic database programming, and I think—or at least hope—I've accomplished that. There's a lot more richness to Visual Basic's database capabilities, which you'll discover if you explore database programming in more depth.

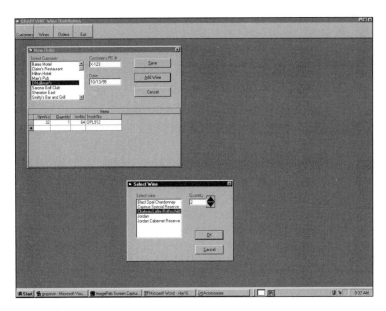

Figure 16.4 *Adding a wine to an invoice.*

Dynamic Data Exchange

Dynamic Data Exchange allows your Visual Basic programs to exchange data with other Windows programs, as well as send them commands.

ynamic Data Exchange (DDE) is a feature of Windows that permits programs to send data back and forth. Within certain limitations, it also allows them to send commands to each other. It can be an extraordinarily useful technique, and in many situations is preferable to the other Windows method for interaction between programs: Object Linking and Embedding. (We'll cover OLE in the next chapter.)

What exactly can DDE do? Once again, an example is the best clarification. I recently wrote a custom program in Visual Basic for the laboratory where I work, a program designed to take measurements from digitized data that was collected from our experiments. The final destination for this data was an Excel spreadsheet that serves for data manipulation and graphing. My first impulse was to have the Visual Basic program save the results in a text file, which could then be imported into Excel. But after a few moments of thought about the capabilities of DDE, I came up with a much better way. The final program uses DDE to accomplish the following:

1. Start Excel and open a new worksheet.

2. Insert labels into specific cells in the worksheet to provide the date, data labels, and other experiment identifiers.

3. Poke analysis results numbers into specific worksheet cells as the analysis proceeds.

4. Place formulas in other worksheet cells to perform the needed calculations.

5. Save the worksheet file under a user-selected name.

Now, when running an analysis, all I need do is Alt+Tab from the Visual Basic measurement program to Excel to find my data ready for analysis and graphing. This is a real time-saver, and it represents the way that Windows programs are supposed to work together.

DDE BASICS

Perhaps the most common way to copy data from one Windows application to another is to use the Clipboard. As handy as the clipboard can be, it does not provide for automatic updating of the data. In other words, each time the data in the original changes, the copied data must be updated. DDE remedies this situation by providing the capability of automatically updating transferred data.

Let's look at a specific example. Suppose we are using a word processor to write a report, and we want to include some numbers from an Excel worksheet. We would start Excel, open the worksheet, select the numbers, and copy them to the Clipboard. Next, we would switch back to the word processor and paste the table into our document. Very convenient, as long as we know the numbers will never change.

In practical application, this is often not the case. Sales figures change, forecasts are modified—how can we be sure that our report is up-to-date? With standard Clipboard copy-and-paste, we have to repeat the entire process of copying the numbers from the worksheet to the document. And what's worse, we may not even know when the numbers have changed if we are on a network where other people can modify the worksheet.

DDE to the rescue! DDE permits us to establish a *link* between the worksheet and the document. This link gives us the ability to copy data *and* information about its source. We don't see this information—it is stored internally—but it enables the program to automatically update the copied information when the source changes. We can establish any number of links between multiple applications. Furthermore, the linked data can be just about anything — numbers, text, or a graphical image, for example. With DDE, we only need to enter data once—the DDE links automatically transfer it to any other place it is needed. The same is true of changes to existing data; manual updates are no longer necessary. End result? We save time and decrease the potential for errors.

Will OLE Replace DDE?

You've probably heard about Object Linking and Embedding, or OLE, which provides sophisticated methods for Windows applications to share data and functionality. Since OLE provides a way for programs to share data, you might wonder if it will eventually replace DDE. Should you ignore DDE and utilize OLE when your Visual Basic programs need to exchange data? I can't predict the future, of course, but my bet is that the answer is "no." Why do I feel this way?

OLE is certainly more powerful than DDE (you'll see what I mean in the next chapter). But unavoidable consequences of this power include a need for greater system resources, more difficulty in programming, and generally slower speed. OLE is always there when we need it; but when DDE will fill the bill, we're better off using it. Why use a half-ton pickup truck to bring home a bag of groceries when your old Volkswagen can do the job, is easier to drive and uses less gas? And considering Microsoft's emphasis on backward compatibility, it is highly unlikely that DDE support will ever be removed from Windows.

DDE Terminology

When you use DDE to link two applications, one application is called the *source* and the other is called the *destination*. As you can guess, the data to be exchanged originates in the source application and is transferred to one or more destination applications. The link is sometimes referred to as a *conversation*. It is always the destination application that initiates a DDE conversation.

To initiate a conversation, the destination application must specify the name of the source application. Each Windows application that can act as a DDE source has a unique name for this purpose. Usually, this is the executable filename, without the .EXE extension. The destination application must also specify the *topic* of the conversation. The topic identifies the unit of data being linked—a designated unit that is meaningful to the source. It often is the name of a data file. While the available DDE topics vary from application to application, one that is almost universally supported is the System topic. Using the System topic, a DDE destination can obtain the other topics that the source supports and other information about the application, including the supported data formats.

Both the application and the topic remain constant throughout a DDE conversation. The conversation will terminate if either the source or the destination attempts to change the application or topic. In contrast, the item of a DDE conversation can change as many times as desired. For example, the same DDE conversation could refer to different spreadsheet cells at different times, as long as they are in the same file (a technique we'll use later).

The term *item* refers to the actualdata being transferred in the DDE conversation. The item must be identified in a way that the source application can understand. Thus, a spreadsheet program such as Lotus 1-2-3 understands the row and column addresses of spreadsheet cells, and a word processor such as Word recognizes bookmark names. Here's an example: For a destination application to establish a link to the contents of cell C12 in the Excel worksheet D:\REPORTS\MAY1995.XLS, the conversation will specify EXCEL as the application, D:\REPORTS\MAY1995.XLS as the topic, and R12C3 as the item (row 12, column 3).

It is most common for the data to be transferred from the source to the destination. As we'll see later, however, it is also possible for data to travel in the other direction — from destination to source. At first glance, having the data move from destination to source may seem contradictory. But remember that the destination application is the one that initiates the DDE conversation; it is usually, but not always, the destination that receives the transferred data.

Updating DDE Links

In addition to specifying the application, topic, and item, a DDE link includes a specification of how the link is updated. Three methods are possible:

> *Automatic link*   The destination is updated whenever the source data changes.

Manual link   The destination must specifically request each update from the source.

Notify link   The destination is automatically notified by the source whenever the data changes, but the data is updated only when the destination requests it.

The type of link utilized depends, of course, on the specific situation.

DDE and Visual Basic Objects

The only Visual Basic objects that can serve as the destination in a DDE conversation are the Text Box, Picture Box, and Label controls. Each of these controls has three properties that determine the details of the conversation:

LinkTopic   specifies the application and topic of the conversation.

LinkItem   specifies the data item.

LinkMode   specifies one of the three link modes (automatic, manual, or notify).

Any Visual Basic form, including MDI forms, can be the source in a DDE conversation. A form's **LinkTopic** property specifies the topic name that the destination application will use to refer to the form in a DDE conversation. The item in a conversation can be a Text Box, Picture Box, or Label control on the form. In the DDE conversation, the destination application specifies the control's **Name** property as the item.

In order to have a Text Box, Picture Box, or Label act as a DDE destination, we use the control's **LinkTopic** property to specify both the source application and the source topic. The property must list the application followed by a vertical pipe character, **CHR\$(124)**, and the topic name. To link a Text Box to data in the Excel worksheet REPORT.XLS, we would write:

```
Text1.LinkTopic = "EXCEL|REPORT.XLS"
```

or

```
Text1.LinkTopic = "EXCEL" + CHR$(124) + " REPORT.XLS"
```

The control's **LinkItem** property specifies the data item to be linked. The precise content and format of the **LinkItem** property vary from one source application to another (refer to the source application's documentation for details). For spreadsheet programs such as Excel and 1-2-3, row and column coordinates are usually meaningful. For word processors such as Microsoft Word, the same is true for bookmark names.

The destination control's **LinkMode** property determines the way in which the link will be updated. The default setting is *0-None*, which specifies no DDE conversation. When you want the control to be an active DDE destination, three settings are possible: 1-Automatic, 2-Manual, and 3-Notify. (We covered the way these three update modes work earlier in this chapter.)

One more destination control property is important to the picture. The **LinkTimeout** property specifies how long a Visual Basic DDE destination control will wait for the source application to respond to a DDE message before generating an error. The wait time is specified in tenths of seconds, and the default setting is 50, or 5 seconds. To obtain the longest possible wait, 65535 tenths of a second (approximately 1 hour and 49 minutes), set **LinkTimeout** to -1.

Using Visual Basic controls as the source in a DDE conversation also involves properties. Because all DDE conversations are initiated by the destination application, in order to act as a DDE source, a Visual Basic application simply responds to the DDE messages that are sent by the destination. To initiate a DDE link, the message sent by the destination must specify three things: the application, topic, and item. How does this information identify a Visual Basic control?

Application The name of the Visual Basic source application. If the application is running in the Visual Basic development environment, it is the project name without the .MAK extension. If the application is running as a stand-alone executable, it is the Visual Basic application name without the .EXE extension. In code, we can use the App object's **EXEName** property to obtain the application name.

Topic The **LinkTopic** property of the Visual Basic form that contains the control with the data to be linked. This property's default setting is in the format Form1, Form2, and so on. If a form will serve as a DDE topic, change its **LinkTopic** property to an appropriate name.

Item The **Name** property of the control (Text Box, Picture Box, or Label) that contains the data to be linked.

The form's **LinkMode** property controls whether a destination application is permitted to initiate a DDE conversation with one or more controls on the form. If **LinkMode** is set to *0-None* (the default), DDE conversations are not permitted with any control on the form. If **LinkMode** is set to *1-Source*, any Label, Picture Box, or Text Box on the form can serve as the source in a DDE link with any destination application that requests it. Once a DDE link exists, Visual Basic automatically notifies the destination application whenever a change occurs in the contents of a linked control. If we set **LinkMode** to *1-Source* at design time, we can change it to *0-None* and back again in code at runtime. If we set **LinkMode** to *0-None* at design time, we cannot change it to *1-Source* at runtime.

Let's look at a concrete example:Our Visual Basic project named SALES.VBP, or the resulting EXE file named SALES.EXE, contains a form with its **LinkTopic** property set to *SalesFigures* and its **LinkMode** property set to *1-Source*. Imagine that this form contains a Text Box with its **Name** property set to *Total.* A destination application could establish a DDE link with that Text Box by specifying SALES as the application, SalesFigures as the topic, and Total as the item.

DDE Events

As you might expect, a number of events are associated with DDE conversations. The specific events and the way we use them differ slightly depending on whether the Visual Basic object is the source or the destination in the DDE conversation.

The **LinkOpen** event will occur when a Visual Basic control acting as destination successfully initiates a DDE conversation. The event procedure looks like this:

```
Sub CtlName_LinkOpen ([Index as Integer], Cancel as Integer)
...
End Sub
```

The **Index** argument identifies the control, if it is part of a control array. The **Cancel** argument is not used for **LinkOpen()** events when the control is the destination. We use the destination control's **LinkOpen()** event procedure to perform those tasks, such as opening files, that are required when a DDE link is established. We can also use this event to assist with program debugging.

The **LinkOpen()** event also occurs when an external destination application initiates a DDE conversation with a Visual Basic source form. Under these circumstances the **LinkOpen()** event procedure has the following structure:

```
Sub FormName_LinkOpen (Cancel as Integer)
...
End Sub
```

If the **Cancel** argument is left at its initial value of *False*, the link is established. To circumvent this link, code in the event procedure can set **Cancel** to any non-zero value, and Visual Basic will not permit the link to be established. You can use the source **LinkOpen()** event procedure to keep track of the number of DDE links sourced by the Visual Basic program, and refuse to establish new links once the total number becomes too large for satisfactory performance.

A **LinkClose** event will occur if the DDE conversation is terminated, for either a destination control or a source form. The event procedure receives no information about why the conversation was terminated.

A **LinkError** event will occur for either a destination control or a source form under certain error conditions. Visual Basic's standard error handling procedures are invoked if a DDE error occurs while Basic code is executing, enabling us to trap and handle the error in the usual fashion (as will be explained in a later chapter). The **LinkError** event is triggered only if an error occurs when no Basic code is executing. Occurrences that can cause errors include transfer of data in a format that the destination cannot handle or operating system resource shortages. We will cover more about handling DDE errors later in this chapter.

A **LinkNotify** event will occur for destination controls where the **LinkMode** property has been set to *3-Notify*. This event is triggered when the source data changes. Code in the **LinkNotify()** event procedure can either use the **LinkRequest** method to update the destination immediately with the modified data, or, when the new data is not needed immediately, a flag can be set indicating that the an update must be performed later.

A **LinkExecute** event occurs when a source form receives a command string from the destination in the DDE conversation. The **LinkExecute()** event procedure format is:

```
Sub Form_Execute (Cmd As String, Cancel As Integer)
...
End Sub
```

The **Cmd** argument contains the command string that was sent by the DDE destination. No defined "DDE Command Language" is shared among applications, and the specific commands and syntax that a particular DDE source understands differ from program to program. To enable our Visual Basic program to respond to such commands, we have to write the code.

The **Cancel** argument passed to the **Execute()** event procedure determines the response sent back to the DDE destination application—the one that sent the command string. If **Cancel** is set to 0, the Visual Basic program sends a positive acknowledgment, usually meaning that the command string was received and acted upon. If **Cancel** is set to any non-zero value, a negative acknowledgment occurs. A negative acknowledgment is automatically sent when the program has no **LinkExecute()** event procedure.

Pasting Links into a Visual Basic Program

One way to create a link in a Visual Basic program is to paste it using the Clipboard. If you have worked with Windows applications such as a word processor, you have probably seen the Paste Link command, which is usually found on the Edit menu. Using this command creates a DDE link with any other DDE-aware Windows application. The general procedure for establishing links using the Clipboard is shown here:

1. Make the source application active and select the data to be linked (for example, a column of cells in a spreadsheet).

2. Still in the source application, select Copy (this command is almost always found on the Edit menu). The Copy command places the data and associated link information on the Clipboard.

3. Make the destination application active.

4. Move to the location where you want the linked data placed.

5. Select Paste Link. An automatic link is established between the two applications.

In this section we'll include a Paste Link command in our Visual Basic programs. This type of DDE support can greatly increase a program's usefulness by permitting users to quickly and easily cut and paste DDE links.

DDE and the Clipboard

In order to use the Copy...Paste Link command sequence to create a DDE link, the Windows Clipboard is required as the intermediate storage location where the link information is kept. A Visual Basic program accesses the Windows Clipboard by means of the Clipboard object.

The Clipboard is not simply a storage buffer that can hold and later return whatever data it receives. No, the Clipboard is actually pretty clever: It has the ability to hold data in several different formats. In fact, the Clipboard can hold more than one data item if they are in different formats. Furthermore, the Clipboard can tell you whether it currently contains a data item of a specified format. The data formats that the Clipboard can work with are listed here:

- Text

- Bitmap (.BMP files)

- Metafile (.WMF files)

- Device-independent bitmap (.DIB files)

- Color palette

- DDE link information

The meaning of the first four items should be clear: Text is, well, text, and the next three are different formats used to hold graphics images. A Color Palette is a set of color values that is used for the pixels in a specific graphic. But what is meant by "DDE link information"? This is the information required to establish a DDE link to the data on the Clipboard. Let's see how this works.

When we use the Copy command, Windows applications that support active DDE links not only place a copy of the selected data (text, a bitmap, or whatever) on the Clipboard, they also place the information—the application, topic, and item information—that is needed to establish a DDE link to the original data. If we switch to another application and execute the Paste command (not the Paste Link command), only the data will be copied from the Clipboard into the destination, and no link will be established. By executing the Paste Link command, however, both the data and the DDE link information will be obtained from the Clipboard and an active DDE link will be created.

How can a Visual Basic application determine if data in a particular format is available on the Clipboard? The Clipboard object's **GetFormat** method is designed for just this task. The method's syntax is:

```
result = Clipboard.Getformat(type)
```

Table 17.1 *Windows Global Constants*

Constant	Value	Format
vbCFLink	HBF00	DDE conversation information
vbCFText	1	Text
vbCFBitmap	2	Bitmap
vbCFMetafile	3	Metafile
vbCFDIB	8	Device-independent bitmap
vbCFPalette	9	Color palette

The type argument specifies the data format, and we can specify type with the Windows global constants shown in Table 17.1.

The **GetFormat** method returns *True* if the specified type of data is present on the Clipboard, *False* if not. For example, we could test for the presence of text data as follows:

```
If Clipboard.GetFormat(vbCFText) Then
    ...
    ' Text data present on clipboard
Else
    ...
    ' Text data not present
End If
```

Being able to determine whether a specific data format is present on the Clipboard can be useful in a variety of situations. A graphics program, for example, could enable a "Paste Picture" command only if data in one of the three graphics formats is present on the Clipboard. For DDE, however, it's the DDE link information that interests us. We need this information for the Paste Link command to work properly. Let's see how we get it.

To retrieve the DDE link information, use the Clipboard object's **GetText** method. This method can be used to retrieve text data from the Clipboard; but if we pass the argument vbCFLink (value = &HBF00), **GetText** returns DDE link information (or an empty string if there is no link information on the Clipboard):

```
LinkInfo = Clipboard.GetText(vbCFLink)
```

The DDE link information is returned in a specific format. The application name comes first, followed by a vertical pipe character (CHR$(124)), then the topic. The topic is followed by an exclamation point; the item is at the end:

```
application|topic!item
```

Some DDE links do not include an item. In this case only the application and topic are returned, separated by a vertical pipe.

Once we have the DDE link information, we can use Visual Basic's string manipulation functions to extract individual strings for the application, topic, and item (if present). Then, follow this procedure to establish the link:

1. Set the destination control's **LinkMode** property to *0-None*.

2. Set the **LinkTopic** property to the application and topic retrieved from the Clipboard.

3. If necessary, set the **LinkItem** property using the item obtained from the Clipboard.

4. Set the destination control's **LinkMode** property to *1-Automatic*.

You can see that the steps required to establish a DDE link with your Visual Basic application as the destination are relatively simple using the Clipboard. It's essential, however, that your program verifies that the operation is valid before attempting to establish the link. Screening out invalid links before they have been established can save headaches later.

Two conditions must be satisfied for a Paste Link operation to be valid. First, DDE link information must be available on the Clipboard. Secondly, the data available on the Clipboard must be in a format that is appropriate for the intended destination control. For example, we can link text data, but not a graphic, to a Text Box control. Similarly, we can link a graphic, but not text, to a Picture Box control. Our program needs to verify that both of these conditions are met before attempting a Paste Link. Enabling or disabling the Paste Link menu command depending on whether these conditions are met is one way to accomplish this.

MAKING PASTE LINK WORK FOR YOU

Now it's time to apply some of the things we have been learning. In this section we'll develop a simple program that can act as the destination for a Paste Link command. To make things more interesting, we'll provide two possible destination controls—a Text Box and a Picture Box—so we can link both text and graphics. We'll also see how to enable or disable the Paste Link command, depending on whether appropriate data is on the Clipboard.

The program's single form is quite simple, containing only three controls: a Picture Box on the left side of the form, a TextBox on the right side, and a Command Button at the bottom. All of the control properties can be left at their default values except for the Text Box's **MultiLine** property, which should be changed to *True*, and the Command Button's **Caption**, which should be changed to *Exit*.

Next, press Ctrl+E to bring up the Menu editor. Using the techniques you learned in an earlier chapter, create an Edit menu; then add a single item, Paste Link, to that menu. The form is now complete. A complete listing of the form's objects and properties is presented in Listing 17.1.

Listing 17.1   Objects and Properties in PASTELNK.FRM

```
Begin VB.Form Form1
   Caption         =   "Paste Link Demonstration"
   ClientHeight    =   5400
   ClientLeft      =   1890
   ClientTop       =   1800
   ClientWidth     =   9315
   Height          =   6000
   Left            =   1830
   LinkTopic       =   "Form1"
   ScaleHeight     =   5400
   ScaleWidth      =   9315
   Top             =   1260
   Width           =   9435
   Begin VB.CommandButton Command1
      Caption      =   "&Quit"
      Height       =   435
      Left         =   7140
      TabIndex     =   2
      Top          =   4830
      Width        =   2115
   End
   Begin VB.TextBox Text1
      Height       =   4110
      Left         =   6300
      MultiLine    =   -1   'True
      TabIndex     =   1
      Top          =   420
      Width        =   2955
   End
   Begin VB.PictureBox Picture1
      Height       =   4110
      Left         =   420
      ScaleHeight  =   4050
      ScaleWidth   =   5415
      TabIndex     =   0
```

```
    Top           =    420
    Width         =    5475
  End
  Begin VB.Menu mnuEdit
     Caption        =    "&Edit"
     Begin VB.Menu mnuEditPasteLink
        Caption        =    "Paste &Link"
     End
  End
End
End
```

Now let's work on the code. The **Click()** event procedure for the Command Button is trivial, containing only the End statement. We also need to define a couple of constants in the general declarations section of the form, as shown here:

```
Const NONE = 0, AUTOMATIC = 1
```

The program's main functionality resides in event procedures for the menu commands. We want to do two things. First, when the menu is displayed, we want to enable the Paste Link command only if the clipboard contains both DDE link information and data in a format that is appropriate for the control that currently has the focus (text data for the Text Box, a graphic for the Picture Box). We accomplish this in the **Click()** event procedure for the Edit menu command.

Code in this procedure first disables the menu command; we will enable it only if the required conditions are met. We begin by using the Clipboard object's **GetFormat()** method with the vbCFLink argument to determine whether the Clipboard contains DDE link information. If not, we exit the sub, leaving the Paste Link command disabled. If the link information is present, we determine whether the type of data matches the current control. Since there are three types of graphics that the Clipboard can hold, we have to check for all three. This check is accomplished by these lines of code:

```
X = Clipboard.GetFormat(vbCFBitmap)
X = X Or Clipboard.GetFormat(vbCFMetafile)
X = X Or Clipboard.GetFormat(vbCFDIB)
```

The first line sets X to *True* if the Clipboard contains a bitmap graphic. Then X is Ored in turn with the result of the questions: "Does the Clipboard contain a metafile graphic?" and "Does the Clipboard contain a device-independent bitmap graphic?" The result is that X is *True* if the Clipboard contains any one of the three graphics formats, and *False* otherwise.

But how do we determine which of the form's controls currently has the focus? First, we need to determine the identity of the control with the focus. This is done with the **ActiveControl** property, which returns the control that has the focus. The **ActiveControl** property applies to the Screen object as well as to Form and MDIForm objects. This is a very useful property, permitting us to access and manipulate the active control no matter which control it is. We will make use of the Screen object's **ActiveControl** property, which returns the control that has the focus on the active form. Note, however, that we can use the Form or MDIForm object's **ActiveControl** property to access the control that has the focus on a form, even when the form is not active.

Once we have retrieved the control that has the focus, how do we determine what type of control it is? By using the **TypeOf...Is** statement. This statement has the following syntax:

```
TypeOf objectName Is objectType
```

In this syntax, *objectName* is any Visual Basic object. It can be a form or control name, but more often the control returned by the **ActiveControl** property is used here. The *objectType* is the identifier for any Visual Basic control object— that is, any control. For a list of the identifiers associated with each Visual Basic control, search for "Object Type" in the Visual Basic Help system.

Now we can put things together. The If statement that follows will execute only if the active control on the screen is a Picture Box:

```
If TypeOf Screen.ActiveControl Is PictureBox Then
...
End If
```

We can do the same thing for a Text Box, ending up with the following code:

```
X = Clipboard.GetFormat(vbCFBitmap)
X = X Or Clipboard.GetFormat(vbCFMetafile)
X = X Or Clipboard.GetFormat(vbCFDIB)

If X And (TypeOf Screen.ActiveControl Is PictureBox) Then
    mnuEditPasteLink.Enabled = True
    Exit Sub
End If
```

The effect of this code is: "If the Clipboard contains a graphic image and the control with the focus is a Picture Box, then enable the Paste Link command

and exit the sub." We do the same thing for the Text Box: Check that the Clipboard contains text data and that the active control is a Text Box. Now, the Paste Link command will be available to the user only under the appropriate circumstances, lessening confusion and the chance of errors. The complete code for this procedure is shown in Listing 17.2.

Listing 17.2 The Click() Event Procedure for the Edit Menu Command

```
Private Sub mnuEdit_Click()

Dim X As Long

' This sub enables the Paste Link command only if the Clipboard
' contains link information and also contains data in a format
' that is valid for the currently active control.

mnuEditPasteLink.Enabled = False

' If the clipboard does not contain valid DDE
' link information, leave the menu command disabled.

X = Clipboard.GetFormat(vbCFLink)
If X = False Then Exit Sub

' Does the clipboard contain a graphic?

X = Clipboard.GetFormat(vbCFBitmap)
X = X Or Clipboard.GetFormat(vbCFMetafile)
X = X Or Clipboard.GetFormat(vbCFDIB)

' If clipboard contains a graphic and the active control
' is the Picture Box, enable the Paste Link command.

If X And (TypeOf Screen.ActiveControl Is PictureBox) Then
    mnuEditPasteLink.Enabled = True
    Exit Sub
End If

' If the clipboard contains text and the active control
' is a Text Box, enable the Paste Link command.

X = Clipboard.GetFormat(vbCFText)
If X And (TypeOf Screen.ActiveControl Is TextBox) Then
        mnuEditPasteLink.Enabled = True
End If

End Sub
```

The only other procedure the program needs is for the Paste Link command —the code that actually establishes the DDE link. We use the procedures explained earlier: Retrieve the link information from the Clipboard and place it in the destination control's properties. Since we are setting the **LinkMode** to *Automatic*, the data itself is retrieved and displayed automatically. The code for this procedure is shown in Listing 17.3. The only wrinkle here is taking into account that some link information does not include an item specification. Comments in the code explain how this is accomplished.

Listing 17.3   Code in PASTELNK.FRM

```
Private Sub mnuEditPasteLink_Click()

Dim LinkInfo As String, X As Long

' Get link information from the clipboard.

LinkInfo = Clipboard.GetText(vbCFLink)

' Locate the "!".

X = InStr(LinkInfo, "!")

' There is a link item only if LinkInfo contains "!".

If X <> 0 Then
    Screen.ActiveControl.LinkMode = NONE
    Screen.ActiveControl.LinkTopic = Left(LinkInfo, X - 1)
    Screen.ActiveControl.LinkItem = Mid(LinkInfo, X + 1)
    Screen.ActiveControl.LinkMode = AUTOMATIC

' If Link does not contain "!" there is no link item.

ElseIf InStr(LinkInfo, "|") Then
    Screen.ActiveControl.LinkMode = NONE
    Screen.ActiveControl.LinkTopic = LinkInfo
    Screen.ActiveControl.LinkItem = ""
    Screen.ActiveControl.LinkMode = AUTOMATIC
End If

End Sub
```

The program is ready to run. Once the program is executing, start another Windows program, preferably one that works with both text and graphics, such as Microsoft Excel. In Excel (or other program), select some text or graphics and copy it to the Clipboard. This usually requires the Edit Copy command. Switch back to the Visual Basic program, and click or tab to move the focus to the Picture Box or the Text Box. When we select Edit, we see that the Paste Link command is enabled only if the data we placed on the Clipboard matches the active control. When we select Paste Link, the data appears in the active control. Move back to the source program and modify the data; when we return to the Visual Basic program, we see the changes have appeared there, too. The program is shown with a linked Excel graph in Figure 17.1.

Pasting Links from a Visual Basic Program

Most Windows programs have a Copy command that copies selected data to the Clipboard. In order to support DDE links, the Copy command must not only copy the selected data to the Clipboard, but also copy the link information that other applications require to establish a link with the data. This information consists of three parts: the application name, the topic, and, in most cases, the item. Another application can then retrieve only the data without a link (usually with the Paste command), or retrieve the DDE link information and use it to establish a link (usually with the Paste Link command). If we want our Visual Basic program to be able to act as the source in an active link, it must copy DDE link information along with the data to the Windows Clipboard when the user selects the Copy command.

Of course, not every occurrence of the Copy command needs to place link information on the Clipboard. Some data may not be appropriate for linking, in which case we would copy the data only to the Clipboard.

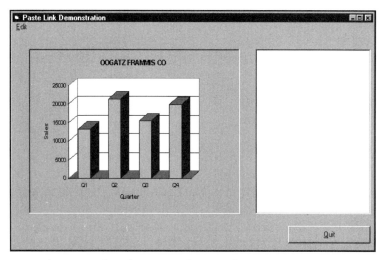

Figure 17.1   *Linking an Excel graph into a Visual Basic application.*

The first step before copying to the Clipboard is assembling the link information. Once again, link information consists of three parts: application, topic, and item. The application is the name of the Visual Basic program, the topic is the **LinkTopic** property of the form containing the control, and the item is the name of the control whose data we want to link. Remember, only Text Box and Picture Box controls can act as the source in a DDE link.

If we are running a program from within the Visual Basic development environment, the application name is the project name (without the extension). If we are running a stand-alone program, the application name is the name of the executable file (minus the EXE extension). In either case, we can obtain the name from the **EXEName** property of the App object:

```
application = App.EXEName
```

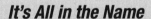

It's All in the Name

You can use the App object's **EXEName** property only if the name of the program's **EXE file** has not been changed. A DDE link requires the program's original name; this is the name assigned in the Make EXE dialog box. The APP.EXEName property, however, returns the application's current EXE filename.

The second piece of information required is the **LinkTopic** property of the form. This can be set at design time or at runtime in code, using just about any name desired. Of course, for purposes of clarity, it should be something that describes the form to which it applies.

A control's **Name** property is not available at runtime. The solution to this problem is to store the control's **Name** in its Tag property during program design. The **Tag** property is not used by Visual Basic in any way—it serves as a storage location for any related data the program may need—in this case, the control's **Name** property. Note that if the source control is part of a control array, the name stored in the **Tag** property must include the control name followed by its array index in parentheses.

These three pieces of information must be combined in a single string with a specific format that you have seen before: the application name followed by a vertical pipe (CHR$(124)), then the LinkTopic followed by an exclamation point and the control name. An example is shown here:

```
LinkInfo = App.EXEName & "|" & LinkTopic & "!" & Screen.ActiveControl.Tag
```

Once we have assembled the string containing the link information, we can place it on the Clipboard.

Copying the DDE Link Information and Data to the Clipboard

When the program user issues the Copy command, our program must copy both the DDE link information and the data itself to the Clipboard. To put the DDE link string on the Clipboard, we use the **SetText** method with the argument vbCFLink. The vbCFLink argument tells the Clipboard to interpret the data passed as DDE link information rather than as regular text. If the link string is stored in the variable LinkInfo, the following code will copy it to the Clipboard:

```
Clipboard.SetText LinkInfo, vbCFLink
```

The next step is to copy the data itself to the Clipboard. Remember, only two controls can act as DDE sources: Text Boxes and Picture Boxes. For a Text Box, use the Clipboard's **SetText** method to copy its text to the Clipboard. The following example assumes that the Text Box is the active control—something the program must verify before executing the **SetText** method:

```
Clipboard.SetText SCREEN.ActiveControl.Text
```

If the source control is a Picture Box, use the **SetData** method to copy the Picture Box contents to the Clipboard. Again, our program must verify that the active control is indeed a Picture Box:

```
Clipboard.SetData SCREEN.ActiveControl.Picture
```

Of course, our program's Copy command should support copying of data from all types of controls, not just Picture Boxes and Text Boxes. These latter types of control are special only in regard to DDE links. When the Copy command is executed while another type of control is active, the code can copy the control's data to the Clipboard but not DDE information.

Demonstrating Copy Link

Thanks to the inner workings of Windows, copying link information to the Clipboard where it can be retrieved by other programs is a relatively simple matter. The program COPYLINK.VBP demonstrated how this is accomplished. The program, which is shown in Figure 17.2, contains only a Picture Box and a Text Box, along with two Command Buttons. Both controls are loaded with

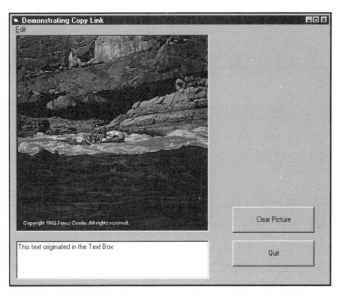

Figure 17.2   *The COPYLINK demonstration program with Microsoft Word in the background showing text linked from the demo.*

some data at design time. For the Picture Box, I used a bitmap image that I had on my disk from a previous project; you can use any bitmap you like, including the ones provided with Visual Basic. Remember, set the Picture Box's **Picture** property to specify its image.

A few other properties need setting during program design. The **Tag** property of the Picture Box and the Text Box must be set to the control's **Name** property. Since these are left at their default values, we have Picture1.Tag = "Picture1" and Text1.Tag = "Text1". Also the form's **LinkMode** property must be set to *Source* or else it will not permit other programs to establish a link with any of its controls. Note that a **LinkMode** property setting of *None* does not prevent the link information from being placed on the Clipboard—the problem arises when the destination application attempts to establish the link. The form's objects and properties are given in Listing 17.4.

Listing 17.4   Objects and Properties in COPYLINK.FRM

```
Begin VB.Form Form1
    Caption         =   "Demonstrating Copy Link"
    ClientHeight    =   6210
    ClientLeft      =   3555
    ClientTop       =   1935
    ClientWidth     =   8160
```

```
Height          =    6810
Left            =    3495
LinkMode        =    1   'Source
LinkTopic       =    "Form1"
Top             =    1395
Width           =    8280
Begin VB.CommandButton Command2
   Caption         =    "Quit"
   Height          =    645
   Left            =    5670
   TabIndex        =    3
   Top             =    5145
   Width           =    2115
End
Begin VB.CommandButton Command1
   Caption         =    "Clear Picture"
   Height          =    645
   Left            =    5670
   TabIndex        =    2
   Top             =    4305
   Width           =    2115
End
Begin VB.TextBox Text1
   Height          =    960
   Left            =    105
   MultiLine       =    -1  'True
   TabIndex        =    1
   Tag             =    "Text1"
   Text            =    "copylink.frx":0000
   Top             =    5145
   Width           =    4950
End
Begin VB.PictureBox Picture1
   AutoSize        =    -1  'True
   Height          =    4920
   Left            =    105
   Picture         =    "copylink.frx":0025
   TabIndex        =    0
   Tag             =    "Picture1"
   Top             =    0
   Width           =    4950
End
Begin VB.Menu mnuEdit
   Caption         =    "&Edit"
   Begin VB.Menu mnuEditCopy
      Caption         =    "Copy"
      Shortcut        =    ^C
   End
End
End
```

The program's code is shown in Listing 17.5. The two Command Button event procedures should be self-explanatory. To clear the Picture Box, we use the **LoadPicture()** function with no argument. In the **Click()** event procedure for the Edit menu, we use a technique similar to the one shown earlier—enabling the menu command only under appropriate circumstances. In this case the proper circumstances exist if the active control is a Picture Box or a Text Box. If the focus is on one of the Command Buttons, nothing is available for copying to the Clipboard!

The real action takes place in the **Click()** event procedure for the Copy command. Depending on whether the active control is a Picture Box or a Text Box, the code copies the appropriate link information and data to the Clipboard. The procedure for doing this is almost identical for both types of control, differing only in the method used (SetText for a Text Box, SetData for a Picture Box) to copy the data to the Clipboard.

To see how the program works, execute it — then select either the Text Box or the Picture Box by clicking on it. Next, select Edit|Copy or press Ctrl+C to copy the data and link information to the Clipboard. Switch to another Windows application that supports DDE links, such as a word processor. If you prefer, use the PASTLINK program that we developed earlier in the chapter. Select the destination program's Paste Link command (or the equivalent) to paste the data and link from the Clipboard. Next, switch back to COPYLINK and modify the linked data by clearing the picture or editing the text. Switch back to the destination application where you will see the changes automatically reflected.

Listing 17.5   Code in COPYLINK.FRM

```
Option Explicit

Private Sub Command1_Click()

' Clear the Picture Box

Picture1.picture = LoadPicture()

End Sub


Private Sub Command2_Click()

' Quit the program.
```

```
        End

    End Sub


    Private Sub mnuEdit_Click()

    ' Enable the Copy command only if the Picture Box
    ' or the Text Box is active.

    If TypeOf Screen.ActiveControl Is TextBox Or TypeOf Screen.ActiveControl Is
    PictureBox Then
        mnuEditCopy.Enabled = True
    Else
        mnuEditCopy.Enabled = False
    End If

    End Sub


    Private Sub mnuEditCopy_Click()

    Dim LinkInfo As String

    ' Clear the Clipboard

    Clipboard.Clear

    ' If the active control is the Text Box copy its text and
    ' DDE information to the Clipboard.

    If TypeOf Screen.ActiveControl Is TextBox Then
        LinkInfo = App.EXEName & "|" & LinkTopic
        LinkInfo = LinkInfo & "!" & Screen.ActiveControl.Tag
        Clipboard.SetText LinkInfo, vbCFLink
        Clipboard.SetText Screen.ActiveControl.TEXT
    End If

    ' If the active control is a Picture Box copy its picture and
    ' DDE information to the Clipboard.

    If TypeOf Screen.ActiveControl Is PictureBox Then
        LinkInfo = App.EXEName & "|" & LinkTopic
        LinkInfo = LinkInfo & "!" & Screen.ActiveControl.Tag
        Clipboard.SetText LinkInfo, vbCFLink
        Clipboard.SetData Screen.ActiveControl.picture
    End If

    End Sub
```

MORE DDE MAGIC

DDE offers a great deal more capability than is possible to cover here. However, I would like to finish this chapter with one more use for DDE—something that I find very useful. Using the power of DDE, we can use Visual Basic to create extensions to existing programs, circumventing omissions or shortcomings in their design and capabilities.

For example, we may like to use the Microsoft Excel spreadsheet program for manipulation and graphing of numerical data. And why not? Excel has a wide range of powerful features, and trying to duplicate even a few of them in a Visual Basic program would be a major programming challenge. However, in my opinion, Excel falls short in one area: data entry. Typing large amounts of data into the spreadsheet's row and column structure can be an exercise in frustration and error. As you know, however, Visual Basic makes it easy to create attractive, easy to use forms for data entry and other purposes. By using DDE, we can create a Visual Basic data entry program that sends the data to an Excel spreadsheet. We get the best of both worlds—the convenience of a Visual Basic data entry form and the analytical capabilities of Excel.

Using DDE in this way is quite different from the material we covered earlier in the chapter. DDE is used to transfer data, but no link is established. Once a piece of data is "sent" to Excel, we have no link back to the Visual Basic program—the end result is exactly the same as if the data had been typed directly into Excel. In addition to sending data to other programs, we'll see that DDE can be used to send commands, instructing programs to perform various actions. The first action we will need is the ability to start a program if it is not already running.

To start another Windows application from within a Visual Basic program, you use the **Shell** function. The function syntax:

```
result = Shell(CommandString [, WindowStyle])
```

The CommandString argument specifies the name of the program to execute, including any required arguments or command line switches. If the program name in CommandString doesn't include a .COM, .EXE, .BAT, or .PIF file extension, .EXE is assumed. The WindowStyle argument specifies the style of the application window when the program starts, such as maximized or minimized. We can omit this argument, and the program is opened minimized with the focus. The possible values for WindowStyle and the defined constants are shown in Table 17.2.

Table 17.2   *WindowStyle Values and Constants*

Constant	Value	Description
vbHide	0	Window is hidden and focus is passed to the hidden window.
vbNormalFocus	1	Window has focus and is restored to its original size and position.
vbMinimizedFocus	2	Window is displayed as an icon with focus.
vbMaximizedFocus	3	Window is maximized with focus.
vbNormalNoFocus	4	Window is restored to its most recent size and position. The currently active window remains active.
vbMinimizedNoFocus	6	Window is displayed as an icon. The currently active window remains active.

If the application is successfully initiated, the **Shell** function returns the application's task identification, a unique number that identifies the running application. If the **Shell** function is unable to start the named application, an error occurs.

When using the **Shell** function, remember that it runs other applications asynchronously. This means that we can't be sure that a program started with **Shell** will have completed its start-up procedures before the code following the **Shell** function in our Visual Basic application is executed.

Sending Commands to Another Program

Once we have established a DDE link, we can use the link for more than transferring data. We can also use it to send commands to the other applicaton using the **LinkExecute** method. The **LinkExecute** method is applied to the control that is maintaining the link—the active destination control. That's just a syntax requirement, however, as the control has nothing to do with the command that we are sending. The syntax for the **LinkExecute** method is shown here:

```
ControlName.LinkExecute Command
```

ControlName is the name of a control that is the destination in an active DDE link. The Command argument is a string that contains the commands to be sent to the DDE source application. The legal commands depend on the specific application. In other words, no universal "DDE command set" exists that contains commands for use with all applications. You'll need to refer to the documentation for each source application for information on the commands it accepts. Excel, for example, accepts any of its macro commands enclosed in brackets.

Sending Data to Another Program

Once an active DDE link is established, we can send data from the destination program to the source program. Note that this is the reverse of the more typical data flow in a DDE conversation, which is from source to destination. To send data from the destination to the source, use the **LinkPoke** method. The procedure is as follows:

1. Put the data to be transferred in a Text Box or Picture Box control.

2. Set the control's **LinkMode** property to *0-None.*

3. Set the control's **LinkTopic** and **LinkItem** properties to identify the location where you want to poke the data.

4. Set the **LinkMode** property to *2-Manual.*

5. Execute the **LinkPoke** method.

For example, the code here will poke the text "Testing LinkPoke" to cell B2 in the Excel spreadsheet TESTDATA.XLS:

```
Text1.Text = "Testing LinkPoke"
Text1.LinkMode = 0
Text1.LinkTopic = "EXCEL|TESTDATA"
Text1.LinkItem = "R2C2"
Text1.LinkMode = 2
Text1.LinkPoke
```

Note the use of "R2C2" to refer to the second row in the second column. For DDE commands, Excel uses numbers for both rows and columns.

A Front End Demonstration

We now have the tools that we need to create a Visual Basic front end. We know how to start another Windows program, to send it commands, and to send it data. The demonstration program developed here is fundamental; but even for a full-featured front end, you'll be surprised at how easy it is to create. This program is designed for use with Excel, but the same techniques will apply to other applications as well. FRONTEND's data entry form is shown

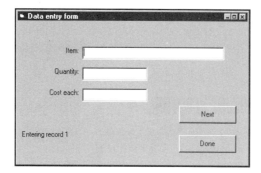

Figure 17.3 *A Visual Basic program for data entry into an Excel spreadsheet.*

in Figure 17.3. Here are the tasks we want it to perform:

• Start Excel.

• Display three Text Box controls for data entry.

• Poke data in the three Text Boxes to columns A, B, and C in the Excel spreadsheet, starting in the first row.

• Poke subsequent entries into the same columns in row 2, row 3, and so on.

• Display an updating label on the form that informs the user of the current record number.

• On exit, prompt for a filename entry and then send commands to Excel to save the spreadsheet under that name; then terminate.

The program's one form contains three Text Boxes, four Labels, and two Command Buttons. The Text Boxes and Command Buttons are control arrays. The form's objects and properties are shown in Listing 17.6. For convenient data entry, ensure that the tab order has the three Text Box controls in the 1, 2, and 3 positions, and the Next button in the 4 position.

Listing 17.6   Objects and Properties in FRONTEND.FRM

```
Begin VB.Form Form1
   Caption          =   "Data entry form"
   ClientHeight     =   3555
   ClientLeft       =   1710
   ClientTop        =   1425
   ClientWidth      =   5970
   Height           =   3960
   Left             =   1650
```

```
LinkTopic        =      "Form1"
ScaleHeight      =      3555
ScaleWidth       =      5970
Top              =      1080
Width            =      6090
Begin VB.CommandButton Command1
   Caption       =      "Done"
   Height        =      435
   Index         =      1
   Left          =      4200
   TabIndex      =      8
   Top           =      2835
   Width         =      1485
End
Begin VB.CommandButton Command1
   Caption       =      "Next"
   Height        =      435
   Index         =      0
   Left          =      4200
   TabIndex      =      7
   Top           =      2100
   Width         =      1485
End
Begin VB.TextBox Text1
   Height        =      330
   Index         =      2
   Left          =      1680
   TabIndex      =      6
   Top           =      1680
   Width         =      1695
End
Begin VB.TextBox Text1
   Height        =      330
   Index         =      1
   Left          =      1680
   TabIndex      =      5
   Top           =      1155
   Width         =      1695
End
Begin VB.TextBox Text1
   Height        =      330
   Index         =      0
   Left          =      1680
   TabIndex      =      4
   Top           =      630
   Width         =      3690
End
Begin VB.Label Label4
   Alignment     =      1    'Right Justify
   Caption       =      "Cost each:"
   Height        =      330
   Left          =      420
   TabIndex      =      3
```

```
        Top          =   1680
        Width        =   1170
     End
     Begin VB.Label Label3
        Alignment    =   1  'Right Justify
        Caption      =   "Quantity:"
        Height       =   225
        Left         =   420
        TabIndex     =   2
        Top          =   1155
        Width        =   1170
     End
     Begin VB.Label Label2
        Alignment    =   1  'Right Justify
        Caption      =   "Item:"
        Height       =   225
        Left         =   420
        TabIndex     =   1
        Top          =   630
        Width        =   1170
     End
     Begin VB.Label Label1
        Height       =   330
        Left         =   105
        TabIndex     =   0
        Top          =   2730
        Width        =   2430
     End
  End
End
```

The program's code is presented in Listing 17.7. You can see that the code is rather short. A flag named **ExcelRunning** is maintained: *True* if Excel has been started and *False* otherwise. This flag is used to prevent the program from trying to send commands to Excel if a DDE link has not been established (which occurs when the user "saves" the first record), which would cause an error. The remainder of the code is straightforward and should be clearly understandable from the comments.

Note that I have used the **On Local Error** statement: When an error is detected, an error handing routine is executed that contains simply a **Resume Next** statement. This tells Visual Basic to ignore errors without reporting them (you will be learning more about Visual Basic error handling in Chapter 19). This step was necessary because the program would sometimes report a "DDE time out" error, meaning that Excel had not responded to the DDE request within the allotted time limit. However, Excel was responding and everything was working fine. We can also prevent this type of error by increasing the destination control's **LinkTimeOut** property.

This demonstration program omits most of the error handling and other "idiot proofing" code that should be included in any program designed for distribution. Even so, it's a good illustration of how Visual Basic and DDE can be teamed up with commercial applications to provide the best solution to a customer's needs.

Listing 17.7   Code in FRONTEND.FRM

```
Option Explicit

Const NONE = 0, MANUAL = 2
Dim ExcelRunning As Boolean


Private Sub Command1_Click(Index As Integer)

Dim Cmd As String
Dim Filename As String
Dim Prompt As String
Dim X As Long
Dim Item As String
Static Row As Integer

On Local Error GoTo Errorhandler

Select Case Index
    Case 0        ' Next
        If Not ExcelRunning Then
            ' Start Excel minimized without focus.
            X = Shell("C:\OFFICE95\EXCEL\EXCEL.EXE", vbMinimizedNoFocus)
            ExcelRunning = True
        End If

        ' Poke the data to the Excel spreadsheet. Loop once
        ' for each Text Box in the control array. Excel always
        ' starts with the default spreadsheet name SHEET1.
        Row = Row + 1

        For X = 0 To 2
            Text1(X).LinkMode = NONE
            Text1(X).LinkTopic = "EXCEL|SHEET1"
            Item = "R" & Right$(Str$(Row), Len(Str$(Row)) - 1)
            Item = Item & "C" & Right$(Str$(X + 1), Len(Str$(X + 1)) - 1)
            Text1(X).LinkItem = Item
            Text1(X).LinkMode = MANUAL
            Text1(X).LinkPoke
        Next X

        ' Clear the Text Boxes.
        For X = 0 To 2
            Text1(X).TEXT = ""
        Next X
```

```
         ' Set focus to the first Text Box.
         Text1(0).SetFocus

         ' Update the counter label.
         Label1.Caption = "Entering record" & Str$(Row + 1)

    Case 1        ' Done

         ' If Excel is running, save workbook and close.
         If ExcelRunning Then
            ' Get the name for the Excel file.
            Prompt = "Name for Excel file (no extension)"
            Filename = InputBox(Prompt, "File name", "")
            Filename = Filename & ".XLS"

            ' Save the spreadsheet. CHR$(34) is the double quote character.
            Cmd = "[SAVE.AS(" & Chr$(34) & Filename & Chr$(34) & ")]"
            Text1(2).LinkExecute Cmd

            ' Close Excel.
            Text1(2).LinkExecute "[Quit()]"
         End If
         End
End Select

Exit Sub

Errorhandler:
    Resume Next

End Sub


Private Sub Form_Load()

' Display record number.
Label1.Caption = "Entering record 1"

ExcelRunning = False


End Sub
```

Object Linking and Embedding

Object linking and embedding makes the software component approach available to the end user as well as the programmer.

You've probably heard a lot about the promise of software components, at the very least, in this book! And if you've been paying attention for the last 17 chapters, you should be aware that the ability to combine prewritten functional software modules into a final application is a powerful approach to programming, indeed. But what about non-programmers—the end users? Can the software component paradigm be extended to them as well? That's the goal of Object Linking and Embedding, or OLE.

OLE BASICS

Microsoft has decided that its major tool in the quest toward software components will be OLE. OLE is a technique that permits Windows applications to cooperate in the manipulation and presentation of data. Each Windows program that supports OLE becomes a component that can be utilized in other programs. Visual Basic programmers are already accustomed to the software component approach to program development. The controls in the tool palette are software components, as are the dozens of commercially available custom controls. The magic of Visual Basic comes from the fact that we can create programs largely by stitching these components together. With OLE 2.0, not only controls but entire programs can be combined to create the most efficient solution to our data processing needs.

The potential advantages of this approach are significant. Previously, programmers had little choice but to implement their own versions of many major software subsystems. For example, if a program required the ability to edit text files, the programmer had to write the editor code as part of the overall project. This was a significant waste of time and effort for the programmer, and also forced end users to deal with the differences between the various editors in the various programs. The advent of the Windows operating environment provided a partial solution to this problem by offering interface standards for various common software features, such as menus, cursor movement, and dialog boxes. But while Windows programs may be easier to use, they are certainly more difficult to write. The challenges that programmers face in creating Windows applications emphasize even more strongly the benefits of the software component approach, where time is never wasted reinventing the wheel (or, in this case, text editor!).

eXPLORER TIP

OLE versus DDE

OLE is similar to DDE (Dynamic Data Exchange) in some respects, but they have more differences than similarities. The two standards should not be viewed as competing methods for achieving the same thing, but rather as two different tools that are appropriate for different tasks. In almost all cases, the nature of the task we need to perform will determine whether we use OLE or DDE.

What Does OLE Do?

At this point you may be thinking "Sounds great, but I still don't know exactly what OLE does." Rather than describe it in the abstract, let's look at a concrete example. Suppose that we are using Microsoft Word to write a document, and we want to include a technical diagram created with the Micrografx Designer technical illustration program. Before OLE, we would have to create the diagram in Designer, save it in a format Word can import, then switch to Word and import the figure into our document. If we later needed to modify the diagram, we had to make the changes in Designer, save the file, and re-import it into Word.

With OLE the process is a lot simpler, and is centered more on our document and less on the individual applications used to create it. We use the Insert Object command to insert a Designer diagram in our document. A blank, sizable window appears in the document at the selected location, displaying an empty Designer diagram. We are still in Word, but Word's menus and Toolbars have been replaced by Designer's menus and toolbars. We now have all of Designer's tools and commands available to work on the diagram *even though we have never left Word.* After creating the diagram, click in the document outside the diagram window and Word's own menus and toolbars reappear, permitting us to continue working on the text part of the document. To modify the diagram, double-click it and Designer's menus and toolbars display again.

OLE in Visual Basic

As you might imagine, OLE is terribly complex under the hood. Fortunately, Visual Basic programmers don't have to look under the hood! The OLE container control makes OLE ridiculously easy, since all the complex workings of OLE are hidden within the control. All we have to do is drop the control in our Visual Basic program and we have OLE at our fingertips. OK, it's not quite that easy, but there's no doubt that the benefits are worth the effort.

OLE really has two parts. The linking and embedding part, described above, is similar in concept to the older style OLE that has been around for a while. The other part, called OLE Automation, is a relatively new addition to the standard. In the first part of this chapter, we will cover the fundamental concepts and terms of the linking and embedding part of OLE. Later in the chapter we'll deal with OLE automation.

What about VBX Controls?

It's not quite accurate to say that VBXs are totally dead. Visual Basic 4.0 includes a 16-bit version of Visual Basic—or, more accurately, a version of Visual Basic that produces 16-bit applications. Applications created this way can run under either Windows 95 or Windows 3.1, and can incorporate VBX custom controls. This compatibility is due to the fact that Microsoft built into Windows 95 the ability to run older—that is, 16-bit—Windows programs. Thus, we have a choice: Develop 32-bit Visual Basic applications for Windows 95 only and forego our favorite VBX controls, or develop 16-bit applications that can execute under either version of Windows but lack the speed and other advantages of 32-bit code.

OLE Terminology

OLE has a terminology all its own. This section will present these terms and explain some of the details of how OLE works.

Containers, Servers, and Objects

OLE interactions involve two Windows applications known as the *container* and *server*. In the example presented earlier, Word was the container and Designer was the server. The unit of data that can be manipulated using OLE is called an *object*. In the earlier example, the Designer diagram was the object. Data objects are provided, or *exposed*, by various applications such as word processors and drawing programs. A server is an application that can expose OLE objects.

Earlier versions of OLE have a slightly different terminology; and if you happen to be familiar with it, you may get confused. The container application used to be called the *client* or the *destination*, and the server application was called the *source*.

In OLE, the term *object* is simply a fancy way of saying data. More precisely, an OLE object is any item of data that can be displayed by an OLE container application. An object can be almost anything—an entire graphic diagram, a section of a word processing document, or a single spreadsheet cell. The characteristics of a data object are defined by the server application where the data object originates.

Every OLE object has a *class* that specifies the name of the server application that exposes the data object. In addition to the server application name, the class also specifies the object's data type and the server's version number. For example, a chart object exposed by Microsoft Excel version 5 has the class "Excel.Chart.5." When you install applications under Windows, they provide Windows with information about any OLE objects they can expose. This information is kept in the Windows registry, and is used by container applications to determine the type of OLE objects that are available on the current system. You can see a list of the classes that are registered on your system by placing an OLE control on a VB form and selecting its **Class** property in the Property window. You'll see the same list if you run a container application, such as a word processor, and issue the command to insert an OLE object (in Microsoft Word, the command is Insert Object). Figure 18.1 shows the Insert Object dialog box in Microsoft Word, showing the OLE objects that are available on my system.

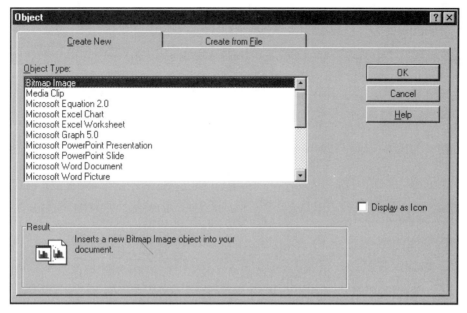

Figure 18.1 *A container application obtains information about available OLE objects from the Windows registry.*

It's Really Linking OR Embedding

OLE should really be called Object Linking or Embedding, because linking and embedding are two different ways of sharing data. We do not link and embed an object—we either link it or embed it. The difference between linking and embedding has to do with where the data is stored and whether other applications have access to it.

Both linked and embedded objects are displayed in the container application and can be edited using the server application. The container application contains a place holder for a linked object, but does not contain the data itself. The data is stored elsewhere, in a file associated with the server application. When an object is embedded, the container application actually contains the data; and the data is stored as part of the container application's data file.

Let's look at this distiction in terms of the example presented earlier. If we had linked the Designer drawing to the Word document, the drawing would exist as a separate file in Designer's standard data file format. The Word document would exist as a separate file in Word format, containing a placeholder for the Designer diagram. If we had embedded the diagram, there would not be a separate Designer file containing the diagram. Rather, the diagram data would be part of the Word data file—it would be saved in the same file with the document text.

Linked and embedded objects also differ in terms of the accessibility of the data object. A linked data object, since it exists in its own independent data file, can be accessed and modified by multiple container applications. For example, an Excel spreadsheet object could be linked to a Visual Basic container application and a Microsoft Word container document at the same time. Either of these container applications (the Visual Basic program or Word) could access and modify the spreadsheet, and the changes would appear in the linked object in the other container the next time it was used. We could also open and modify the spreadsheet using Excel as a stand-alone application; and these changes, too, would appear in both the Visual Basic and the Word containers.

An embedded object's accessibility is much more restricted. It is accessible only to the one container application in which it is embedded. Other applications cannot access or modify the object's data.

Both embedded objects and linked objects originate in the server application that exposed it. Consider a Microsoft Excel spreadsheet object. Whether linked or embedded, the object becomes a part of the container application, but in different ways:

- If we link the spreadsheet object, the container document contains links to the spreadsheet file as well as a visual image of it for display purposes. The spreadsheet data itself is stored in the original Excel spreadsheet file, just like any other spreadsheet. If that spreadsheet file is modified, the container document will display the changes. The container application saves the link information and an image of the data object, but does not save the actual data.

- If we embed the spreadsheet object, the data is included as part of the container document. If the embedded data originated in an existing spreadsheet file, it becomes totally separate and independent from the original file. If the original file is modified, the container does not reflect the changes. The container can, however, use the server application to modify its own copy of the object. It is the container application's responsibility to store the data on disk.

Obviously, whether we use linking or embedding depends upon the specific situation. Linking permits data from a single source to be automatically updated in one or more container application that depends on it. This sounds similar to DDE, but OLE has the advantage over DDE in that an OLE container has quick and direct access to the server application for modification of the linked data. Embedding is not useful for automatic updating of data, since only one application (the container) has access to the data. Embedding is used when we want to provide a single application (the container) with access to the data manipulation and presentation abilities of a variety of server applications.

At the risk of generalizing, DDE is most suitable when our program code needs access to the data, and OLE is preferable when we only need to display the data and edit it using the original application. Like all generalizations, I'm sure exceptions exist; but it usually serves as a pretty good guide.

In-Place Activation

The new OLE standard supports in-place activation, which permits editing of an OLE object within the container application as described earlier. With previous versions of OLE, activating an object caused the server application to start in its own window with the activated object displayed for editing. After completing the necessary editing tasks, we closed the server and were returned to the container application with the modified object displayed.

OLE Containers in Visual Basic

One of the delights of Visual Basic programming is that previously complex tasks are rendered easy or even trivial. Implementing an OLE container is no exception. We let a control—in this case, the OLE Container control—do the work for us. This control has many properties that you have already used with other controls, such as those controlling its size and visibility. There are also several specialized properties that relate specifically to OLE, which we will cover in this section.

Visual Basic Programs as OLE Servers

Until the current version, Visual Basic programs could act only as OLE containers. It was not possible to implement an OLE server in Visual Basic. This has changed now with Windows 95 and Visual Basic 4.0. Using Class Modules, we can define data objects that are available to other container applications. This is an advanced topic, however, and is beyond the scope of an introductory book.

The Windows Registry

For a Visual Basic program—or any program, for that matter—to act as an OLE container, it must know about the OLE server applications that are available. A container application cannot assume that a particular server application is available. Information about OLE servers is kept in the Windows *registry*. This information is maintained automatically. When an OLE server is installed, part of the installation process is registering itself by placing certain information in the registry. This information includes the server command line, the OLE protocols it supports, the class names of the objects it supports, and so on. This, of course, is exactly the information that is required by any program trying to establish itself as an OLE container. By obtaining this information from the registry, a container application can be sure that it will attempt to establish an OLE relationship only with servers that are available. A Visual Basic program uses the OLE control to access the registry.

 **The Deleted Servers Problem**

Problems can arise if an OLE server is deleted by simply easing its program files. Its registration information will still be present in the registry, so container applications may still try to establish an OLE relationship with it. The result, of course, is an error. Whenever possible, use an application's Setup program to uninstall it. Properly designed uninstall programs not only remove the program files but the registry entry, preventing future OLE errors.

Inserting an OLE Object

The OLE control permits an OLE object to be inserted during program design (by the programmer) or while the program is running (by the user). Of course, the program must include the code for the latter action. At runtime, the OLE process can be controlled by the user, working with dialog boxes, or by program code setting properties of the OLE control. Depending on the circumstances, one of these methods will be more appropriate.

There are three ways to go about inserting an object into an OLE container. These three methods apply to both linking and embedding.

- Paste the object into the container using the Paste Special command (or equivalent). This is possible only if a valid OLE object is on the Windows clipboard. This object must have been copied to the clipboard by the server application—for example, a range of cells in an Excel worksheet.

The Paste Special command lets us embed the object with the Paste option, or link the object with the Paste Link option. For certain types of objects, only the Paste option is available.

- Create a new object, a blank whatever-it-is that we're embedding (linking is not possible with this method). Specify the server application, which will start (in-place, if supported). Then use the server's tools and commands to create the object and switch back to the container application.

- Insert the object from an existing file, a data file belonging to the server application. Specify both the file name and whether the object is to be linked or embedded.

These three methods of inserting OLE objects can be used at both design and runtime.

Inserting an Object at Design Time

If we insert an OLE object at design time, the link is fixed to the specified object and cannot be switched to another object while the program is running. For example, if we want a specific Excel workbook linked to or embedded in our Visual Basic application each and every time it runs, we would use this approach.

To insert an object during program design, place an OLE control on the form. Visual Basic will display the Insert Object dialog box, which is shown in Figure 18.2. If we want to create a new, blank object, select the type of object from the list, then click the OK button (remember, new objects can only be embedded, not linked). The server application associated with the selected object will start, and a blank object will display in the OLE control, or in its own window if you selected the Display as Icon option (discussed below). Use the application's tools and commands to create and edit the data, or leave the object blank. The server application's menu is displayed, but lacking the File menu. Since the data object is embedded and will be stored within the OLE container, we have no need for the File menu commands.

The exact details depend on the specific server. If we insert an Excel spreadsheet, for example, a grid of cells displays in the OLE control and the Excel menu appears at the top of the Visual Basic form. In any case, we can click on our form outside the OLE control to return to Visual Basic program design.

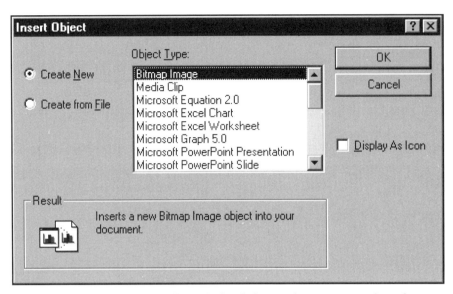

Figure 18.2 *The Insert Object dialog box is displayed when we place an OLE control on a form.*

If we want to insert an object from an existing file, we select the Create from File option in the Insert Object dialog box. The dialog box will change as shown in Figure 18.3. Enter the name of the desired file in the File box, or click the Browse button to select the file. Click the Link option to link the object; otherwise the object will be embedded. Click the OK button and the selected object will be displayed in the OLE control. If we select an invalid file —one that is not associated with a registered OLE server—an error message will be dislayed.

To have the object display an icon in our application rather than the data, select the Display as Icon option in the Insert Object dialog box. We'll still be able to activate the object for editing by double-clicking the icon, but we won't be able to view the data in the Visual Basic application. If we don't need to view the data, this choice can speed up screen display.

If we don't want to insert an object now, click the Cancel button in the Insert Object dialog box and Visual Basic will place an empty OLE control on our form. We can still insert an object later during program design. To do so, right-click the OLE control and select Insert Object from the menu that is displayed. The Insert Object dialog box will be displayed, and we can proceed as described above.

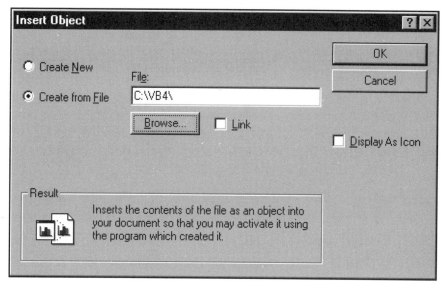

Figure 18.3 *We can also use the Insert Object dialog box to insert an object based on an existing file.*

Restricting OLE Type

An OLE control can hold either a linked or an embedded object. If we want to restrict it to one type or the other, we set the **OleTypeAllowed** property to Linked or Embedded (the default setting is Either). The setting of this property affects object insertion during program design and at runtime.

Using Paste Special During Program Design

Another option during program design is to place an object in an OLE control using the Paste Special command. This method is necessary when the object we want to link does not correspond to an entire data file. For example, we can create an object from a single paragraph of a word processing document or a block of cells in a spreadsheet. Start by placing the OLE control on your Visual Basic form, leaving it empty. Then follow these steps:

1. Start the server application and select the data that you want to link or embed.

2. In the server application, select Cut from the Edit menu.

3. Switch to Visual Basic.

4. Right-click the OLE control and select Paste Special from the pop-up menu. The Paste Special dialog box is displayed, as shown in Figure 18.4. If the Paste Special command on the pop-up menu is disabled, it means that the data you copied to the clipboard is not a valid OLE object.

5. In the dialog box, the As list displays the server applications that are associated with the data object on the clipboard. In most cases this list will contain only one application. If it displays more than one, it means that two or more servers are registered on your system for the type of data on the clipboard. Select the one that you want associated with the data object.

6. Select the Paste option to embed the object. Select the Paste Link option to link the object. For certain types of objects, only one of these options will be available.

7. Select the Display as Icon option if desired (this option was explained earlier in the chapter).

8. Select OK.

Inserting an Object at Runtime

If we don't want the OLE objects in our Visual Basic application to be fixed, they must be inserted while the program is executing. The OLE control is left

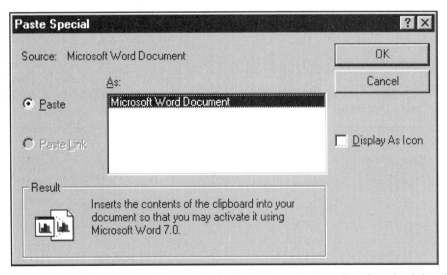

Figure 18.4 *Use the Paste Special command to load an OLE control with an object from the clipboard.*

empty during program design; when the program runs, the desired data object is placed in it either by program code or by the user.

The CreateEmbed and CreateLink Methods

To create an embedded object, use the OLE control's **CreateEmbed** method. This method allows us to create a new embedded object or one that is based on an existing file. The syntax of the **CreateEmbed** is as follows:

```
object.CreateEmbed sourcedoc [class]
```

The identifier object specifies the name of the OLE control. If we want to embed an object based on an existing file, sourcedoc specifies the file, and class can be omitted (or, if not omitted, is ignored). If we want to create a blank object of a certain class, class specifies the class and sourcedoc must be an blank string. Here's an example: If we have an OLE control named OLE1, the command

```
OLE1.CreateEmbed "c:\data\report1994.xls"
```

creates an embedded object based on the spreadsheet file REPORT1994.XLS in the folder C:\DATA. In contrast, the command

```
OLE1.CreateEmbed "", "Excel.Sheet.5"
```

creates a new, blank object based on an Excel version 5 workbook.

Use the **CreateEmbed** method only if the OLE control's **OLETypeAllowed** property is set to *Embedded* or *Both*. Executing this method will erase any object currently in the OLE container without warning. As we'll soon see, it is your program's responsibility to save the existing object.

The **CreateLink** method is used to create a linked object. The syntax is as follows:

```
object.CreateLink sourcedoc [, sourceitem]
```

The argument sourcedoc, which is required, specifies the data file to which the object is to be linked. The optional argument sourceitem identifies the link data item within the file. Let's look at a couple of examples. The statement

```
OLE1.CreateLink "Evaluation.Doc"
```

creates a link to the entire Microsoft Word document Evaluation.Doc. The command

```
OLE1.CreateLink "Evaluation.Doc", "Bookmark6"
```

creates a link to the text in the same document that is identified by the bookmark named Bookmark6. The **CreateLink** method can be used only if the OLE control's **OLETypeAllowed** property is set to *Linked* or *Both*.

Successful use of both of these methods requires that the specified data file is present, and (when required) the specified link item is present in the file. If not, an error occurs. Also, the class specified for the **CreateEmbed** method must be a valid class that is present in the system registry.

Using a Dialog Box to Insert an Object at Runtime

We explained earlier in the chapter how to use the Insert Object dialog box during program design to insert an object in an OLE control. We can display the same dialog box during program execution by executing the OLE object's **InsertObjDlg** method. This dialog box permits the user to embed or link a new object of a specified class or an object based on an existing file. However, if the OLE control's **OLETypeAllowed** property is set to *Linked* or *Embedded* (rather than to *Both*), only the specified action will be available in the Insert Object dialog box.

Using Paste Special at Runtime

We can also implement a Paste Special command in our VB program, permitting the user to paste OLE objects into an OLE control at runtime. Of course, a valid OLE object must be on the clipboard for this method to work. Then we have two approaches. One is to use the OLE control's **Paste** method. This method is usually executed in response to a Paste command on the application's Edit menu. The required steps are as follows:

1. Set the OLE control's **OLETypeAllowed** property to either *Linked* or *Embedded* depending on whether we want the object to be linked or embedded.

2. Verify that the control's **PasteOK** property is *True*. If not, it means that the clipboard does not contain an object that is appropriate for the control's **OLETypeAllowed** setting.

3. Execute the control's **Paste** method.

The second and perhaps easier approach is to execute the OLE control's **PasteSpecialDlg** method. Executing this method displays the Paste Special dialog box; this is the same dialog that is displayed when you select Paste Special from the OLE control's pop-up menu during program design. In this dialog box, the user selects from the As list (necessary only if more than one server is listed), chooses between the Paste and Paste Link options (to embed or link, respectively), then selects OK. If the OLE control's **OLETypeAllowed** property is set to *Linked* or *Embedded*, or if the object on the clipboard permits only linking or embedding, only one of these options will be available.

Inserting an Object with Drag and Drop

For a very user-friendly interface, we can implement an interface that permits an object to be inserted in an OLE control with drag-and-drop. The OLE control's **OLEDropAllowed** property must be set to *True*. The user selects data in the server application, drags it to the VB application, and drops it on the OLE control. The result is the same as if the user had copied the object to the clipboard and then executed the OLE control's **Paste** method. If the user is dragging an appropriate object, the mouse pointer displays a special "drop" icon when it is over the OLE control. Not all objects are appropriate for drag-and-drop, however.

Saving and Retrieving OLE Objects

It is the responsibility of the VB program to save the data in its OLE controls. Neither embedded nor linked OLE objects automatically save themselves. If the user closes a form containing an OLE control, the OLE object's data is lost. With an embedded object this is the actual data, and with a linked object it is the information defining the link to the file that contains the data. For an OLE object to be available the next time the program is run, the data must be explicitly saved and then reloaded into the OLE control the next time the program is executed. Capabilities that are built into the OLE control simplify this task.

Saving OLE Objects to Disk

The data associated with each OLE object is saved in its own file. This is a standard Basic file, opened in Binary mode using the file commands that we covered in Chapter 8. Once the file is open, call the OLE control's **SaveToFile** method, passing the number of the open file as an argument. For example, for an OLE control named Ole1, the following code will save its data in a file named MYOLEFILE.DAT:

```
FileNum = FreeFile
Open "MyOleFile.Dat" For Binary as #FileNum
Ole1.SaveToFile FileNum
Close #FileNum
```

The procedure for saving an OLE object is the same for both linked and embedded OLE objects; but as mentioned above, the nature of the saved data differs. For a linked OLE object, an image, or picture of the data is saved to the file along with the link information identifying the source data file. The object's actual data, you'll remember, is maintained by the server application in that source file. For an embedded OLE object, the actual data is saved in the Basic file.

Be aware that the OLE control does not keep track of whether or not its data is saved. If we load a new object into the control, any existing data will be overwritten without warning. It is the responsibility of our program to keep track of an OLE object's data status, and either save it automatically or prompt the user to save when necessary.

Retrieving OLE Objects from Disk

Retrieving an OLE object from disk is primarily the reverse of the procedure used to save it. Open the data file in binary mode, then call the OLE control's **ReadFromFile** method, passing the file number as an argument. Here's an example:

```
FileNum = FreeFile
Open "MyOleFile.Dat" For Binary as #FileNum
Ole1.ReadFromFile FileNum
Close #FileNum
```

Other OLE Control Properties, Methods, and Events

For an OLE container that contains a linked object, the possibility always exists that the data in the linked file has been modified by another program (it could be the server application or another OLE container application that is linked to the file). To be sure that the OLE control displays the current version of the data, execute the OLE control's **Update** method. This may not be necessary, however, depending on the OLE control's **UpdateOptions** property setting. There are three possible settings for this property:

0 - Automatic (the default)   The OLE control is updated whenever the linked data changes.

1 - Frozen	The OLE control is updated whenever the user saves the linked document from within the server application.
2 - Manual	The OLE Client control is updated only when the **Update** method is invoked.

If the setting is Automatic, clearly the **Update** method will never be necessary. Of course, the **UpdateOptions** property applies only to linked OLE objects. Since embedded objects store their own data, there is never a need to update them.

You can use the OLE control's **Updated** event to detect when an OLE object has been updated by the server application. This event is triggered each time the server application updates an OLE object. The syntax for this event procedure is:

```
Sub OLE_Updated (Code As Integer)
```

The Code argument indicates how the OLE object was updated. Its possible values are as follows (the constant names in parentheses are predefined Windows constants that we can use in our code):

0 (vbOLEChanged)	The file the object is linked to has been modified.
1 (vbOLESaved)	The file the object is linked to has been saved by the server application.
2 (vbOLEClosed)	The file the object is linked to has been closed by the server application.
3 (vbOLERenamed)	The file that the object is linked to has been renamed by the server application.

This event procedure is frequently used to inform the program that the data in a linked OLE control has been changed since it was last saved. Code in the **Update()** event procedure can set a global "data changed" flag. The program can test this flag, for example on exit, to determine if the data needs to be saved.

Activating OLE Objects

Activating an OLE object means to start its server application to manipulate the object. For an OLE control, the default method of activation is to double-click it or to move the focus to the OLE control and press Enter. Other activation methods are possible, depending on the details of the server application and on the setting of the OLE control's **AutoActivate** property. The possible settings of this property are shown in the Table 18.1.

Putting OLE to Work

This book is called the *Visual Basic Explorer*, but so far all you've been doing in this chapter is sitting around looking at maps. Impossible to avoid, but hardly exciting! There are plenty more OLE details I could present, but you've already learned the important stuff, more than enough to put OLE to work in a real-world Visual Basic application. So let's get to work and try OLE out for ourselves. Anyway, I believe that this is the best way to learn—roll up your sleeves and try it out. In this section we'll develop a basic OLE container application that demonstrates how some of the techniques presented earlier are applied in a real program. You'll see how to create a new embedded object, how to edit an existing object, and how to save and retrieve objects on disk.

OLE_DEMO.VBP consists of a single form containing only an OLE control and a menu. Other than changing the form's **Caption** property to *OLE Demonstration*, we can leave all object properties at their default values. There are two menus: a File menu with Save and Exit commands and an Object menu with Insert and Delete commands. The form's objects and properties are given in Listing 18.1.

Table 18.1 *AutoActivate Property Settings*

Constant	Value	Description
vbOLEActivateManual	0	Manual. The object cannot be automatically activated. You must activate the object in code using the OLE control's DoVerb() method.
vbOLEActivateGetFocus	1	Focus. If the OLE control contains an object that supports single click activation, the server application is activated when the OLE control receives the focus.
vbOLEActivateDoubleclick	2	(Default) Double-Click. If the OLE control contains an object, the server application is activated when the user double-clicks the OLE container control or presses Enter when the control has the focus.
vbOLEActivateAuto	3	Automatic. If the OLE control contains an object, the server application is activated according to the object's normal method of activation, either when the control receives the focus or when the user double-clicks the control.

Listing 18.1   Objects and Properties in OLE_DEMO.FRM

```
Begin VB.Form frmOleDemo
   Caption         =   "OLE Demonstration "
   Begin VB.OLE OLE1
   End
   Begin VB.Menu mnuFile
      Caption         =   "&File"
      Begin VB.Menu mnuFileSave
         Caption         =   "&Save"
      End
      Begin VB.Menu mnuFileSep
         Caption         =   "-"
      End
      Begin VB.Menu mnuFileExit
         Caption         =   "E&xit"
      End
   End
   Begin VB.Menu mnuObject
      Caption         =   "&Object"
      Begin VB.Menu mnuInsert
         Caption         =   "&Insert"
      End
      Begin VB.Menu mnuObjectDelete
         Caption         =   "&Delete"
      End
   End
End
```

The program code is shown in Listing 18.2. It starts by declaring a few constants and global variables in the form's General Declarations section. For simplicity's sake, I have defined a constant for the name of the OLE data file, OLE_DEMO.DAT. Here's how the program works. When it's running, the user can select the Object Insert command to display the Insert Object dialog box, then use this dialog (as described earlier in the chapter) to insert either a new object or one based on an existing file. The inserted object can be activated and edited using the server application; pressing Esc ends in-place activation and returns to the program's own menu. For example, Figure 18.5 shows an inserted Excel spreadsheet activated for editing. Note how the Visual Basic program displays Excel's menu.

Once an object has been inserted, you can use the File Save command to save it to disk under the predefined file name. The Object Delete command deletes the object from the OLE control. The program keeps track of whether the inserted object has been saved to disk. Use Object Insert to insert a different object, if desired.

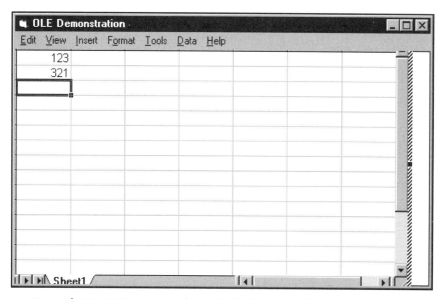

Figure 18.5 *The OLE_DEMO program with an embedded Excel spreadsheet activated for in-place editing.*

When the program begins, it checks to see if the data file exists on disk. If it does, we are offered the option of loading it into the OLE control. I assume that the fie name OLE_DEMO.DAT will not conflict with an existing file on your disk. If it does, change the constant definition in the program to use another name.

This program is a good demonstration of how the capabilities of the OLE control make it easy to program OLE support into our Visual Basic programs. And with OLE, a whole new world of possibilities is opened up. The power of our programs is no longer limited to the code we have the time and skill to write, or to the custom controls that we can afford to buy.

Listing 18.2   Code in OLE_DEMO.FRM

```
Option Explicit

Option Explicit

' Constant for OLE object type.
Const OLE_EMBEDDED = 1

' Constant for the OLE data file name.
Const FILE_NAME = "OLE_DEMO.DAT"

' Global variables and flags.
```

```
Dim DataSaved As Boolean
Dim ObjectPresent As Boolean


Private Sub Form_Load()

Dim FileNum As Long, Reply As Integer

ObjectPresent = False
DataSaved = True

' See if the OLE data file exists. If it does, offer
' the option of loading it.

If Dir$(FILE_NAME) <> "" Then
    Reply = MsgBox("Load OLE data from disk?", vbYesNo + vbQuestion,
            "Load Object")
    If Reply = vbYes Then
        Screen.MousePointer = 11
        FileNum = FreeFile
        Open FILE_NAME For Binary As #FileNum
        OLE1.ReadFromFile FileNum
        ObjectPresent = True
        Close #FileNum
        Screen.MousePointer = 0
    End If
End If

End Sub


Private Sub Form_Resize()

' Size the OLE control to fill the form.

OLE1.Move 0, 0, frmOleDemo.ScaleWidth, frmOleDemo.ScaleHeight

End Sub


Private Sub mnuFile_Click()

' Enable Save menu command only if an object exists.

If ObjectPresent Then
    mnuFileSave.Enabled = True
Else
    mnuFileSave.Enabled = False
End If

End Sub


Private Sub mnuFileExit_Click()
```

```
Dim Reply As Integer

' If the object has not been saved, offer the option.

If Not DataSaved Then

    Reply = MsgBox("Save OLE object before quitting?",
            vbYesNoCancel +  vbQuestion, "Delete Object")
    If Reply = vbYes Then
        Call SaveObject
    ElseIf Reply = vbCancel Then
        Exit Sub
    End If

End If

End

End Sub


Private Sub mnuFileSave_Click()

Call SaveObject

End Sub


Private Sub mnuInsert_Click()

Dim Reply As Integer

' If an object is already present in the OLE control,
' ask the user if it should be deleted. If the
' reply is no exit sub.

If ObjectPresent Then
    Reply = MsgBox("Delete current object?", vbYesNo + vbQuestion,
            "Insert Object")
    If Reply = vbYes Then
        Call mnuObjectDelete_Click
    Else
        Exit Sub
    End If
End If

' Permit only embedded objects.

    OLE1.OLETypeAllowed = OLE_EMBEDDED

' Display the OLE Insert Object Dialog.

    frmOleDemo.OLE1.InsertObjDlg
```

```
        ObjectPresent = True
        DataSaved = False
        Screen.MousePointer = 0

End Sub


Private Sub mnuObject_Click()

' Enable the Delete menu command
' only if an object is present.

If ObjectPresent Then
    mnuObjectDelete.Enabled = True
Else
    mnuObjectDelete.Enabled = False
End If

End Sub


Private Sub mnuObjectDelete_Click()

Dim Reply As Integer

' If the object has not been saved, offer the
' user the option of saving it.

If Not DataSaved Then

    Reply = MsgBox("Save the object before deleting it?", vbYesNoCancel _
            + vbQuestion, "Delete Object")

    If Reply = vbYes Then
        Call SaveObject
    ElseIf Reply = vbCancel Then
        Exit Sub
    End If

End If

' Delete the object.

OLE1.DELETE
ObjectPresent = False
DataSaved = True

End Sub


Private Sub OLE1_DblClick()
```

```
' The OLE object is automatically activated
' for editing because its AutoActivate property
' has been left at the default value of 2. Otherwise
' we would have to execute the DoVerb method to activate it.

DataSaved = False

End Sub


Private Sub OLE1_Updated(Code As Integer)

' If the data is changed by the server,
' clear the Saved flag.

DataSaved = False

End Sub

Private Sub SaveObject()

Dim FileNum As Integer

' Save the OLE object.

FileNum = FreeFile

Open FILE_NAME For Binary As #FileNum

OLE1.FileNumber = FileNum
OLE1.SaveToFile FileNum
DataSaved = True

Close #FileNum

End Sub
```

OLE AUTOMATION

The first part of this chapter presented two sides of the OLE triangle, linking data objects and embedding data objects. These are powerful tools indeed—but since we know that triangles have three sides, there must be something else. There is, indeed, and it is called *OLE Automaton*. This is the newest component of OLE, and in some ways may be the most powerful. In the remainder of this chapter we'll take a look at the basics of OLE Automation in Visual Basic.

How Does it Work?

At the heart of OLE automation is a special kind of data object called a *programmable* data object. Programmable data objects have the capability to be embedded or linked in a container application, just like non-programmable objects. What makes them special is the ability to accept messages from other applications. These messages can contain commands instructing the data object to perform actions on its data. The messages can also pass data (both to and from) the programmable object.

Here's a simple example. We need to add up a column of numbers in our Visual Basic program. Rather that writing the code ourselves, we could use OLE Automation to send the numbers to an Excel spreadsheet object, instruct it to add them up, then return the result. We wouldn't use OLE automation for such a simple task, of course, but it gives us the idea of what it's all about. Server applications that expose programmable objects can be thought of as custom controls whose capabilities are available to other applications.

Let's look at a hypothetical example, something for which you might actually use OLE automation. Imagine that you are writing an application for a stock market analyst who needs to download market data from an online service, perform calculations on the data to come up with various economic predictions, then email the resulting report to a list of clients. Using Visual Basic alone, this would be a formidable programming job. Using OLE automation, however, things would be much easier:

- Send commands to a communications object, instructing it to download the required data.

- Send the data to a spreadsheet object.

- Send commands to the spreadsheet object, instructing it to perform the modeling calculations.

- Retrieve the results from the spreadsheet object and send them to an email object.

- Send commands to the email object instructing it to mail the data to a specified list of recipients.

We can use OLE automation by itself or along with linking or embedding. If we link or embed a programmable object, we'll have the option of sending it commands using OLE automation or in-place activation (or both). The method we select will depend on the needs of the project. As Visual Basic programmers, we can think of programs that support OLE automation as custom controls. The functionality that these programs expose through the OLE interface are control methods, and the program variables and settings that control its operation are its properties. In fact, the custom controls supported by Visual Basic 4 utilize OLE technology, and each one can be thought of as a specialized "mini-server."

Creating an OLE Automation Object

As with embedded OLE objects, we can create a new OLE automation object or open an existing one based on a disk file. In a Visual Basic program, an OLE automation object is identified by a variable of type Object. The first step in creating an object, therefore, is to declare a variable of this type:

```
Dim MyObject As Object
```

Next, we create a new, empty OLE automation object by using the **Set** statement with the **CreateObject()** function. This function has only one argument, specifying the application name and the class name of the object to be created. For example, the statement

```
Set MyObject = CreateObject ("Word.Basic")
```

creates an object based on the Microsoft Word application and the Basic class. We must provide both the application name and class name, because some applications expose more than one class of object.

We create an OLE automation object based on an existing file by using **Set** with the **GetObject()** function, as shown here:

```
Set MyObject = GetObject("c:\data\finance.doc")
```

GetObject() can accept a second, optional argument specifying the object class name. This argument is required only if the specified file contains two or more object types. An Excel spreadsheet file, for example, can contain both sheet and chart objects. To specify the sheet object in an Excel file, we would write

```
Set MyObject = GetObject("C:\WORKSHEETS\ANNUAL.XLS", "Excel.sheet")
```

where Excel is the server application name and sheet is the object type.

OLE automation is relatively new, and not many OLE automation objects are "out there." The few that exist all come from Microsoft. I expect that the list of objects will grow rapidly as other software publishers adopt the OLE automation standard. An application's documentation or on-line help should provide information about the objects it exposes and the methods and properties associated with them. Table 18.2 lists the OLE automation objects that are available from major applications programs as of this writing.

Just like different Visual Basic controls, objects exposed for OLE automation differ in their capabilities. A Word.Basic object, for example, does not permit access to the contents of a document using OLE automation unless the object is also embedded in an OLE container control. An Excel.Sheet object is different, since it does not need to be embedded in order for us to use OLE automation to access its contents.

Obtaining Object Information

Visual Basic provides two tools that we can use to find information about the objects available on our system. These tools are extremely useful, since a big problem when working with OLE automation is determining the details of the objects that are available, their methods and properties, and how to use them. For a separate applications program, the best source of information is usually the program's own documentation or help system. For online information within Visual Basic, we can use the References list and the Object Browser.

The References list is displayed by selecting References from the Visual Basic Tools menu. This dialog box is shown in Figure 18.6. The list displays all of the object sources, or libraries, that are available on our system. The ones marked with an X in the adjacent box are available in the current Visual Basic project. We can add or remove a library from the project by clicking its box.

Table 18.2 *Available OLE Automation Objects*

Application	Object Type	Class
Microsoft Access	Application	Access.Application
Microsoft Excel	Application	Excel.Application
	Worksheet	Excel.Sheet
	Chart	Excel.Chart
Microsoft Project	Application	MSProject.Project
Microsoft Word	WordBasic	Word.Basic

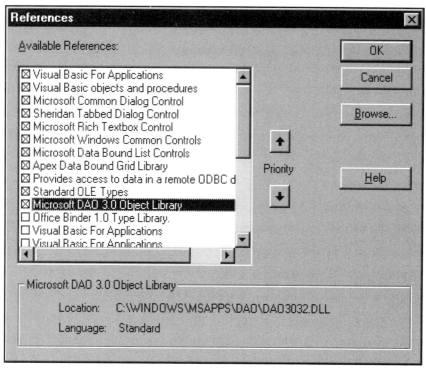

Figure 18.6 *The References list shows the object libraries that are available on our system.*

Since a typical system has a lot of object sources available, it would not be efficient to load them all into every Visual Basic project. By selecting only the ones we need, we minimize memory use and maximize speed. If we try to remove a library that is in use, Visual Basic displays a warning message.

If an object library is selected in the references list, it does not necessarily mean that the library is used by the project—only that it is available. When Visual Basic encounters a reference to an object in our code, it searches the object libraries selected in the References list in top-to-bottom order for a matching object. If two or more applications or libraries expose objects with the same name, Visual Basic uses the first one that is found. If we deselect unused object libraries in the References list, Visual Basic's search process will be speeded up since it has fewer libraries to search. We can also use the Priority buttons in the References dialog box to move frequently used libraries to the top of the list for an additional speed improvement.

Visual Basic will not permit us to deselect a library that is used in the current project. This includes libraries providing objects that are referenced explicitly, as well as libraries used by all custom controls that are installed using the Custom Controls command on the Tools menu. We can never delete the "Visual Basic for Applications" and "Visual Basic objects and procedures" references, because they are necessary for running Visual Basic.

The References list tells us what object libraries are available, but it tells us nothing about the objects in those libraries. For this we need the Object Browser, which we display by pressing F2 or selecting View Object Browser. This dialog box is shown in Figure 18.7. Its parts are described here:

The Libraries/Projects list displays all of the object libraries that are checked in the References list. The name of the current Visual Basic project is displayed also.

The Classes/Modules list displays the classes that are available in the selected library or project.

The Methods/Properties box lists the methods and properties for the item selected in the Classes/Modules list.

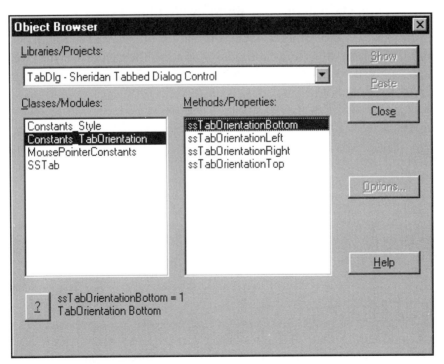

Figure 18.7   The Object Browser.

You may have noticed that many of the items listed in the Object Browser and the References list seem to be related to the various custom controls that are part of Visual Basic. This reflects the fact that the new 32-bit controls, the so-called OCX controls, are in fact implemented using OLE automation technology. Unfortunately, the Object Browser's usefulness for OLE automation programming is limited because it shows all of the system's objects and not just those that are OLE automation capable. We cannot readily use the Browser, therefore, to locate OLE automation objects.

However, if we already know the server and class that we'll be using, we can use the Browser to obtain details on the object's methods and properties. There are two buttons in the Object browser dialog box that can help us:

- Click the Paste button to paste the item selected in the Methods/Properties list into the current Visual Basic code window at the location of the cursor (this Paste is direct and does not go through the clipboard).

- Click the ? button to view the help information related to the selected item.

Properties and Methods of OLE Automation Objects

Like other Visual Basic objects, OLE automation objects are manipulated by means of their properties and methods. Of course, the details of what we can do with an object depend on the object itself, but the basic procedure is similar to working with Visual Basic controls. Each object has its own set of methods and properties. For example, if we had created a word processing document object called MyObj, we could manipulate it as follows:

```
MyObj.Insert "Dear Mr. Gates:"        ' Insert some text.
MyObj.Italics = True         ' Make it italics
MyObj.SaveAs  "LETTER_TO_BILL.DOC" ' Save to disk
```

Here we make use of the object's **Insert()** and **SaveAs()** methods and its **Italics** property. The same general principles hold for all objects, and if you're used to working with Visual Basic controls, you'll find little difference with OLE automation objects.

Using OLE Automation

I mentioned earlier that OLE automation can be used with objects that are embedded as well as with objects that aren't. In this section, I will demonstrate both types of OLE automation. These are simple demonstrations, not the sort of tasks that OLE automation would be required to perform. Again, my purpose is to show how it's done—and for that purpose, these programs serve perfectly well.

OLE Automation with a Non-Embedded Object

For the non-embedded object, I will use an Excel Sheet object. In order to run this program, you must have Microsoft Excel installed on your system. Other Windows spreadsheet programs may support OLE automation by the time you read this. If you have another spreadsheet program, look through its documentation to see if it supports OLE automation and identify the corresponding methods and properties.

This project is called OLEAUTO1.VBP, and it is shown executing in Figure 18.8. It has one form that contains two Text Boxes, two Labels, and one Command button. Enter new **Caption** properties for the Form, the Labels, and the Command button as shown in the figure, and delete the **Text** property values of the two Text Boxes. Otherwise, the object properties can be left at their default values. Be sure to put the "Enter a Number" label next to the Text Box named Text1.

We declare a type Object variable in the form's General Declarations section. The **Form_Load()** event procedure performs the two required initialization steps: Creating the Excel Sheet object, and outputting the calculation formula in cell A1 of the spreadsheet object. Note that in Excel itself, columns are referred to by letters; but in OLE automation, commands are referenced by numbers (1 = A, 2 = B, and so on.) The two lines of code are shown here:

```
Set XLObj = CreateObject("Excel.Sheet")
XLObj.Cells(2, 1).Formula = "=A1^3"
```

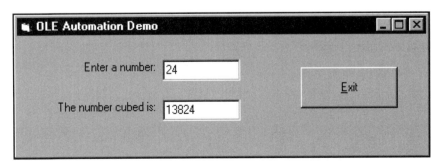

Figure 18.8   *OLEAUTO1 uses an Excel Sheet object to calculate the cube of a number.*

The spreadsheet is now set up to perform the desired calculation. Since the formula we entered in the spreadsheet refers to cell A1, we must put the input value there. We want the calculation to be performed when the user enters or changes a number in the "Enter a Number" Text Box. We'll place the needed code in the Text Box's **Change()** event procedure. Once we send the input value to cell A1 of the spreadsheet, the Sheet object immediately performs the calculation and the answer is waiting to be retrieved from cell A2. Put that value in the second Text Box and we're complete:

```
' Clear the results text box.
Text2.TEXT = ""

' Put the input value in cell A1 of the spreadsheet.
XLObj.Cells(1, 1).VALUE = Val(Text1.TEXT)

' Retrieve the answer from cell B1.
Text2.TEXT = XLObj.Cells(2, 1).VALUE
```

In order to save the spreadsheet to disk, we would execute the object's **SaveAs()** method:

```
XLObj.SaveAs "test.xls"
```

We don't want to save the file, however, so all that's necessary before quitting the program is to destroy the object:

```
Set XLObj = Nothing
```

The complete code listing for OLEAUTO1.FRM is given in Listing 18.3.

Listing 18.3   Code in OLEAUTO1.FRM

```
Option Explicit

Dim XLObj As Object

Private Sub Command1_Click()

' If we wanted to save the object, here's how.
' XLObj.SaveAs "filename.xls"

' Destroy the object.
Set XLObj = Nothing

' Exit the program.
End
```

```
End Sub


Private Sub Form_Load()

' Create the Excel sheet object.
Set XLObj = CreateObject("Excel.Sheet")

' Put the cube forumla in cell B1.
XLObj.Cells(2, 1).Formula = "=A1^3"

End Sub


Private Sub Text1_Change()

' Clear the results text box.
Text2.TEXT = ""

' Put the input value in cell A1 of the spreadsheet.
XLObj.Cells(1, 1).VALUE = Val(Text1.TEXT)

' Get the answer from cell B1.
Text2.TEXT = XLObj.Cells(2, 1).VALUE

End Sub
```

OLE Automation with an Embedded Object

In order to demonstrate OLE automation with an embedded object, I will use a Microsoft Word document object. The technique of combining OLE embedding with OLE automation is a powerful and flexible technique. This simple demonstration gives you a small taste of what is possible. The program does the following:

- Creates a blank Word document embedded in the Visual Basic program's OLE control.

- When the user clicks a Command Button, starts the letter by entering the date, return address, and greeting.

- Activates the document for in-place editing, permitting the user to add the body of the letter and format it with Word's tools and commands.

- When the user clicks another Command Button, finishes the letter by adding the closing.

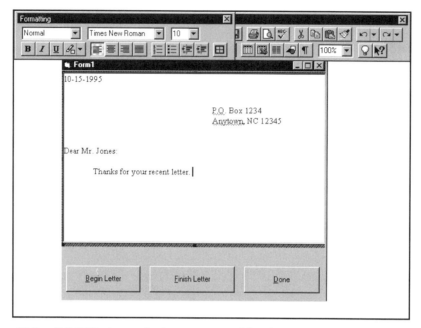

Figure 18.9 *OLEAUTO2, showing the document activated for editing.*

- When the user clicks the Done button, asks whether the letter should be printed and saved. If the user requests either one, uses OLE automation commands to instruct Word print or save the document.

This demonstration program is shown in Figure 18.9. This figure shows the document activated for editing. Notice that with the document activated, Word's toolbars are displayed, providing access to Word's formatting and editing commands.

The program's objects and properties are presented in Listing 18.4, and the code is in Listing 18.5. Rather than walk you though the code a line at a time, I suggest you try to figure out what's going on by yourself. The code is actually fairly simple, so you shouldn't have any problems.

Listing 18.4   Objects and Properties in OLEAUTO1.FRM

```
Begin VB.Form Form1
   Caption        =    "Form1"
   ClientHeight   =    5325
   ClientLeft     =    375
   ClientTop      =    525
   ClientWidth    =    6375
   Height         =    5730
```

```
    Left            =   315
    LinkTopic       =   "Form1"
    ScaleHeight     =   5325
    ScaleWidth      =   6375
    Top             =   180
    Width           =   6495
    Begin VB.CommandButton Command1
        Caption         =   "&Done"
        Height          =   615
        Index           =   2
        Left            =   4440
        TabIndex        =   3
        Top             =   4560
        Width           =   1815
    End
    Begin VB.CommandButton Command1
        Caption         =   "&Finish Letter"
        Height          =   615
        Index           =   1
        Left            =   2160
        TabIndex        =   2
        Top             =   4560
        Width           =   2055
    End
    Begin VB.CommandButton Command1
        Caption         =   "&Begin Letter"
        Height          =   615
        Index           =   0
        Left            =   120
        TabIndex        =   1
        Top             =   4560
        Width           =   1815
    End
    Begin VB.OLE OLE1
        Height          =   4215
        Left            =   120
        TabIndex        =   0
        Top             =   120
        Width           =   6135
    End
End
```

Listing 18.5   Code in OLEAUTO2.FRM

```
Option Explicit

' The Object variable.
Dim WordDoc As Object

Const vbOLEPrimary = 0


Private Sub Command1_Click(Index As Integer)
```

```
Dim Reply As Integer
Dim s1 As String, s2 As String

' Five tabs.
s1 = Chr$(9) & Chr$(9) & Chr$(9) & Chr$(9) & Chr$(9)

Select Case Index
    Case 0        ' Begin Letter
        ' Insert the date into the document.
        WordDoc.INSERT Date$
        WordDoc.InsertPara
        ' Insert two blank lines.
        WordDoc.InsertPara
        WordDoc.InsertPara
        ' Insert the return address preceded by tabs.
        s2 = s1 & "P.O. Box 1234"
        WordDoc.INSERT s2
        WordDoc.InsertPara
        s2 = s1 & "Anytown, NC 12345"
        WordDoc.INSERT s2
        WordDoc.InsertPara
        ' Insert two blank lines and the greeting.
        WordDoc.InsertPara
        WordDoc.InsertPara
        WordDoc.INSERT "Dear "

        ' Activate for in-place editing.
        OLE1.DoVerb (vbOLEPrimary)

    Case 1        ' Finish Letter
        ' Add the closing at the end of the letter.
        WordDoc.InsertPara
        s2 = s1 & "Yours truly,"
        WordDoc.INSERT s2
        WordDoc.InsertPara
        WordDoc.InsertPara
        WordDoc.InsertPara
        WordDoc.InsertPara
        s2 = s1 & "Peter G. Aitken"
        WordDoc.INSERT s2
        WordDoc.InsertPara

        ' Activate for in-place editing.
        OLE1.DoVerb (vbOLEPrimary)

    Case 2        ' Done
        ' Does the user want to print? If so, instruct
        ' Word to print with the default settings.
        Reply = MsgBox("Print letter?", vbYesNo + vbQuestion)
        If Reply = vbYes Then WordDoc.FilePrintDefault

        ' Does the user want to save? If so, instruct
        ' Word to display the Save As dialog box.
        Reply = MsgBox("Save letter?", vbYesNo + vbQuestion)
```

```
            If Reply = vbYes Then
                WordDoc.FileSave
            End If

            ' Destroy the object.
            Set WordDoc = Nothing
            End
End Select

End Sub


Private Sub Form_Load()

' Position the OLE control to fill the width of the form
' and 3/4 of the height.
OLE1.TOP = 0
OLE1.Left = 0
OLE1.Width = ScaleWidth
OLE1.Height = ScaleHeight * 0.75

'Create a new embedded Word document.
OLE1.CreateEmbed "", "Word.Document.6"

' Activate the object(required for OLE automation).
OLE1.DoVerb (vbOLEPrimary)

' Create the OLE automation object.
Set WordDoc = OLE1.object.Application.WordBasic

End Sub
```

OLE and System Speed

As you might expect, the intricacies of OLE place a lot of demand on your system. My computer is pretty fast; but even so, some of these OLE operations move about as fast as a one-legged snail. Perhaps the release version of Visual Basic will be faster than the beta I am using, but take these factors into account when designing your programs. The convenience and power of using OLE may be offset by the sacrifice in performance, so give careful consideration to the trade-off involved.

Error Handling

This is one of the shortest chapters in the book, and you may think it's one of the least interesting. In truth, it may be the most important chapter.

Error handling code is undoubtedly the least interesting part of programming. The code doesn't do anything interesting or flashy—no multimedia extravaganzas, no lightning-fast math calculations, no clever user interfaces—but the fact remains that a program without well-designed and carefully implemented error handing code is almost guaranteed to have its users clamoring for the programmer's blood. And that person, my friend, is *you*! Pay attention to this chapter, and you may live to a ripe old age.

WHAT ERRORS NEED HANDLING?

Computer programs are rife with possibilities for errors. And, in fact, several types of errors can occur. *Syntax errors* happen when you make a mistake writing the program, such as using an undeclared variable (only when using Option Explicit, of course, which you always should do!), passing the wrong number and/or type of arguments to a function, or misspelling a function name. Pesky as these types of errors are, they are rarely a serious problem because Visual Basic catches them as soon as you try to run the program in the Visual Basic development environment. Depending on the specific error, Visual Basic will highlight the offending line of code or will display a dialog box displaying a description of the error. In the latter case, click the Debug button to go to the line of code where the error occurred. These built-in capabilities of Visual Basic make it so easy to find and fix syntax errors, they almost never survive in a program to cause problems for the end user.

There are other types of errors that are not so easily handled. They usually don't crop up during program development where we can fix them. Rather, they wait until the program is in the hands of the end user. The reason that these errors are so difficult to deal with is that they usually depend on factors that are out of our control. Here are a few examples:

- We prompt the users to enter a number but they enter a string instead.

- The program tries to read from a file that a user has accidentally deleted.

- The user enters data that results in an attempt to divide by zero.

- The program tries to write data to drive A: when there is no diskette inserted in the drive.

- The program tries to access a network when the user does not have sufficient access rights.

The list could go on and on. Literally hundreds of these runtime errors can occur, and no programmer—regardless of how clever—can ensure that none of them will occur. What a programmer can do is provide error handling code in the program. In this way, any errors that might crop up will not have serious consequences for the user. This task is done using Visual Basic's error trapping capabilities.

What happens if we don't trap errors? If we're running the program in the Visual Basic development environment, most errors result in display of a dialog box describing the error, as shown in Figure 19.1. The dialog box displays the error number and a brief description of the error. The program at this point is suspended. If we click the End button in the dialog, the program terminates. If we click Debug, the cursor is positioned on the line of code that caused the error. We can edit the code to try to eliminate the error, then press F5 to continue the program execution where it stopped. (Certain types of

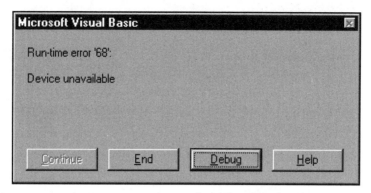

Figure 19.1 *Untrapped errors are reported in Visual Basic by a dialog box like this one.*

changes to the code do not permit continuing program execution, but require that the program be restarted from the beginning. Visual Basic informs us when this is the case.)

If we are running the Visual Basic program as a stand-along EXE file, untrapped errors are also reported by a dialog box giving the error number and a brief description. Of course, no option exists to edit the code to correct the error. Since our end users will be executing our programs as stand-alones, they are faced with a terse message and a non-functional program when an error occurs. This problem is the very situation that we are trying to avoid with error trapping.

Trapping Errors

Trapping errors is similar in some respects to handling events. If you think of an error as an event, and error handling code as an event procedure, you'll have a good start at understanding how Visual Basic deals with errors. The difference is that an error does not trigger a discrete event procedure. Rather, we use the **On Error** statement to specify where in our code execution is to pass when an error occurs. Here's an example. The statement

```
On Error Goto ErrorHandler
```

tells Visual Basic that when an error occurs, execution passes to the line of code identified by the label ErrorHandler. Labels that identify locations in code consist of a name followed by a colon, as shown in these three examples:

```
ErrorHandler:
IfError:
OJSimpson:
```

The rules for line labels are the same as for Basic variable names; the only difference is the colon at the end. Each procedure's error handling code is traditionally placed at the end of the procedure, between the last "regular" statement in the procedure and the **End Sub** or **End Function** statement at the end. We must place an **Exit Sub** or **Exit Function** statement just before the label identifying the error handling code to prevent execution from falling into the error handling code.

The line label identifying the error handling code must be in the same procedure as the **On Error Goto** statement that specifies it. This means that error handling code is local to procedures (both event and general procedures). You might think that this is a bad idea—wouldn't it be better to have a single comprehensive error handler that deals with errors occurring in all parts of the program? Not really. Since each procedure tends to deal with one discrete aspect of the program (or at least it does if we're programming properly), the type of errors it has the potential to generate will be limited. A Text Box's **Change()** event procedure may need to deal with improper data entry, but it will never be faced with a disk access or printer error. Therefore, each procedure's error handling code can be relatively simple and concise—dealing only with that procedure's potential errors. In addition, by including error handling code in procedures, each procedure becomes an independent entity that is not dependent on code elsewhere in the program.

Two variants are possible on the **On Error** statement. If we execute

```
On Error Goto 0
```

error trapping will be disabled, and the program will respond to errors in the default manner by displaying the terse dialog box described above. If we execute

```
On Error Resume Next
```

the program is instructed to continue executing with the statement that immediately follows the one that caused the error. This does not mean that we are ignoring the error (a bad idea to be sure!), but that we are deferring handling of the error for the moment. This technique is used in situations where the information needed to accurately diagnose the error is not available immediately when the error occurs.

You now know how to trap errors—to direct program execution to a special section of code when an error occurs. There are still several questions to be answered—for example, how do we know *which* error has occurred, and what can we do about it? We'll deal with these soon, but first let's look at a sample procedure that contains error trapping code, just to give you a feel for how it works. This sample procedure is presented in Listing 19.1. The comments in the code explain how it works. There's no "real" code in this procedure, just the error trapping statements and comments.

Listing 19.1   How Error Trapping Works

```
Private Sub MyDemoProcedure()

' At this point, before any On Error has been executed,
' errors will be reported by dialog box in the default fashion.

On Error Go To ErrorHandler:

' In this section of code, when an error occurs execution will
' pass to the location identified by the ErrorHandler label.

On Error Goto 0

' In this section of code error trapping is disabled. Errors
' will be reported to the user in the default dialog box format.

On Error Resume Next

' In this section of code error trapping is deferred.


On Error Go To ErrorHandler:

' In this section error trapping is again directed to the code
' following the ErrorHandler label.

' The Exit Sub is required so execution does not fall into the
' following error handling code.

Exit Sub

ErrorHandler:

' The error handling code is placed here.

End Sub
```

In a Visual Basic program, error handling is said to be active from the time a trapped error occurs until a **Resume** statement is executed.

The ERR Object

Much of Visual Basic's ability to deal with errors comes from the ERR object. Each Visual Basic program automatically has a single ERR object associated with it. The ERR object has global scope, meaning it can be accessed from anywhere in our program. At any moment, the ERR object contains (in its properties) information about the most recent error that has occurred. The two properties we'll need most often are described here:

Number   A type Long that identifies the specific error that occurred.

Description   A brief text description of the most recent error.

Two properties of the ERR object provide the same numerical code and text description that are displayed in the error dialog box when an error occurs and error trapping is not enabled. As such, they do not provide a great deal of information. Their value lies in giving your program access to them in code, enabling it to determine which error occurred and then take appropriate action.

Let's look at an example. If our program attempts to open a file on a diskette drive, a common error we should trap is not having a diskette inserted in the drive. If we try to open a file under these conditions, the error number is 71. Our code would look something like Listing 19.2.

Listing 19.2   Using the ERR Object's Number Property to Identify the Error

```
Private Sub SaveData()

Dim f As Long

On Error GoTo FileError

f = FreeFile

Open "a:\junk.dat" For Binary As #f

' Write data here.

Close #f

Exit Sub

FileError:

If Err.Number = 71 Then
    MsgBox ("Please insert a diskette in drive A:, then click OK")
```

```
      Resume
End If

End Sub
```

If there is no diskette in drive A: when this procedure executes, error #71 will occur when the Open statement attempts to execute. Execution will pass to the FileError label, and the ERR object's **Number** property will be tested against the value *71*. Since it matches, the program will display a message box prompting the user to insert a diskette. When the user closes the message box, the **Resume** statement will cause execution to continue with the statement that caused the error—in this case, the **Open** statement. Since there's now a diskette in the drive, the statement will execute with no error.

While the above code works, it is not something we would place in a real program. If a different error occurred, execution would still pass to FileError; but the If condition would not be True, so the associated statements would not be executed. Instead, execution would leave the procedure, and the error would be left hanging.

Does this mean that the error handling code in each procedure must explicitly deal with every single possible error? No—that's impractical. I'll show you how to create a more generic error handler, but first we need to examine the Resume statement.

Sometimes our error handling code will test the value of ERR.Number as soon as the error is trapped (as in the previous example). Other times, the numerical error value will not be tested immediately. When this happens, retrieve the value of ERR.Number and save it in a regular variable. Why is this? Remember that the ERR object contains information about the single most recent error. If a second error occurs between the time of the first error and retrieving the value of ERR.Number, we receive the numerical code for the second error—information about the first error is lost.

As you might well imagine, Visual Basic has a whole slew of trappable errors. How do you find out about them? Activate the Visual Basic Help system and search for "trappable errors." You receive a list of error message categories, such as OLE Automation Messages and Miscellaneous Messages. Select the desired category for a list of related errors and their numerical codes. Select an individual error message to view more details on the causes and possible remedies (if any) for the error condition.

The Resume Statement

You saw the **Resume** statement used in the previous example. **Resume** can only be used within error handling code, or else an error occurs. The **Resume** statement controls where execution goes once the error processing is completed. When used by itself, it means "try again to execute the statement that caused the error." This is sometimes appropriate, in situations like the example where one can assume that the cause of the error has been fixed. In other circumstances, however, this is not possible. If we want execution to continue somewhere other than the statement that caused the error, we have two choices.

Resume Next continues execution immediately after the statement that caused the error.

Resume label continues execution with the program line identified by *label*. The argument *label* must be in the same procedure as the **Resume** statement (the same procedure where the error occurred).

Which variant of **Resume** we use depends on the nature of the error we have trapped and the details of our program. Sometimes we may want to give the user a choice. Listing 19.3 shows an improvement on the previous example.

Listing 19.3   Improved Error Handling Code

```
Private Sub SaveData()


Dim f As Long, Reply As Integer
Dim msg As String

On Error GoTo FileError

f = FreeFile

Open "a:\junk.dat" For Binary As #f

' Data writing code goes here.

Close #f

Exit Sub

FileError:

If Err.Number = 71 Then
    msg = "Please inert a diskette in drive A:, then click Retry."
    msg = msg & Chr$(13)
    msg = msg & "Or click Cancel to try again later."
```

```
    Reply = MsgBox(msg, vbRetryCancel, "Disk error")
    If Reply = vbRetry Then
        Resume
    ElseIf Reply = vbCancel Then
        Resume Finish
    End If

    ' Other error handling code goes here.

Finish:

End If

End Sub
```

Now, when error #71 is trapped, a message box is displayed offering the users the choice of inserting a disk immediately, or canceling the save operation and trying again later (a desirable option if, say, they are out of diskettes and must go fetch one). If the user selects Retry, the **Resume** statement is used to re-execute the **Open** statement. If the user selects Cancel, the Resume *label* is used to direct execution out of the procedure.

 **Message Boxes and Line Breaks**

Sometimes the message we want to display in a message box is too long to fit on one line. To break a long message into two or more lines, place the Chr$(13) character in the message at the desired break points. If we place two of these characters one after the other, we'll skip two lines, in effect giving us a blank line in our message.

Using On Error Resume Next

As I have mentioned above, executing **On Error Resume Next** is used when we want to defer error trapping. When this statement is in effect and an error occurs, execution continues with the statement immediately following the one that caused the error. This type of deferred error trapping is most useful when our program is accessing objects, such as OLE automation objects, because it permits us to unambiguously identify the object that caused the error. The basic sequence of code is as follows:

1. Execute On Error Resume Next.

2. Access or manipulate the object.

3. Immediately test Err.Number to see if an error has occurred; if so, handle it.

Listing 19.4 illustrates this technique. The code attempts to use the **GetObject()** function to access a non-existent object. This causes error #432, defined as "File name or class name not found during OLE Automation operation." The If statement tests for this value in Err.Number; and if it is found, displays a dialog box with a message and the name and source of the error. The error source is obtained from the Err object's **Source** property, which contains the name of the object or application that caused the most recent error. In this example, it will return the name of the Visual Basic project. In other cases, such as passing a non-supported command to an existing OLE automation object, the object name will be returned.

Finally, the **Clear** method is executed to clear all of the Err object's properties. This ensures that the old information from this error will not "hang around" and be misinterpreted later. The **Clear** method is invoked automatically whenever an **On Error**, **Resume**, **Exit Sub**, or **Exit Function** statement is executed.

Listing 19.4   Demonstrating Deferred Error Handling When Accessing Objects

```
Private Sub AccessObject()

Dim MyObj As Object
Dim msg As String

On Error Resume Next    ' Defer error trapping.
' Try to start a non-existent object.
MyObj = GetObject("MyWord.Basic")

' Test for error 432
If Err.Number = 432 Then    ' OLE Automation error.

    ' Tell user what happened.
    msg = "An error occurred attempting to open the OLE object!"
    msg = msg & Chr$(13)
    msg = msg & "Error source: " & Err.Source
    msg = msg & Chr$(13) & "Error number: " & Err.Number
    MsgBox (msg)
    ' Clear the Err object properties.
    Err.Clear
End If

End Sub
```

General Error Handling Code

As I mentioned earlier, it is not practical to explicitly test for every individual error that might conceivably occur in each procedure. Does this mean that we just ignore other errors? Not necessarily. We may not be able to explicitly handle an unexpected error, but at least we can inform the users of the nature of the error so they can report it to us. The goal is to provide information about the nature of the error and where it occurred—both in terms of which form and which procedure. The name of the form can be obtained from Screen.ActiveForm.Name. As for the procedure, we'll have to declare a string variable and load it with the procedure name. An example is shown in Listing 19.5.

Listing 19.5   Code for Reporting Information on Untrapped Errors

```
Dim ProcName As String
ProcName = "Form_DblClick"

On Error GoTo ErrorHandler

' Other code here

ErrorHandler:

msg = "An untrapped error has occurred. Please make a " & Chr$(13)
msg = msg & "note of the following information." & Chr$(13) & Chr$(13)
msg = msg & "Error number: " & Err.Number & Chr$(13)
msg = msg & "Description: " & Err.Description & Chr$(13)
msg = msg & "Location: " & Screen.ActiveForm.Name & Chr$(13)
msg = msg & "Procedure: " & ProcName
MsgBox (msg)
```

The burden for well-designed error handling, more than any other aspect of a Visual Basic Program, may rest with the programmer. There are no clever controls that you can drop in to take care of it for you. The errors that need to be addressed and the way they are handled depend to a large degree on the specifics of your program. It's tempting to skimp on error handling or to leave it for the end of the project. Bad ideas! Keep error handling in mind from the very start so it is built into the program—not tacked on at the end as an afterthought. You'll save time and grief in the long run.

Accessing the Windows API

By accessing the Windows Applications Programming Interface, or API, your Visual Basic program can tap the full power of windows.

In working with Visual Basic, you've seen how it has a lot of built-in procedures that perform such commonly needed tasks as string manipulation, graphics, and mathematical calculations. In a similar fashion, the Windows operating system also has a large collection of built-in procedures. By calling these API procedures directly from your Visual Basic program, you can provide additional functionality with relatively little programming.

WHAT IS THE WINDOWS API?

The Windows API is a huge collection of procedures that can be called by any program running under Windows. In fact, a great deal of what any Windows program does is accomplished by means of the API. Displaying screen windows, using the printer, displaying text, using menus–it's all done by the API. There's no way to overestimate the importance of the API. From a programmer's perspective, Windows *is* the API.

When you write a Visual Basic program, you are accessing the API indirectly. You create your program by placing controls, setting properties, executing methods, and so on. When the program runs, Visual Basic translates your instructions into calls to the appropriate API procedures, which perform much of the actual job of the program. You can also call API procedures directly, a task that is not too much different from calling a regular Basic procedure.

Why call the API directly? As powerful as Visual Basic is, it does not provide access to all of the capabilities of the Windows API. If you know what's available in the API, and how to get at it, you'll have just that many more tools available when creating a Visual Basic program.

The API procedures are located in files called *dynamic link libraries*, or DLLs. DLL files are installed on your disk when you install Windows, and are loaded into memory whenever a Windows application calls them. Many applications install their own DLL files, but we are interested in those that are a part of the Windows 95 operating system. There is only a single copy of each API procedure, which is shared by all programs that need it. This is called *dynamic linking*–hence the name dynamic link library.

The Windows API contains a huge number of procedures to perform just about any task you can imagine, and a lot that you can't! There are procedures for window management, file manipulation, printer control, menus and dialog boxes, memory management, graphics drawing, multimedia, string manipulation...well, you get the idea. Reference material on the API runs to multi-volume sets with more than a thousand pages. There's no way I can provide information on even a small fraction of the API procedures that are available. Rather, my goal in this chapter is to show you the general methods for calling API procedures from your Visual Basic programs. For information on the specific procedures that are available, I suggest you turn to one of the API reference books that have been published. Be sure you get a book on the Windows 95 API, not the older Windows 3.1 API.

eXPLORER TIP — Online API information

The Professional Edition of Visual Basic 3.0 included an online reference to the Windows API, which was extremely useful. The Visual Basic 4.0 beta that I used to write this book has no such reference, but may be added in the final commercial release version. Check your Visual Basic installation. If you have a C/C++ programming tool for Windows 95, such as Visual C++, it will almost certainly have online API reference information.

Accessing the Windows API

Calling an API procedure from a Visual Basic program is not much different from calling a general Basic function or subprocedure. If the API procedure is a function—that is, if it returns a value to the calling program—you use the function name on the right side of an assignment statement, assigning its return value to a variable of the appropriate type. For an API subprocedure that does not return a value, you use the Call statement. As with any procedure, you must pass it the correct number and types of arguments.

Let's look at a simple example. If **MyAPISub** is an API subprocedure, and **MyAPIFunc** is an API function that returns an integer, we would call them as shown here (we'll ignore arguments for now):

```
Call MyAPISub()
RetVal = MyAPIFunc()
```

Before you can call an API procedure, it must be declared in the program using the **Declare** statement. The **Declare** statement informs Visual Basic about the name of the procedure, and the number and type of arguments it takes. The Declare statement takes one of the following forms depending on whether the API procedure is a subprocedure or a function:

```
Declare Sub APIProcName Lib DLLname [([argumentlist])]

Declare Function APIProcName Lib DLLname [([argumentlist])] [As type]
```

APIProcName is the name of the API procedure, and **DLLname** is a string literal specifying the name of the DLL file that contains the procedure. The *type* at the end of the function declaration declares the data type of the value returned by a **Function** procedure. *argumentlist* is a list of variables representing arguments that are passed to the **Sub** or **Function** procedure when it is called. Most arguments to API procedures must be passed with the ByVal keyword. The list has the following syntax:

```
ByVal argname1 [As type] [,ByVal argname2 [As type]]...
```

It is essential that the components of the **Declare** statement be specified exactly, or the statement won't work. If there's an error in the **Declare** statement, when you run the program, the call to the API procedure generates a "Reference to undefined function or array" error message. The **Declare** statements required by many API procedures are rather long and involved. Here's a real example:

```
Declare Function SendDlgItemMessage Lib "user32" Alias "SendDlgItemMessageA"_
  (ByVal hDlg As Long, ByVal nIDDlgItem As Long, _
  ByVal wMsg As Long, ByVal wParam As Long, lParam As Any) As Long
```

For now, don't worry about the **Alias** keyword, which I'll explain later, or about what the function of this API procedure is. I'm just using this as an example of a real API procedure declaration. I'm glad to report that you will rarely if ever need to type them into your programs yourself. Visual Basic includes a program called the API Text Viewer, which provides a complete listing of **Declare** statements for all of the API functions. You can simply copy the **Declare** statement to the Clipboard and paste it into your program. The API Text Viewer is started by clicking its icon in the Visual Basic program group that was created when Visual Basic was installed. Please refer to your Visual Basic documentation for information on how to use the viewer.

Declare statements should generally be placed in the general declarations section of the module that calls the procedures. See the section below on the **Private** and **Public** keywords for more information on the location of **Declare** statements.

 **DLL Procedure Names Are Case-Sensitive**

In Windows 95, DLL procedure names are case sensitive. All it takes to get a runtime error is one letter typed in the wrong case. There's no alternative but to be careful when typing procedure names.

The Alias, Private, and Public Keywords

These three keywords are optional components of a **Declare** statement. The **Alias** keyword lets you define an alternate name, or alias, for the DLL procedure. The result is that you'll use a different name to call the procedure, a name other than the one it is assigned in the DLL. For example, the statement

```
Declare Function APIProc1 Lib "MyDLL" Alias "APIProc2" () as Long
```

declares that the DLL named **MyDLL** contains a procedure named **APIProc2** but that we will call it by the name **APIProc1** in the program.

Why are aliases necessary? The most common reason is that some DLL procedures have the same name as a Visual Basic reserved word. In this situation, trying to use the DLL procedure under its "real" name can cause confusion and errors. By assigning an alias, you can use both the DLL procedure and the reserved word without conflict. Other uses of **Alias** are internal to the API and are not related to Visual Basic itself. **Declare** statements that you copy from the API Text Viewer are already provided with the required aliases. The only time you'll need to add one yourself is if a DLL function name conflicts with a Basic function or procedure in your program.

You use the **Public** and **Private** keywords to control where in your program an API declaration is effective. This determines which of the program's modules can use the declared procedure. If a procedure is declared **Public**, you can use it in all of the program's modules. **Public** is the default, so including the keyword in the **Declare** statement is optional. A procedure declared **Private** can only be used by code in the module that contains the **Declare** statement. The **Public** or **Private** keyword goes at the beginning of the **Declare** statement:

```
Public Declare Sub APIProc1 .....
Private Declare Function APIProc2 .....
```

Within a form module, only **Private** procedure declarations are allowed, which means that you can place **Public** declarations only in code modules. The primary use for making a procedure declaration **Private** occurs when you are writing a form module that you intend to use in other programs as a software component. A software component needs to be completely portable, which means that any API procedures that it uses must be declared within the module, which requires use of the **Private** keyword. This ensures that the module is completely self-contained.

Declaring API Functions as Subprocedures

Most of the procedures in the API are functions—in other words, they return a value to the calling program. While your program will often need the return value, sometimes it won't. When an API function's return value is not needed, you can declare and use the API procedure as a subprocedure that does not return a value, which simplifies its use in the program. For example, the **SetTextAlign** API procedure specifies the alignment of text that is printed on the screen. It is a function, and its declaration is as follows:

```
Declare Function SetTextAlign Lib "gdi32" (ByVal hDC As Long, ByVal wFlags As
Long) As Long
```

A Visual Basic program would call it like this:

```
RetVal = SetTextAlign(...)
```

The value that this API function returns is the previous text alignment setting. This value is not of much use to most programs. To use **SetTextAlign()** as a subprocedure, you would declare it as follows

```
Declare Sub SetTextAlign Lib "GDI" (ByVal hDC As Long, ByVal wFlags As Long)
```

and call it using the **Call** statement:

```
Call SetTextAlign(...)
```

You cannot define an API procedure as both a function and a subprocedure in the same program with the same name. If you want use an API procedure both ways, you can declare it with an *Alias* name:

```
Declare Sub SetTextAlign Lib "GDI" (…)
Declare Function SetTextAlignFunction Lib "GDI" Alias "SetTextAlign" (…) As Long
```

You can then call it using whichever declaration fits the situation at hand:

```
Call SetTextAlign (…)
```

Or

```
RetVl = SetTextAlignFunction (…)
```

An API Demonstration

The program I will develop in this section not only shows you a real example of using an API procedure, but does something useful. It's related to the limitations of Visual Basic's **Print** method. When you use this method to display text on a form or a Picture Box, the position of the text is determined by the object's **CurrentX** and **CurrentY** properties, which give the horizontal and vertical position of the *current position*. The text is always left-aligned with respect to this position. Visual Basic itself provides no other alignment options.

You can, however, use a Windows API call to obtain different types of text alignment, both vertical and horizontal. This is done with the procedure **SetTextAlign()**. Its declaration is:

```
Declare Sub SetTextAlign Lib "gdi32" (ByVal hDC As Long, ByVal wFlags As Long)
```

The argument *hDC* specifies the **hDC** property of the object that you are printing to, and the argument *wFlags* contains the flags specifying the desired text alignment. These flags specify the text justification with respect to the object's current position. You can specify both vertical and horizontal justification. The possible values for horizontal alignment are defined by the following Windows global constants:

TA_CENTER	Centers the text on the current position
TA_LEFT	Positions the left edge of the text at the current position (the default)
TA_RIGHT	Positions the right edge of the text at the current position

You can also specify vertical alignment. To understand vertical alignment, consider the total vertical extent that characters can span, using these terms:

BOTTOM	The lowest any character extends, such as the descenders on g and y
TOP	The highest any character extends, such as tall uppercase letters or diacritical marks such as Ä and é
BASELINE	The bottom of characters that don't have descenders, such as a and c

The vertical alignment options are defined using these terms, as follows:

TA_BASELINE	The font baseline is aligned with the current position
TA_BOTTOM	The font bottom is aligned with the current position
TA_TOP	The font top is aligned with the current position (the default)

Because the available text alignment settings operate with respect to the object's current position, the **SetTextAlign()** procedure does not align text with respect to the edges of the print area, like a word processing program does. If you want to specify alignment with respect to the object edges, you must do some fiddling in code. For example, to right-align text in a Picture Box so that the right edge of the text lines up with the right edge of the Picture Box, you must set the Picture Box's **CurrentX** property to the right edge (obtained from the ScaleWidth property), then use the **SetTextAlign()** procedure to set right alignment before displaying the text with the Print method. Similarly, to center text in a Picture Box you would first set **CurrentX** to the center of the box (ScaleWidth/2) and then use **SetTextAlign()** to specify center alignment.

Now let's get to the demonstration program. This program displays text in a Picture Box. First, vertical and horizontal lines are drawn to mark the center of the box. Two sets of option buttons let you select both vertical and horizontal text alignment. All alignment is with respect to the box center that is marked by the two lines.

Start a new project. On the form, add a Picture Box, a Command Button, and two Frame controls. On each of the Frame controls, create a control array of three Option Buttons. The object properties are shown in Listing 20.1, and the form's code is shown in Listing 20.2. The program is shown executing in Figure 20.1.

Note how we draw the lines in the box. First, the Picture Box's **DrawStyle** is set to 3-Dash-Dot, which will give us lines with a dot-dash pattern. Then, in code, we use the Line method to draw the lines, obtaining the needed coordinates from the control's **ScaleHeight** and **ScaleWidth** properties:

```
Picture1.Line (0, Picture1.ScaleHeight / 2)-Step(Picture1.ScaleWidth, 0)
Picture1.Line (Picture1.ScaleWidth / 2, 0)-Step(0, Picture1.ScaleHeight)
```

When you use this method to set text alignment, be aware that the alignment that you set with **SetTextAlign()** is guaranteed to be in effect for only a single Print method. If, for example, you change text alignment and then execute these statements

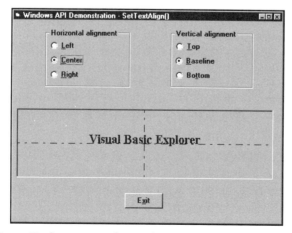

Figure 20.1   *Using a Windows API procedure to align text.*

```
PictureBox.Print "text1"
PictureBox.Print "text2"
```

The specified alignment may not be used for the second message. You must call **SetTextAlign()** before each and every **Print** method. Because Visual Basic treats multiple arguments to a **Print** method as two distinct **Print** methods, the following still may not work:

```
PictureBox.Print "text1";"text2"
```

Avoid the potential problem by concatenating the strings before executing **Print**:

```
PictureBox.Print "text1" & "text2"
```

Listing 20.1   Objects and Properties in ALIGNTXT.FRM

```
Begin VB.Form frmTxtAlign
   BorderStyle     =   1  'Fixed Single
   Caption         =   "Windows API Demonstration - SetTextAlign()"
   Begin VB.CommandButton cmdExit
      Caption        =   "E&xit"
   End
   Begin VB.PictureBox Picture1
      DrawStyle       =   3  'Dash-Dot
      BeginProperty Font
         name            =   "Times New Roman"
         size            =   15.75
      EndProperty
   End
   Begin VB.Frame Frame2
      Caption         =   "Horizontal alignment"
      Begin VB.OptionButton HorizAlign
         Caption         =   "&Left"
         Index           =   0
      End
      Begin VB.OptionButton HorizAlign
         Caption         =   "&Center"
         Index           =   1
      End
      Begin VB.OptionButton HorizAlign
         Caption         =   "&Right"
         Index           =   2
      End
   End
   Begin VB.Frame Frame1
      Caption         =   "Vertical alignment"
      Begin VB.OptionButton VertAlign
         Caption         =   "&Top"
         Index           =   0
      End
```

```
        Begin VB.OptionButton VertAlign
            Caption         =   "&Baseline"
            Index           =   1
        End
        Begin VB.OptionButton VertAlign
            Caption         =   "Bo&ttom"
            Index           =   2
        End
    End
End
End
```

Listing 20.2   Code in ALIGNTXT.FRM

```
Option Explicit

Const TA_LEFT = 0
Const TA_RIGHT = 2
Const TA_CENTER = 6
Const TA_TOP = 0
Const TA_BOTTOM = 8
Const TA_BASELINE = 24

Const MESSAGE = "Visual Basic Explorer"

Private Declare Sub SetTextAlign Lib "gdi32" (ByVal hDC As Long, ByVal wFlags As
Long)


Private Sub cmdExit_Click()

End

End Sub


Private Sub Form_Load()

' Set default option button.

HorizAlign(0).VALUE = True
VertAlign(0).VALUE = True

End Sub


Private Sub HorizAlign_Click(Index As Integer)

' If THE alignment option has been changed,
' repaint the Picture Box.

Picture1_Paint

End Sub
```

```
Private Sub Picture1_Paint()

Dim wFlags As Long

' Clear the picture box.
Picture1.Cls

' Draw centered vertical and horizontal lines.
Picture1.Line (0, Picture1.ScaleHeight / 2)-Step(Picture1.ScaleWidth, 0)
Picture1.Line (Picture1.ScaleWidth / 2, 0)-Step(0, Picture1.ScaleHeight)

' Place the current position at the intersection of the lines.
Picture1.CurrentY = Picture1.ScaleHeight / 2
Picture1.CurrentX = Picture1.ScaleWidth / 2

' Set wFlags to reflect the alignment options selected.
If HorizAlign(0).VALUE Then wFlags = TA_LEFT
If HorizAlign(1).VALUE Then wFlags = TA_CENTER
If HorizAlign(2).VALUE Then wFlags = TA_RIGHT

If VertAlign(0).VALUE Then wFlags = wFlags Or TA_TOP
If VertAlign(1).VALUE Then wFlags = wFlags Or TA_BASELINE
If VertAlign(2).VALUE Then wFlags = wFlags Or TA_BOTTOM

' Set the new alignment.
Call SetTextAlign(Picture1.hDC, wFlags)

' Display the text.
Picture1.Print MESSAGE

End Sub

Private Sub VertAlign_Click(Index As Integer)

' If the alignment option has been changed,
' repaint the picture box.

Picture1_Paint

End Sub
```

Appendix:
What's On the CD?

The companion CD-ROM for this book contains all the source code from the book as well as huge assortment of sample custom controls. Many of the sample custom controls can be used right off of the CD. If you like them, contact the manufacturer for details on purchasing the full packages.

Here is a breakdown of the directory structure of the CD:

CONTROLS\VBX	Custom controls that can be used with the 16-bit version of VB4
CONTROLS\OCX	Custom controls that can be used with the 32-bit version of VB4
DEMOS	Applications that demonstrate the capabilities of custom controls
SOURCE	All the source code from the book
SYSTEM	A few files you may need to put into your WINDOWS\SYSTEM directory if you didn't do a complete VB4 install.

Now, let's take a look at a few of the custom controls on the CD that you can try out.

Control: *Connectivity Custom Controls*
Format: 32-bit OCX

Where on CD: \CONTROLS\OCX\TOUPIN

Where On-Line: http://www.toupin.com/~etoupin/welcome.html

Description: This group of OCX custom controls can really make your life easy if you want to do any Internet-related programming. It's all here; FTP, GetHost, SMTP, everything! You can develop your own news reader application or even build the next hot Web browser. Ed Toupin, the creator of these controls, has done a wonderful job of putting together some very robust controls that he has allowed us to offer to you. His only request is that if you use them in any applications, that you register the software with him for a nominal fee. If you plan on doing Internet programming, you can not afford to not look at these controls.

Control: *Connectivity Custom Controls*

Company: ProNexus

Format: 16-bit VBX

Where on CD: \CONTROLS\VBX\PRONEXUS\VBVOICE

Where On-Line: CompuServe (GO PRONEXUS)

Description: This demo system is a fully functional copy of VBVoice, a powerful telephony custom control, with the exception that the voice card driver is not included, and the voice editor, Announce, has been crippled. You can run the demo programs, and design and test your own using the simulation mode, which uses a sound card. When simulation mode meets a situation where it normally gets status information from the telephone system, a dialog pops up to ask you which response you would like to test.

Control: *Graphics Manipulation Controls*

Company: ImageFX

Format: 16-bit VBX

Where on CD: \DEMOS\IMAGEFX

Where On-Line: http://www.imagefx.com/imagefx/

Description: The demo version of FXTools/VB Professional Edition includes nine custom controls that add professional effects to images, text, shapes and video. You can display 19 image file formats including Iterated Systems, Inc.

Fractal Image File (FIF), and LEAD Technologies, Inc. (CMP). Plus, you can easily control WAV and MIDI sound; control and display AVI and QuickTime movies with special effects on any frame; and move text along a predefined path. Over 100 special effects are provided along with the ability to cancel an effect and receive notification that an effect has completed with or without a time delay. Delayed Effect Notification (DEN) is built into all FXTools/VB Professional controls that display special effects. If you are doing any multimedia programming, then this package is a must!

Control: *Graphics Manipulation Controls*

Company: VideoSoft

Format: 16-bit VBX

Where on CD: \DEMOS\VIDEOSFT

Where On-Line: CompuServe (GO VIDEOSOFT)

Description: This demo shows you some of the features of VideoSoft's group of custom VBX controls. These are not cutting edge controls with a bunch of incredible features. They are, however, incredibly useful controls that do some specific tasks very well. For example, the FlexString control that comes with the VSFlex package allows you to incorporate regular-expression text matching into your VB programs. This allows you to easily parse complex text input or to offer regular expression search and replace features such as those found in professional packages such as Microsoft Word. Another control, the **vsElastic** control that comes in the VSVBX package is a versatile smart container that automatically resizes to the left, right, top, bottom, or to fill its container, be it a form or another control. Play around with this demo and you will see what big time savers these controls can be.

INDEX

A

Absolute value function, 103
Access databases
 field properties, 347
Access keys, 121
 coding, 48
Additive colors, 173
Alias, 245, 502
Alignment, 94
American Standard Code for
 Information Interchange, 118
ANSI to ASCII, 390
API. *See Applications Program Interface.*
Applications Program Interface (API),
246, 499
 calling from VB, 501
Arguments
 numeric, 101
 procedure, 100
Arithmetic operators, 71
Arrays, 87-89
 control, 94
 sequential access files, 198
ASCII. *See American Standard Code
 for Information Interchange.*
Attribute classes, 310

B

Basic coding
 commenting code, 70
 constants, 60
 debugging, 90
 decision structures, 76
 end statements, 18
 history of, 59-60
 line wrapping, 76
 logical expressions, 73
 loop structures, 79
 modules, 272
 operators, 70
 numeric variables, 61
 variables, 60
BAS extension, 57, 382
Basic modules, 272
 adding, 273, 382
Baud rate, 230
Binary access files, 192
 pointer, 205
 reading, 206
 structure, 205
Binary search, 312
Bitmaps, 170
Blank records, 284
Bookmark property, 383
Boolean variables, 66
BorderStyle property, 39, 50, 93, 374
Buffer, 234
 input,235
 output, 236
Buttons
 adding, 12
 caption property, 275, 382
 changing fonts, 96
 option, 42
 View Code, 15
 View Form, 93
Byebye procedure, 277

C

Capability command, 250
Caption properties, 9
 command buttons, 13

515